Revelation

visions for today

A New Covenant Commentary

By the same author:

Hebrews: A New Covenant Commentary
Fields White for Harvest
Romans: A New Covenant Commentary
Galatians
John: Gospel of the New Creation
Covenant and Creation
Search for Order
Faith of Israel

Revelation

visions for today

A New Covenant Commentary

By
William J. Dumbrell

WIPF & STOCK · Eugene, Oregon

Wipf and Stock Publishers
199 W 8th Ave, Suite 3
Eugene, OR 97401

Revelation: Visions for Today
A New Covenant Commentary
By Dumbrell, William
Copyright©2011 by Dumbrell, William
ISBN 13: 978-1-5326-4320-0
Publication date 11/14/2017
Previously published by Redeemer Baptist Press, 2011

Contents

Introduction 1
   Reading Guide 4
Revelation 1 7
   Revelation 1:1–3:22 7
      Prologue 1:1–8 7
      Revelation 1:1–3 Superscription 7
      Revelation 1:4–6 A Letter to Seven Churches 14
      Revelation 1:7–8 The Expectation of the Book 21
      Revelation 1:9–20 The Son of Man and the Churches 24
Revelation 2 35
   Revelation 2–3 Prophetic messages to the Seven Churches of Asia
      Minor 35
      Revelation 2:1–7 Ephesus 40
      Revelation 2:8–11 Smyrna 42
      Revelation 2:12–17 Pergamum 43
      Revelation 2:18–29 Thyatira 44
Revelation 3 49
      Revelation 3:1–6 Sardis 49
      Revelation 3:7–13 Philadelphia 51
      Revelation 3:14–22 Laodicea 54
   Summary of the Seven Prophetic Messages 57
Revelation 4 59
   Revelation 4–5 In the Throne Room of Heaven 59
   Revelation 4 Judgement on the World Anticipated 59
Revelation 5 77
   Revelation 5 The Lamb Takes the Scroll to Implement World
      Judgement 77
Revelation 6 97
   Revelation 6–9 The Common Features of the Seals, Trumpets (and
      Bowls) 97
   The Seals, Trumpets and Bowls as Judgement on a Fallen World 98

Revelation 6:1–9 The Seals Leading to the Opening of the Scroll
. . . . 108
The Rationale for the Three Series 114
Revelation 6 The Seals 115
    Revelation 6:1–2 The First Seal 117
    Revelation 6:3–4 The Second Seal 118
    Revelation 6:5–6 The Third Seal 119
    Revelation 6:7–8 The Fourth Seal 119
    Revelation 6:9–11 The Fifth Seal 120
    Revelation 6:12–17 The Sixth Seal 122

Revelation 7 . . . . **125**
Revelation 7 The Church in Two Modes 125
Revelation 7:1–8 The Saints Protected for Battle 125
Revelation 7:9–17 The Earthly Church from a Heavenly
    Perspective 130

Revelation 8 . . . . **139**
Revelation 8:1, 3–5 The Seventh Seal 139
Revelation 8:2, 6–9:21 The First Six Trumpets 139
Revelation 8:2, 6–9:21 The Trumpets Sound 141
Summary 144
The Interrelationship of the Three Series 146
    Revelation 8:7 The First Trumpet 150
    Revelation 8:8–9 The Second Trumpet 150
    Revelation 8:10–11 The Third Trumpet 150
    Revelation 8:12–13 The Fourth Trumpet 151

Revelation 9 . . . . **153**
Revelation 9:1–12 The Fifth Trumpet: Demonic Locusts . . . 153
Revelation 9:13–21 The Sixth Trumpet—Demonic Horses . . 157

Revelation 10 . . . . **163**
Revelation 10 The Open Scroll 163

Revelation 11 . . . . **173**
Revelation 11–13 The Church Age 173
    Revelation 11:1–13 A Summary of Christian Witness 173
    Revelation 11:3–13 Two Witnesses 178
    Revelation 11:14–18 The Seventh Trumpet Sounds the End . 189

Revelation 11:19–15:5 Summary: The Centrepiece of Revelation 192
Revelation 12. .... **195**
  Revelation 12–13 The Church Under Persecution 195
  Revelation 12 Satan's Release 195
    Revelation 12:1–6 The Woman, the Child and the Dragon .. 196
    Revelation 12:7–12 War in Heaven 200
  Excursus: The Fall of Satan 205
    Revelation 12:13–18 The Pursuit of the Woman 205
Revelation 13. .... **209**
  Revelation 13 The Worship of World Power 209
    Revelation 13:1–10 The Antichrist 209
    Revelation 13:11–18 The Land Beast and 666 216
  Summary of Revelation 11–13 222
Revelation 14. .... **225**
  Revelation 14–15 Victory and Judgement 225
    Revelation 14:1–5 The Lamb and His Army on Mount Zion .. 225
    Revelation 14:6–13 The Process of Judgement 229
    Revelation 14:14–20 The Divine Harvest 233
Revelation 15. .... **235**
  Revelation 15 The Seven Bowls and the New Exodus 235
    Revelation 15:2–4 The Song of Moses and the Lamb 235
  Heaven Excursus 244
Revelation 16. .... **247**
  Revelation 16:1–19:5 World Judgement: The Fall of Babylon the Great 247
  Revelation 16 The Judgement of the Bowls 247
    Revelation 16:2 The First Bowl 252
    Revelation 16:3 The Second Bowl 252
    Revelation 16:5 The Third Bowl 253
    Revelation 16:8–9 The Fourth Bowl 254
    Revelation 16:10–16 The Fifth and Sixth Bowls 254
    Revelation 16:17–21 The Seventh Bowl 258
Revelation 17. .... **261**
  Overview of Chapters 17–19 261
  Revelation 17 The Great Fall of Great Babylon 262

Introduction. 262
   Revelation 17:1–6 266
   Revelation 17:7–18 The Interpretation of the Mystery 270
Excursus: Worship in Revelation 276
Revelation 18. . . . . **279**
   Revelation 18 The World Lament over the Fall of Babylon . . . 279
   Revelation 18:1–8 Introduction 279
   Revelation 18:9–20 The Lament of her World over Babylon. . 281
Revelation 19. . . . . **285**
   Revelation 19:1–6 Hallelujah by Heaven and the Saints. . . . 285
   Revelation 19:7–10 The Marriage of the Lamb. 286
   Revelation 19:11–20:15 The Splendour of the End: The Transition
      from Babylon to the New Jerusalem 288
   Revelation 19:11–21 The Messianic War 288
Revelation 20. . . . . **295**
   Revelation 20 The End of World History 295
   Revelation 20:1–3 The Release of Satan 295
   Revelation 20:4–6 The Rule of the Saints. 297
   Revelation 20:7–10 The Attack on the Camp of the Saints . . 299
   Revelation 20:11–15 The Last Judgement 305
Revelation 21. . . . . **309**
   Revelation 21–22 The New Jerusalem as The New Creation. . . 309
   Revelation 21:1–8 The New Heaven and Earth: The Church as
      the Bride of Christ 309
   Revelation 21:9–21 The Bride and her Adornment 318
   Revelation 21:22–27 The New Temple 323
Revelation 22. . . . . **327**
   Revelation 22:1–5 The New Eden. 327
   Revelation 22:6–9 The Epilogue to the Book 330
   Revelation 22:10–17 The Final Prophecy: A Call to Holiness of
      Life. 331
   Revelation 22:16–21 Finale 332
   Summary 334
Bibliography **335**

Introduction

Our understanding of Genesis 1-2 is affected by the process of history introduced by the Fall in Genesis 3. But Genesis 1-2 looks forward to the reconstitution of the world. The seventh day of creation (Genesis 2:1-3) differs from the previous six days in that there is no record of beginning or ending. So the seventh day begins when the sixth day ends, but then continues until the end of history. This is confirmed by Hebrews 4:4-9 in which the seventh day is associated with God's rest (cf. the fourth commandment, Exodus 20:11). In Hebrews, rest means entering into the full dimension of the promised permanence of the final Promised Land. Rest is, therefore, full and eternal life in God's presence. The world was created for redeemed humanity. And at the return of Jesus (the Parousia), saved humanity will fully experience eternal life in God's presence in the new creation. Thus redeemed humanity, at the Parousia, will realise what had always been the divine intention revealed in Genesis 1-2 in the creation of the universe.

The understanding of this divine intention, although evident in Genesis 1-2, is thwarted by human ability to decide its own future. Humanity took on this deciding role when confronted by an evil presence in the original Eden. The point of the Book of Revelation is to unfold how God's original intention is finally realised by the operation of the full significance of the cross at the return of Jesus, and the final defeat of Satan and evil.

Thus the Book of Revelation is the final biblical response to Genesis 1-3. Without Revelation, the plan of the Bible would be conspicuously incomplete. All that is in between Genesis 1-3 and Revelation is needed for us to comprehend the divine intention and fulfilment. But Revelation is magnificent theological literature which lays bare the character of the historical church, exalts the cross, and presents the naked strength of evil and the utter sinfulness of humanity. And through it all, Revelation reveals the firm control of God over history and the final victory of the Holy Trinity. Without Revelation, the Bible would be an enigma.

Revelation reflects the biblical account of cosmic combat in which the empires of the world embody the demonic threat of chaos and evil against divine order. This is the plot that orders the book of Daniel, upon which Revelation is heavily dependent. Out of the chaos that is this world emerges, by the defeat and eradication of evil, the complete operation of the new covenant and the great company of the redeemed in the new creation. Revelation reveals the execution of the plan of God through the witness of Jesus to the word of God and his sovereign rule over creation, the defeat of evil, the judgement of the wicked, and the vindication of the upright.[1] Consistently, the whole book is called a prophecy (1:3; 22:7,10,18,19).

The visions in this visionary book do not advance in time but provide greater focus and clarity in the one general vision from 4:1–22:5. The prologue to the book (1:1–8) contains a letter opening (1:4–6), marking Revelation as a true letter. And the epilogue ends with a letter conclusion (22:21). The whole book recounts a single vision that took place at Patmos on the Lord's Day (1:9). The structure suggested by Dan Lioy[2] (2003, 59) is followed here:

Prologue 1:1–8
Throne Room Scene 1:9–20
Prophetic Messages to Seven Churches 2:1–3:22
Throne Room Scene 4:1–5:14
Seven Seal Judgements 6:1–8:1
Throne Room Scene 8:2–6
Seven Trumpet Judgements 8:7–11:18
Throne Room Scene 11:19
Mother Israel, the Dragon, and Their Seed 12:1–14:20
Judgement of the Bowls 15:1–16:17
Destruction of Babylon 16:18–18:24
The New Creation, New Jerusalem 19:1–22:5
Closing and Epilogue 22:6–21

The book identifies itself in 1:4 as a Pastoral Letter to seven churches in Asia Minor. It majors on the question asked then and now: who is Lord over a world that seems to lie in the hands of the evil one? Despite what seems to be, God rules the world and is

---

1   Lioy, 2003, 83.
2   Ibid., 59.

coming to overthrow the Roman and other evil historical empires. God will establish his kingdom.³ This paradox of God's rule—contradicted in John's day by the notion of the supposed divine rule of the Roman Empire—provides an understanding of how progressive godless world government reaching down to the end of time will be resolved by God's ultimate triumph over evil and the visible establishment of his eternal kingdom.

The continuity established with Israel's past indicates that God is completing through the true Israel the purposes always in his mind for creation. The revelation that God gives connects the unfolding history of the world from the cross to the Second Coming, effected through Jesus and his bond-servants and their witness (1:1, 5). We cannot understand the history of the period other than in the light of the goal towards which history is heading. The already decided end of human history will unfold by the emergence of the new creation in divine time, that is, 'shortly'.

The two major views on the date of the book are either during the reign of Nero (c.A.D. 68) or Domitian (A.D. 81–96). The majority opinion favours Domitian but the apparent existence of the temple (cf. 11:1–2) may provide evidence for an earlier date. J.A.T. Robinson (1976) argued that the whole of the New Testament was produced beforeA.D. 70, noting that the actual fall of Jerusalem is never reported or alluded to by the New Testament writers. Moreover, the persecution of Christians is better placed under Nero than Domitian. There is no record of Domitian having imprisoned or executed those who refused to worship him.⁴ If the argument falters on the quick deterioration of the Christian church (Revelation 2–3) as difficult to comprehend pre-A.D. 70, Corinthians is an example of a congregation that lost their first love early in the first century. So a date in the later 60s seems preferable.

Finally, the book answers the important question of 'God's ways' in history and salvation, for which God is praised in the hymn anticipating the end (15:3). Why did God permit and tolerate world rebellion for so long? And, by his creation of the human species, why did God make world rebellion possible? The answer that Revelation gives is that humanity must come to recognise,

---

3 Rowland, 1982, 126–135.
4 Morris, 1987, 36.

throughout the long run of its history, the futility of its attempts since Babel (Genesis 11:1–9) to build a better but godless world. The kingdom of the beast represents the ultimate attempt in world sophistication, ingenuity, discovery, and technology to develop a Utopia. But the attempt to develop Utopia founders, like all previous endeavours by world conquerors, on the problem of the effects of the Fall (Genesis 3). The difficulty of human self-reference and thus national self-reference is intractable.

There seems to be no final battle beyond the beast and his followers turning in upon the world system that they had erected (17:16–17). The Parousia of Christ ends human history and ushers in the visible kingdom of God over all. But the manifestation of God's ways will only be recognised after the event. God had given humanity latitude to construct its own history; hence the final recognition of total human incapability of achieving its goal. Out of the failure of history, God's new world would arise.

Reading Guide

Revelation 1 indicates that the book unveils the future by God through Jesus. Jesus is both the Son Man and the Ancient of Days, that is, God. Revelation 2–3 presents the future of the Church of God throughout Christian history by the typical experience of seven Asian churches. Revelation 4–5 majors on the future as the judgement of God on the world through the medium of the scroll to be opened with world judgement (Revelation 4) in reaction to the death and resurrection of the Lamb (Revelation 5).

Revelation 6–9 contains details of ongoing world punishments: the seals and trumpets, with the seven bowls as the finale to come. In a preface to the judgement series—seals, trumpets and bowls—I argue for the Fall as the source of all human sin and judgement. Revelation 7, in two sections (1–8, 9–17), is an interval within Revelation 6–9. 7:1–8 views the task of the 144,000 believers as keeping faith in a sinful world throughout the ages. 7:9–17 offers a view of the saints before the heavenly throne and then details how they get there.

Revelation 9 uses two pictures to graphically present the evil which only God can conquer, and thereby prepares the reader for a final divine intervention. In Revelation 10 the scroll opened by the Lamb in heaven is brought down by the mighty angel from heaven to earth, and henceforth becomes John's message. This indicates that the seals and trumpets were not part of the scroll of Revelation 5 (previously opened by the Lamb but brought down in Revelation 10). The scroll of Revelation 5 is concerned with the history of the church from the Resurrection to the Second Coming. Revelation 10 begins the Lamb's messianic war anticipated in Revelation 5. The Lamb's war leads to the overthrow and extinction of evil, which has already been defeated by the cross.

Revelation 11 presents the ministry of the church (the two witnesses) in the church age. The church is also presented as succumbing, eventually, to persecution. The death and resurrection of the witnesses precipitates the end of the world systems and the ushering in of the visible kingdom of heaven. Revelation 12–13 shows how Satan, thrown out of heaven by the work of the cross, is restrained during the church age—that is, the thousand years—so as not to deceive the nations (cf. 20:1–3). But later, 'shortly' before the Parousia, Satan is given free reign to deceive (12:7–9; 20:1–3). Through the agency of two beasts (Revelation 12–13), the age of Satanic freedom begins on earth. But Satan, pledged to world deception, is unable to complete his aims.

In Revelation 14, the conclusion to the church's ministry is evident with the 144,000 standing victorious with the Lamb on Mt Zion (the new Jerusalem). The remainder of Revelation 14 tells: how the 144,000 reached their end; and that world judgement must occur.

Revelation 15 describes the victory of the church as a new exodus to come, finally, through the unleashing of the last judgements.

Revelation 16 narrates the pouring of the seven bowls, the last series of judgements. The seven bowls represent intensification of all historical punishments on humanity for idolatry. The effect of the bowls leads to the collapse of the world system, which turns in on itself. And the result will be the victory of the Lamb (cf. 17:14).

Revelation 17 details the end of the world system, which is described as the whore or Babylon the great. The description of the world system as the whore prepares the reader for the contrasting presentation of the bride of Christ (Revelation 19, 21). Revelation

18 offers a world lament over Babylon's fall. Revelation 19 shows that Babylon's fall promotes world rejoicing, bringing on the marriage of the Lamb, and the final victory of the Lamb.

20:1–3 presents the history of Satan from the cross onwards. Satan is bound and then released before the end. 20:4–6 describes the work of the saints in heaven between the Fall and the Second Coming. 20:7–10 presents events which are parallel to the final battle (19:11–21). 20:11–15 presents the last judgement.

Revelation 21 provides a description of the bride of Christ, the people of God in the new creation, the heavenly Jerusalem.

Revelation 22:1–5 presents the new creation as the new Eden—the end of the beginning (cf. Genesis 1–2)—but with a huge overplus. The epilogue (22:6–21) concludes Revelation.

The theme of Revelation is the witness of Jesus (1:5) glorifying God through his life and death (Revelation 5), and through the witness of his church. That is why two chapters (Revelation 2–3) are devoted to a survey of the expected character of the church of Christ. The paradoxical result is that the advent of the new creation is to be brought about by God in Christ alone; but God also uses the oftentimes weak and faltering witness of the visible church. The witness of the church to Christ conveys the great biblical hope of the advent of the kingdom of God. This hope is the essence of the proclamation of the eternal gospel of sovereignty. So it is by the witness of the church that the eternal gospel convulses the world.

My thanks are due to all who cooperated in the production of this commentary. Bryan Hardman and the late Denis Ryan made it publishable and provided much guidance on the way. My thanks, especially, are due to Russell Bailey and friends from Redeemer Baptist Church for skilful editing and final presentation.

Revelation 1

Revelation 1:1–3:22

Prologue 1:1–8

In the Revelation of God's plan for world history, the vision of the exalted Son of Man (1:12–16) identifies Jesus with God. This is the focus of Revelation 1. Jesus is equipped with power over death and Hades, as he must be, for his ministry of world judgement. Furthermore, Jesus will present his witness to the world through the church whom he protects and enables. It is through this witness of Jesus that the work of the cross is brought to its final conclusion in the new Jerusalem. Revelation 1 draws attention to the immense Trinitarian power which accounts for the fact and purpose and continued survival of the church.

Revelation 1:1–3 Superscription

Revelation claims the authorization of Jesus. It is thus not entitled The Revelation of John. It is, rather, *The Revelation of Jesus Christ* (1:1a). It received its canonical title later.[1] It is a revelation from Jesus Christ (subjective genitive), who makes known his role beyond what has previously been made known in the coming of the kingdom. Jesus' role will culminate in his glorious Parousia, his second coming. Then, with God—following the visible defeat of evil—Jesus will take acknowledged charge of the universe. The book depicts the struggle between good and evil in our world. Jesus' person, work and mission is at the centre of this struggle.

The book is a revelation. It does not come from human thought or imagination. The term 'revelation' suggests an apocalyptic genre. The content and symbolism of the book exhibit clear apocalyptic affinities. The first word of the book (*apocalypsis*) states clearly that the book is an unveiling of what is to come. The source of the revelation is God himself. It is a revelation from God to Christ to show, through the medium of an angel to his servant 'John', what must come to pass. The 'servants' to whom the Revelation is addressed seem to be prophetic figures, probably the

---

1   Fiorenza, 2002, 7.

leaders of the churches addressed. The heavenly revelation concerns God's activity in history to complete his eschatological purposes for the world. The book is John's witness to the divine unveiling revealed to him as a vision (1:1–2). What has always been true and expected, God is now making plain.

The singular noun 'apocalypse' together with the aorist infinitive *deixai* ('showed' 1:1) suggest one great vision that Christ offers to John. God himself is the author of what is revealed. The content is 'the things which *must* happen', that is, by the divine will. The 'must' that soon is to take place is the fulfilment of his purposes for humanity and the world. Nothing will prevent this fulfilment. For human history, with all its failures, is the progressive expression of God's purpose. The 'must' indicates God's absolute sovereignty over all creation that will be expressed through Jesus. The content of the vision is elaborated in 4:1–22:5. And then the same phrase of divine necessity ('the things which *must* happen') occurs at the closing of the book in 22:6, referring to what John has 'seen'.

Semaino (1:1, cf. Daniel 2:28–30,45) means 'show by a sign'. When not used in the general sense of make known, *semaino* occurs only[2] in the introduction to Daniel's description of the king's dream about the flow of world history (LXX Daniel 2:23,30,45).[3] So the symbols in the Revelation vision are meant to be deciphered. This is confirmed by the use of *deiknumi* (show, 1:1). There is extensive use of symbolism in the Old Testament which is deciphered. John sees the beast rising from the sea (Revelation 13) to take control of the world in the period before Jesus' Parousia. There must be interpretation of such symbolism to convey the message of the book.

The book is to be approached with three genres in mind (1:3). It is a letter, in prophetic language, communicated by typical apocalyptic symbolism.

As a letter, John writes to emphasise that the future belongs to a righteous remnant whom God will protect through hardship and persecution. The symbolism—required to communicate transcendent reality, with which apocalyptic is concerned—was familiar to

---

2 cf. Beale, 1999, 50–51.
3 cf. Dumbrell, 2002, 305–6.

Jewish readers of the Old Testament. The socio-political use of two cities (Rome and the heavenly Jerusalem) represents combat between two worlds, indicating that the book has more affinity in genre with apocalyptic than with prophecy. However, it is prophetic in the way in which it addresses a concrete historical situation. And it is a letter from John. Revelation is not pseudepigraphical, as per the genre of other apocalypses. Rather, John is conscious of his inspiration and writes in his own name within a continuing prophetic tradition conveying the fulfilment of Old Testament unfulfilled prophecy.

Apocalyptic literature offers a transcendent view of the world, questioning human understanding which is conditioned by the world of physical appearance. History is predetermined, yet human beings within history seem to be free moral agents.[4] The present age is characterised by seductive evil that will reach its zenith at the end of history when God will intervene. The Christian community is urged to remain faithful and is warned of the consequences of unfaithfulness. Furthermore, they are consoled by the assurance that God has not forgotten them. He is aware of their circumstances and one day he will reward their unwavering commitment to him. They are to avoid idolatry with its concomitants of immorality and compromise. Instead they are to embrace humility, love, and perseverance.

As an apocalyptic revelation, the book will offer encouragement to Christians threatened by persecution as well as offering an understanding of the meaning and the task of the church within history. This genre is used to provide an explanation for the problem of evil. Evil is used in the plan of God to bring about the destined new creation.

The Apocalypse stands squarely in the eschatological and apocalyptic traditions that preceded it. It covers the past, present and future eschatological flow of salvation history, drawing heavily on the Old Testament to promote Old Testament expectations in the light of the death of Christ. In keeping with the free use of symbolism in apocalyptic literature, there is significant use of Old Testament symbolic background in Revelation.

---

4   Foerster *axios*, TDNT 1. 379.

John also describes the book as a prophecy (1:3, cf 22:6–7, 11–16) about the imminent inaugurated fulfilment of Old Testament prophecies about the kingdom to come finally, visibly in Christ.

The word 'prophecy' occurs seven times (1:3; 11:6; 19:10; 22:7,10,18,19). The book is therefore seen to be the complete fulfilment of biblical prophecy, bringing the forward-looking message of the Bible to a conclusion; not only the fulfilment of unfulfilled Old Testament prophecy, but also the fulfilment of prophecy projected in the New Testament. This fulfilment will usher in the new Jerusalem—that is, the new creation—and the completion of an Eden experience for humankind (cf. 22:1–5 with Genesis 2:9–14).[5] This completes canonical revelation.

The agent through whom the disclosure (revelation) is made to the world is Jesus Christ. The order of the two names 'Jesus Christ' emphasises that the revelation stems from the ministry and death of Jesus who—by his resurrection and ascension—now sits at the right hand of God as king of the universe, that is, as Christ (cf. Romans 1:4; Philippians 2:5–11). The only earthly act of Jesus that is mentioned in Revelation is his death. This death is pivotal for the understanding of all history. Jesus' death was God's testimony to his control over history. For in the death of the Lamb slain and by the resurrection, God in Jesus had demonstrated his conquest of death. The key to the book is understanding the person and role of Jesus Christ, past and present, in the continuity of events divinely destined to happen. The book begins and ends with Christology (1:1; 22:21), for Jesus is the continuing content of the revelation.

The message was, appropriately, cast in symbolism (1:1, *esemanen*). Its interpretation was not to be dependent upon the concrete features of any particular period in history, but would be true for all periods. Symbols are essential to convey messages in multiple layers for continual application through to the end of history. Symbols go beyond the limitations of physical existence and thought; they are trans-historical. Thus Revelation incarnates its meanings in images, events and visions, preferring the imagina-

---

[5] cf. Beale, 1999, 183.

tive to the propositional.⁶ With evocative power the symbols of Revelation invite imaginative participation in the book's symbolic world.⁷ An exclusively literal approach will lead to disastrous misunderstandings, as will any attempt to position the book solely in a particular history.

The new creation is presented through biblical symbolism of the church. God speaks through dreams, visions and cosmic excursions with angelic guides. In this symbolism, numerology is a prominent feature: 1 = unity; 2 = division, contrast; 3 = completion, purity or its contrast, or parody; 4 = sacred significance, universality; 5 = incomplete or of a limited duration; 7 = perfection, completion, fulfilment; 10 = of sizeable proportions but indefinite; 12 = fullness of God's people. There is also symbolism in time: three and one half years = indefinite period but with a fixed end in sight.⁸

It is often proposed in modern interpretation that symbols are not to be transferred into propositional language since propositional language is not capable of expressing truths about the transcendent God. In Revelation, Christ as a lion and a Lamb is not propositional. But the symbol requires interpretation in association with the progressive symbolism of the book. It is further suggested that attempts to interpret symbols robs them of their persuasive power. However, by putting the progressive pictures together and understanding the general sense of Revelation, the reader can arrive at meaning, which is necessary when dealing with metaphorical language.

The Greek words *en taxei* ('in order', but also 'soon', 1:1) indicate that the process of spiritual warfare between the world and the church of God leading to the new Jerusalem has begun. God's disclosure of what is to happen at the end of days (1:1; cf. Daniel 2:28–29),⁹ signifies that the book as a whole is about to elaborate on issues raised in Daniel 2. What will be 'shown' to John is the vanquishing of evil kingdoms and the vindication of the righteous in the inauguration of the visible kingdom of God (cf. Daniel 2).

---

6   Ryken, 1993, 458.
7   cf. Beale, 1999, 50–69.
8   Lioy, 2003, 42.
9   'to show...the things which must soon take place', Beale, 1999, 182.

Revelation, like Daniel 2, deals with events that must take place in the purpose of God before the disordered and rebellious world will give way to the fulfilment in Christ of God's full purposes for creation in the advent of the new Jerusalem.[10] For history is not haphazard or quixotic. The angel sent to John (1:1) is the angel sent to the churches (22:16).

1:2 appears to be amplifying 1:1, referring to the testimony to the word of God by John that Jesus gave (cf. 19:10). The content, coming to John through Spirit-inspired prophetic vision, is the witness that Jesus was to the word of God. This had led to his death. Here and elsewhere the book presents Jesus as the revealer who will address the seven churches of Asia, open the scroll of destiny (5:5,7) and disclose its contents (6:1,3,5,7,9; 8:1).

The word 'witness' (1:2) refers to John's verbal witness to the truth of God (1:2,9; 6:9; 20:4, cf. 12:11), along with his obedience to God's commands (12:17). It is strongly implied that faithful witness will lead to death (2:13; 11:7; 12:17), just as the sequence of titles in 1:5 indicates that Jesus' witness led to his death. However, when John wrote Revelation the Greek word *martus* did not mean martyr, that is, a witness leading to death. But Jesus' work is continued in his followers. Jesus' followers are not only called his witnesses (17:6) but also are said to hold the witness of Jesus (12:17; 19:10). The witness of Jesus is the content of their own witness (6:9; 12:11). Theirs will be a witness to the true God, a witness to his righteousness that exposes the falsehood of idolatry and the evil of those who worship the beast. Their witness will be a call to submit to the sovereignty of God, that is, to the preaching of the gospel. Revelation and John's Gospel share a major theme, namely, that the world is a courtroom in which the issue is 'who is the true sovereign of the universe?'.

In his life, Jesus raised the vital issues that humankind must confront. The church is to continue that theme in its witness to him. And at the Parousia, Christ becomes the judge of world reaction to this witness. The witness of Jesus given through his life, death and resurrection is the theme of Revelation. Christ, the faithful and true witness (3:14), will be faithful and true in judgement (19:11). In its context, the title 'the faithful witness' (cf.

---

10 Beale, 1984, 415–416.

Psalm 89:37) ascribed to Jesus (1:5) portrays a judicial content in which the claim of Yahweh to be the only true God, the Creator, and the Lord of history will be vindicated. The people of the true Israel are the continuing witnesses (cf. Isaiah 43:10,12; 44:8), called to testify to the nations that Yahweh alone is the true God and Saviour.

John uses the Old Testament comprehensively, but he does not cite texts. Old Testament texts are simply made part of the Christian story by taking Jewish tradition and language and enfolding them into Christian tradition and language.[11] John thereby makes the claim that Christians are the ongoing Israel. Restored Israel is called to maintain this continuity in Revelation. John derives his content for witness through the visions he receives. His message is about the future course of history and the great denouement to come at its end. But that future course has been set since the Fall by the godless idolatry of the nations from which the nations will not deviate. This idolatry will demand rigid examination and judgement.

The message of Revelation is contained in a letter to seven churches under angelic supervision. Accordingly, the message comes to John through an angel. Angels are envoys from the heavenly court who feature prominently throughout the book in communication, interpretation and heavenly worship. As members of Yahweh's heavenly court, they serve and praise him there. There is a hierarchy of angels in Revelation. These angels reveal visions and provide interpretation (cf. Daniel).[12]

Such was the importance of the book's content, which could not be altered or added to (22:18), that a blessing (1:3) is offered to those who read it aloud (that is, to the leader of the congregation) and to those who keep it. Presumably, the substance of this blessing will be belonging as citizens to the new Jerusalem. The sure hope of participation in the end-time city will provide the continuing content of present blessing. However, reading by itself will not be enough; blessing will come when life is shaped by the certainty of the worldview that Revelation offers. 1:3 is the first of seven blessings (14:13; 16:15; 19:9; 20:6; 22:7,14), all of which relate to

---

11 cf. Stevenson 2001, 238–9.
12 cf. Smalley, 2005, 28–30.

hearing and obeying the word of God and the witness that Jesus had offered. Blessing will finally win out, for the book begins with the church in tribulation and ends with cosmic reconciliation under the rule of God to which believers are to look forward. Tribulation and patience are the notes that the book continuously strikes for believers, since these are the necessary characteristics of the people of God within history.

Revelation is a prophecy written in apocalyptic vein. No such claim is made for any other piece of New Testament literature. John is claiming spiritual continuity with the divinely inspired Old Testament prophets through whom the word of God came. His understanding of his role—for the book is written after the event of inspiration through him—is to disclose the divine way in which the triumph of the Lamb will bring history to an end.

The historical moment (*kairos*, 1:3) when the kingdom of God will be ushered in visibly (cf. Mark 1:14–15) is near. The end is imminent (cf. 22:6,7,12,20). There is a sense of urgency. John's message is relevant as the time is near, whatever the particular historical period of the reader.

Revelation 1:4–6 A Letter to Seven Churches

1:4–5a opens as a conventional letter stating the name of the writer and a list of those to whom the letter is addressed, followed by a greeting in the form 'grace to you and peace'. The text places the revelation that follows under the eternal sovereignty of God. Grace (1:4) is the consciousness of God's favour extended through the Spirit with resulting peace: the restored harmony between God and man that can only come from him. The full Trinitarian identification of the divine underscores the seriousness with which the book must be taken. The strong references to deity in Revelation 1 serve to underline the authority which backs the writer of the letter.

The conclusion (22:21) confirms the letter form. The entire book is thus a circular letter to the seven churches in Roman Asia. The letter to the seven churches (to which John is no stranger) contains John's visionary revelations, reported prophetically. The seven churches—as the number seven suggests and the later information endorses—are representative, in their potential and problems, of the church throughout history. John sees himself as standing in the tradition of Old Testament prophecy (cf. 10:7, 'servants the prophets' seems to refer to the Old Testament prophets; cf. Amos 3:7).

John is on the small island of Patmos (1:9), 16 square miles in area and 40 miles west-south-west of Miletus. Patmos, in the Icarian sea, was one of the Dodecanese (12 islands). It provided the last stopping place when travelling from Rome to Ephesus. 1: 9 suggests, and tradition concurs, that John was in penal exile on Patmos. But if 'on account of the word of God' (1: 9) refers back to 1:2, then it could be that John was in Patmos to receive the vision there.

The seven churches (1:4)—Ephesus, Smyrna, Pergamum, Thyatira, Sardis, Philadelphia and Laodicea (1:11)—are in geographical order for a messenger starting from Ephesus. The particular Christian audience is clearly defined in the seven letters, although the content of the letters is also of general interest to all churches. The four references to the seven churches (1:4,11,20,20) suggest a universality about them ('four' = universal, 'seven' = complete). The revelation is addressed to the seven churches. But the entire revelation addressed to the seven churches concerns the whole world throughout history. The global, transhistorical relevance of the revelation rests on the assumption that the seven Asian churches are representative of Christian people throughout history. Each of the letters concludes with an indication that the message is generally directed to all churches. Most of Revelation is intended for all churches, but Jesus introduced seven letters with particular messages to each of the seven churches. Each letter was relevant to its own situation. And the letters expose temptations, problems and successes that relate to the church of all times. Each church, since all seven are differentiated, is then addressed by the whole of the book that follows.

John had probably spent his last years in the Province of Asia, the western part of modern Asian Turkey that the Seleucid Attalus III had transferred to Rome c.133 BC. Because of God's grace (1:4), John knows that peace for his people may follow. In the Trinitarian presentation of 1:4–5, denoting the source of blessing, the threefold description of the Godhead exhibits the customary use of three in Revelation as the number of the divine (= God in Trinity; or its counterfeit, the demonic trinity, cf. 16:13).

1:4b and 1:8 encase the complete ministry of Jesus (1:5–7): his earthly ministry leading to his death; his resurrection; his redemption and establishment of the true Israel with the same commission as had been given to Old Testament Israel; and, finally, his Parousia. 1:4b and 1:8 deal with the eternal reign of God within which history occurs, and with the Spirit through whom revelation will be communicated.

The description of God (1:4) encompasses three tenses beginning before time and space and continuing after the renewal of the world (21:1). God's unchangeable eternity is underlined by the lack of concord between the preposition and pronoun ('from him', but nominative, *Ho On*). The purpose of this lack of concord in syntax may be to highlight the detail of the Old Testament reference (Exodus 3:14).[13] But, primarily, John's desire may have been to emphasise, ungrammatically, God as unchanging. God is eternally (*ho on*), continually directing and governing. As Creator and Sustainer, God was (*ho en*). And God is to come, pointing to a final further theophany which is a conclusive confrontation with evil. God's governance of history is affirmed by what follows in Revelation. He was and is always coming, in past and present, but these comings are the manifestation of him who always is. Historical past, present and future are comprehended in his eternal being. He is always the subject, never an object; what happens, happens because he wills it; he is never acted upon.[14] Nothing is beyond his control. In a disorderly world, God's order is operating. This formula occurs five times (1:4,8; 4:8; 11:17; 16:5) and is an interpretation of the divine name Yahweh (cf. Exodus 3:14).

But 'who is to come' is not referring to God's future existence. The reference is to his continual coming into the world in salvation and judgement, consummated in his final coming into this present world to bring its disobedient history to a close. When the eschatological coming of God is being described (11:17; 16:5), the formula is logically abbreviated to 'who is' and ' who was'. God's

---

13 cf. Beale, 1999, 188.
14 cf. Caird, 1966, 16.

final coming will mean his eschatological rule over the world. So this threefold sequence describes God's eternity.

The reference to the seven spirits before the throne (1:4) draws upon Zechariah 4:1–14[15] in its presentation of the seven lamps on the lampstand (that is, Israel) as a symbol for the complete fullness of the divine Spirit in the gift of covenant grace.[16] 'Seven' (55 times in Revelation, out of 88 New Testament occurrences) = completion, plenitude, fullness and totality. In the Old Testament, the Hebrew word *ruach* ('spirit') does not refer to Yahweh as he is in himself but as he communicates his power, his life, his wrath in judgement, his will, his very presence to the world. Spirit in the Old Testament does not customarily denote Yahweh's essence.[17] In the Old Testament, 'Spirit' generally denotes God's action as an extension of his personality. 'Seven spirits' indicates the fullness of God in his powerful working in the world. The sevenfold Spirit before the throne identifies the Spirit as the one always ready and able to manifest the presence of God in the world (4:5).

God's worldly rule is thus to be imposed not by might but by the Spirit (Zechariah 4:6). Since his Spirit will act in and with the human spirit, God will principally carry out his intention by interaction with human beings. The Spirit is now the presence and power of the Lord in the world, bringing about God's kingdom by implementing the Lamb's victory throughout the world.

The seven lamps of Zechariah's lampstand (Zechariah 4:2) become the seven spirits of God blazing before the throne (4:5). But this is the function of the Lamb (5:6; cf. 4:5); the seven spirits are eyes of the Lamb which range through the whole world. The Lamb is the lamp of the new Jerusalem (21:23). Christ radiates the Spirit into the world. The Spirit is now the Spirit of Christ (cf. Acts 2:33; Romans 8:9–10) working the will of God in history. Since the Spirit is predicated of God and Christ (3:1; 5:6), the book establishes the procession of the Holy Spirit to be from Father and Son. The seven Spirits are also the power of Christ through the church's prophetic witness to the world, for the seven churches

---

15 or perhaps the sevenfold gifts of the Spirit in Isaiah 11:2.
16 Hoeksema, 2000, 20.
17 However, cf. Isaiah 40:13 where the Spirit is the intelligent centre of God's being.

are represented as seven golden lampstands (1:12). Zechariah's one lampstand is thus divided. In Revelation there are thirteen references to the Spirit (1:10; 2:7,11,17,29; 3:6,13,22; 4:2; 14:13; 17:3; 21:10; 22:17).

In this Trinitarian presentation (1:4–5) the coupling of the name Jesus with the royal name, Christ, serves to emphasise his glorified humanity (cf. 11:15; 12:10; 20:4,6). Grace and peace is the Father's gift based on Jesus' work. This gift of grace and peace is affirmed by God through the resurrection and communicated by the Spirit to bring about the wholeness of person (Hebrew *shalom*), which is the ultimate gift of God.

1:5–7 majors on three statements. First, that the ministry of Jesus was the basis of all future claims for him (1:5). Secondly, that the death and resurrection of Jesus instituted the new covenant and brought to the new covenant people the covenant blessings given to Israel for ministry to the world (1:6; cf. Exodus 19:5–6). Thirdly, that Jesus' return at the end of the age in great power and authority is to usher in the new world and rule under God (1:7).

In 1:5 there are three titles of Jesus Christ which are characteristic of deity (cf. 1:1). These titles refer to his human past (witness), present (first born of the dead), and future work in a visible stage to come (ruler of the kings of the earth, cf. Psalm 2:7). All of these titles refer to the Messiah (Psalm 89:27,36–37).[18] The name 'Jesus' occurs fourteen times in Revelation and thus his humanity is stressed. Seven of these references occur as a phrase, 'witness of Jesus', emphasising the witness he offered in his humanity. The word 'Christ' also occurs seven times indicating that Jesus' fulfilment of Davidic hopes is a prominent feature in the book. The role of Christ in Revelation is to establish God's kingdom on earth, thereby turning the kingdoms of the world into the kingdom of our Lord and his Messiah.

As the faithful witness (cf. Isaiah 55:4; Psalm 89:37), Jesus is the eschatological witness (*martus*). 'Faithful witness' is in the nominative but is in apposition with 'Jesus Christ' (genitive), indicating again the subjection of concord to theological emphasis. At this stage in the history of the church, the primary meaning of

---

18   Beale, 1999, 190.

martus is the witness of the church as the legatee of Israel's role (cf. Isaiah 49:6; Acts 1:8). And Jesus fulfils Israel's role. The context in Revelation determines whether death is to be associated with that *martus* (witness).

Psalm 89:19-37 concerns the anointed king who would reign over defeated enemies. The anointed king's seed would be established on his throne forever as fulfilment of the prophecy about the permanent throne of David (cf. 11:15; 12:10; 20:4,6; 2 Samuel 7:8-16). Jesus bore witness by his non-violent sacrificial death[19]— like the enduring witness of the moon (Psalm 89:37)—to God's covenant intentions for his messianic kingship (cf. Psalm 2:7). The message from Jesus and of Jesus thus leads believers to the new Jerusalem.

By his resurrection Jesus is also 'the first born of the dead': the beginning of the new human sequence and its pre-eminent head, the inaugurator and the representative of the new creation. Jesus thereby exhibited the beginning of the final transformation to come upon all Christians, and thus was both the file leader of the new creation and sovereign over it.[20] He is now ruler of the kings of the earth,[21] but with a future dimension to this third item. The reality of this rule over the kings of the earth is in the future (19:16), when final expression is given to the victory of Psalm 2:7-9. In Revelation, John delivers from Jesus how this rule will be finally implemented. Some suggest that Christ's rule over the kings of the earth refers to his rule over believers (1:6) who have now assumed the role of Adam and Israel (Exodus 19:6), that is, believers who are now the true Israel in this new messianic age. However, the expression 'kings of the earth' in Revelation usually expresses political opposition (cf. 6:15; 17:2; 18:3,9; 19:19). So the message here is that Christ will have visible rule over all political opposition.

After the threefold blessing (1:5-6) that has resulted from the present work of Jesus, a doxology—characteristically Jewish at the mention of the divine name—follows. Christ's activity, the

---

19 op. cit., 1999, 190-191. cf. Antipas' his death, 3:14.
20 cf. Romans 1:4; Colossians 1:18; Acts 2:29-32.
21 cf. Psalm 89:27, the Davidic king.

blessing of his work as opposed to the enumeration of his person, is summarised by three participial phrases (1:6–7).

First, Jesus loved us. The aorist carries the meaning that the cross was the supreme example of his continuing love. And Jesus' death on the cross is the universal Day of Atonement.

Secondly, and following on from the first, Jesus ransomed us. The Old Testament exodus is likened to Jesus redeeming us by his atonement. The Greek word *louo* ('washed') has strong textual support but the Greek aorist *luo* ('loosed') fits better contextually. Jesus did all this 'by his blood' (probably meaning 'at the price of his blood'), that is, by his sacrificial death. Redemption was from the presence and consequences of sin, as sin is a slave-master.

Thirdly, and consequentially, Jesus has installed us as a new kingdom (1:6). Jesus has considered us as resurrected and exalted and reigning. New covenant believers are like the Old Covenant believers at Sinai: covenantally set forth in priestly terms, showing by their purity their separation from the world (cf. Exodus 19:6). There is textual support for each of the Greek words *basileia* ('kingdom') and *basileus* ('king'). But *basileia* fits better contextually as it provides a collective emphasis (cf. 1 Peter 2:9): a kingdom of kingly subjects with direct priestly access to serve God. Jesus has dignified us with this new status. Christians are a priestly kingdom under the dominion of God. This was formerly intended primarily for national Israel but the place of national Israel has been surrendered by her unbelief. In Exodus 19:6 the concept of Israel being a priestly kingdom is in the future. But in 1:6 the tense is past. This is the significance of the cross for believers. The rule of believers in the new kingdom makes them servants of all (cf. Matthew 20:25–28), members of the new covenant witnessing to and overcoming the world as Jesus did. Believers are victorious in Christian warfare (7:1–8) as Jesus was in his sacrificial death. Jesus reigns as king by his selfless conquest of sin and death (Romans 1:4). Believers will fulfil their roles in this kingdom by their sacrificial witness in the world and by their reign over sin and, finally, death.

Individually, Christians are now priests consecrated for divine service; corporately they are a kingdom.[22] Christians are now heirs to the covenant relationship and promises given to Israel. John indicates that Christians are now the people of God who will serve God in his eschatological temple (1:6).[23]

The priestly kingdom role of believers in the new Jerusalem is the major note on which Revelation ends (22:3–5). Particularly, therefore, the priestly-royalty legacy of Adam[24] and national Israel is pertinently applied to believers (1:6; 5:10; 20:6). This indicates that the book is concerned with a revelation of the consequences of the death of Christ, his heavenly rule resulting in the inclusion of believers in a ruling activity within the wide framework of the new creation. This would realise all the blessings God had intended for mankind (cf. Genesis 1:26–28; 2:9–17). Mankind will then fulfil as kings the royal role specified for Adam in Genesis 1, and that of priesthood performed by Adam in Genesis 2.

The doxology which follows is to God from whom the blessing that is Jesus has come. It is now concluded with a formal amen, which is the believers' assent and confirmation. There is a two-fold doxology to the divine person here ('glory and dominion'). This increases to a threefold doxology (4:11, 'glory and honour and power'), a fourfold doxology (5:13, 'blessing and honour and glory and power'), and a sevenfold doxology (7:12 'blessing and glory and wisdom, thanksgiving and honour and power and might'). 'Glory'—that is, total recognition of God's deity and dominion, world recognition of his rule for all eternity, credit for all that has happened in history—is what the believers are continually to offer to the one who sits upon the throne.

Revelation 1:7–8 The Expectation of the Book

The commencement 'behold' signals a special divine intervention. We move from what Christ has done (1:5–6) to the shape of the future. Christ's second coming provides the topic of expectancy for the whole book. He comes with clouds. Clouds are

---

22 cf. Exodus 19:6; Isaiah 61:6; and 1 Peter 2:9, where *basileion hierateuma* indicates a kingdom of subjects comprising a body of priests.
23 Stevenson, 2001, 240.
24 cf. Dumbrell, 2002, 21.

heavenly messengers, the symbols of majesty and judgement,[25] used only of God in the Old Testament (Psalm 104:3; Isaiah 19:1) and attesting his heavenly glory. 1:7 combines a reference to Daniel 7:13 and Zechariah 12:10–14. Jesus will return as the Son of Man, the judge of the end-time. Those who will not see Jesus as their crucified Messiah will see him one day arriving as their Judge. The ultimate issues of the kingdom of God—life and death, salvation and damnation—turn on people's response to Jesus Christ.[26] Dominion and a kingdom (Daniel 7:14) has now been given to Jesus, the fulfilment of the divine intention of Genesis 1:26–28. The human race, in the light of the universal lordship of Christ, will recognise the tragedy of their rejection of the cross and will admit their culpability. While the whole human race sees the return of Christ, those who pierced him (Jews and Romans) are singled out. They are a class within 'every eye' of those who opposed and oppose Christ. All the tribes of the earth shall mourn over prospective judgement (cf. Matthew 24:30). This is a grim preview of what is ahead. 1:7 ends with an affirmation of divine certainty.

The emphasis is on the return of Christ, visibly coming in judgement of the whole human race. But we must not exclude continuing historical applications of comings within history such as the fall of Jerusalem (cf. Mark 13:26 with the application of Daniel 7:13). These historical applications mark a coming of Christ to judge within continuing history. Revelation indicates many incidents within history which mark a coming of Christ to judge. Jesus' return is the topic of Revelation. The Parousia is the arrival of Jesus after the defeat of the evil kingdoms, the final enemies of the true Israel.

In the future all will recognise him for what he is: the one pierced (cf. Zechariah 12:10). Nothing, however, is said about conversion; only that they shall mourn, possibly over prospective judgement. They will admit their culpability in the light of the manifested universal lordship of Christ.

God now speaks before the onset of John's vision (1:8). God introduces the plan for the new creation with a word, just as he had

---

25 Hoeksema, 2000, 28.
26 Webb, 2003, 49.

brought the world into being by his word. In Revelation, God speaks again at 21:5–8. The first speech sets the movement towards the new creation in train; the second speech announces the completion of the new creation (21:5–8). Thus, by inclusion, God opens and closes the book. However, he is never described as present among the churches on earth (he was said to be present in the earthly temple). God's direct presence is only to be realised in the eschatological age (21:1–3).[27] Christ, who preceded all things as their source, will also bring in God's eschatological fulfilment of all things. The inter-changeability of the divine titles between God and Christ (cf. 1:8 with 22:13; 1:17) clearly presents Christ as God.

God's speech (1:8) adds an exalted three-fold affirmation of his person (cf. 21:6). The consummation of the divine purpose for creation is to result from the return of Christ (1:7). As almighty, God directs creation to its fulfilment. The eternal gospel, the call to the world to submit to the benign sovereignty of God (14:6), is the gospel of God (Romans 1:1–2). More than that, God is redeemer in Christ reconciling the world unto himself (2 Corinthians 5:19). And it is to God, in the end, that Christ will hand over the kingship of the universe (1 Corinthians 15:28). In Paul's letter to the Corinthians, this handing over of the kingship is so that God may be all in all, which is also the design of Revelation.

The universe in its historical beginning and end is grounded, as all things are, in God. God is the Alpha and Omega (referring to the first and last letters of the Greek alphabet), the beginning and the end of human history but also the director of everything in between. God is the first and therefore, as unchangeable, is also the last since history is to end. He is thus responsible for and sums up all things. God is responsible for the beginning of history and all beyond its end. He has had the first word in creation and will have the last word in the new creation.[28]

As such God is *Pantokrator* (invincible), the sovereign director of history, the Lord God, the Almighty. This is the divine title of

---

27 cf. Stevenson, 2001, 239.
28 Bauckham, The Theology of the Book of Revelation, 1993, 27 cf. Mathewson, 2003, 79.

the Old Testament.[29] There is no God other than he (Isaiah 44:6). God is the one who is, who was, and who is to come. This repetition of the threefold relationship of God to all that is, is in regard to the eschatological fulfilment of all things. This threefold declaration sums up the goal for history, emphasising that God orders this world despite the appearance of disobedient disorder.

Thus, three of the four most important designations for God in Revelation are incorporated in 1: 8. There is a corresponding declaration of Christ as first and last (1:17; cf. 22:13 the Alpha and Omega, the beginning and the end, the first and the last). With the inclusion of 2:8, Revelation contains seven self-declarations by God and Christ. It is at Christ's Parousia that God, the beginning of all things, will also come in judgement as the end of all things. The introduction to Revelation concludes with this self-declaration of his incontestable sovereignty (1:8). This understanding of the divine presence will govern what follows in Revelation.

The emphasis at the beginning (1:5–8), carried even further in 1:12–16, is the inevitability of the end. Evil, conquered by the cross, will finally be eliminated from human experience. New covenant believers will therefore experience the divine purpose and provision—which was clear from the beginning in Genesis 1–2—of life in a new Eden.

Revelation 1:9–20 The Son of Man and the Churches

These verses: form the introduction to Revelation 2–3; contain the promise structure of the book that is responded to in fulfilment (19:1–22:5); and contain John's commission to write, with a specific injunction from Jesus (1:19). John is a brother in Christian experience (1:9). John identifies himself with his readers, using one article to govern the three following datives. All three datives have their reference 'in Jesus'. Christians possess eternal life. John reminds his readers that the duality of Christian existence in Jesus is that the present reality in the world is, at the same time tribulation, being a citizen of the new Jerusalem, and perseverance until the fall of Babylon. The middle term,

---

29 cf. the seven instances of the title at 1:8; 4:8; 11:17; 15:3; 16:7; 19:6; 21:22. The only other mention of this divine title in the New Testament is at 2 Corinthians 6:18.

'kingdom' (1:9a), conveys knowledge of the heavenly order. This provides the faith rationale for the other two datives, tribulation and active perseverance. All three terms are qualified by being in Jesus, through the Spirit. So Christian tribulation is the necessary state for the possession of the coming kingdom. Therefore tribulation must be met with courageous, patient endurance that looks towards final fulfilment of life in the kingdom. 1:9 also indicates that the reason for John's exile was his commitment to witness to the fulfilment of God's word in Jesus, presumably in Asia Minor.

The sounding of the trumpet-like voice (1:10; cf. Exodus 19:16 at Sinai) finds John facing in the wrong direction and requiring reorientation. He is summoned (Greek aorist) to direct encounter with the heavenly world. This spiritual awakening occurs on the Lord's Day (1:10), the first Christian occurrence of a term used by later writers to refer to the Christian Sunday.[30] This resurrection day could form the eighth day of the original creation, the beginning of the new creation.

John tells his readers that he 'became'—that is, experienced rapture or possession by the Spirit—'in the Spirit', a phrase occurring three times later at major transitions (4:2; 17:3; 21:10). The phrase seems to signify the experience of the Spirit's power in prophetic revelation (Matthew 22:43; Luke 1:17; 2:27; Acts 19:21) whereby sensory experience is replaced by spiritual audition and vision (cf. 4:2). John is claiming that Revelation is the product of a real visionary experience. However, this experience was not merely personal. The effects of the experience are never fully described. The issue here is the validity of his prophetic experience and thus the fidelity of his communication. The introductory 1:10–11 points by analogy to Ezekiel's call. 'Write in a book' reflects the command that Yahweh gave to his prophetic servants for judgements to be communicated to Israel.[31] The voice and the trumpet point by analogy to Sinai (Exodus 19:16, 19–20), indicating a theophany.

John is required to record on a scroll what he sees (1:11)—that is, what he experiences—the complete vision. The book is then to

---

30   cf. Didache 14:1; Evan Pet 35; Ignatius Ad Mag 9:1.
31   cf. Exodus 17:14; Isaiah 30:8; Jeremiah 30:2; 36:2, 28 (Beale, 1999, 203).

be sent to the named seven cities. These seven cities are at the centre of postal districts that could send the book further. Ephesus, as the administrative capital of the region and the major metropolis, comes first. The coastal Smyrna is followed by inland cities, working back in a circuit to Ephesus.

John sees a Christophany (1:12–16); a vision of the suffering but exalted one like a Son of Man (Daniel 7:13). The title 'Son of Man' was the title chosen by Jesus to explain his earthly ministry (John 1:51). Jesus would be elevated to the throne of God (Daniel 7:13); and given glory, dominion, kingship, and rule over all. This Son of Man is now the conqueror of death; he is the ruler and judge of the world; he is now, also, the Ancient of Days before whom—as the end-time judge of all (Daniel 7:9–13)—the books had been opened. This heavenly function of Christ presumes that he is sharing the divine throne (cf. Daniel 7:9). Christ's deity is plain. The term Son of Man, chosen by Jesus to describe his earthly mission and the meaning of his death, is now chosen to present his rule over the world through the church. Jesus' earthly ministry, his final surrender to the cross, and then his resurrection accounts for the beginning of the Christian church and sustains the church through her history. In his death, Jesus had taken the Adamic race to the cross; Jesus was the sinless and inclusive representative of the Adamic race on the cross. In his resurrection Jesus had been the beginner and, in continuation, the begetter of the new human race as the first born from the dead.

1:12–20 introduces the following letters to the seven churches, whose ministry is based on the authority of this vision.[32] judgement for the world will occur on the basis of the church's testimony to the Son of Man. 1:12–16 thus focuses on the Son of Man as divine and as the corporate representative for the saints. By his resurrection, Jesus has fulfilled the expectations of Daniel 7:9–13. This presentation of the Son of Man as the Son of God is the narrative emphasis of the first chapter. Christ moves in the midst of seven lampstands having conquered sin, the world, and the devil. John's Gospel has dealt with the expectations surrounding the title Son of Man, providing a clear link between the title and future

---

32 cf. Boring, 1989, 63.

judgement.³³ The vision of the exalted Son of Man (1:13–16), with the background in Daniel 7:9–13, sets the Christological tone for the world judgement dealt with in Revelation. The enthroned Son of Man will indeed 'draw all mankind to him' (John 12:32) for their response to the cross. The response to the cross is the judgement bar within history that will decide their eternal future. But his coming will also mean the vindication of the saints (Daniel 7:27).

The initial vision (1:12–16)—together with John's response (1:17a) and Christ's further word (1:17b–20)—presents Christ as eschatological judge, heavenly Lord, and God. The themes of suffering, kingdom and priesthood are developed with the new theme of Christ having received universal dominion as Son of Man (Daniel 7:14) and thus as judge. Christ says to John: 'do not fear' (1:17a), which is the main point of 1:12–16. 1:17b–18 is the basis for the exhortation not to fear. 1:19–20 is Christ's exhortation to record the vision. Christ commissions John, presents his credentials as God, and exhorts John to take courage (1:17a).

As the new temple and its builder, Christ is at the centre of seven golden lampstands just as God's presence was thought to pervade the earthly Jerusalem temple. The number seven denotes the perfect communion of the church with God. There is now a heavenly essence of this perfect communion of the church with God. The lampstands are probably arranged in a circle representing the seven churches in their ideal position gathered around Jesus, whose seven eyes is their source.³⁴ This is like Israel's experience of the glory of the Lord in the tabernacle and temple (Exodus 40:34–38; 1 Kings 8:10–11). The lamps burn continuously as Jesus, the light of the world, supplies the 'oil'.

John's imagery is dependent on Zechariah 4. However, whereas in Zechariah there is one seven-branch golden lampstand (Zechariah 4:2), there are now in Revelation seven golden lampstands representing the true Israel. The lampstands represent Israel dispersed (representative of the universal church of all ages). And in the midst of the dispersed Israel, sustaining them, stands the empowering presence of the Lord of the earth. The

---

33   cf. John 5:27ff; 3:13; 12:32–36 (Dumbrell, 2006).
34   Aune, 1997, 89.

spiritual endowment of Israel in Zechariah 4 was symbolised by the two 'pipes' from the two olive trees who were the two anointed ones (Zechariah 4:14). The two anointed ones—the king, Zerubbabel; and the high priest, Joshua—are the designated sources of blessing for Israel. In the new covenant, the offices of these representatives are now combined in Christ. And all within the seven churches, representative of the true Israel, are now kings and priests. In Revelation, the source of power for the seven lamp-stands (the seven churches) is the lamps, and the seven lamps are the seven eyes of the Lord (1:4; 4:5) which through the seven spirits of God are to be sent out into all the world (5:6).

The Son of Man walks in the midst of the seven lampstands. He is the reason for their existence. The seven lampstands are symbolic of the new temple; they are the people of God from every nation manifested in individual congregations as the true Israel. They live not by might nor by power but by God's Spirit (Zechariah 4:6).[35] Each congregation is a lampstand witnessing to the world by the Spirit-light from its lamp. The gold of the lampstand represents the people of God in their preciousness and purity. The shift from one lampstand in Zechariah to seven lampstands in Revelation is a shift from Israel to the universal church. The light that the Old Testament lamps shed as the lampstand stood in the temple represented God's presence with Israel. If the churches do not retain their priestly-kingdom witness (cf. 11:1–13) to the testimony of Jesus, Christ will judge them. But if they are faithful, they will worship in the presence of the Lord.

Gradations of light affect the narrative. The brightest light is at the centre and this is the source of life for those at the perimeter. The intensity of light changes for the lampstands at the perimeter.[36] They are able, however, to provide light for a darkened world. At the centre, as the light of the world—lighting the lampstands—is the intense, searing, blinding brilliance of one like unto a Son of Man (cf. 1:16). The seven stars, the angelic leadership of the seven churches, are held in the palm of Christ's right hand (1:16). The image is not only of protection, stability and

---

35 Beale, 1999, 207.
36 Resseguie, 1998, 38–39.

order but also of active power. Without Christ, his people can do nothing.

As John turns to 'see the voice' (1:12), his whole orientation is changed. The new temple (the seven golden lampstands) is sustained in the present dark world by the light received from Jesus (the Son of Man figure in the midst of them). The force of the church's witness depends upon the figure at the centre (1:13). Thus the vision then turns at once to indicate the manner of the Son of Man.

John sees a human form in the middle of the lampstands. Christ is that human form. Christ's priestly ministry is to tend and care for the churches. The title and descriptions given to Jesus (1:12–18) find their place in each of the seven letters except the letter to Laodicea (3:14–22). The vision will assure the church in the world that Christ is able to meet her needs and respond to her circumstances.

Christ is clothed down to his feet. This points to his rank, dignity and high priestly significance. This is the only reference in Revelation to Christ acting as priest. The outer appearance of this Son of Man describes the reality of his inner nature.[37] The Greek word *poderes* (a long robe or tunic) is found several times in the LXX referring to: the ephod of Israel's high priest (Exodus 25:7; 28:4,27,31; 29:5; 35:[8]9); and the high priestly robes (Zechariah 3:[5]4). The Hebrew word *me'il* was also used for a common garment for men of high rank (1 Samuel 18:4; 24:5,11; Ezekiel 26:16). Christ was 'girded at the breast with a golden girdle' like the Israelite high priest, who wore a priestly girdle on the breast a little below the armpits (Exodus 28:4; 29:5; 39:29; Leviticus 16:4; cf. the divine messenger Daniel 10:5; and the angels of the last plagues, Revelation 15:6). Royally robed, Jesus bears remarkable similarities to the divine personage of Ezekiel 9:2 who administered protection to the faithful by sealing them with a protective sign before the destruction of Jerusalem. In the same way, Christ may be seen walking among the seven golden lampstands as a heavenly high priest. The lampstands are his churches gathered around him. His clothing thus indicates that he has both a priestly and a kingly role.

---

37 cf. for the robe, Ezekiel 9:2–3; and the parallel for rank at Daniel 10:5.

The detail of 1:14 is drawn from a view of the heavenly throne-room (cf. Daniel 7:9–14).[38] With head and hair as white as snow in its purity (1:14; cf. Daniel 7:9), Christ is clearly identified with the Ancient of Days: the eternal majestic and divine figure of Daniel 7:9; the end-time judge before whom the books are opened. Christ tends the ecclesial lampstands—as was the priestly role in the Old Testament—by commending, correcting, exhorting and warning that the churches continue to be light-bearers in a dark world.

Christ's eyes are as flames of fire, threatening judgement, for he is the end-time judge. Christ has penetrating divine vision (cf. Daniel 10:6) and supernatural intelligence. His feet are like burnished brass (cf. Daniel 10:6), providing the position for strength and stability. Put together, the presentation suggests the irreversible character of his judgement. Christ moves in the midst of the churches with a divine presence and a moral purity that befits the Lord of the churches. His voice (1:15) is as the sound of many waters (cf. Daniel 10:6). This description echoes the awe-inspiring, powerful sound of the deity returning to his end-time temple (Ezekiel 43:2). The seven churches are held in his right hand which is the place of favour, protection and strength. They are sustained by him and one in him. They are united and indestructible.[39] The gates of hell will never prevail against his church. At his Second Coming, Christ will gather the righteous and judge the wicked.

A two-edged sword proceeded from Christ's mouth (1:16; cf. 2:12,16; 19:15; Ephesians 6:17; Hebrews 4:12). This sword is the incisive word of God (cf. Isaiah 11:4; 49:2). By this sword the Son of Man figure is now identified with the servant of Isaiah (Isaiah 49:2) and the messianic shoot of David[40] (Isaiah 11:4) in his fulfilment of judgement. This sword coming out of his mouth is symbolic of Christ being the Word of God. The symbol also tells what he uses to wield divine judgement. This sword will be the only weapon that he will need. Christ will fight his enemies with this sword in the future great battle on his return (cf. 19:15). The

---

38 Lacocque, 1979, 124–6.
39 cf. Wilcock, 1975, 42.
40 cf. Beale, 1984, 162.

climax to the vision is Christ's face shining like the sun in its strength (cf. Judges 5:31, referring to victorious Israelite warriors). Christ's face is brilliantly dazzling in its righteousness; fearsome, awesome, and dangerous (cf. 10:1 referring to an angel; and Matthew 13:43 referring to the righteous). An anticipation of this splendour had been seen by the Apostle John and others on the Mount of Transfiguration (Matthew 17:2).

The vision leaves no misapprehensions. John has seen the victorious Christ: risen, exalted, and now represented in his world by his church set within the tribulations of the present age. Any uncertainty about the significance of the presentation in 1:12–16 is cleared away by 1:17. Jesus Christ is God, the first and last (cf. Isaiah referring to Yahweh 41:4; 44:6; 48:12). Jesus Christ is the sovereign Creator and Lord of history. Jesus Christ is the Living One elevated from death. As a result of his exaltation, death and Hades are chained and imprisoned (1:18). Jesus Christ suffered, died and rose from the dead for the joy that was set before him. This provides suffering Christians in all history with the hope that transcends death. The end of the book has already arrived in this spectacular beginning.

At the onset of the vision, John is completely overwhelmed (1:17). But Christ reassures him. Christ lays his almighty right hand—the hand that holds the seven stars—on John and, with this confirmation from Christ, John begins his prophetic mission. John exhibits the four-fold pattern of Old Testament prophets receiving prophetic commissions: he sees a vision; he falls down in fear; he is strengthened by a heavenly being; and, finally, he receives further revelation from a heavenly being.[41]

Jesus' self-declaration (1:17–18) begins by asserting his participation in the eternal being of God. Jesus said of himself: 'I am the First and the Last'. This title is used in Isaiah 40–55 to indicate that God is eternal, without beginning and without end, the Creator of all things, and the sovereign Lord of history. God precedes all things as their Creator and he will bring all things to eschatological fulfilment. He is the origin and goal of history. He has the first word in creation and the last word in the new creation. In Revelation, 'the first and the last' is not used of God. But the

---

41 cf. especially Daniel 10:5–11, 12–20; Beale, 1999, 213.

synonymous 'the Alpha and the Omega' is used both of God (1:8) and of Christ (22:13). In the latter reference, 'the first and the last' and 'the Alpha and the Omega' are both used of Christ in the one sentence. Christ participates with God in Lordship over creation. He preceded all things as their source with God and shares with him in eschatological fulfilment. The title 'first and last' in Isaiah 40–55 is exclusively monotheistic. The title in Revelation does not designate Christ as an alternative deity; rather, it includes him in the eternal being of the one God of Israel who is the only source and goal of all things.

Jesus is now alive forevermore (1:18) and has the keys of death and Hades (cf. Job 38:17). God has unlimited power over all things (1:8). Likewise, Christ has power over death (the fact) and Hades (the state). To have the 'keys' of death and Hades (1:18)—by his death and resurrection—is to determine the future of humanity, and to finally destroy all evil. John had experienced this: he fell at Christ's feet as though dead (1:17) and Jesus raised him up in a figurative resurrection. As the Living One (1:18) who had been dead, the ever-human Jesus shares God's eternal and communicable livingness. Christ said of himself that he is 'the first and the last' and he has 'the keys of Hades and of death'. Christ's control of history is connected with his resurrection (1:18). Christ's death and resurrection were integral to the purpose of history. God is the 'Living One'.[42] Jesus, also, is the living one as the Father's life is communicated to him in his incarnation and as he shares in the fullness of the Godhead.

Jesus had been dead but now, through his resurrection, is in a state of continuous and available life. However, the man Jesus is also now the Christ. He is, as he always was, the Eternal One. He has always had life in himself. He has the power to give life, to consign to death, or to recover from death. At the Parousia the redeemed creation will share in his livingness. He has rescued humankind, who always feared death (Hebrews 2:14–15). Christ is now presiding over the realms that Satan had ruled.

---

42 Joshua 3:10; Psalm 84:2; Hosea 1:10; Matthew 16:16; 26:63; Acts 14:15; Romans 9:26; 2 Corinthians 3:3; 6:16; 1 Thessalonians 1:9; 1 Timothy 3:15; 4:10; Hebrews 3:12; 9:14; 10:31; 1 Peter 1:23; cf. Deuteronomy 32:40; Isaiah 49:18; Jeremiah 5:2; Daniel 12:7.

The ever-living Christ sustains the church in the palm of his hand (1:16). Christ walks in the midst of the churches (2:1). Christ chastises a church for wavering faith and, if necessary, Christ removes that lampstand (church, 2:5). Furthermore, the ever-living Christ promises those who exercise unswerving dedication the blessings of a new creation. But only after Christ's work is finished do we find him sitting with God on his throne (22:1). It is clear that Christ's presence among his churches is also the presence of the living God.

'Therefore' (1:19) resumes the earlier command (1:11) to 'write', referring to the whole book (as indicated by the plural relative in both 1:11 and 1:19a). Suggestions about the purpose and meaning of 1:19 abound. Since past, present, and future references are found throughout Revelation (the contents of the book are a continual reflection in apocalyptic symbolism on the whole era between the resurrection and the Parousia), it is unlikely that 1:19 proposes a three-fold chronological division of contents. Rather, 1:19 seems best interpreted (cf. 1:1; 4:1; 22:6) as an allusion to Daniel 2:28–29 (cf. Daniel 2:45):[43] 'there is a God in heaven who reveals mysteries, and he has made known to King Nebuchadnezzar what will take place in the latter days'. As an allusion to these verses in Daniel, 1:19 becomes the account of how God's kingdom rule—presently expressed through struggling Christian groups—will finally, universally control the new world.

So John is to write what he had seen (1:19 aorist, cf. 1:11). John is to write the whole visionary sequence—the things which he has already seen, the things which he is now seeing, and the things that he will yet see in the vision—after the entire sequence has been presented to him.[44] The command therefore refers to the present relevance of what had been received in the vision with its apocalyptic emphasis on what will be at the end of history, that is, at the coming into being of the new creation.

The divine meaning of what John saw (1:16) is now disclosed (1:20). The seven stars in Christ's right hand are revealed as the seven angels of the seven churches. The reference is to Christ's Lordship in his active care and intimate awareness of the

---
43   Beale 1984, 413–423.
44   cf. Beale, 1999, 168–170.

churches, with their faults and merits.[45] The churches are dependent upon heavenly direction from the messengers for their existence (Daniel 12:3; Jude 13). The servants of the churches are in Christ's right hand. This indicates Christ's total protection of the churches and their dependence upon him through his Spirit. The lampstands refer to the church as light-givers.[46] Thus, Revelation 1 presents all three members of the Trinity. But the focus is on the Son of Man who will bring about the demise of evil through a suffering church.

---

45 Caird, 1966, 30.
46 cf. Smalley, 2005, 58.

Revelation 2

Revelation 2–3 Prophetic messages to the Seven Churches of Asia Minor

The message to each of the seven churches opens with what Jesus says and closes with what the Spirit says, indicating that the voice of Jesus speaking through the Spirit has come to John. The seven messages from Christ in the Spirit direct the lives of the Christian communities towards Christ's future coming. The structure of Revelation 2–3 with respect to the seven churches is: the first and last church risk losing their identity (2:5; 3:16), but these two churches are also commended for a few things; the second and sixth churches have no weaknesses, they are encouraged to continue; the third, fourth and fifth churches are mixed, commended for some good things but also warned about serious problems which threaten their existence as a church. The main point of the structure is their beginning and the end. Only a small part of the entire church is always faithful (Smyrna and Philadelphia).

The purpose of the seven letters is to review the effectiveness of the church in the world. The course of the church through history has been chartered, positively and negatively, by the patterns of worship and belief formed by these early congregations in Asia. The messages to the seven churches are not ordinary letters as they lack salutation and closing. Rather, they are prophetic messages addressed to an angel—an emissary of Christ—of each church. The angels represent the inner character of each church. The prophetic messages set the political and spiritual scene for the events within the book. The promises contained within the messages to the 'victors' look towards the advent of the new Jerusalem. Indeed, many of the promises in these messages are repeated in the description of the new Jerusalem (Revelation 21–22). Each letter is addressed to the angel of the church. This address is followed by a customary Old Testament prophetic formula: 'thus says' (*tade legei*). Each prophetic message is then prefaced by a self-declaration of the heavenly Christ, carefully diagnostic and directed to what will be Christ's response to the problem of that church. Christ is the stability and the source of spiritual life for believers. He is the one who opens doors, controls the churches and walks in their midst. Christ has not abandoned them to deal with evil in the world by themselves.

In each letter Jesus reveals his knowledge of the church's stability or infidelity in an 'I know' (*oida*) section. The body of Christ's edict to each church, introduced by 'I know', contains two closely interrelated parts. The first part reminds the addressees that the Lord is aware of the precise situation in each church. The second part, which is longer, contains detailed points of praise and blame. The 'I know' section is followed by a commendation for commitment and/or condemnation for slackness. Only two churches, Smyrna and Philadelphia, do not receive a command to repent; only one church, Laodicea, receives no praise. The judgement and/or salvation formula emerges unmistakably in this portion of the edict.

Jesus walks in the midst of the churches. Therefore Jesus has intimate knowledge of the churches and the churches can be assured that, if they reflect the light of Christ who is among them, then they will be the light of the world. However, Christ finds the seven churches—with one exception—unequal to the covenant task of preaching the gospel to the world. But Christ is in their midst so heavenly help is available to rekindle their lost love. The future of the church depends on Christ's presence. In the Old Testament, the light from the lampstand before the tabernacle holy of holies represented God's presence mediating blessings for Israel. Israel was then to mediate God's blessings to the world. The primary meaning of lampstand in Revelation is also witness. The lampstand set 'before the Lord' in the tabernacle (11:4) refers to the prophetic witness of the church.

The exhortation to 'hear' what the Spirit is saying to the churches is a call to internalise Christ's message and to respond obediently. For those who obey and thereby overcome, there are promises. The promises in each of the seven prophetic messages (Revelation 2–3) are applied later in the book as rewards in the new Jerusalem for overcoming (Revelation 21–22). Thus Revelation 2–3 is integrated with the comprehensive vision that follows (4:1–22:5).

John presents Christian life as a struggle against the world, the flesh, and the devil. Thus the paired concluding elements of challenge and promise. In each prophetic message the call to conquer is a call to faithfully engage in the eschatological battle with the world unto death. Some have already done this. And each promise has an appropriate fulfilment in the new Jerusalem: the promise of the paradise of God (2:7) is responded to by the tree of life in the paradise of God (22:2); the promise of freedom from second death (2:11) is responded to at the judgement (20:15, 21:8); the promise of possession of a white stone and new name (2:17) is responded to by foundation stones of the new Jerusalem with the names of the twelve apostles of Jesus written on them (21:14); the promise that Christ will rule the nations with a rod of iron (2:26–27) is responded to with the rule of the King of kings and Lord of lords (19:15, 16); the promise of the believer's enrolment in the book of life (3:5) is responded to by those who are given entrance to the new Jerusalem (20:15; 21:27); the promise of endorsement of the faithful with the name of the new Jerusalem (3:12) is responded to in the name of the bride adorned for Christ (21:2); and the promise of enthronement with Christ (3:21) is responded to in the thrones of believers judging and reigning with Christ (20:4).

The practice and performance of the churches in Revelation 2–3 accords with the onset of early degeneration within the church that is evident in other books of the New Testament.[1] The seven prophetic messages, dealing with the practice and performance of the churches, are interrelated as each forms an introduction to the entire book. These historical churches were representative of Christian involvement in a cosmic conflict between God and evil. This conflict is over the eschatological purpose of God for the whole of creation.

While the common call is to conquer or to be victorious (2:7,11,17, 26; 3:5, 12, 21), the meaning of this victory is not explained until the formula 'he who overcomes' is found just once more in the vision of the new Jerusalem (21:7). Those who are by faith victorious in a godless world enter into the divine city. A war must be waged in which believers are involved in the great tribulation in fallen Babylon. So the call to conquer is the call to seek first

---

[1] cf. especially the Pastorals, 2 Peter and Jude.

the kingdom of God and his righteousness in all circumstances, as Jesus did, particularly those circumstances where devilish opposition would not be readily identified (5:5–6; John 16:33). The call is to engage in the eschatological battle described by John in Revelation. This call to overcome in the eschatological battle is for the whole church in its witness throughout history. To each church the message is the same: believers can only enter the new Jerusalem by faithfulness unto death! Thus, *nikao* (conquer, 21:7) is applied to receiving all the blessings of salvation. The prophetic messages make clear that the whole Christian life is to be characterised by overcoming in the face of persecution. This overcoming is not just at the moment of death since the call was to 'the one who keeps on overcoming' (present tense), that is, the one who keeps on winning the victories that must characterise the life of faith (cf. 1 John 2:13–14; 5:4–5).

The number seven (=perfection, completion, fulfilment), and the fact that each letter is concluded with a message to all the churches, confirms that in John's mind Revelation is about the ongoing problem of the participation of the church in the world throughout history. The problems that face the churches of John's day are bound up with common factors that will continue to plague Christian witness in the world throughout its history.

The prophetic messages to the seven churches assume great prominence at the beginning of the book since they present the church as it ever will be in history: never dominant in its society, beset with problems, and called to a suffering ministry. The prophetic messages to the seven churches also detail the promises that are to be fulfilled (21:1–22:5). The defeat of evil will not be achieved by the world church as its human constitution will always be part of the problem. But much can be done by the Spirit of God through the church, despite its human weakness. Thus these prophetic messages, with their common concluding promises, should be taken as a group.

Complacency, apathy, compromise, deception and religious infidelity are the problems. Despite these difficulties in the church, John is confident that the church will triumph. It is God's church. In history the church will provide the paradoxical biblical continuum of God's victory being expressed through human weakness.

The work of the church is already finished in heaven (cf. Revelation 4), even while its historical witness is being imperfectly executed on earth. In history the church will suffer and die and be resurrected (11:1–13), journeying through an exodus of testing before it reaches the Promised Land. This is the exodus to which the message of biblical redemption points.

Slaughtered saints must wait patiently (6:9–11). Those that conquer the beast must pass through a Red Sea of blood before they sing the victory song on the other side (15:2). John's message to the churches is that the victims of the world may be God's victors. The outcome of the inevitable conflict between the church and the world has already been determined in heaven. The blood of the Lamb and the word of the churches' testimony will conquer Satan. In its best moments, members of the church do not cling to life in the face of death (12:11).

The war can be won by God without the church. The war will not be won by the church. But God has chosen to enlist the church in the battle, and it will be spiritually protected during the beast's onslaught (11:1–6). The church is not protected from physical danger to fulfil its role as witness. The way to be spared from physical harm is by swearing allegiance to the beast. But if the church swears allegiance to the beast, she falls into idolatry and ceases to be the church. Some elements within the historical church will face spiritual destruction. But overall the church is Christ's body and—though sinful—it belongs to him and it expresses his rule. The church may be threatened, but it will never fail since Christ holds the seven stars (the seven angels) in his right hand and walks in the midst of the seven golden lampstands.

The order of the messages is probably determined by geographical considerations, but there are also chiastic inter-relationships between them. All of the churches were under tremendous political, religious and social pressures. An intended order has been suggested in which: Ephesus (first) and Laodicea (seventh) struggled with the problem of increasing wealth and decreasing zeal, engendering apathy; Smyrna (second) and Philadelphia (sixth) patiently endured affliction while maintaining devotion to Christ; Pergamum (third) and Sardis (fifth) were confronted with the temptations to compromise; and Thyatira (fourth), perhaps necessarily at the centre in the chiastic structure, was rife with immorality and doctrinal compromise.[2] D. E. Aune maintains that, in terms of genre, the letters do not follow Hellenistic conventions but are a type of royal edict that also evinces a prophetic form of a salvation-judgement oracle.[3]

John wants his readers to be under no illusions about the church. It will always be called to witness to the same heavenly realities; however, throughout history it will also always be subject to the same temptations to idolatry, self-preservation and pursuit of temporal security. Like the world, the church could be enamoured of its self-importance and so pursue worldly goals. So the problems that beleaguer the churches are compromise, inertia, abandoned love, idolatry, fornication, complacency and self-deception. And these problems all relate to lack of Christian perseverance.

Leon Morris has identified the following pattern in the letters to the churches: churches 1 and 7 are in grave danger; churches 2 and 6 are in excellent shape; but churches 3, 4 and 5 are middling, neither very good nor very bad.[4] This pattern calls attention to the churches that are middling. The seven churches display responses to the fallen order ranging from total capitulation (Sardis and Laodicea) to apparent perfect discipleship (Smyrna and Philadelphia). This is the nature of the crisis for John's readers: they constantly expend their energy in struggles against forces that threaten to undo their faith.[5]

Revelation 2:1-7 Ephesus

Christ introduces himself, with a reference to 1:20, as the one who holds the seven stars in his right hand: he is familiar with their dealings; he is in firm and absolute control over the congregation and its leadership;[6] he holds the seven stars completely within (*kraten*, Greek accusative) his right hand, indicating his entire protection. Christ walks among the seven golden

---

2   Lioy, 2003, 85.
3   1990, 184.
4   1987, 57–58.
5   Wall 1995, 69.
6   Morris, 59, 1992.

lampstands, that is, he rules and sustains all the churches and moves among them personally in his unseen presence.

Christ reproves this church for losing its first love (2:4). 'First love' is, most likely, a reference to their loss of commitment to witness to Christ.[7] 'Endurance' (*hupomonen*, steadfastness under trials) is the only praiseworthy attribute that is repeated (2:2,3) in the message to the Church at Ephesus, perhaps indicating in the repetition that the absence of perseverance was a problem.[8] There is mention of evil doers and self-styled apostles (2:2c) whom they do not tolerate. These false apostles, presumably libertarian itinerant missionaries,[9] seem not to be identical with the threat from the Nicolaitans (2:6).[10] The Nicolaitans may have been a widely known libertine pre-Gnostic sect. For the Gnostics, the human body did not matter; what counted was spiritual illumination. The resurrection was or would be no more than an enlightened transformation. For the Gnostics and those who preceded them, sexual excesses were irrelevant.

The threat from Christ is the removal of their lampstand 'from its place' (2:5). And this will happen unless they repent, that is, unless they admit their fault and turn again to do their first works. They must return to their fruitful origins. The loss of the lampstand means that they will no longer be able to witness to the world and thus this church will be extinct. The lampstands represent the power of the Spirit given primarily to effect their witness to the faith. To the one who overcomes, not to the church as a whole, the Lord gives the promise of access to the tree of life (2:7).

Close attention is called to what the Spirit is saying through Christ (1:7). 'He who has an ear' suggests that not all will hear, but if they do hear there is a promise of salvation. There is a battle to be fought and the foe is devious, deceptive and powerful. However, in common with all seven of the prophetic messages, overcoming is to be their constant way of life.

In this first prophetic message, overcoming means eating from the tree of life (2:7). Ultimately, the tree of life is the cross bearing

---

7   cf. Matthew 24:12–14; Beale, 1999, 230.
8   Smalley, 2005, 61.
9   loc. cit.
10   cf. op. cit., 62–63.

the fruit of salvation, namely: inclusion in the resurrection of Christ; eternal salvation; and continuing blessings.[11] God's garden paradise symbolically includes the present abode of the just in the heavenly kingdom (cf. Luke 23:42–43), and the future new creation for those who overcome at the final resurrection (cf. 22:2).

Revelation 2:8–11 Smyrna

In telling the Smyrnaeans that he is 'the first and the last' (2:8), Jesus appropriates a title equivalent to 'Alpha and Omega' (1:8). This is a title that belongs to God alone. Jesus is proclaiming his absolute deity and lordship. Christ is the beginning and end of the redemptive process of recreation. Christ mentions his own death and resurrection (2:8) in his salutation to the church of Smyrna. Indeed, his death is to be re-lived in their Christian experience as the key to their future life (2:10).

The Smyrnaeans' main problem, shared with Philadelphia, was slanderous hostility from the Jews. The point of contention may have been that Christians claimed to be the new covenant continuation of old covenant Israel. Until the second half of the first century, Christians were protected from persecution. Christians were seen to be under the umbrella of Judaism. In the Roman Empire the worship of Caesar as a god was mandatory. But Jews were not forced to worship Caesar. Instead, they were allowed to offer sacrifices in honour of the Emperors as rulers. Around about the time of the Neronian persecution, Christians came under suspicion and persecution of Christians by the Romans began. The faithfulness of Smyrna's Christians during this trial was evidence of their true spiritual riches. The issue for the Smyrnaeans was extreme: persecution and poverty, probably due to their refusal to participate in Emperor worship.

The ten-day tribulation (cf. Genesis 24:55; Daniel 1:12) stands for an indeterminate but relatively short period, divinely permitted to make the church stronger and more resolute. This period of persecution included imprisonment and, for some, even death (2:10). On the other hand, as tribulation and poverty are adjoined to each other in 2:9, the pressure against the Smyrnaeans may have been economic repression due to the fact that they were not

---

11   cf. Hemer, 1989, 55.

members of a recognised religious group. The prophetic message states that the church, not the synagogue, is conveying the true traditions of Judaism. Christians constitute the genuine Israel. As the inheritors of God's promises, the Christians in Smyrna have become the real Jews (cf. 1:9).

In the midst of their tribulation they are urged to be faithful unto death (2:10). Then the overcomers will receive not the fading laurel wreath of sporting fame but the incorruptible victor's crown (*stephanos*) of eternal life; the heavenly kingdom (20:6) that entails freedom from the second death (11b, cf. 20:6,14) and, thus, eternal life.

Revelation 2:12–17 Pergamum

Jesus presents himself as one who has a sharp two-edged sword (2:12), the symbol for divine judgement. With this sword he conquers; with this sword he will wage war on evildoers and apostates (2:16). Christ is the messianic warrior-judge who will do battle with false prophets (cf. 2:16). Pergamum was a centre of paganism. In Pergamum the believers are being opposed by a satanically inspired culture. But this church had shown forthright commitment to the name of Jesus—his person and work (2:13 cf. 'you hold fast to my name, and did not deny [Greek aorist] my faith')—even when the witness Antipas was martyred. Antipas was, most likely, a prophet; an individual Christian who had been publicly executed. This event would have provoked great difficulties for the church.

However, this apparently faithful church seems to have succumbed to idolatry by entertaining 'the teaching of Balaam'. The 'teaching of Balaam' (2:14) is probably another way of saying 'the teaching of the Nicolaitans' (2:15). This probably meant closer relationships with pagan cults, particularly the imperial cult and institutions. The issue was probably not food offered to idols but, rather, some other compromise with idolatry. Christ makes it clear that moral conduct cannot be separated from religious beliefs.

Appropriately, after this mention of food offered to idols, the Lord's promise to the victors features religious banquet imagery. The overcomer will receive the hidden manna (cf. John 6:31–34):

participation in the heavenly banquet, which is a symbol of participation in the future world of eternal life.[12] This is the banquet shared with Christ who is the Lord and bread of life (cf. John 6:30–58). The hiddenness of the manna suggests that this may be, perhaps in other forms, the food of Paradise (cf. Exodus 16:32).

Overcomers thus have a new spiritual status: they have a new name even before death and the final tribulation. Perseverance of believers brings a fuller identification with Christ. The new name (2:17, *kainos*, meaning new in point of time and new in quality) is an allusion to membership of the true Israel (cf. Isaiah 62:2; 65:15). With this new name, overcomers: participate in Israel's future kingly status (Isaiah 62:3); having been restored, are brought into Yahweh's covenantal presence (62:4a); and enter into the new married relationship to Yahweh (62:4b–5). Overcomers have access to the character and power represented by their new name. 'Written on a white stone' perhaps indicates that this is their ticket of admission to the heavenly banquet.

That no one knows the name except the one receiving it expresses, apocalyptically, a special personal prerogative and breathes an aura of mystery. Nevertheless, there is identification with Christ and the sharing of his new name means sharing in the new status of Jesus that the Parousia will reveal (19:12).

Revelation 2:18–29 Thyatira

Jesus addresses this church uniquely, with a title that is not used elsewhere in Revelation, as 'Son of God'. The opening salutation suggests that sovereign judgement is to follow, for the Son of God has: eyes like flaming fire (2:18; cf. 1:1 and Daniel 10:6) to search minds and hearts (2:23; Jeremiah 17:9–10); and feet of blazing metal (2:18; cf. 1:15a), referring to divine strength and stability.

The title 'Son of God' means that Jesus is the true Son, as opposed to current pagan claims for local deities.[13] The title is a claim to full equality with God, also indicating the intimate relationship between God and Christ. Finally, the suggestion of sovereign judgement in the title prepares for the promises to the victor

---

12 cf. Spatafora, 1997, 134.
13 Beale, 1999, 259.

(2:26–28): to receive power to rule from the Son, just as the Son has been given authority to rule from the Father (Psalm 2:6–11).

The basic virtues of the Thyatirans are seen in the growing witness of 'their works'. And their works speak of their love and faith (2:19). Even so, there is much that is wrong with the community. A prominent self-proclaimed 'prophetess' is given a cursed biblical label for she is a self-indulgent enemy of the true prophets, a symbolic Jezebel (1 Kings 18:13; 19:1–3; 21:5–26; 2 Kings 9:21–37). This woman, like the Old Testament Jezebel, seduces Christ's servants into false religion. Just as her name is probably metaphorical, in the same way 'her children' (2:23) is probably a metaphor for the deviant community that has been seduced by her teaching.

References to Balaam and Jezebel in the prophetic messages recall historical incidents when the Jews were led into immorality and idolatry (1 Kings 16:31–33; 21:25–26; Numbers 31:16; 25:1–2). In the churches of Asia, individuals were teaching Christians to eat food sacrificed to idols and to commit fornication (2:14, perhaps a metaphorical reference to an alliance with Roman imperial society that led to immoral behaviour and idolatry).[14] Christians were becoming complacent in their attitudes towards surrounding cultures, thereby losing their distinctiveness.

The church is accused of tolerating the activity of false teachers (2:20) who are influencing church members to compromise with elements of pagan society and to indulge in the idolatrous practices and sexual excesses of their culture. The sins of the Jezebel group are probably like those of the Nicolaitans and the followers of Balaam (2:14–15). An essential component of this corrupt teaching was that they might know the 'deep things' of Satan—plumbing evil to its depths (2:24)—an expression presumably used by the false teachers themselves to denote the extremes of their practices. It may have been suggested that believers could participate to some degree in idolatrous situations, thereby having a little experience and understanding of the demonic satanic realm in their culture without being harmed spiritually by such participation. This teaching may have been directed towards the same attitude as was being corrected in the earlier Corinthian letters: conduct in the material world was seen not to be important,

---

14 Stevenson, 2001, 228–229, cf. Caird, 1966, 39.

rather, the spiritual world was emphasised such that if one's relationship with God was firm then even involvement with the demonic realm could not shake it. Those who follow this attitude are in mortal danger. The Thyatirans are blamed for being indifferent towards those within their community who conducted themselves in a way totally at odds with the norms of Christian morality. Christ had warned (we are not told how) these false prophets to repent. But they had rejected his command (2:21–23).

Jezebel will be cast onto a bed, which is probably a metaphor for future great distress and debilitating suffering. This is an appropriate punishment for her spiritual adultery. Her followers also will be cast into great tribulation and, indeed, destroyed. The teaching of Jezebel attracts a severe punishment. This tribulation of Jezebel and her followers will become so well known (2:23) to all the churches that it will be evident that Christ, with his penetrating knowledge (2:18), has been the judge. This pre-Gnostic movement will therefore be destroyed (2:23).

Some in Thyatira have not yet been led astray (2:24–25). Christ emphasises that their only real concern should be to hold fast the faith until he comes. In particular, they must reject this false teaching which supposed that Christians must experience vice (the deep things/mysteries of Satan, 2:24) in order to overcome it. In Thyatira this entailed participation in various cult practices associated with the pagan guilds.

Jesus' assurance to the victor—the one who stands fast, keeping Jesus' words in constant practice (works) and in witness to the end of one's life on earth—is that they will share in his kingly power. Those who overcome throughout life and persevere to the end will reign with Christ in his messianic kingdom (2:26). This is now the precise definition of 'overcoming', namely, that which leads to inclusion in the messianic rule (cf. Psalm 2:7). Revelation uses *poimaino* (2:27, tend like a shepherd) which follows LXX instead of MT 'smite' (Psalm 2:9). Believers will have unquestioned rule over the world. When and how this is to be is not explained; it may be referring to the new creation. Believers know that they are risen with Christ and the world is under judgement. The *exousia* (authority) given to believers over the nations is later explained to be authority to witness; this involves suffering (11:7).

The saints overcome by maintaining faithful witness unto death (cf. 12:11).

To 'smash' the nations (2:27) is to look forward to the final messianic triumph. Christ will give the believer the 'morning star' (2:28), which is possibly either a reference to the servant community of Daniel 12:3 or the symbol of messianic rule. Numbers 24:14–20 describes the future eschatological leader of Israel as a rising star and a sceptre (cf. 2 Peter 1:17–19, which uses the Numbers' allusion). In 22:16, however, the morning star is identified as Christ himself—the one ruling over a messianic kingdom—who brought light after the darkness of world unbelief. The believer (overcomer) is thus being promised full possession of a nature transformed by Christ himself. The prophetic message concludes with the customary warning to 'hear'.

Revelation 3

Revelation 3:1–6 Sardis

Jesus introduces himself as 'the one who has seven spirits' (1:4; 5:6), referring to the Holy Spirit in all his fullness (seven = perfection, completion, fulfilment). As the one who holds the seven 'stars', Christ has sovereign and omnipresent control over churches.

The church of Sardis presented an image of being spiritually active and significant in its community as a church. But the problem is that there is no substance to their reputation (3:1). This church is not alive; it is dead, though not altogether (3:1–2). The problem is that Sardis is not even a work in progress. Christian activity had begun but nothing had been completed 'before God' (3:2), therefore nothing merited God's commendation. The situation was critical; there is no word of praise. But the position is not hopeless (3:4). The reference to 'remaining things' (or 'people', 3:2)[1] suggests that some people in the church have engaged in a life of faithful service.

Four imperatives are used to stir the church into life (2:2–3): wake up (be watchful); remember what has been received from Christ; keep it; and repent. The reality of their position is that they had heard the gospel (Greek aorist), received the gospel (Greek perfect), and still have the gospel. Now they are to obey the gospel (3:3).

There is a core of people within the church who have not soiled their garments. These core persons have not been compromised by idolatry (3:4; cf. 14:4). They have, no doubt, sustained the church. On the basis of this core, the church as a whole is now exhorted to come to life and to be alert for the future. Otherwise, the Lord's unexpected visitation—to come, like a thief—will catch them unawares. The Lord does not hesitate to present himself as one who will intervene decisively in the lives of those too dulled to deal with their own need for security (cf. 16:15; Matthew 24:43; Luke 12:39; 1 Thessalonians 5:2; 2 Peter 3:10). He does not say how, but they are to strengthen the things that remain since there

---

1 cf. Smalley, 2005, 81 on the Greek expression *ta loipa*.

is still hope (3:4). To avoid the decisive visitation from Christ, the church of Sardis must remember their previous position, when they had received and heard Jesus' message (3:3). They must reverse their now deficient works to provide proof of their faith. Such repentance involves not just sorrow for past infidelity but rather a change of mind and heart (3:3, *metanoia*) that must come through the Spirit and will set them on a renewed course of how they should live in the sight of God.

But some have not defiled themselves. They will in the future walk in white (symbolising perfection) beside Jesus (3:4b); not behind him as disciples but with him as companions. Like Jesus, who loved not his life unto death, they will be 'worthy' (cf. 5:9). The rest of the congregation in Sardis soiled their clothes, indicative of their inward condition of compromise with their idolatrous culture. Complacent and comfortable, they are at home with the values of this world. They need to become spiritually alive by strengthening the things that are going to die (3:2). They need inward transformation by the Spirit of Christ in order to qualify for wearing white robes (cf. 7:9–14). They will then follow the example of the faithful core at Sardis who are already destined for wearing these non-contaminated robes of spiritual purity.

The promise to the victor who has persevered is public proclamation of the victor's name before Christ's Father and before his angels (3:5). The promise of inclusion in the book of life (3:5b) constitutes a firm promise of salvation. Those who falsely claim the name of Christ—who therefore do not have a true Christian name—will be exposed on the final day of judgement when the names in the book of life are 'confessed' (read out) before God by Christ (cf. Matthew 10:32 = Luke 12:8). In the Old Testament, only the righteous who persevered (Exodus 32:32–33) were found in God's census book of those who were to enter the land. In Isaiah's prophecy (Isaiah 4:3), the faithful remnant are those who are written among the living in Jerusalem. In Revelation the names of overcomers, those who are faithful until death (2:26), will be written in the citizen roll of the new Jerusalem; their names will never be removed (3:5). 'Names' indicating Christian standing have figured prominently in this prophetic message to the church in Sardis (3:1,4,5). Names are used as metaphors for the assurance of their salvation (cf. 13:8; 17:8).[2] The concluding warning to the church in Sardis is the same as in each of the other prophetic messages.

Revelation 3:7–13 Philadelphia

As elsewhere (2:8, 3:1), Jesus introduces himself in this message to the church in Philadelphia with titles used for God (3:8), namely, the holy and true one (*alethinos* meaning 'reality' as opposed to what is 'unreal'). Jesus is above everything in an unholy world, in a fallen creation (6:10). Jesus' word is just and will surely be effective. Unlike the other prophetic messages, Jesus does not use a description from 1:9–20 to introduce himself. Rather, he uses an allusion to Isaiah 22:22 which states that he has kingly authority as head of the royal household (the key of David) to regulate the right of entry into the messianic kingdom (3:7). The scope of this title is echoed in the body of the proclamation; the Lord has opened a door for this church in the context of what had been a particularly closed and implacable Jewish community. They had 'little strength': the church's prestige and influence in its area were small. But they were a strongly spiritual church for they had kept Christ's word and had not denied his name. Thus they had maintained the truth of the gospel, confessing their Christian faith (3:8), and they have access to the divine presence because of their faithfulness (3:7–8). They had magnified Christ, implementing by their witness his call to obedience under patient suffering. No one can shut the open door of entrance into the kingdom (cf. 4:1) which Christ had set before them. But the time will come when no one can open it (3:7).[3]

Philadelphia and Smyrna are the only two churches that receive praise. However, they share a pressing problem also. Both suffered from exposure to persecution by those of the Jewish race. The persecutors were no longer genuine Jews, they were not God's people. Rather, they were now headed by Satan, God's arch-enemy and the enemy of those in the church at Philadelphia. Those who claim to be Jews (from the local synagogue) are 'liars' and a 'synagogue of Satan' (3:9). The Jews who denied Jesus'

---

2   Beale, 1999, 280.
3   Lioy, 2003, 129.

claim to divinity would do anything to deny the right of Christians to claim as their own the traditions and promises made in regard to Israel and the messianic kingdom.[4]

These enemies will be overcome (3:9; Isaiah 60:14) and the situation will be reversed just as Israel had been told by the prophets (Isaiah 45:14; Ezekiel 36:2). As in the case of Smyrna, a test is in the offing. But this time the test is much more general, on the whole inhabited world. The Philadelphian church will be kept from this hour of trial (3:10), an ordeal in which all must choose whom they will serve. In this sixth prophetic message—somewhat as with the sixth element in the subsequent groups of seven seals, trumpets and bowls—the reader is alerted to the worldwide test to come. The powerful witness of the church in Philadelphia will bring Jews of the synagogue of Satan into the true Israel (cf. 3:9). In a surprising reversal of Jewish expectations, Jews will do what the Gentiles were to have done before Israel in the last days (Isaiah 60:14): the persecuting Jews will bow before the feet of the believers. This will be evidence that Christ loves the church, that God has chosen those who believe in Christ (cf. 3:9). So this Gentile church in Philadelphia will be used, as Paul had foreseen (Romans 11:11), to bring about Jewish salvation.

They have kept Christ's word. Now Christ's power will keep them from the hour of testing to come upon the whole populated world (3:10, *oikoumene*), affecting Christians and all who 'dwell on the earth'. This phrase in Revelation invariably refers to the whole of rebellious mankind (6:10; 8:13; 11:10; 13:8,14; 17:8). Through such testing the Philadelphian believers will be spiritually refined, but not physically protected. Jesus is coming to his church 'soon'. His presence, to be manifested fully at his Parousia, will also be felt in the uncertain future ahead. Their fidelity during the future struggle will determine whether they retain possession of their victory 'crown' at the end of the struggle (cf. 1 Corinthians 9:25). Within history, churches may fail; but redeemed individuals will not fail to finish (John 10:10).

Jesus' promise to the individual victor—to become a pillar in the temple of 'my God' (cf. Galatians 2:9), part of the permanent structure of the new temple—fits well in this prophetic message

---

4   cf. Stevenson, 2001, 242–243.

which has emphasised Christian access to God's presence. This promise may also refer back to the promise to the royal steward (Isaiah 22:22–23) of an honoured place in his father's house. The believer is assured of a place of stability and permanence that they will never lose as a pillar in God's temple.

This is the first mention of the temple motif in Revelation. Throughout the book, the temple stands as the great symbol for God's sovereign and transcendent presence. From this centre, beginning with Revelation 4–5, the inexorable divine movement from the death, resurrection and ascension of Christ until the advent of the new Jerusalem is presented.[5]

The temple in this prophetic message represents the heavenly abode of the saints, not their final transformation as the new Jerusalem come to earth. The overcomer will never leave the temple; their eternal standing is certain. According to the imagery of the time, pillars—like statues—had inscriptions celebrating either those to whom they were dedicated or family members. The 'names' written on the pillars show their permanent heavenly state. The pillars bear 'the name of my God': they belong to God and honour God and reflect his nature. This is assurance of God's continued presence into eternal life. Believers also bear the 'name of the city' of the new Jerusalem (3:12), and this new Jerusalem comes down out of heaven from God. Thus believing Jews and Gentiles have a new nature: they are now citizens of heaven sharing that new relationship. Through the Spirit, believers will now reflect the character of Christ. In this way, those with little power—apparently impotent before their adversaries—can rely on the stability and power that the Lord will guarantee them. As members of the new Jerusalem, believers will receive the divine nature in all its fullness: both God's name and Jesus' new name (referring to Jesus' equality with God, 19:12).

There are only two churches who are not given a command to repent: the Philadelphians and the Smyrnaeans. To the Smyrnaeans, Jesus had offered freedom from fear. To the Philadelphians, he gives an exhortation to hold fast. Both are assured of the crown of life for their fidelity (2:10; 3:11). The Philadelphian

---

5   cf. op. cit., 212.

church is to carefully reflect on what has been communicated in all seven prophetic messages (3:13).

Revelation 3:14–22 Laodicea

The seven prophetic messages begin with Ephesus—a church in decline—and end with a church that Christ is about to spit out of his mouth. The first and last prophetic messages may reveal something about the history of the church as a whole. The point of the seven letters is not a presentation of the developing history of the church, rather, it is an analysis of what the church will always be. It is, therefore, a salutary warning to the visible church that the last message concludes with such a negative description. The message to Laodicea completes the cycle: no word of commendation for Laodicea; Smyrna and Philadelphia doing well despite their plight in the face of religious persecution; the four other churches partly reproved and partly commended.

Christ is presented as the Amen ('firm', 'true', 3:14), a title without parallel in the New Testament. Following the 'Amen' title are two adjectives—faithful and true—describing the 'Amen'. This 'Amen' title for Jesus is equivalent to the Hebrew 'God of truth' (cf. Isaiah 65:16). By his death, Jesus shows himself to be the faithful and true witness. In 1:5, Christ the 'faithful witness' is followed by Christ the 'firstborn of the dead'. In 3:14, the 'faithful and true witness' is followed by 'the beginning (*arche*, the first in time and rank) of the creation of God'. The sequence suggests that if the Laodiceans do not become faithful witnesses then they will not form part of the new creation that had its origin in Jesus' Lordship (cf. Colossians 1:15). Jesus Christ was the prime source of all creation (John 1:1–3). His role in the original creation is fulfilled and consummated in the redemptive 'new creation'. By his resurrection and ascension, Christ inaugurated and exercised sovereignty over the coming new creation. The promise to the victor in this prophetic message is to reign with Christ.

Beale suggests that the salutation from Christ as the inaugurator of the new creation and sovereign over it in his resurrection means that the new creation prophecies of Isaiah

(43:18–19; 65:17) have begun to be fulfilled.[6] God, Israel and the Servant are all 'witnesses' to the coming restoration of Israel from exile (Isaiah 43:10). And the exodus theology of the Bible always had the future of an Israel in view. Christ's Parousia will be the real fulfilment, when the real exile of mankind from the presence of God will be corrected by the new creation. To share in this inheritance of the new Promised Land, Gentiles must become part of Israel (cf. Ezekiel 47:22–23) by incorporation into the risen Jesus who is the true Israel.

The stress of this last prophetic message is that the Laodiceans need to be renewed as new creatures (3:18–20) in their relationship to Christ. They are to become members of the new creation and give uncompromising testimony to Jesus. If this happens, they will receive the reward of heavenly enthronement (3:21; cf. 20:4–6).

There is no commendation for the church of the Laodiceans in this prophetic message; only severe reproof. They are so corrupt that Jesus uses the jarring image of vomiting them out of his mouth. Like the lukewarm water that flowed over the cliff facing Laodicea from the hot springs of Hierapolis—lukewarm water that induced nausea—the Laodicaeans are neither stimulating (hot) nor refreshing (cold), but sickening and good for nothing (lukewarm).

Laodicea had grown as a town because its geographic position was conducive to commerce, but the water was far from good. The members of the church of Laodicea were affluent; they had evaluated themselves to be without serious need but they did not know how spiritually poor, blind and naked they really were (3:17). Jesus refers to the wealth of this congregation: their medical profession was famed for its eye ointments and their linen and wool products were valuable commodities in the ancient world (3:17–18). But like Israel in Canaan[7]—where Israel had prospered as a merchant by oppression—the members of the church of Laodicea deceive themselves. The Laodiceans use the same words to describe their wealth as are used later in Revelation to describe idolatrous Babylon (18:3,15,19). If Smyrna was poor but

---

6   1999, 300–301.
7   cf. Hosea 12:8, of Ephraim, 'I have become rich'.

spiritually rich, then Laodicea was rich but spiritually poor. Their inability to perceive the reality of their poverty was occasioned by their spiritual obtuseness and a corrupt inner nature. The church in general must always deal with this dilemma. Just like the lukewarm water of their affluent city induced vomiting, in the same way the effect of the conduct of these affluent Christians would induce Christ to spit them out of his mouth.

These affluent Laodiceans are to heed the threefold exhortation of 3:18 in order to become truly rich. They are to buy gold from Christ, refined in the fire—a biblical idiom for purifying the life (Job 23:10; Proverbs 27:21; Malachi 3:2-3)—with all impurities burned away. Thus they will have the means to acquire: the white robes of victory and purity; and 'eye-salve' with which they will be able to exercise spiritual discernment and thereby rightly evaluate their world. Repentance will follow (3:19). They need to cover the shame of their nakedness, probably referring to their participation in idolatry (cf. Isaiah 47:3; Ezekiel 16:36; 23:29; Nahum 3:5 cf. Isaiah 20:4), with the white robes of victory and purity.

The indictments are really signs of Christ's love for them (3:19, cf. Proverbs 3:12). Jesus' message is for reproof and discipline, not judgement. They are still loved by Christ! Nevertheless, Jesus' spiritual commodities have a price: repentance and uncompromising witnesses. The deception under which the Laodiceans had been led astray is so powerful that only Christ can provide the remedy. The Lord jolts them to an awareness of their need for renewed spiritual concern (zeal) and to a change of heart and mind (*metanoia*, repentance).

Jesus now offers to be the self-invited dinner guest, depending on their response. Now he stands continually (Greek perfect tense) outside of the church, knocking on the door. He will not force his way in. But if they respond in obedience to the threefold exhortation (3:18) then Christ stands before the door ready to establish personal, familial contact. In Canticles 5:2 (LXX), the beloved's voice is heard when he knocks on the door and asks for admission. The closing part of the prophetic message to the Laodiceans appears to allude to this heart-warming passage from the Canticle. There is no word of commendation to this church but, if they follow Christ's exhortation, there is an invitation to enter into intimate friendship with Christ himself!

Anyone who overcomes will rule with Christ in the kingdom upon completion of their faithful witness at death or at his Parousia (3:21; cf. Luke 22:28–30; Matthew 19:28). They can overcome the pressures of their situation based on Christ's victory (Greek aorist tense) at the cross.

This prophetic message to the church of the Laodiceans ends with the familiar injunction to all the churches to 'hear'. Religious infidelity, deception, complacency, somnolence and compromise are problems in the churches. Each prophetic message provides a way for the church to overcome: repent (2:5,16; 3:3,19), remain faithful (2:10), and hold fast (2:25; 3:3,11). The church as a whole needs to demonstrate the life of the new Jerusalem.

Summary of the Seven Prophetic Messages

The prophetic messages to the seven churches (2:1–3:22) summarise the role and plight of the church in the world in every age. The genre of the seven messages is unlike the clear symbolic apocalypticism of the remainder of the book. However, the seven messages provide background reality of the church in the world which makes the book always relevant. Each church is subject to the same temptations to idolatry, self-preservation and pursuit of temporal security. Like the world, the church could be enamoured of its self-importance. The seven churches indicate how the church in the world is prone to failure and defeat. After the seven prophetic messages, Revelation returns to the uncertain course of the church in the world (4–22:1–5).

We are under no illusions about who will achieve the final victory to usher in the new world. The church is prone to failure and defeat. Yet the church is Christ's body and, though sinful, it is his church and in his control. Albeit imperfectly, the church draws the attention of the world, in all ages, to Christ. Through this witness of the church and the witness of Christians to Christ—in paradoxical ways—under God, Christ will finally bring in the kingdom. Through the weakness of the church the power of God prevails, evil will ultimately be eliminated, and the New Eden will arise.

Despite the problems of the church engendered by its fallen humanness—notwithstanding the weakness and failures of Christ's human witnesses—God will triumph through the church's defeat by the world (cf. 11:7). Just like our Lord, the church must pass through its passion on the way to vindication. Like Jesus, the church will suffer and die and be resurrected. The church will journey through an exodus of testing before it reaches the Promised Land. God has enlisted the church in the battle against the world, the flesh and the devil. The church will be spiritually protected for its role as witness during the beast's onslaught (11:1–6). But the church is not protected from physical danger. The seven prophetic messages make the point that God gets victory through an historically weak and often divided church. This is the point of the prominence given to the witness of these seven churches as a model of the church through history.

Revelation 4

Revelation 4–5 In the Throne Room of Heaven

Revelation 4 Judgement on the World Anticipated

Revelation 4–5 are located at the divine throne in the heavenly temple. Revelation 4 reveals a vision of God's eternal purposes accomplished. Revelation describes how the new creation will bring in the total sovereignty of God as it is seen now, in heaven, at the beginning of the vision. The location is not the realm of space and time but a vision of the transcendent spiritual realm in which God dwells. The picture is of the harmony, blessing and order which is finally to prevail on earth (cf. Revelation 21–22). It is clear from the presentation of the fragmented earthly church in Revelation 2–3 that the church will not bring in this kingdom of God.

The timeless character of John's vision makes it difficult to determine the function of the heavenly council scene within Revelation.[1] The indications, within Revelation 4, that it presents—at the beginning of the book—the end achievement of the new creation (Revelation 21–22), are: the world of chaotic evil, the sea, now lies subdued before the throne; the presence of the rainbow around the throne suggests no further need to guarantee the fulfilment of the covenant with creation (Genesis 6:18; 9:13); and the assembled, representative church around the throne (4:4). Revelation 5 shows the manner in which the victory of Revelation 4 will be achieved: the kingdom will come through the Lamb by his victory over evil. In Revelation 5 there is the delivery of the scroll of destiny which reports this victory.

Thus, the lengthy vision of the future given to John from 4:1–22:5 is based on Revelation 4–5. From this point on the one vision is divided into seven sections: two groups of three and a climax (19:11–22:5). The first group of three visions (4:1–8:1; 8:2–11:18; 11:19–13:18) culminates in general tribulation throughout the world. Christians are directly involved (11:1; 13:16–18). The presentation gives some indication of—but is not controlled by—historical order, chronology and the passage of

---

[1] Beale, 1999, 329.

time. The second group of three visions moves to judgement against the opponents of Christians (14:1–20; 15:1–16:21; 17:1–19:10). The seventh vision (19:11–22:5) ushers in the end. In this way the entire vision (4:1–22:5) projects the failures and successes of the church set in the context of the effect of evil throughout world history. The church is always facing the same failures as the majority of the seven churches (Revelation 2–3). Rarely is any church a true identity of the people of God. Even so, the church is sustained through history by Christ and God's purposes in Christ. The victory of the Lamb in the seventh vision following the judgements is based on Revelation 4.

John is called up, like one of the Old Testament prophets, into the timeless realm of the heavenly council (Isaiah 6:1–8; 1 Kings 22:19ff; Zechariah 3). There are concomitants of the holiness of the divine presence in 'flashes of lightning and thunder' (4:5; cf. 11:19). Daniel 7:9–13 projects similar imagery of the throne room in heaven as the centre of reality. Revelation states seven times—using the same expression, 'him who sits on the throne'—that God sits enthroned (4:9; 5:1,7,13; 6:16; 7:15; 21:5; cf. 4:2,3; 7:10; 19:4; 20:11). This indicates his total and decisive sovereignty over all things. That God sits enthroned is central to the structure of the book. The word 'throne' occurs seventeen times in Revelation 4–5, and thirty-eight times in Revelation 4–22. All judgements in Revelation 6–16 issue from the throne (6:1–8, 16; 8:3–6; 16:17). The throne is, indeed, at the centre of John's cosmology.[2] The circular assembly around the throne emphasises God's universal and cosmic kingship. All heavenly beings find their significance in their placement around the throne. This harmony in heaven under divine sovereignty indicates the outcome that the book will project for all creation.

Thus, the first scene of the vision (Revelation 4), presents the reign of God through Christ totally concluded.[3] This is the fundamental message of Revelation: the kingdom of God come in its fullness. This provides the reader with a perspective of the 'events' which will proceed in heaven and on earth. The message of Revelation is that the decisive salvation event in the history of the world

---

2   Hendriksen, 1962, 101–3.
3   Beale, 1999, 1031.

has taken place through the death and resurrection of the Lamb (cf. 5:9ff, 12). But, in fact, he was the Lamb slain before the foundation of the world (13:8).

John is still in the same state as at 1:10, that is, 'in the Spirit' (cf. Ezekiel 2). The voice that summons John to heaven (4:1) is the same voice as at 1:10–11. Thus 4:1 is a transition within a single visionary experience. At the close of the vision (cf. 22:9) John is still in the Spirit (4:2), indicating the holistic nature of this experience; it is a continuous vision with symbolic development. The vision now begins to deal with what God had eternally destined for the future, a plan that is fixed and certain.

The vision of John from 4:1–22:5 unfolds the future of the world resulting from the death of Christ. Jesus has already identified himself as the one who was dead and lives forever and has the keys of Death and Hades (1:18). Thus the door to heaven is open and remains open (Greek perfect tense) because of Jesus' death and resurrection. The vision of Christ (1:12–20) who defeated death and Hades results in the open door into the throne room in heaven leading to further visionary revelation. Each of the three parts of the heavenly vision begins with John's experience of openness in heaven (4:1–5:14, open door; 11:19–15:5, open temple; 19:11–21:8 open heaven). Thus Revelation 4–5 becomes the dominating first of the sequences of the heavenly vision in which the mystery of human existence and its future is projected. The vision shows what must happen hereafter, that is, imposed by divine necessity (Revelation 4) in the light of the death of Christ (Revelation 5).

Revelation 4–5 are bound together with the implementation of world judgement in the Lamb. Judgement is necessary to bring about the divine purposes for a new creation. From the throne room, the reaction of divine holiness against the rebellious world is initiated. Heaven is the ordered new creation (Revelation 4) brought into being by the death of Christ in history and by the application of the judgement of the cross (Revelation 5).

The allusion to Daniel 2:28–29 in 4:1 (cf. 1:1; 1:19) is a clue to the macro-structure of the book.[4] Revelation 4 presents the structure of relationships within the new creation resulting from the judgements (Revelation 5) which will occur in the projected world struggle.

Revelation 4–5 follows the outline of Daniel 7:9–28, namely: throne set; God seated; God's appearance; fire; a host surrounding the throne; books opened before the throne; a divine messianic figure approaching the throne; the seer's emotional distress; the seer's instruction from a heavenly presence; the saints given authority to reign over the kingdom; and God's eternal reign.[5] But these chapters in Revelation are also like Ezekiel 1. In expressing the note of divine judgement on the sinful world, Revelation 4–5 enacts the movement of Daniel 7. World government is brought to account before the eternal reign of God and Christ in the new creation.

In Revelation 4, God's sovereignty is seen as acknowledged in heaven and demonstrated by the order proceeding out from and around the throne. God's sovereignty is displayed as the ultimate reality behind all earthly appearances. The book will be concerned with the manner in which this sovereignty is finally to be accepted by all creation. The vision presents God's reign over the world through Christ:[6] an ordered cosmos based on the divine throne that must ultimately prevail throughout the universe. God's throne, the symbol of divine sovereignty, is a picture of the ruler himself as the ultimate reality behind all earthly appearances. The unknowable transcendence of God is protected by focussing on the throne and on what goes on around it. Everything finds its significance in its relationship to the throne. The vision of 4:1–22:5 concludes with God enthroned (22:1) on earth in the midst of the new creation.[7]

The throne room scenes in Revelation (1:9–20; 4–5; 8:2–6; 15:1–16:1; 16:18–21; 19:1–10) also operate as structural markers introducing important literary movements in the book, taking the

---

4   Beale, 1992, 360–387.
5   cf. Beale, 1999, 314–5.
6   cf. Revelation 5 and Beale, 1999, 1031.
7   R.J. McKelvey, 1989, 85–100.

reader through to the completed vision: the emergence of the people of God as the new Jerusalem. In Revelation 4–5, John understands that the throne room—in which the vision takes place—is the holy of holies of the heavenly temple (4:2; cf. allusions to Isaiah 6 at 4:8; 11:19; 15:5ff).[8] God sits on the throne as the absolute sovereign. God's actions are described in Revelation using divine passives. He is unassailable. Avoiding the divine name, John accentuates the unknowable mysterious transcendence of God. God's form is not described since no one has seen or can ever see God. The image is theocentric: God reigning at the centre of the universe, the architect of creation, and the provider of the redemption in Christ designed to bring in the new creation. God is unseen and unknowable, but he is unmistakably present. As the source and goal of creation, just and trustworthy, to worship God is the natural response of all creation.

God sits enthroned within the heavenly temple. The temple is the symbol of the divine presence and, by housing the ark in the holy of holies, the temple is also the symbol of God's covenant relationship with his people.[9] In Revelation 6–16, all judgements issue from the throne. God's throne was a dominant concept in the Old Testament temple. Whenever the Old Testament mentions God as enthroned (1 Kings 22:19; Psalms 9:4; 11:4; 47:8; Isaiah 6:1; Ezekiel 1:26; Daniel 7:9), it is invariably connected with divine judgement. In Isaiah 66:1 heaven itself becomes his throne (cf. Jeremiah 17:12–13). The picture of the throne room merges with that of a heavenly temple in Revelation (16:17; cf. 7:15; Psalm 18:6; Micah 1:2; Habakkuk 2:20). In both Old and New Testaments, the temple (divine palace) and God's throne are carefully interrelated. The word 'throne', used to signify God's sovereignty, occurs thirteen times in 4:1–11. The frequent reference to 'throne' throughout the book stresses God's sovereign presence. The sovereign presence of God is to be exercised on the great white throne of universal judgement (20:11).

The image of the throne is both political (the place where God rules over all creation) and cultic (the divine throne room is the holy of holies of heaven itself, cf. 11:19; 15:5–8). God's holiness

---

8   Beale, 1997, 315.
9   cf. Stevenson, 2001, 2–6.

will always mean judgement on evil. The one who sits on the throne is the holy God of the Sinai covenant who demands obedience to his righteous will. The activities around the throne proceed from God himself. The throne is also the Lamb's throne (3:21; 5:6; 7:17). And the throne is at the heart of the new Jerusalem (22:3). A major purpose of the book is to declare God's judgement from the throne upon evil: upon Babylon the great harlot (Revelation 18); and then, finally, upon Satan and evil (20:11–15).

The resplendence surrounding the throne (4:3) alludes to Ezekiel (1:26,28; 9:2 (cf. Ezekiel 10:1, 28:13), together with connections in Exodus (24:10; 28:17–20). Each of these references to precious stones mentions a sapphire in connection with a theophany. God is thus presented in terms of the brilliance of resplendent light. All three stones—jasper, carnelian and emerald (4:3; cf. Ezekiel 1, 28; Exodus 28)—represent and anticipate the precious stones in the foundations of the new Jerusalem (21:10–11, 18–23). Their brilliance collectively speaks of the mysterious transcendence of God. They also represent the divine glory (21:10–11). Jasper is the last and carnelian the first stone in the high priest's breastplate of judgement. The emerald in the breastplate represented the tribe of Judah. The mention of emerald in 4:3 may be to represent Jesus as the Lion of the tribe of Judah.

The rainbow around the throne (4:3), like an emerald, is an important feature which has significance that can be easily overlooked. The rainbow was the sign—given by God to Noah (Genesis 9:13)—that God's covenanted purposes for creation to become a total Edenic Paradise (cf. 22:1–5) stood firm. The rainbow represented the multi-characteristic grace of God, as great as his majesty, prevailing in tempering judgement with mercy. In Revelation the rainbow is set in the heavens around the throne of God, which is further evidence that this vision to John is the logical result of God's faithfulness to his covenant pledge to Noah. In Genesis the rainbow in the sky was called into service to represent the restoration of the firmament division between the upper and lower waters (Genesis 1:6); a guarantee of God's purposes for creation. In Revelation the presence of the rainbow, now around the throne, indicates that God's purposes for creation which have been sustained throughout history have now prevailed! Beale observes that the precious stones together with the rainbow are an incipient hint: this vision will not only issue, eventually, into a new creation but the vision also portrays, already, the advent of the beginning of the new creation.[10]

The twenty-four elders and the four living creatures who surround the Trinity at the throne (4:4,6; cf. Revelation 5) provide the inner structure of praise within which the Trinity dwells (cf. 7:9–17; 11:19; 15:5). This anticipates the access of all the redeemed into the holy of holies. In a sense, this is the continuation of the divine council of the Old Testament (cf. Genesis 3:22; 1 Kings 22:19; Job 1:6; 2:1; Isaiah 24:23). True knowledge of God is inseparable from worship of God. God is to be worshipped. This is the natural response of all creation. The most notable characterization of any face-to-face encounter with God, any experience of his holy presence, is worship. Also around the throne are the heavenly hosts (5:11) and the multitude of the redeemed (cf. 7:9, 15; 14:3). The water of the river of life, eternal spiritual blessing for believers, comes forth from before the throne (cf. 22:1). The altar of incense for the offering of prayers of the saints is also before the throne (8:3).

The twenty-four elders—a term occurring twelve times (4:4,10; 5:5,6,8,11,14; 7:11,13; 11:16; 14:3; 19:4), always associated with the four living creatures—surround the throne in a scene unparalleled in Jewish apocalyptic visions. As elders (church leaders), they represent the heavenly church. The number twenty-four indicates that the elders represent the elect community of both Testaments, the combination of twelve apostles and twelve tribal patriarchs: the completion of God's purposes in redemption.[11] Since they are called 'elders', the twenty-four are probably men. The elders are always distinguished from angels (cf. 5:11; 7:11), and the angels are differentiated from the redeemed (5:9; 7:13). As members of the heavenly council, the elders are given a prominent place in the vision. These apostles and tribal patriarchs represent the entire church, the one true Israel. This combination of patriarchs and apostles also occurs in the new Jerusalem names of gates and foundations (21:12–14).

---

10 1999, 321.
11 Hurtado, 1985, 114.

The elders are sitting on their thrones. This seems to contrast with the apocalyptic picture of the heavenly retinue, who are always standing. So the elders are given honour and status previously denied to the highest angels. By the time that the Revelation was written, the term 'elder' was understood by the readers to mean a leader of the Christian congregation. They have crowns of gold (*stephanous*, not *diademata*). They are now kings and priests. However, these crowns emphasise not their royalty but their victory. The crowns they wear as victors make them an association of redeemed men. The number twenty-four indicates that this association of redeemed men are the elect in the Old and New Testaments, the faithful of all ages who have kingly and priestly privileges.

The elders announce the appearance of the sacrificed Lamb (5:5), identify the elect (7:13–17), and lead the chorus of praise at the announcement of the triumph of God on behalf of the saints (11:15–19). This suggests the heavenly role of the redeemed. The fact that there were twenty-four courses of priests in the Old Testament (1 Chronicles 23:3–4; 24:4; 25:9–31) signifies that the number of elders may also be alluding to the priestly status of the redeemed. The thrones on which they sit probably also allude to the royal rank of the faithful. Thus the redeemed are acting in their prescribed eschatological role of kings and priests (1:6; 5:10; 20:4–6; cf. 22:4–5).

The fact that the elders are enthroned signifies that Christ's exaltation has occurred. The elders, enthroned as kings, are vested in the white robes of priesthood. These white robes are also the garb of the saints (3:5,18). In Revelation the white robes are worn by none other than the redeemed. The elders' vestments indicate their conformity to the image of Christ and, as kings and priests, that they are fittingly successors of the elect Israel (Exodus 19:5–6).

As they wear what the redeemed have been promised—white robes of redemption (3:5) and victory crowns (3:11)—and occupy a throne (3:21), Revelation 4 reinforces the promises of Christ to the overcomers of the seven churches. The overcomers participate in the vision of God as the ancient elders of Israel participated at Sinai's initial covenant conclusion (Exodus 24:10; cf. Isaiah 24:23

LXX which mentions God ruling in Zion in eschatological victory, glorified before his elders). The twenty-four elders each have a harp (the heavenly instrument) and a golden bowl of incense (the prayers of the saints that they present before the throne, 5:8). As their own thrones and crowns suggest (Psalm 8:5), the elders are rulers in the new age.

John presents a development of Ezekiel's vision of the throne (4:5; cf Ezekiel 1:13), alluding to the thunderstorm that accompanied God's self-manifestation on Mount Sinai (Exodus 19:16; 20:18). Moreover, the formula used at 4:5a is also used at the opening of the seventh seal (8:5), the sounding of the seventh trumpet (11:19), and the pouring out of the seventh bowl (16:18–21). All are portents of God's judgement, confirming the judgement theme of Revelation 4. God's holiness is manifested in his judgement on evil, now completed.

The seven lamps of fire correspond to the flames of the always lit seven-branched lamp, standing in the earthly temple before the veil of the holy of holies (Exodus 40:25). The seven Spirits (4:5) correspond also to the seven lamps in Zechariah's vision (Zechariah 4:2). This symbolism represents the presence of the Holy Spirit.

The sea of glass like crystal before the throne (4:6–8a) together with the rainbow provide an interpretive key to Revelation 4. While nothing similar to a sea of glass has previously been associated with heaven, there is mention in Ezekiel 1:22, 26 of the likeness of a firmament shining like crystal. And at Exodus 24:9–10 there is a pavement in the appearance of a sapphire stone, like the very heaven for clearness.

The sea of glass (4:6) may be symbolic of the final harmony reflected in the heavenly scene. Again, this is prospective for the world. God will have removed evil from the world and overcome death. At the beginning of the second of the three heavenly visions (13:1), a threat of a foreboding presence for the world arises as the beast from the sea. Here the sea is the realm of chaos and the habitat of ocean monsters (Psalms 74:13–14; 89:10; Isaiah 27:1). Thus from the turbulent sea as the traditional realm of rebellion (cf. Daniel 7:2; perhaps also Genesis 1:2) emerges the blasphemous beast, upon whom the fallen Babylon is later to be seated. The sea had also formed the barrier that redeemed Israel must pass to reach the Promised Land.

At the end of the second heavenly vision (Revelation 15), John sees something like a glassy sea mixed with fire. And those conquering the beast and its image, who were victorious over the number of its name, are standing on it. They hold harps of gold and are singing the song of Moses and the Lamb (15:2-3). They had moved in the final exodus out of the chaos realm of the beast where the worship of the beast's image and the shaping of its mark prevailed. However, there the sea is mingled with fire (15:2): God's cleansing and purification of evil was still intended (cf. Isaiah 1:25).

At the close of the third vision there is no more sea (21:1). John sees the descent of the heavenly Jerusalem as the complete substitute for the new creation. It appears that the ordering of the world has now reached the result that 4:6 had indicated. In the ideal order, all evil will have been eliminated and cast into the lake of fire (cf. 20:11-15). The calmed sea before the throne (4:6) indicates that the chaos threat is now tamed. Perfect order finally prevails as God had always intended. Thus, in this prospective new creation, chaos will have been overcome because the evil that comes from it will have been destroyed and death abolished. Now the sea, once a hostile enemy and relic of the old order—standing for everything that is recalcitrant to the will of God—is as glass before God, a centre of calm in the new order when the anticipated end has happened (21:1).

The picture of the living creatures at the throne (4:7ff)—cherubim attendants as a mark of natural creation's share in humanity's redemption (Romans 8:19-21)—reinstitutes the symbolism of the Old Testament. In the earthly temple, God was deemed to be enthroned on the wings of the cherubim with the Ark of the Covenant as his footstool. The four living creatures in Revelation seem to be attached to the throne, variously positioned as in the middle of the throne and around the throne. They are perhaps like the Old Testament cherubim: appurtenances of the mercy seat and the ark-throne (Exodus 25:17-22; 37:6-9), an integral part of the throne.[12] The living creatures are angelic cherubim representing the worship of animate, non-human creation. In the 'middle' of the throne, they are at the centre of the universe and witness events taking place where heaven and earth symbolically meet.[13] The living creatures are positioned as the seraphim of Isaiah 6:2 had been, as leaders of the heavenly liturgy in the judgement scene. The living creatures in Revelation lead a praise circle that includes: the twenty-four elders; many angels; and, in the outermost circle, every other creature in heaven and earth.

Like the vision of the Seraphim in Isaiah 6:2, each of the four living creatures has six wings. The four creatures in Revelation also refer back to Ezekiel 1, but with differences: in Ezekiel each living creature had four faces, whereas in Revelation the face of only one of the living creatures is mentioned; the cherubim in Ezekiel 10:2,14,20 only had four wings; and the cherubim below the throne in Ezekiel 1 carried the throne but in Revelation the four beings attend the throne, surround it, and move with it. The four living beings in Revelation are full of alert, knowing eyes which represent unceasing watchfulness that searches the earth.

These four creatures seem to represent the transformation of the new created order (4:8). By divine authority they inaugurate the judgements on human beings until the consummation (6:1–8; 15:7). Like Isaiah 6, the living beings participate in the judgement scene. But in Revelation 5 the scene is now the world at large and not, as in Isaiah 6, the impending exile of Judah and the Davidic kingdom.

The living creatures, central to the throne, are mentioned fourteen times in Revelation. They are the heavenly antitypes of the two cherubim who flanked the mercy seat in the holy of holies in the earthly temple (Exodus 25:18–22), but in Revelation they are also given the six wings of the Seraphim of Isaiah 6. Their existence—like that of every creature in heaven and earth (5:13)—is entirely fulfilled in the worship of God. The number 'four' symbolises sacred significance, universality. Thus the living creatures act for the universal new creation. They bear witness to God's sovereignty over all creation.

---

12 cf. Hall 1990, 609–613.
13 Tonstad, 2006, 121–123.

Each of the four living creatures is the head of its species, with faces like: a lion, most noble; an ox, strongest of creatures; a man, most intelligent; and an eagle, swiftest (cf. Ezekiel 1). The living creatures represent each part of the animate creation and participate in the administration of divine justice (6:1,3,5,7). Their participation is an indication of the constituent role of justice in a biblical concept of creation.

All animal life is represented in the four living beings. Nobility, strength, wisdom, and speed all symbolise divine empowerment of creation. They also symbolise the divine power that upholds and pervades—and also transcends—creation. Irenaeus identified the four living creatures with the four Gospels: human face = Matthew; eagle = Mark; ox = Luke; lion = John. Another less likely suggestion is that the four faces are attributes of God, namely: human face = wisdom, intelligence, compassion, sympathy; eagle = soaring aspiration; ox = patience, strength, faithfulness; and lion = courage, bold and victorious, striving after ideals. Whereas God is distinct from his world, the four living creatures are reminders of divine immanence in creation. Their name *zoa* (living beings) is derived directly from Ezekiel 1:5. The living beings in Revelation are, therefore, interchangeable with Ezekiel's cherubim.

The living beings ceaselessly proclaim the deity and the sovereignty of God over history (4:8). The fullness of eyes—back and front, around and within—emphasises their alertness, watchfulness, and comprehensive knowledge combined with penetrative intelligence. However, this knowledge is not the same as the omniscience that is God's alone. With their six wings they are analogous to the seraphim in Isaiah 6:1–3: two wings covering the face in awe; two wings covering the feet in humility; and two wings for flight in obedience. The living creatures are ready to carry out divine commands. They are constantly vigilant over God's creation. Their ascription of praise to God (4:8) is the same as that of the seraphim in Isaiah 6:3. The living beings offer incessant praise, night and day (cf. 4:8).

When the four living creatures sing their song (4:8)—which closes with reference to God as *ho erchomenos* (who is to come)—the elders fall down before the divine presence who is the Creator and also the one who will bring eschatological salvation.

Praise is primary in the presence of God, and the praise song of the four living creatures begins the worship structure. It focuses on three aspects of God's essential nature: his holiness, his omnipotence, and his eternity. 'Lord God Almighty' stresses divine omnipotence and power and thus God's position to administer creation with justice. In the threefold celebration of his eternity (4:8b), God's past existence (*ho en*) is given more attention than in 1:4 (where *ho on*, the one who is, was first). In 4:8 it is the uniqueness of God the Creator that is being celebrated. *Ho on* (who is) signifies the drama of redemption. Whilst there is no mention of redemption in Revelation 4, this is implied by the eternity of the Creator in the outworking of his creation purposes.

This hymn of the four living creatures (4:8) sums up the vision. It is symmetrically patterned in three parts to reflect the perfect splendour of God. First, the trisagion 'holy, holy, holy' emphasises God's complete distinction from anything created. Secondly, the threefold designations 'Lord, God, Almighty' presents God as the ruler over all things including earthly rulers. And thirdly, the threefold presentation 'which was and is and is to come' speaks of the divine eternal omnipresence. Angels later join in the heavenly chorus with a seven-fold acclamation (5:11). True knowledge of who God is stems from, and is inseparable from, the worship of God. God controls history and he will bring it to its triumphant conclusion. Then all the world will be aware that he has brought in the kingdom visibly.

J. L. Resseguie notes the symmetrical character of the hymn of the four living creatures (4:8).[14] The worship of the four living creatures and of the twenty-four elders expresses the two primary forms of awareness of God: awed perception of his numinous holiness (cf. Isaiah 6:3), and the consciousness of utter dependence upon God for existence itself. No part of animate creation is absent from the heavenly chorus. All other claims to worship are fraudulent and are attempts to usurp authority, power and glory that belong to God alone. These early chapters praise God as the source and goal of creation; the later chapters offer praise because his judgements are just and true.

---

14 1998, 109–110.

4:9–11 project a scene of total obeisance in which living creatures as the central worshippers lead in worship that widening circles then take up. The praise of the four living creatures (4:9) is for glory (incomparability of his deity), honour (reverence, respect as God's alone), and thanksgiving due to God (with the articles suggesting completeness). Their praise is for the perfection of God: his holiness, omnipotence and eternity. Gratitude for the gift of creation is what the whole of creation should present to God. Cultic imagery is prominent because the throne room is the heavenly sanctuary, the holy of holies of the heavenly temple (cf. 11:19; 15:5–8). Wider circles will expand this ceaseless worship that is at the heart of reality. This worship finally includes all creatures in the cosmos (5:13). The eschatological goal of God's purpose for creation is anticipated in this worship of God and the Lamb by the whole of creation.

Whenever the four creatures worship, the elders also offer praise (4:10). Their response to this first call to worship from the living beings (4:8) is the first of six times in Revelation when the elders will prostrate themselves before God or the Lamb (4:10; 5:8, 14; 7:11; 11:16; 19:4). The elders worship in an act of obeisance. They get down from their thrones and remove their crowns thereby acknowledging their derivative victory and displaying deep reverence. All human dignity must submit before the divine throne in this way. The affirmation of God's eternity ('who lives forever', 4:10) appears to be related to Daniel 4:34 and 12:7. If so, the affirmation may also imply that the final elimination of all evil rule has occurred.[15] So the elders are now casting their crowns in allegiance and obedience, surrendering their royal reward to the giver of it. The crown represents honour and reward for victory. Casting the crown means total yielding of life in worship to the one who lives forever.

The song of the twenty-four elders (4:11) takes its cue from the four creatures (4:8), but is more focussed on the wonders of God's creation. In contrast to the four living beings, the elders address God directly, indicating that they have a closer relationship to God. There is now continuous worship of the twenty-four elders, expressing awed perception of God's numinous holiness and

---

15 cf. Beale, 1999, 334.

conscious dependence upon God for existence. This worship is in response to God's display of power in creation.

The acknowledgement of 'our Lord and God' (4:11) exactly echoes the words of Dominus et Deus Noster, which was a required expression in Roman emperor worship. 'Lord God Almighty' is an expression of divine infinity and sovereignty over history. However, acknowledging God is not necessarily worship. To worship God is to acknowledge God as God, to allow God to be God of the whole life, and to yield all to him. Worship is acknowledging God's worth with complete commitment, as the elders do here. Worship as a recurring motif in the book is anticipated here by the Greek word *hotan* (4:9, whenever). God and the Lamb are to be praised in an all-embracing way (cf. 5:13). This all-embracing praise is seen again at 7:9–17, with the great multitude with palm branches; 11:15–19, where voices in heaven proclaim God's reign; 14:1–5, with the assembly of the 144,000 on Mt. Zion; 15:2–8, with the Song of Moses and the Lamb; and 19:1–8, with the loud voice of the multitude in heaven. All these occasions are liturgical and function as a commentary on what is happening on the earth. The vision tells us that even in the dynamic of rebellious creation, God is working his purposes out.

God created all (4:11), so he is 'worthy'. The Lamb, as the one who will bring in the new world and its order, is also praised for being 'worthy' (5:9). By the use of the Greek imperfect (4:11, 'they existed') there may be indication that creation had existence in God's mind before creation. Creation came into being as an expression of God's will, and reveals his power. The throng acknowledges that, as created beings, their authority is wholly derivative from God and so God alone is to be worshipped as the source of all power and authority. There is a tilt here against the cultic/political power in the system of Roman emperor worship. Rome represented and propagated its power in religious terms. Loyalty to the gods of Rome and the deified emperor was expressed through worship. Thus Rome absolutised power, claiming for itself ultimate divine sovereignty over the world. In effect, Rome contested God's power on earth. But in Revelation 4 John sees God's power acknowledged in heaven. This conflict of sovereignty is often portrayed in the remainder of the book in terms of worship. Rome's usurpation of divine rule is indicated by the universal worship of the beast (13:4,8,12), whereas the coming of God's kingdom is portrayed by the universal worship of God (15:4, cf. 19:5–6).

Every stage of God's victory through Revelation 7–19 is accompanied by worship in heaven (5:13; 7:9–17; 11:15–19; 12:10–12; 14:1–15:5; 15:2–4; 19:1–8). The issue of true and false worship is fundamental to John's prophetic insight into the power structures of the world in which his readers lived. Revelation pronounces the incompatibility of the exclusive monotheistic worship portrayed in Revelation 4 with any kind of idolatry. Hence the challenge: either share Rome's ideology promoted by Roman propaganda as typical of world attitudes or see Rome's pretensions unmasked by the perspective of heaven. Revelation portrays the Roman Empire as a representative system of violent oppression founded on conquest and maintained by brutal force.[16] Rome is representative of the control exercised by godless political authority throughout history.

Revelation 4 presents a picture of one God with an ordered creation and the church in heaven. The remainder of the book, beginning with Revelation 5, will disclose how this order is to be imposed. The Old Testament provides background to this portion of the vision. The fulfilment of the Daniel 7 vision brings the judgement of all world power, the kingdom given to the Son of Man, and the reign of the Son of Man with the saints.[17] The expectation is that the books will be opened, judgement will be passed, and the kingdoms of this world will become the kingdoms of Christ.

The prophetic messages to the seven churches (Revelation 2–3) describe the fate of the visible church on earth. Saints struggle with temptation and persecution as the council in heaven proceeds to wind up history. But the universal reign of the Son of Man with the saints—presented as accomplished in Revelation 4–5—is already in the process of happening within the struggling seven churches of Asia. The church is exposed in the world but she is, paradoxically, powerful in all her weakness. The now of Revelation 2–3 is flanked by what will be (Revelation 1 and Revelation

---

16 Beale, 1997, 35.
17 Beale, 1984, 227.

4–5). Around the seven letters there is the commission of Revelation 1 and the heavenly vision of Revelation 4 that depicts the end, followed by Revelation 5 which depicts the necessity of history. This forms an inclusion. The divine plan for the rule of the saints is seen against the background of God's sovereign purposes for creation. Bringing this divine plan to pass requires the opening of the scroll by him who alone is worthy, the Lamb (5:1–5). The fulfilment of God's purposes is continually acknowledged, with certainty, by the throne room company in their worship of the Creator. This corresponds to the heavenly temple scene of Isaiah 6.

The throne scene in Revelation 4 represents the beginning of the end and, indeed, the shape of the end of the beginning. Revelation 5 will make it clear that the judgement of humankind that must precede redemption has already taken place by the cross. But this judgement is yet to be pronounced and applied. The elders, the fruits of redemption, are already around the throne and they have surrendered their crowns. However, the world judgement through which the church of Christ must pass is still to come. The Lamb, the agent of both judgement and redemption, is missing in the vision of Revelation 4. The Lamb is the inaugurator, by the cross, of the consummation of revelation which is the new creation. So God is presented as Sovereign Judge (Revelation 4) and the source of redemption (Revelation 5). And he is both Sovereign and Redeemer because he is Creator. In God's plan, finality for creation and thus the new creation must come about by redemption (re-creation).

Revelation 5

Revelation 5 The Lamb Takes the Scroll to Implement World Judgement

The heavenly throne scene continues in Revelation 5, taking the eschatological setting of Revelation 4 further and informing the reader of the divine manner in which that setting has been achieved.

'And I saw' (5:1) begins a new dimension of the vision introducing the sealed scroll, written on both sides and sealed with seven seals (cf. Daniel 12:4, 9). The number 'seven' signifies the absolute completeness of the contents of the scroll. The scroll conveys the subsequent course of human history. It lies in the hand of the Almighty Presence who sits on the throne. Again, the redemptive process that leads to the new creation begins from the throne. Creation and redemption are inextricably linked as the initiation and development of the divine plan designed from the beginning to lead to the new creation. God's purpose in bringing about the new creation is already achieved in Christ, but only partially experienced by the believing community. God's purpose is to lift humanity from their self-imposed bondage by the complete unfolding of the new creation, already inaugurated by Christ's death.[1] The throne room scene of Revelation 4 presents judgement having been effected; Revelation 5 provides for the movement to the new creation through the enactment of judgement. Judgement is accomplished by the slain Lamb. Revelation 4 focuses on the Creator; Revelation 5 focuses on the Redeemer. God's sovereignty recognised and praised by the totality of the universe (Revelation 4) is now expressed in the death of the Lamb that initiates the world judgement to bring about the advent of the kingdom of God (Revelation 5).

It is sometimes suggested that Revelation 5 deals with the enthronement of Christ: his exaltation (5:5); his presentation (5:6); and his enthronement/authority (5:7). Yet Revelation 1–3 had already recognised him as fully empowered with God. So, rather

---

1   cf. Wall, 1991, 97.

than enthronement, Revelation 5 speaks of Christ's authorization: his investiture to open the scroll. By his death as the Lamb, humankind will be called to account before the judgement bar that is the cross (cf. John 12: 32). What must lead to the advent of the new creation is the complete creation of a new humanity. The human world must take responsibility for its rejection of the sovereignty of God. This rejection of God's sovereignty had distorted and corrupted the vision that God had set before humankind (Genesis 1–2).[2] Only by the judgements flowing from the death of the Lamb—by which the overthrow of evil has been achieved—can the purposes of God for creation (Revelation 4) be realised.

There are four new scenes in Revelation 5 (5:1,2–5,6–10, 11–14). All are introduced by *kai eidon* (and I saw). John saw both God (5:1,7,13) and the Lamb (5:6,8,12–13). The Spirit is also associated with the throne (5:6). The scroll of the future thus receives Trinitarian backing. The scroll lies on the open right palm of the one sitting on the throne. This is similar to Ezekiel 1–3: the prophet sees a vision of the divine throne; there is a prophetic call; there is the scroll of a book in the hand stretched out to the prophet; there is a message involving the open scroll; and there is the demand to eat the scroll (10:9–10; cf. Ezekiel 3:1–2), symbolising the prophet's absorption of the entire message. In Revelation, the position of the scroll in God's right hand emphasises: the divine source of the scroll; the supreme authority of the revelation in the scroll; and the assurance of complete power to translate the contents of the scroll into action.

The description 'written on the inside and on the back' fits an unrolled scroll.[3] It is written back and front, so the contents are full: nothing needs to be added; nothing can be added. The scroll contains extensive and comprehensive divine decrees for the ushering in of the kingdom. It will reveal God's purposes relating to world judgement delivered through the Lamb's victory. This will lead to the advent of the new Jerusalem.

The scroll is sealed (*kata* = comprehensively) by seven seals, a hint of the profundity of the mystery contained in it which is now

---

2 cf. Dumbrell, 2002, 13–27.
3 This is not a codex. The codex came into being in the late first century at the earliest (Beale, 1997, 343).

to be revealed. The seven seals protect and guarantee the fulfilment of the contents of the scroll. The scroll sealed with seven seals represents the total presentation of what must occur in this eschatological period after the death of Christ and before the Parousia. Since the content of the gospel had been revealed to the Old Testament prophets (Romans 1:2), then the content of the Revelation scroll will have been—in some way—anticipated by them in their message to Israel of judgement to come, paving the way for redemption beyond judgement. The purpose of the opening of the scroll is therefore to bring to fulfilment previous revelation. A sealed scroll written on both sides makes the fulfilment of the divine intention totally unchangeable.

In addition to what has previously been revealed generally, the scroll contains further aspects of the divine purpose. Smalley is probably correct when he states that the scroll contains the finality of God's covenant purposes.[4] God will sustain his intention to bring in an Edenic world in which there is no evil presence: God's covenant with creation will prevail.[5] In John's contemporaneous world, God's rule was hidden and contested by the powers of evil. But to no purpose, as the throne scene (Revelation 4) indicates that through judgements God's sovereignty will be implemented upon earth. Through the judgements loosed by the cross upon a rebellious world, the kingdom of God is to come to earth. This is strongly implied by the song of the living creatures who proclaim God as the one who was and who is and who is to come (4:8): that is, God has already established and will finally visibly establish his kingdom rule. God was sovereign from the beginning.

The voice of the strong angel (5:2, cf. 10:1; 18:21)[6] brings the decree relating to judgement and redemption. The strong angel puts the question to the entire world: 'who is worthy to open the scroll?'. The word *axios* (worthy, capable) means 'of proper weight'. The Greek word refers to a quality of being, person, power, or attainment. The threefold examination of creation (5:3) is comprehensive: no created being has the worthiness required to

---

4   2005, 128.
5   Dumbrell, 1984, 31–33.
6   Beale very plausibly relates this Revelation strong angel to the angelic representative from the heavenly council in Daniel 4:13–23 (1999, 338).

open the scroll since to open the scroll is to execute the contents of the scroll. Only deity is worthy (cf. 4:11) to implement this plan of deity.

The imperfect tense (*edunato,* 5:3) indicates ongoing inability of the inhabitants of creation to open the scroll. The reason is clear: God's purposes transcend the created order and cannot be understood by anyone within the created order who is not completely identified with God's purposes. This is why the Lamb is the only one who can open the scroll. It is only by his victory of the cross that implementation of the divine plan is possible. The Lamb is the means by which rebellious creation is overcome, for he is at the very centre of God's purposes. The credentials necessary for opening the scroll are not messianic rank but character and action. The Lamb's credentials are his character of perfect moral purity together with his action of self-sacrifice.

Most suppose that the scroll is progressively revealed as the Lamb opens the seven seals in order. This may be the case if breaking the seals is also implementing the contents of the scroll. However, as all seven seals must be broken before the scroll can be read,[7] it is only when the last seal has been broken that the totality of God's purposes are clear. The opened scroll appears again, later in the vision (10:2,8–10).

The scroll must contain the mystery of the divine purpose which is to be revealed when the scroll is opened. Revelation 4 showed God's sovereignty manifest and acknowledged in heaven. But God's sovereignty is presently hidden on earth where it is contested by the powers of evil. The 'how' of the scroll in Revelation 5 is the mystery: how God's sovereignty is visibly implemented on earth. God's purposes that the new world will come have been revealed (Revelation 4). The important question is, 'How will it come about?' (Revelation 5). This is taken further by the song of the living creatures (4:8) who—instead of proclaiming like the Seraphim of Isaiah 6:3 that the earth is already full of God's glory—proclaim God as the one who was and who is and who is to come, that is, God will establish in the future his kingdom. The

---

[7] Bauckham, 1993, The Theology of the Book of Revelation, 248 (cf. Beale, 1999, 347, who disagrees with this view).

scroll (5:1) contains God's hitherto secret purpose for establishing his kingdom on earth.

The Lamb is worthy to open the scroll for he has won the comprehensive victory for God against all evil. The coming of God's kingdom will be the outworking of this victory. The scroll is about how the Lamb's victory is to be implemented. It will perhaps come as a surprise that victory does not come by the restraint of evil, nor is victory won by the gradual overcoming of evil. At times we feel that we live in a world where God does not care since evil seems to be able to destroy Christian witness. And this Christian witness seemed to us to be the key to the end. But the scroll does not tell how Israel or the church contribute to the end through their witness or restraint of evil. Rather, the scroll reveals that the church was never able of itself to bring in the end. The scroll reveals that God can and he will bring about his divine purpose to usher in the new creation.

John is distraught to find that no one can open this scroll (5:4). He is distraught because the contents of the scroll are so important; he is distraught because the opening of the scroll will unfold and put into effect the shape of the future. John feared that the scroll would not be opened, that the events would remain unfulfilled, that God's final and decisive action would be—unthinkably—indefinitely postponed. But an elder who is part of the heavenly company (5:5) reassures John that there is one, and one only, who is worthy to open the scroll: the one who has conquered, the Lion of the tribe of Judah, the offspring from David. The imagery of the Lion and the Davidic overtones introduce the major purpose of the scroll, which is messianic war. Though the victory will be won by the slain Lamb, the Lion symbolism portends conquest and sovereignty. Thus the divine judgements of Revelation 4 will be instituted by the invocation of messianic war on the world, which stands under divine judgement for its continued refusal to recognise divine sovereignty.

The Lion of Judah—a messianic title suggestive of leadership, strength, fearless aggression and conquest—looks back to Genesis 49:8-10 (cf. 4 Ezra 12:31-2). The expectation is that leadership will come from the tribe of Judah in the eschatological war against the enemies of God's purposes. Messianic war is in view. 'Lion' evokes a strong, militaristic and nationalistic image of the Davidic Messiah as the conqueror of the nations. The 'Lion' will destroy the enemies of God's people. Since the Old Testament prophetic expectation was of a new world and a new world order, this messianic victory will bring that new world order into being.

The lion image (Genesis 49:9) suggests kingly might, boldness and victory. The Messiah who stems from David (cf. Isaiah 11:1) is the heir to David's throne (cf. 1:17–18, 22:13,16). According to the prophet Isaiah, the Messiah who leads in the final Davidic kingdom has human origins (Isaiah 11:1–16). The Lion is a messianic symbol taking up Jewish hopes for a descendant of David who is anointed by God as king and military leader of his people. This Messiah will fight a war against godless humanistic oppression. The Messiah will liberate and restore Israel and establish the rule of God. And this rule of God is also the rule of God's Messiah and God's people. The Messiah will lead the armies of the saints against the enemies of Israel.

The key concept of conquering derives from the militant Messiah. The Messiah conquers (3:21; 5:5; 17:14); and the Messiah's people share in his victory (2:7,11,17,26; 3:5,12,21; 12:11; 15:2; 21:7). Note the importance of the Messiah's army. The battle with Satan will be history-long. Even so, that battle against Satan is already won. The Messiah's followers will defeat the beast (15:2). But the beast also defeats the Messiah's followers. However, even when defeated the Messiah's followers are the victors (11:7; 13:7). The language of conquering is used in all three stages of the Messiah's work: he conquered in death and resurrection (3:21; 5:5); his followers conquer in the time before the end (12:11; 15:2); and he will conquer at the Parousia (17:14). This image of messianic war describes the whole process of the establishment of the messianic kingdom. For Judaism, this messianic war is future. But, in reality, the messianic war has already been fought and the Messiah has already won. His followers are exhorted to continue the battle in the present. The Messiah will fight through them. Thus under the theme of Davidic messiahship, the hopes of the Old Testament prophetic tradition are focussed on the eschatological vision centred on Jesus.

Psalm 2—often seen as referring to the Messiah in the New Testament—is critical to understanding Revelation's key concept of conquering. The psalm presents God's Son as king on Mount Zion, resisting and overcoming the rebellious nations (Psalm 2:7–8). The Messiah will subdue the rebellious nations with a rod of iron (Psalm 2:9; cf. 2:18,26–28; 11:15,18; 12:5,10; 14:1; 16:14,16; 19:15). John saw the Messiah's army, who will share in the Messiah's victory standing with the Messiah on Mount Zion (14:1). This is the fulfilment of Psalm 2:6. The Messiah gains victory over 'the kings of the earth', that is, victory over political powers opposed to God (1:5; 6:15; 17:2, 18; 18:3,9; 19:19; 21:24; cf. 16:14). The Messiah overcomes the world (3:21; 5:5; 17:14). The Messiah conquered by his death (3:21; 5:5) and by his death he will conquer at the Parousia (17:14). The Messiah has already won the decisive victory and now his followers are summoned to continue the battle in the present.

So it is Israel's Messiah—the Lion of Judah, having completed his conquest of the prince of the world, now having all power in earth and heaven—who is accounted worthy to open the scroll. His victory makes implementation of the scroll's contents possible. The turning point in human history has now taken place. The scroll is to reveal the way in which, according to the hitherto secret purpose of God, Christ's victory over death through death is to become effective in establishing God's rule. The scroll will reveal the way in which evil will be defeated and the disobedient world will be judged. Followers of the Messiah are to participate in the coming of God's kingdom by following him in witness, sacrifice, and victory over death. The Messiah by his death and resurrection has conquered all that stands in opposition to God in the world, including the defeat of the final enemy death. So the Messiah is the one who can reveal to his followers how they too will conquer death. The scroll is how the conquest of evil and death will come about, and how this conquest will bring in the kingdom of God in which God's will alone will be done. Israel's Messiah is the divine agent to execute the Father's will by bringing in, through judgement, the new Jerusalem.

Then (5:6), graphically, John sees a Lamb standing (Greek perfect tense, that is, 'stationed') 'as slain', with all the indication of powerlessness and defeat. But this slain Lamb stands in the throne circle, so he has conquered. The Lamb is positioned in the middle of the throne (NEB), surrounded by the four living creatures and then by the elders. In the final victory, the triumphant Lamb of God will share this throne (cf. 3:21; 22:1). He has been slain (Greek perfect tense, that is, the results of that sacrifice of atonement are presently and always available). The resurrected Lamb still bears the scars of his mortal wounding. He stands conquering by his death before the throne which is at the very centre of the universe.

The lion image had presented the theme of messianic conquest. But John doesn't see a lion; he sees a slaughtered Lamb (5:6)! There will be messianic conquest, but the manner of its implementation defies prediction. The Lion who conquered is the slaughtered Lamb, conquering by faithfulness unto and in death. He conquers for his followers. The Lamb of God conquers by crucifixion. The ultimate power of God is expressed in the crucifixion. By his resurrection he is shown to be the conquering Lion, able to display all the characteristics of strength and power.

Following the Lamb's conquest, he comes to the throne (5:7) for his investiture or exaltation.[8] The Lamb's work is the explanation of how God works in the world, to be further divulged in the opening of the scroll. The Lamb's position before the throne relates him to the judgmental purposes of God. The Lamb's coming to the divine throne and his reception of authority to bring in the end (5:7) indicates his enthronement now as ruler of the kings of the earth (1:5).[9]

This transference of imagery from Lion to Lamb is the movement from Judaism's expectations of the majesty of a powerful deliverer to the Christian reality of the gentleness and meekness of the Lamb. The Lamb is equipped with: seven horns—the perfection of royal power—as conqueror and overcomer; and fullness of eyes (seven eyes), betokening omniscience. The twenty-eight (seven by four) occurrences of Lamb in the book indicate the worldwide scope of his complete victory. Seven of these

---

[8] cf. Romans 1:4 where Paul refers to Christ's heavenly office equipped with kingship over the universe (cf. my *Romans*, 2005, 11–15).

[9] Smalley, 2005, 362.

occurrences are coupled with God and the Lamb (5:13; 6:16; 7:10; 14:4; 21:22; 22:1,3).

The use of *arnion* (lamb) as the word to describe the slain Messiah in Revelation relates to Isaiah 53:7; but *amnos* is used in Isaiah. *Amnos* is also used in John's Gospel and elsewhere in the New Testament. In Revelation, the diminutive *arnion* may be used to emphasise the degree of difference between a lion and a lamb: but, as a counter to this suggestion, *arnion* can be used to represent a sheep of any age. Perhaps *amnos* was too restrictive for the purposes of Revelation because of its sacrificial connotation: but, as a counter to this suggestion, in Revelation the Lamb is described as the one who was slain four times, and the effectiveness of the blood of the Lamb is stressed three times. So the primary emphasis in the image of the Lamb in Revelation is sacrificial. But sacrifice is not the whole story. In Revelation Christ is more than a sacrificial victim. The Lamb slain is also the apocalyptic warring Lamb (17:14, cf. 1 Enoch 90) with omnipotence and omniscience (5:6), the powerful conquering Lamb who leads his army to victory. The cross is thus presented as the Armageddon by which all principalities and powers inimical to the kingdom of God will be overthrown.

It is likely that Revelation 5:6,9 alludes to Isaiah 53:7—like a lamb that is led to the slaughter...yet he did not open his mouth—and to the Servant as the sacrificial Lamb. Thus the Suffering Servant is the Passover Lamb of the new exodus (cf. Isaiah 40–55), a notion which is prominent in John's Gospel. The exodus was a key salvation event for Israel in which God, liberating them and destroying their oppressors, made Israel his own people and led them to theocratic independence in a land of their own. So the exodus was a natural model for apocalyptic and prophetic hopes. Revelation develops this common New Testament application of the exodus. In Revelation it is clear that the Lamb slain means the sacrificed Passover Lamb, since the Lamb 'ransomed' a people and made them a 'kingdom and priests to God' (5:9–10). Also, when Revelation treats the blood of the Lamb as the price of redemption, this is consistent with the role of the blood of the Passover Lamb.

John had drawn on all the lamb associations, including that of 1 Enoch 89–90 where the people of God are seen as God's flock and the deliverer is David. The Lamb in Enoch becomes—as in Revelation—a seven-horned ram, the powerful conqueror. This created a new symbol in Revelation: a victorious military figure that, in the paradox of all history, conquers by self-sacrifice; a victorious military figure who willingly gives up his life to become the faithful and true witness. The Warrior Lamb as the slain Lamb (mortally wounded in defeating an enemy) is appropriate for Revelation. Its strong message is that those who conquer are those that remain faithful to death, holding the testimony of Jesus even when confronted with death. The securing of divine purposes will be achieved by suffering and sacrifice, not by power. The Paschal Lamb, the Suffering Servant, connotes cultic atonement sacrifice. But the Lamb is also the messianic conqueror by his faithful witness unto death.

Christ now reigns as heavenly regent/Messiah overcoming the world through his church. The object of the conquest is left undefined in Revelation 5 as the victory is boundless in its scope. All that is opposed to God's rule has been defeated by the Lamb slain, faithful unto death. By the cross, Satan is a defeated enemy. However, in the continuing plan of God at the end of the church age, Satan is loosed to bring about by deceit his own conquest of the nations and then his final doom.

The sacrificial death of the Lamb (5:6) was to inaugurate a new exodus to a new promised land for a new Israel, to conquer Satan, and to bring in the new creation over which God and the Lamb will be jointly enthroned (22:1).[10] The Lamb has redeemed people from all nations (5:9–10): by his death for all sin which denies Satan the role of accuser of the brethren; in his conquest over Satan; and by his resurrection defeating the last enemy, death.

The people of the Lamb were redeemed to conquer. By their faithfulness to the Lamb they conquer the world, the flesh and the devil. This in itself would be a great moral victory, even if there were nothing more. However in God's gift there is more, all won through the Lamb's victory, namely: the final conquest of death, the advent of the new creation, and membership of the new

---

10 Resseguie, 1998, 131–133.

Jerusalem. All of this is to come to the overcomers, but not to the world. In the new Jerusalem, the overcomers will know as they have been known in the world; they will know that it had been by the power of the seven-fold Spirit in them that they had honoured Christ. The overcomers, in their struggle against the flesh, had worked out their own salvation in fear and trembling. This was proof that God had worked within them (Philippians 2:12–13) to bring them to glory.

The Lamb stands sacrificed but now resurrected; immediately before the throne, at the place of power, and by his sacrifice expressing that power. But the emphasis is neither on his elevation nor his enthronement. The emphasis is on the judgements that will be unleashed by the opening of the book. And these judgements are to be based on world reaction to the Lamb slain. The continuing and ultimate victory of God over evil, which the rest of Revelation describes, is no more than the working out of the decisive victory of the Lamb on the cross.

The image of the Lamb reinterprets that of the Lion, overturning conventional expectations of messianic victory. Victory occurs not by might and power but by obedience and faithfulness to divine truth. This is also the way that the readers of Revelation will achieve victory over death: by their faithfulness (cf. 12:11). The startling element is that the emphasis is on the Lamb as slain. This feature precedes all others in John's description. This is how the fullness of the power and presence of God has occurred, both in the vision and also within history.

The language of 'slain' (Greek perfect participle) is not merely the language of sacrifice, but of struggle and conflict. There is life through death for the resurrected Lamb. The image points to the necessity for the Christian army to find its strength by spiritual identification with the Lamb's death, to overcome the spiritual opposition in the world by participating in the resurrection life of the Lamb.

The Lamb's messianic activity results in victory over evil in both the political and the spiritual spheres. The Lamb's eyes are represented as the seven spirits. Richard Bauckham makes the point that, in the Old Testament, Yahweh's eyes speak of his omniscience and power (Zechariah 4:10b; 2 Chronicles 16:9).[11] Bauckham suggests that in Revelation the connection between eyes and power is made explicit by adding seven horns to the Lamb. The dragon and beasts also have horns which represent their power (12:3; 13:1,11; 17:12-13). For the slaughtered Lamb, these seven horns represent the power won by his victory (5:5-6). Thus the eyes are symbolic of the Lamb's discernment and the horns are symbolic of his power.

The fullness of the Spirit of God relates to the Lamb as eyes relate to a person. The Spirit of truth emanates from the Lamb in response to needs and problems of believers in the world.[12] The Lamb's equipment, seven horns (cf. 1 Enoch 90:9, 37-38), marks the plenitude of his power. Having conquered death, the Lamb is victorious. For that reason the Lamb is worthy to open the sealed book (5:6-9). Through the Spirit of Christ, the omniscience and power of Yahweh is being conveyed. The Spirit's power in Zechariah, actively empowering the building of the second temple, is opposed to the horns of the nations (Zechariah 1:18-21). In the same way the Lamb's power in Revelation is opposed to the horns of the dragon and the beasts (12:3; 13:1,11). The Lamb who overcomes is the new temple. He will complete the erection of the new temple.

How are the seven Spirits of God, with which the Lamb is endowed (5:5), sent into all the earth? In heaven the seven Spirits burn before the throne of God (1:4; 4:5) like the seven-branched lampstand that burned before the Lord in the earthly temple (Exodus 40:25). The answer is that the seven Spirits, the horns and the eyes of the Lamb will be active throughout the earth through the Lamb's followers. They will bear witness to his victory through his death. In them, the Spirit of prophecy maintains the witness of Jesus in the world. They are not only olive trees filled with the Spirit, but also lampstands (1:20; 2:1,5; 11:4) burning with the light of the Spirit in the world.

The 'seven Spirits' (5:6) is therefore not referring to the Lamb's omnipotence independent of his church. Rather, the 'seven Spirits' refers to the Lamb's presence with those whom his death has ransomed for God (5:9); through their witness the Spirit

---

11   1993, The Climax of Prophecy, 164-166.
12   cf. Spatafora, 1997, 236.

of God goes out into all the earth, continually expressing the Lamb's conquest. The ministry of the Lamb by the Spirit in the churches (2:1) is through the effectiveness of believers as his witnesses in the world (11:3ff).

The Spirit mediates the victory of the exalted Christ, the Lamb, through his church. The Spirit declares Christ's word to his people in vision and prophetic oracle. The Spirit leads the prayers of Christ's people. The Spirit inspires the missionary witness of Christ's people to the world. The Spirit's role is eschatological, constituting the Christian churches as the community of the age to come. The eschatological outpouring of the Spirit into the world is derived from the victory of Christ in his death and resurrection (5:6). In the same way, the Spirit's activity in and through the churches is directed towards the fulfilment of this victory of Christ in the eschatological future.

Even so, the real point in the vision is that the Lamb has been slain and is now standing. Through the grace of God, Christ's death has provided the means for world redemption[13]—by the conquest of death—for an amazing resurrection has occurred! Now his redeemed no longer live their lives under the fear of death, for the 'wages of sin' will no longer be extracted from believers. It is in this sense that believers will also 'conquer' death. The death of the Lamb indicated the extent of the love of God. However, the Lamb 'standing' before the throne indicates God's affirmation of the purpose of the death. The Lamb's death paid the debt for human sin throughout all history. It is the effective witness of Christ through believers that will finally overcome the rebellious world. The whole world will, finally, revolt against the rule of evil (cf. 17:15–18).

The Lamb's coming to the throne and his receipt of the scroll (Greek perfect tense, implying his power to keep and implement it) resonate with the Old Testament Son of Man picture (Daniel 7:13). This brings about a change in the world situation. Christ is authorised to take the scroll and to execute its contents. The scroll is comprehensively sealed (*katesphragismenon*). This implies that

---

13 cf. Lioy, 2003, 135.

the purposes of God cannot be thwarted.[14] And, significantly, the scroll is in the right hand of God: the hand which had brought creation into being (Isaiah 48:13), the hand which delivered Israel from Egypt (Exodus 15:6,12), the hand which gave to Israel their land (Psalm 44:3). Now the right hand of God will bring victory for the people of God as the restored Israel over all their enemies (cf. Psalms 60:5; 118:15). Through the scroll God reveals that he holds those who rebel against him (cf. Psalm 21:8) accountable, but he upholds the faithful (cf. Psalm 63:8). The right hand of God is thus an image for the powerful action of God in the fulfilment of his purposes.

Christ receives worship from the heavenly host (5:8–10) for accepting his unique role as redeemer when he took the scroll. The setting is the heavenly throne room where ceaseless worship is offered to God. The elders—the representative church in heaven—hold harps, the celestial instrument (14:2; 15:2). The worship of Christ is explicitly divine worship, as the parallels between 4:9–11 and 5:8–10 make clear. The emphasis has moved from the scroll and the Lamb (5:1–7) to worship, by the innumerable heavenly host, of the Lamb as Redeemer. The Lamb's reception of the scroll evokes an overwhelming response from the orders of creation (5:8), a thrill of satisfaction by all creation. Taking the scroll represents initiation of proceedings to convert the contents of the scroll into reality, that is, ushering in the final kingdom.

The golden bowls—recalling the receptacles on the Old Testament altar of incense (Zechariah 14:20)—are now full of incense: the sweet odour of prayer rising up, the prayers of the saints of all ages. The prayers of the saints represent the presence of the redeemed as new participants in the praise of God in heaven. The great throng encompasses the totality of animate and redeemed creation. The worship of the seven churches—the universal church—is brought into deeper focus (Revelation 4–5) as their worship of God and the Lamb takes place in heaven. The three hymns are of ever growing and ascending praise by gradually larger groups (5:9–10,12,13). The hymns anticipate what is to come. The praise is for the redemption that the Lamb has

---

14 Smalley, 2005, 128; Aune, 1998, 338–346.

achieved. The four living creatures and the elders prostrate themselves and extol the worth of the Lamb—who is worthy as God is worthy (4:11)—for redemption through his sacrifice. Following their redemption, they will rule (5:10). Thus as the new Israel, when the fullness of the kingdom of God is finally revealed, they will fulfil the mandate given to the old Israel (Exodus 19:5–6).

The redeemed have immediate access to God as priests and kings for praise and worship. 'Reign' (5:10) is future tense. The redeemed will reign eschatologically *on earth*, that is, in the new creation (22:4–5). With immediate access to God as priests, their lives will be marked now by continuing praise and thanksgiving (cf. Romans 12:1–2). The Christian royal priesthood, presented initially at 1:6, is presented again in 5:9–10 but with two significant additions. First, the Gentiles are included (5:9). Secondly, if the future tense is accepted, the Christian royal priesthood will reign 'on earth'. The Revelation states that they will serve day and night in the heavenly temple (cf. 7:15). So, taking both 1:6 and 5:9–10, Revelation claims that the priestly status of the redeemed is both present and future reality.

The innumerable combined company of all around the throne and on earth (5:11–14) offers universal tribute. First, the sevenfold ascription of praise of the entire heavenly assembly is for divine purposes fulfilled in the sacrifice of Christ (5:12). And the responsive praise of all creation addressed to both God and the Lamb serves as a praise summary of the two chapters.[15] The establishment of the Lamb as redeemer, world ruler, and judge is celebrated in their praise.

The new song (5:9–13) of praise is for an entirely new order through redemption. This redemption is qualitatively without precedent (cf. 5:9, *kainen*). The new song has three movements. In the first movement, the redeemed—represented by the elders and the four living creatures—praise God and the slain Lamb for redemption from Babylon and participation in the new Jerusalem (5:9–10) as the true Israel. The Lamb's worthiness is matchless: he accepted his sacrificial death; he paid the necessary ransom for all enslaved humanity; he made the true Israel a kingdom of priests, God's special possession (Exodus 19:6) as a new servant

---

15 Carnegie, 1982, 251.

community.[16] The focus is the slain Lamb. The consequences are redemption for humanity from the rebellious order and the creation of a new order on earth. The Lamb's death has earned him honour, glory and praise. The Lamb's death gave him the power to bestow incalculable riches and to resolve the mystery of the future. Christians experience a new exodus brought about by Christ's victory.

Christ's worthiness is based on his death. His death and his messianic office are inseparably linked (5:5). The elders and the living creatures sing in celebration of the great fact of the redemption of the true Israel (cf. 5:10). Later, the full complement of the redeemed who follow the Lamb sing the new song (14:2–3). And then the conquerors of the Beast will stand by the sea with harps and sing the 'song of the Lamb' (15:2–3). Their song is about sacrifice and redemption that lead to total re-creation. The redeemed have come from every conceivable background: from common ethnic descent (tribe) out of every language setting (tongue); out of every political order; out of every race or stock (people); out of every geographical location (nation). They are destined as a kingdom and priests unto God for God's service in the new Jerusalem. They receive their authority from Christ the king, who is now enthroned.[17]

The creatures and elders sing (literally, 'speaking' a song, perhaps conveying the continuous present of unceasing worship) a new song (*kainos*, new in quality and time). The song (5:9–10) celebrates the opening of the scroll which is the beginning of the Lamb's rule in the inaugurated kingdom. The Lamb *was* slain, that is, he has been victorious over death, redeemed his people, and made his people rulers. Just as Moses and Israel sang a song on the shores of the Red Sea to commemorate the deliverance from Pharaoh (Exodus 15:1–18), so the twenty-four elders sing a new song to commemorate the new final act of redemption. Israel was redeemed from slavery to be a priestly nation (Exodus 19:6);

---

16 Wall, 1991, 104.
17 Beale, 362, 1999.

the Lamb redeems a new nation of kings and priests that is God's anti-empire commissioned to conquer the empire of the beast.[18]

In 5:10 the verb 'reign' could be present or future tense, but the future tense is preferred as the verse moves from present redemption to glorification. Rule and dominion are associated. The rule of the redeemed cannot occur prior to the full operation of the new covenant after the return of Christ. As stated previously, Revelation 4 indicates what will be and Revelation 5 indicates how it will be achieved. So in 5:10 'reign' seems to be an aspiration. This will be a spiritual kingship. The quality of their lives will demonstrate the result of the abundance of grace and the gift of righteousness (cf. Romans 5:17). The reign of believers on the transformed earth will be in service to Christ. So the Collect for Peace in the Morning Prayer Service (1662) of the Church of England reads 'whose service is perfect freedom'. But this collect could be rephrased: 'whom to serve is to reign'.

The allusion in 5:11 to Daniel's picture of a mighty heavenly throng (Daniel 7:10) signifies that world judgement is about to begin.[19]

In the second movement of the song, one Greek article governs the sevenfold offering of praise (5:12). This suggests that all seven qualities belong intrinsically to Christ. The slain Lamb is praised for his: power (the ability to act); wealth (unconditional ownership of all, 2 Corinthians 8:9); wisdom (the attribute of God that demonstrates itself in conscious and purposeful creation and government of all the world, appointing limits and goals in the execution of his will and the moulding of destiny);[20] strength (power in reserve, available whether exerted or not); honour (God's rightful possession); glory (divine and heavenly radiance, majesty and being of God); and blessing (acknowledgement in praise for all that the Lamb intrinsically possesses).

Some like to view the first four attributes as objective: qualities that the Lamb assumes now. The last three attributes may then

---

18 cf. Resseguie, 1998, 131.
19 cf. Lioy, 2003, 136.
20 Wisdom establishes the rule of righteousness on earth and is the moral power pervading and affecting the progress of world history. For believers, Christ is the wisdom of God (1 Corinthians 1:24,30).

be viewed as subjective human acceptance of the Lamb expressed in worship. In this view, the Lamb's death has earned him honour, glory and praise. However, the whole series is governed by the one Greek article. This suggests that all seven attributes are qualities of Christ, as opposed to the last three being human responses.

The death of Christ has liberated Christians from sin (1:5) and made them an eschatological people of God (1:5; 5:9–10). So the church must now play its role in the universal coming of the kingdom. Believers are now in prospect, but will be, priests and kings. God's rule realised in the present church is not the ultimate victory. While evil powers still dominate the earth, that victory has still to reach its goal.

The work of Christ is depicted in Revelation 5 using two motifs: messianic war and the exodus. There is a third motif depicting Christ's earthly ministry: the faithful witness. The relationship of all three motifs can be seen in what is said about the way Christians share in Christ's victory over Satan. The continuing and ultimate victory of God over evil is the working-out of the decisive victory of the Lamb on the cross. But evil powers still dominate the earth. Victory has still to reach its goal.

The whole of creation, designated in a fourfold way (4 = universality), is now involved. In the third movement of the song, as a climax to Revelation 4–5, the circle of worship expands to encompass the entire creation.[21] Revelation 4 presented God on the throne; 5:1–12 is about the Lamb; 5:13–14 presents both God and the Lamb together, with God enthroned. When the work of redemption is finally completed, the Lamb will share the throne. The heavenly gathering now comprises all intelligent creatures united in a brief but forceful song. The worship offered to God is worship offered to Christ. Each term of praise has the article and stands emphasised by itself. The doxology is addressed to both God and the Lamb, uniting the praise of God (4:9–11) and the praise of the Lamb (5:12). In addition to blessing and honour and glory (5:13), the might (*kratos*)—active power as contrasted to strength in reserve (*ischus*)—of God and the Lamb is praised.

5:9–12 anticipated the goal of God's purpose through Christ, which is universal worship in the new heaven and earth. The

---

21 Resseguie, 1998, 91.

conjunction of God and the Lamb in 5:13 indicates that within a monotheistic structure Christ cannot be a second object of worship alongside God. Thus, the specific worship of Christ (5:9–12) leads to the joint worship of God and Christ as God. God retains primacy and Christ shares the glory due to God. Elsewhere Christ is presented as sharing God's throne (3:21; 22:1,3). But in 5:13, God—as ultimate—is the one who sits on the throne.

Mention of God and Christ together in Revelation is followed by a singular verb (cf. also 11:15) or singular pronoun (22:3ff). The functional unity of God and Christ is such that Christ cannot be an alternative object of worship. Christ shares in the glory due to God (5:13). This equality between the Father and the Son is the purpose of the Christology in Revelation 5. Fittingly, the four living beings who pronounced the first doxology (4:8) also close the doxology (5:14). In this vision in the throne room, worship is directed towards God and the Lamb in heaven. This gives new perspective to the churches as they live in rebellious Babylon.

The four living creatures who continually express creation's worship add their own 'amen' (5:14) to the wider worship of God and the Lamb by the whole creation (5:13). Creation is theocentric, oriented in its worship towards the Creator. Humankind, on the other hand, is shown in these chapters to be radically displaced from the centre of things. The four living creatures are not anthropomorphic beings. The third creature is the only one that has a face resembling a human face. Their representative function is to worship on behalf of all, and this function is fulfilled when the worship circle is enlarged to include all animate creation (5:13).

These introductory scenes (Revelation 4–5) are then followed by a preview of the history of the fallen world with particular reference to the period between the Resurrection and the Second Coming. The preview includes: the contents of the seven seals (6:1–8:1, 8:2–5); a temple altar scene (8:2–5) in which seven trumpets are given to the seven angels who stand in the temple (8:2; 15:6); a further temple scene (11:19); a symbolic overview of the state of the church under extreme satanic opposition in the world (Revelation 12–13); Satan freed (20:1–3) and able to seduce the nations during the time directly preceding the Second Coming

(Revelation 13); inauguration of the final judgement on history (14:1–5) in the seven bowls that come from the heavenly temple (15:5–16:21); and the finale of history (19:11–21).

Revelation 6

Revelation 6–9 The Common Features of the Seals, Trumpets (and Bowls).

Revelation 6–16 contains a threefold series of seals, trumpets and bowls. The seven judgements in each series indicates completeness (7 = completion, fulfilment). The climax of each series is the seventh and final act of judgement. These divine judgements are against deviant humanity and operate either directly or through nature. The first four judgements in each series produce reactions or reflections that follow in the last three judgements of each series.

The opening of the seven seals is immediately after the declaration of the Lamb's messianic war on evil (Revelation 5). This reveals the inner dynamic of history, the greater context in which the cross has meaning, and the nature of the world in which the messianic war will take place. The visionary sequence of the seals commences with John's words, 'and I saw ... and I heard' (6:1). So the scroll is not being read. Rather, the contents of each of the seals in series is described as the scroll is being opened. Indeed, the scroll cannot be read until all seven seals have been broken. So the content of the seven seals must be dissociated from the content of the scroll of Revelation 5. In my view—for reasons that I shall provide—the trumpets, likewise, are not part of the scroll.

The contents of the scroll are related to the Christian age, specifically how evil is to be confronted. But the seals and trumpets seem to refer to the whole course of human history. Undergirding the content of the three series is the continuation of judgements operating in history from the Fall. These judgements were imposed on humanity for their misuse of creation and the gift of human life. In the case of the seals and trumpets, the judgements are only partial. They could have had much deeper effects. So it seems that the disorder which is in the world and used by Satan is under divine restraint. At the end, in the last sequence of the bowls, this divine restraint is removed.

Humanity has failed to understand that to use God's world requires God's tendered grace. The bowl series represents the extreme intensification of 'natural' calamities. The absence of controlling grace had and would result in distortion. In history, this distortion is introduced by human self-direction.

The Seals, Trumpets and Bowls as Judgement on a Fallen World

I now turn to the origin and purpose of the judgements in the three series. I argue that the three series are divine punishments which are administered through human transgression against— and misuse of—nature and human relationships, the interaction of humanity with each other and with the world outside the garden after the Fall.

The point of the three sets of seven apocalyptic style judgements—seals, trumpets and bowls—beginning directly after Revelation 5, is to comfort the readers: humankind is under judgement but the future of believers is assured by the Lamb's conquest of evil and reversal of the Fall. The scroll cannot be opened until the seventh seal has been broken.[1] So seals (6:1–8:1) and trumpets (8:1–9:21) do not form part of the content of the scroll (the scroll is not presented as open in Revelation until 10:2). Furthermore, the seals and first six trumpets are not specifically summoned into operation. The character of their operation seems to indicate that they represent the continuing character of world judgement, beginning from the Fall (Genesis 3).

The first four items in each series (seals, trumpets, bowls) are judgements incurred by the human world generally. In the last series—the bowls, by which history is concluded—the first four items appear to be grouped evils progressively punished that have been concurrently operating through time, and then intensified at the end. The last three items, on the other hand, are directly related to the end of history. And history is bound to come to an end, because of human transgressions. The seventh judgement in each series has a similar function in that: the seventh seal functions to introduce the trumpets; the seventh trumpet announces the end

---

1 cf. Ulfgard, 1989, 28.

of history and the advent of the kingdom of God, and presupposes the bowls; and the seventh bowl ends history.

In the series of seals, the first four judgements are human calamities. Under Satan's world control (the first seal), these human calamities have been operating since the Fall. Under Satan's control these human calamities motivate divisions within humanity which lead to warfare with attendant consequences, such as famine, culminating in death (seals two to four). Thus seals two to four are dependent upon the preceding world-conquering figure of seal one.

In the next two series, trumpets and bowls, the first four judgements affect the natural world. These latter series assume—but do not state specifically—that the judgements occur in a world that is generally under Satan's provocation. Thus the first four items in each of the three series (seals, trumpets, bowls) present pictorial descriptions of the results of universal rebellion against principles of divine order in creation. The Bible emphasises that the historical course of human failure to respond to the grace of God—stimulated by Satanic deception—will produce progressive judgements that will continually afflict the world (cf. Romans 1:18-32). The fifth and sixth judgements in each series (seals, trumpets, bowls) indicate the deeply deleterious spiritual effects of humanistic society and culture upon humanity throughout history. Humanity has failed to understand that Satanic deceptive control resulting in misguided and sinful human actions has been the cause of difficulties throughout history.

The three series of punishments go back to the great misuse of human opportunity—by Satanic deception—that the Garden of Eden narrative displays. The decisions made by the human pair in Genesis 2 were a Satanic motivated attack on the divine order of creation. The first result of an evil influence in the garden was division in the relationship between man and woman in the garden. The result of this division is to bear fruit in a continually divided world. The bitter fruit for human history is encapsulated in the series of seals, trumpets, and bowls.

The Garden situation of Genesis 2 represented the divine intention for the whole world. The 'edenization' of the world, by divine intervention at the end of human history, appears as the climax of the new creation narrative (22:1–5). The narrative of Genesis 1–3 presumes that the world outside the Garden needed to be 'edenised' through obedient human dominion within Eden. Eden is a description of what human history was to be like: a developing, beautiful creation in which—at the beginning—there was an evil principle embedded. That evil principle affected all of human history.

This principle of evil at work in the human spirit was the cause of the Fall and will be the ultimate cause of all difficulties that will ensue in the world outside the Garden. Presumably, human procreation could have occurred within Eden and Eden's boundaries could have gradually extended. However, this is hypothetical projection. The divine intention is revealed in the direction of the biblical narratives.[2]

The presence of evil within creation and in the Garden meant that Eden of the beginning was not God's final word or model for creation. Evil must be expelled before the Eden of the end can be manifested (22:1–5). Eden was cut off from the outside world by one point of guarded entry (Genesis 3:24). This meant a different world outside;[3] the world of continual human experience. This is the arena where the punishments on the participants of Genesis 3 would be continually imposed.

In the symbolism of the creation narrative (Genesis 2–3), humankind is expelled from the Garden as 'like God'. Humans now know good and evil but are also open to Satanic influence. There is a new independence from God, an ability to make decisions apart from God. Human development happens in the volatile world outside the Garden. That world outside was different in character from Eden. Our present world outside Eden is neutral in character. But, since evil was present in the Garden, we must suppose that the potential for evil is also present in the outside world. As always, evil only needs the triggering mechanism of fallen human intelligence. In addition to this evil triggered by fallen human intelligence, the sequence of trumpets and then bowls shows that regularly occurring natural phenomena present destructive forces which also affect individuals and nations.

---

2 I refer to my *Faith of Israel* (2002, 13–27) for a full statement of the case.
3 Dumbrell, 2002, 18–23.

The human failure of the Fall (Genesis 3) affected humanity and its world. Adam and Eve, driven out from the Garden, were to find the ground beyond the Garden cursed for their sake.[4] The world outside the Garden—never, by divine intention, a perfect world—always needed the operation of godly dominion (Genesis 1:26–28).[5] This world outside Eden became affected by sinful humanity. Sinful humankind, excluded from the Garden, continued to exercise decision-making power that they retained in the outside world (cf. Genesis 3:22–24). But this decision-making power was exercised under the general dominion of Satan. After the Fall humans were unable to conduct ideal personal relationships and instead exercised selfish, perverted, exploitative dominion which was forever inflicting ecological damage. The human pair went out of the Garden still possessing dominion over nature as their basic role in the world. However, they were now without the guidance of the divine presence which they had encountered in the Garden. Humans were under Satanic stimulation and direction which would be ingrained by procreation. Thus humans would be unable to exercise a godly dominion that protectively managed the world. So humans would be unable to ensure their own enjoyment of the world.

The point is that there was a world beyond the Garden that, from the beginning, was and still is incomplete. It would be blessed or cursed by human intervention. It would be blessed with, or cursed without, divine grace. The differentiation of Eden from the world outside—and from the new creation (22:1–5), expressed in Edenic terms—indicates that the world outside the Garden was at the beginning a work in progress.[6] The effect of the Fall was that the human pair, still in possession of dominion over creation, were placed in the wider world outside the Garden (cf. Genesis 3:22–24). The humans were in control of their world outside the garden. Human expulsion from the Garden subjected this world to disastrous human decisions, such as the human decisions in Genesis 3. To be in dominion, humans needed to have the mind

---

4   Genesis 3:17, 'because/on account of you'.
5   Dumbrell, 2002, 13–23.
6   For a critique of the general notion of a 'perfect world' affected and thus fallen because of humankind's fall, see Dumbrell, 1994, 20–30.

of God. But, ejected from the Garden, they didn't have the mind of God. Hence the dereliction of creation and inter-human relationships in our own days.

In the outside world, the human pair—still 'like God' (Genesis 3:22–24)—would exercise a decisive role for themselves, making distorted decisions for management of the world and for human interrelationships. Human decisions would disregard divine prerogatives. But administration of the world requires, then and now, human submission to the known will of God or patient intercession for God's will. Now the fallen pair outside the Garden retain a knowledge of 'good and evil' (Genesis 3:22) and thereby possess a measure of likeness to God. But there were also great areas of unlikeness. In exercising human control over the world, without the guidance of the divine presence, humans could never be sure that their choices for or demands on nature were right decisions that would produce right consequences. As Paul makes clear in his general judgement of rebellious humankind (Romans 1:18–32), the wrath of God operating in the fallen world would be nothing other than subjecting disobedient humankind to the consequences of its own cumulative rebellious choices. Affliction arises when humans interact with each other and with their habitat outside Eden. Humanity lives in a world that needs to be brought under progressive dominion. This was the human task from within the Garden. But now, independent of God, the human pair was unable to exercise godly dominion. And so the Fall would bring critical divisions within humanity itself (cf. Genesis 3 and especially Genesis 4). Throughout history these divisions would generate personal and international conflict with all the associated spiritual, psychological and social problems.

Eden (Genesis 2) represented what the world could become with the elimination of evil. At the return of Christ there will be a 'universal Eden' (cf. 22:1–5). An exegesis of Genesis 3:17 which points to man's presence in the world as the cause of its problems is preferable to the common notion of a 'fallen' world happening, in some way, as a consequence of the fall of humankind.[7]

There was not, and could not be, any sickness or suffering for unfallen humanity in the Genesis Eden since Eden was a

---

7   For the critique of such a view cf. Dumbrell, 2002, 23.

reflection of God's order to be brought about for the total creation. The presence of evil in the Garden indicated the manner in which movement to the end would occur: by the overcoming of evil and removing it from the final Eden. The unfallen Adam and Eve, having the relational power to overcome evil, could have lived forever. When they were expelled from Eden, the human pair had a continuing knowledge of God by which the created world could be controlled. But, separated from God's guidance, they took decisions in a non-Edenic world that were deleterious to themselves and their world. They gradually brought upon themselves the legion of misfortunes that Leviticus and Deuteronomy correctly catalogue as 'covenant curses' resulting from a broken covenant. The covenant that was broken was God's covenant with creation.[8]

Thus the disastrous series of human choices that have resulted in our modern world began with the Fall. Potential harmful factors in the world outside Eden—such as disease and plague—needed to be controlled. But, instead, human mistakes and human selfishness and self-direction in handling each other and the environment have resulted in baneful human involvement with the created world. This is not discussed in Genesis, but the effects of disastrous human choices are clearly present and rampant from then on. The world now has to cope with poor human decisions, causing perils and human suffering that would not have been present in Eden.

The burden of ecological problems arise from human sin and human corruption. This mismanagement of nature has engendered huge and complex problems for humankind itself. Disease and suffering come from this interaction between sinful humankind with each other and with an imperfect world outside of the garden. In addition, the divisions within humankind result in conflict (Genesis 4). Hence war, famine, disease, and death: the order of the first four seals. These first four seals, attended by induced human suffering, are the unavoidable general representations of the legacies of the Fall. All elements of the three sequences of seals, trumpets, and bowls proceed towards the removal of evil at the final transformation.

---

8   cf. Dumbrell, 2002, 25–26.

From the beginning, outside the Garden, humanity has brought upon their world—by their long series of unguided ecological decisions—results that in our time have brought the natural world to the brink of self-destruction. After the Fall, difficulties in the world outside the garden increased exponentially with the increase in humankind. These difficulties arose from a combination of the imperfect world outside the Garden, human misuse of the world and their bodies, and human inability to live in harmony. Until the Eden context for our world is restored by divine transformation,[9] the descriptive judgements of the three series (seals, trumpets and bowls) represent the natural and personal disorders within the world to be removed from believers by the advent of the new creation. Well may creation rejoice at the final transformation of human nature in those who are redeemed (Romans 8:19), for only then will creation's earnest expectations be achieved!

There are also interesting Old Testament connections in the history of Israel with the Revelation series of judgements. Leviticus 26:18–28 presents the punishments to be inflicted upon Israel for breach of covenant through disobedience and idolatry. The sevenfold series of punishments project progressively worse outcomes: drought and crop failure (Leviticus 26:19–20); wild beasts (Leviticus 26:22); sword, death, famine, pestilence, captivity (Leviticus 26:25–26); and even more profound human aberration (Leviticus 26:29). The early affects of the Fall upon a world in which the imagination of the human heart was only evil continually necessitated the flood (Genesis 6:5). But there was no indication of general human moral improvement in that new beginning (cf. Genesis 9:20–29).

Ezekiel 14:21 is a summary of previous trials experienced by Israel: conquest, sword, and famine. This is similar to the woes in the Synoptic gospels: deception; wars; international strife; earthquakes; famines; persecutions; and cosmic changes in sun, moon, and stars (cf. 6:2–17 with Mark 13:7–9, 24–25; Matthew 24:6–8, 29; Luke 21:9–12, 25–28).

Jesus refers to natural disasters which are clearly known to the disciples—such as earthquakes—when speaking to his disciples

---

9   cf. 22:1; Romans 8:22–23; cf. Dumbrell, 2005, 90–91.

about the shape of the future. These impending natural disasters are associated with the prophesied fall of Jerusalem (Matthew 24:7; Mark 13:8; Luke 21:11). These are in addition to the man-made disasters which Jesus refers to in the same passages, namely, wars and famines. But these natural and man-made disasters were not present in Eden, nor will they be present in the Eden of the new creation. 1Kings 19:11 refers to an earthquake directly related to a divine revelation. Isaiah 29:6 refers to thunder and an earthquake as a divine punishment. Matthew 27:51-54 refers to an earthquake associated with the death of Jesus. Acts 16:26 tells of a great earthquake associated with the release of Paul and Silas from prison, with the prisoners unharmed. There is a great earthquake at the opening of the sixth seal (6:12), which is in keeping with God's power and control over creation and its future (cf. 8:5; 11:13,19; 16:18). God's power is also evident in extraordinary biblical incidents such as the flood (Genesis 7-8). This is God's world. He created it. The believer trusts God's provident care through all of life. The glories of redemption are eagerly accepted. And the question of God's ultimate control over all that is happening in creation and impacting the life of the believer is also accepted by faith.

The underlying rationale behind all this is given in Deuteronomy. Israel, as an obedient and compliant nation in the Promised Land—a potential new Eden—was to expect exemption from the disorders that appeared to dominate life outside of the Promised Land. Perfect obedience was not required of Israel; this was impossible after the Fall. But a sacrificial system had been provided. So, rather than perfect obedience, God required an obedient national response to the covenant with forgiveness available through the sacrificial system for confessed sin. Covenant faithfulness, confession and forgiveness would result in: the land producing abundantly, satisfying all their physical needs (Deuteronomy 7:13); blessing of the Israelites above all peoples, with ever fruitful flocks and herds (Deuteronomy 7:14); freedom from affliction with the sicknesses or diseases that they had known in Egypt (Deuteronomy 7:15); and every need supplied (cf. Deuteronomy 8:8–9; 11:11). The Promised Land (Deuteronomy 8:7ff) was a land of: brooks and water; fountains and springs;

wheat and barley; fig trees and pomegranates; olive oil and honey. It is a land in which Israel will not lack anything. There will be iron and copper, and their herds will multiply.

In short, in the Promised Land—as Adam and Eve were in Eden—covenant obedient Israel is to be free from want or distress and exempt from physical affliction or suffering. However, if covenant obedience does not occur and the covenant is broken (Leviticus 26, Deuteronomy 28:15-68) without forgiveness, as was permanently the case, Israel would be subject to the same covenant curses as afflicted the outside world. The curses are the divine judgements for the world outside the Promised Land. The curses (judgements) are brought on by human rejection of the divine order. The divine order is God's covenant with creation.[10] When humans reject the divine order they misuse creation and thereby break the covenant with creation. The results of the breach of covenant include disease, suffering, famine and deprivation. These covenant curses are pandemic in the world outside the Promised Land, but they were not in the original Eden. According to Deuteronomy, the Promised Land could be free of the curses. So the covenant curses would seem to be the result of human failure outside of Eden to understand or manage its environment or each other.[11] Within the Promised Land there would be national lapses. Even so, if Israel repents of idolatry—always the main human temptation and the primary cause of human world difficulty—God would forgive (Leviticus 26:1,30-31).

Thus the Bible shows that the Fall and subsequent Satanic influence results in sinful human self-assertion. This is the source of all human problems, tensions, divisions, sicknesses, sufferings and all difficulties relating to human disorders, human relationships, and the management of creation. The verdict of the Bible is that we can neither manage our world nor ourselves. This verdict is true but it is totally unacceptable personally, nationally and internationally. The biblical gospel of the kingdom of God—which will be universally recognised when it comes—requires the witness of the church to the world, not simply in terms of reaction to individual needs but in a message to the world at large of the

---

10 cf. Dumbrell, 2002, 25-26.
11 cf. Dumbrell, 2002, 22-23.

sinfulness of human world decisions at personal, national, and international levels. Human control of the world has plotted its course through history in a Babel-like way, establishing itself without reference to the Sovereign who controls history. The natural world groans to be delivered from this bondage of corruption. Deliverance will occur for creation with the full bodily redemption of believers at the final world transformation (Romans 8:23)!

It follows that the complex of environmental threats facing our world today are all drawn from the failure of humanity to exercise godly dominion over creation or to live at peace with one another. We have used our power for sinful self-gratification. This has produced our present dire environmental and personal problems. The mind of God is required to solve problems; they are beyond human control. We can have no confidence that we can achieve world co-operation to put into effect attempted solutions, even if the solutions are cogent. Moreover, we are committed to a future controlled by technology invented by and in the hands of human ingenuity. History gives us no confidence that the amazing results of new technology opening new horizons will bring only blessing to the world. Revelation makes it clear that humanity will finally overreach itself and turn in on itself (Revelation 16–17). A humanly directed creation requires divine intervention to bring the original purposes of God (Genesis 1–2) to full fruition in the transformed world of the new creation.

The sequence of the seals and the first six trumpets—which introduce the continuing character of the world judgement, present from the Fall (Genesis 3)—form part of the scroll (cf. 10:1-2). The scroll is opened by the Lamb in heaven. The open scroll, which is concerned with the Christian history of the church, will be brought to earth by a mighty angel (10:1). The judgement is with regard to humankind's sinful disregard of the requirement for man, made in the image of God, to reflect the moral principles written upon the heart of each human being.[12] Richard Bauckham likewise suggests that the majority of the judgements in Revela-

---

12   cf. Dumbrell, 2005, 32–34 on Romans 2:14–16, with particular attention to Romans 2:15.

tion are not special divine interventions.[13] Rather, the judgements are regular evils of human history: imperialism, war, famine and disease, and human failure in interpersonal relationships. Such evils are business as usual in world history.

The punishment (judgement) from God is to leave incorrigible humanity to the consequences of its own ways. The consequent evils are not present in the Garden of Eden. They are the result of leaving humanity to effect its own false choices (Romans 1:18–32). Humankind has engaged in a universal rebellion against principles of divine order at work in creation. The historical course of human failure to respond to the grace of God will invite this progressive series of judgements that will continually afflict the world (cf. Romans 1:18–32). The first four items—the first four seals, the first four trumpets—are general areas of human calamity.

Revelation 6:1–9 The Seals Leading to the Opening of the Scroll

The Lamb in the throne room (6:1), in the exercise of his rule, begins to open the scroll.[14] The seals are associated with the opening of the sealed scroll. And whereas there is interrelationship between the seven trumpets and the seals, the first six trumpets are not part of the content of the scroll.

From the throne room of heaven, one of the four living creatures cries 'come' (6:1). The opening of the seven seals by the Lamb who was slain (5:12) is an outworking of the death of the Lamb. The content of the seals reveals what has been occurring throughout the entire extent of human history. As each of the first four seals is broken, there is revealed a series of preliminary judgements already occurring regularly within the course of history from before the death of Christ until now. But the opened scroll (10:2)—with its new revelation, after all the seals have been opened—seems to be entirely related to the Christian age (11:1–22:5).

The opening of the first four seals is recounted in a couple of brief sentences. The description of the opening of the fifth seal is a little longer. The opening of the sixth seal extends from 6:12 to

---

13 2004, 6.
14 Beale, 1999, 370.

7:17. Each series—seals, trumpets and bowls—reaches the same end. They are not put forward as cataclysmic disasters. Revelation does not convey that these series of judgements occur consecutively. Nor is there any indication that there will be an end to these judgements before the end of history. The seals and trumpets represent the ever-present progressive judgements on human disobedience and lack of proper recognition of divine control of the world. World evil is always getting worse. This progressive development of evil occurs in history together with progressive judgements, climaxing finally in the bowl series of judgements which mock human intellectual and technical advances. In the first two cycles (seals and trumpets), the grace of God reduces the effect of judgements upon the earth. But in the final bowls series, the complete wrath of God is displayed and the effect is total. The judgements are against the misguided human attempts throughout history to use nature for selfish ends instead of using God's providential gift of nature for the glory of God.

The seals are not put into effect by Christ, but are already operating. The number 'one quarter' (6:8) measures specific suffering, or the death rate of humankind when this first series of judgements (the seals) are in operation.[15] This death rate is extended throughout animate and inanimate creation: one fourth withers and/or dies or is replaced. In the case of the trumpets, the operative first four supply further detail of natural difficulties. The trumpets build on the first four seals, operating with the seals. Like the seals, the trumpets and bowls are calamities with great affliction arising from the presence of evil in the world. The result is warfare, famine and death. The death rate advances from 'one fourth' for the seals to 'one third' for the trumpets (8:7). The trumpets are therefore adding natural calamities which are even more difficult, or wider in their range of application, or both. The bowls speak of divine intervention which brings about total death or transformation at the end of history. The nature of the end is fully explained in Revelation 16–20.

The seventh seal ushers in the trumpets, indicating that the trumpets operate as either the continuation of or in combination with the seals. The first six trumpets are all operating before the

---

15 cf. Hoeksema, 2000, 307.

scroll of Revelation 5 is brought down to John from heaven (10:2). Thus these first six trumpets are not part of the scroll. But the end-time bowls are part of the content of the scroll. The relationship of the trumpets and bowls is overlapping, like the relationship of the seals to the trumpets (cf. 11:19 with 15:6–16:1 for trumpets and bowls; 8:1–2 for seals and trumpets). Given the content of the first four items of each series—seals and trumpets, and probably also bowls—it is difficult to escape the conclusion that these have always been present in human history as intensification of God's judgements. The content of the last three seals and trumpets is spiritual reaction to, or reflection upon, the respective first four items.

Each series (seals, trumpets, bowls) has seven items (7 = completion). So each series is inter-related as a complete response to human self determination of its world. Within each series the progressive effect of each item increases. However, the series is visionary experience and therefore the items within each series are not necessarily chronologically presented. For reasons already provided, they are probably all concurrent throughout the world.

The visionary order of Revelation is not necessarily chronological, but the numerology is theological. However, the total vision refers to chronological development (4:1–22:5) of the dereliction of the human order. Items one to four in each of the three series deal with the world within continuing history since Genesis 3, but now within the Christian era. In the bowls, the effect of the judgements is intensified and climactic. Each series (seals, trumpets, bowls) ushers in the end of history: prospectively in the case of the seals (sixth item) and trumpets (seventh item); actually in the case of the bowls (seventh item). Each series is progressively more intimately connected with the throne room.

The seventh seal-opening is linked to the trumpets. When the Lamb opens the seventh seal (8:1) there is silence for about half an hour. After the reference to the silence in heaven (8:1) and the offering of the prayers of the saints (8:3–5), John introduces the seven angels (cf. 8:6ff). There is, therefore, an interlocking of the seventh seal with the trumpets. The first four seals continue to operate within history. The interrelated trumpets and bowls share the same areas of effect on humanity in their first four items, like the first four seals. The trumpets (11:19) and bowls (16:18)—interlocked by 15:1–4—are also both connected to 4:5.

Similar wording introduces each of the first four seal-openings judgements; in each case the content is set in place by a horse and a rider (6:1–8). The four form one set of basic world judgements. The fifth, sixth and seventh seal openings have a much shorter introductory opening. The decisive sixth and seventh seals answer the prayers of the saints (the fifth seal). Revelation 7 interrupts the sequence, but it is closely linked to the sixth seal opening because it answers (especially 7:9) the question at the end of 6:17 (which is, therefore, not a rhetorical question). In each series, the first four judgements concern human interaction with the physical world. The seventh item of the seals and the trumpets introduces the next series, which then has the same structure: four physical judgements, then two spiritual judgements, followed by the end-time seventh item. The seventh item in the trumpets and bowls is directed against unbelievers.

An important feature of the seal series is that it contains no scene of actual judgement (cf. 7:1–4). Rather, the seal series indicates the generality of world problems current throughout history. At the breaking of the fifth seal, the martyr souls each cry out for God to take vengeance. God's reply is to give each martyr a white robe. The martyrs are then told to wait until the number of fellow servants and brethren is completed. Then comes the climax of the seal series, when the whole of humankind—confronted with cosmic woes—seeks refuge from God's wrath (6:15–17). The sixth seal consists of three distinct sections (6:12–17; 7:1–8; 7:9–17). *Meta touto* (7:1) refers to 6:12–17; *meta tauta* (7:9) indicates what is then seen.

The breaking of the sixth seal (6:12–17) places creation on the threshold of the end: great cosmic woes causing high anxiety usher in the end of history. The exclamation that the great day of the wrath (of God and the Lamb) has come (6:17)—and the question 'who can stand before it?' (6:17)—sums up the expectation. The Parousia is here! The fifth seal and the fifth and sixth trumpets present spiritual or psychological issues: general human reactions to God's judgements throughout history which are now specifically related to the Christian era. When the Lamb opens the seventh seal (8:1), the ensuing silence indicates the awe in confronting the end of history, when the new creation will be introduced.

The seal series introduces the nature of God's judgements on earth. However, the seal judgements are not contained within the scroll. Before any judgement may begin there must be the sealing of God's people. This sealing of God's people (7:4) occurs after the seal judgements have already been revealed.[16] This sealing of believers (7:1–4) offers the encouraging message that God will protect his people from spiritual (but not physical) harm throughout the long series of human crises within history. The final judgement has not begun in the seal series, since the first four items of the series present the continuing world situation—which began at the Fall—of disobedience and judgement.

The earthquake and accompanying natural phenomena relate all three sets of judgements to the throne room vision (4:5a), to which has been added: an earthquake at the end of the seal judgements (8:5); heavy hail (11:19) at the end of the trumpets; and huge hailstones (16:18–21) at the end of the bowls.

The reference to the earthquake (4:5) is like the covenant phenomena that accompanied God's self manifestation on Mount Sinai (Exodus 19:16; 20:18). The cosmic happenings in the sixth/seventh item of each series relate the divine judgements of Revelation 6–16 to 4:5a, making Revelation 4–5 the key to the whole book. The final judgement on the unbelieving world—in the integration of the trumpets and bowls with the seven seals—forms the vindicating answer to the plea of the saints and brings judgement upon the world for breach of God's covenant with creation.[17]

Whereas the 'seal' series expresses what has been God's continuing judgement on the world since the Fall, the 'sealing' of God's people must take place before any woes commence. The encouraging message is that the people of God are protected spiritually through the experiences of sickness and suffering that come upon them. The seals and the trumpets are not part of the scroll (cf. the later discussion on 10:1–3), since they have been operating

---

16 cf. Beale, 1999, 404–5.
17 cf. Dumbrell, 2002, 24–26.

throughout history. But the judgement of the seventh trumpet and the bowl series are part of the content of the scroll. In the series of seals and trumpets—but not the bowls—there is an interlude dealing with the history of the church between the sixth and seventh items (7:1–14; 10:1–11:13). In the disordered world brought about by unbelief, the first four items of seals and trumpets have been operating concurrently throughout history. The intercalations between the sixth and seventh items (7:1–14, 10:1–11:13) are about the mission and oppression of the people of God in the midst of all this disorder, and their final redemption.

The trumpet and bowl judgements—sharing the same emphasis as the seals in items 1–4—are modelled on the exodus plagues, roughly in the same order. These plague series reach a crescendo in progressive world judgement, echoing God's intention in hardening Pharaoh's heart. In this way the three series (seals, trumpets, bowls) treat history as a continuing exodus crisis out of which God will eventually withdraw his people for entry into the Promised Land. In the trumpets and bowls, God then demonstrates his omnipotence through the exodus signs. The exodus plagues were not primarily meant to cause the Pharaoh to repent; rather, the plagues were to reveal the incomparability and sovereignty of God. This analogy is to be applied to the judgements of the trumpets and bowls upon the world. The seals pointed to the basic human problem of disobedience to God's will as their cause (i.e. Genesis 3). But the increase of world problems with the trumpets and bowls, beyond the bare inevitability of the seal judgements, point to the need for world redemption in a world gone wrong. The message of the trumpets to the Christian age is that there is still time for individuals within the world structures of governments to come out of them and enter the kingdom of God, for there is no future for these human structures.

The bowls are concerned specifically with the judgement of the beast and his city. They follow the trumpets more intensively, occurring at a later point in history and leading inevitably to the end of history. The first four items in all series refer to world problems current since the Fall. The fifth seal and the fifth and sixth trumpets respond to the first four items respectively. The items of judgement within the two series (seals and trumpets) remain the same, but the intensity and coverage varies. The sixth item in the seals, and the seventh item in the trumpets and bowls, take us to the end of history.

Thus the first four items in all series are aimed at those who are destroying creation and bringing suffering upon the world or themselves. Human failure to honour God in its use of creation will lead to creation being used to express general judgements. This is the emphasis of the trumpets and bowls.

The Rationale for the Three Series

The first four items in each of the series relate to judgements throughout history; they are trans-historical. They cannot be directly applied to particular periods. I have been concerned to relate the first four items of the seals to the corresponding first four of the later series as interrelated human problems all stemming from the Fall. I have argued that the Biblical information allows us to make judgements on the origins of the judgements (seals, trumpets, bowls), indicating indirect divine causation in accordance with the principles of Romans 1:19–24. No particular divine intervention occurs during the opening of the first five seals. But at the breaking of the sixth seal, the wrath of God and the Lamb directly confront humanity. The later two/three items of each series take us beyond the cause and effect of many of the adverse physical features of the world. The movement from the first four items in the last two series (trumpets and bowls) is from physical judgements to spiritual judgements occasioned by direct divine intervention (9:1,13; 16:10,17).

There is recapitulation of concepts in the seals, trumpets and bowls. Within history the basic series of judgements continues beyond the seals, but with the recognition in both the trumpets and bowls that—as history progresses—human misuse of creation multiplies problems for humanity and its world. The first four trumpets (8:7–12; 6:1–11:19) form an obvious group. Between the fourth and fifth trumpets there is a vision of an eagle proclaiming a threefold woe on the inhabitants of the earth (8:13). These three woes are the last three trumpets. The emphatic formulae between the woes (9:12; 11:14) maintains the sequence of the fifth, sixth and seventh trumpets. The indication of the end of the second woe

(11:14) helps to keep the long intercalation (10:1–11:13) in its place in the sequence. The introduction of the last woe (11:14) heralds the coming of the bowls. Because of the events in 11:11–13, humanity acknowledges God's heavenly sovereignty. Nevertheless, humanity remains in unbelief.[18]

I have spoken of the human misuse of creation as the cause of most modern problems. However, there are also natural calamities such as earthquakes, tsunamis and volcanos. It is clear from these natural calamities that humans cannot control God's creation. We are, finally, in the hands of God for our continued existence (cf. Psalm 46:1–3). Psalm 46 shows that humanity—by misuse of its creation charge—has added to these natural calamities. The seals, trumpets and bowls refer to both human and divine causation of judgements occurring imponderably together. We have done our best to trash our world, but the future of the world is ultimately beyond our control. The hope brought to us in Revelation is that God will finally rescue us from ourselves and then bring the universe to the final perfection always contemplated for it.

Revelation 6 The Seals

John sees the visionary sequence of the Lamb in the throne room (6:1) exercising his rule,[19] setting in motion the execution of the scroll. Within history the scroll issues judgements over the disordered world. These judgements are designed to bring about the visible kingdom of God in a new creation. Beale properly states that Christ 'has made the world forces of evil his agents to execute his purposes of sanctification and judgement for the furtherance of his kingdom'.[20] The opening of the seven seals is the outworking of the death of the Lamb. It is the death of the Lamb that now controls the inner dynamics of world history. World history is the context in which judgements have meaning. The opening of the seals reveals self-imposed human causation and divine judgements operating together throughout history. The breaking of the seals

---

18   Beale, 1999, 604 points similarly to Nebuchadnezzar in Daniel 2.
19   Beale, 1999, 370.
20   1999, 385.

introduces a series of preliminary judgements, the first four already occurring regularly within history from before the death of Christ.

The first four seals make one picture, providing a new view of history. Each of the first four seal openings is preceded by an utterance of one of the four living beings followed by the appearance of coloured horses and their riders. The first four seals are a distinct group which together indicate the developing tribulation. The voice of thunder (6:1) indicates that what follows is a judgement from God, like an impending storm. The storm begins with the summons to the first horseman.

Punishment on the rebellious world throughout history always involves the content of the first four seals. The fifth and sixth seals, unlike the first four seals, relate only to the post-cross period. The seventh seal introduces the new series (trumpets). Believers are not exempt from the first four seals; they must accept the continuing trials of the ever present first four seals in a godly manner. Suffering does not occur indiscriminately or by chance. Suffering is destructive, but is brought about within history for the redemption of humanity. The seal judgements show how the power of God operates with respect to concrete earthly events. Various complex and incomprehensible factors—such as aggression—begin outside of the garden (cf. Genesis 4) and occur throughout history in a disobedient world regulated by the will of the divine ruler who guides history to its end.

The four horses are probably sent out together, representing continually current disorders—antithetical to the purpose of creation—that have pervaded the world throughout history. These disorders will ravage the world up to the return of Christ yet, mysteriously, the purpose of these disorders is to fulfil the coming of the kingdom of God. The first four disasters in each of the seals and trumpets series present the same world situation subjected to various sufferings, caused by Satan (first seal) but under divine control (6:1), made worse by human world sinful mismanagement. The fifth seal focuses on Christians suffering. But the fifth and sixth trumpets restrict suffering to unbelievers. As only unbelievers are suffering, trumpets five and six report either the psychological viciousness of evil afflicting unbelievers or a period in history subsequent to the 'death' of the church (11:7).

The imagery of four horses is drawn from Zechariah 1:8–15 (cf. 6:1–8). The predicted afflictions resemble the afflictions in Jeremiah 14:12, 24:10 and 42:17. Jewish exegetical tradition suggests that the four horsemen, upon whom the emphasis is placed, are counterparts of the four evil kingdoms in Daniel 7.[21] Given the dependence of the imagery on Zechariah, the horses are probably sent out simultaneously by divine commission (cf. Zechariah 1:8; 6:1). Being sent together, the woes that they deliver are not consecutive but contemporaneous.

The cherubim creatures around the throne issue a command when each seal is opened: 'Come and see'. These commands indicate the divine source of judgements affecting all people, including believers. The horsemen act when the command has been given. We have already seen that the cherubim lead worship around the throne (4:8–9; 5:8–10,14; 19:4). In the context of God as Judge in the opening of the seals, this action of the cherubim issuing the command preceding judgement is worship: glorifying God's righteous will. The horses are connected with war, conquest, famine, disease and death. They are harbingers of natural calamities. The first four trumpets will also be harbingers of natural calamities, but with an intensification caused by the increasingly selfish use of creation by humans throughout history.

The colours of the horses in Zechariah and Revelation are almost the same. However, in Revelation each colour is metaphorical for the plague that each delivers: white for conquest, red for bloodshed, black for famine, and pale green for death. The four horsemen possess a shared identity as demonic agents of parallel judgements: the parallel judgements depicted in the first four trumpets and bowls. The four horsemen deliver a fourfold covenantal judgement (cf. Deuteronomy 32:23–26 applied in Ezekiel 5 and Ezekiel 14:21).

Revelation 6:1–2 The First Seal

The description of the rider of the first white horse is virtually the same as that of Christ (19:11). Prior to 6:2, only heavenly or

---

21   Beale, 1999, 366–388.

redeemed figures wear victors' crowns in the visions. And white is the usual symbol of victory, righteousness and holiness. Thus a strong case can be made for the rider of the white horse to be Christ (as conqueror, 3:21; 5:5; 17:14). But the rider is not Christ, as Christ has just broken the first seal. These four horsemen probably present a single picture of destruction viewed from four angles.[22] Christ would be out of place in this company. Rather, the rider on the white horse symbolises the false messiah—the world conqueror of Revelation 13—a satanic impersonation wearing a counterfeit crown with a counterfeit righteousness. This false messiah is responsible for the stimulus to disobedience to God to which all humanity is exposed. And this disobedience causes all world ills; this disobedience is the author of all human calamity.

The four riders and horses present as one.[23] The first rider and horse, summarising the roles of the remaining three,[24] is the 'Antichrist'. The white is deceptive, but the bow represents belligerent militarism operating in the world throughout history. This militarism is inconsistent with Christ. The four riders symbolise growing personal and corporate difficulties throughout history. A bow can be a symbol of victory (Zechariah 9:13-14). This first rider, holding a bow, has continuing success even without arrows: a bloodless victory. His victor's crown 'was given' (6:2) by divine authority. So he has been authorised with temporary power for divine purposes. But even though he has authority, he is nevertheless a counterfeit figure. The career of this 'Antichrist' is impressive but the long series of conquests ending in victory are achieved by deception in his struggle against the world (6:3-8). Satan's victory seemed to be achieved at the cross but, paradoxically, the cross was the seal of Satan's defeat. Satan's domination of this world is temporary. The Parousia will bring the world to its intended divine character.

Revelation 6:3-4 The Second Seal

The second seal is broken (6:3) and there is a second summons from a living being. The second rider is on a red horse. The colour

---

22 Beale, 1999, 370-371.
23 Hoeksema, 2000, 190.
24 Beale, 1999, 378.

red represents strife and war, in its worst form, for the world: internal, international and civil. The rider was divinely permitted (passive case) by God to take away peace—the Greek includes the definite article, 'the' peace—from the world. Peace in general as a constituent of world history is taken away and history therefore becomes a tale of internecine strife on earth, including Christians suffering persecution.

Revelation 6:5–6 The Third Seal

The third rider's commission comes from a voice in the midst of the throne. Evidently this third rider's commission is of great importance. The commission features another dimension of Satan's post-Fall influence in the created order: economic injustice and institutionalised inequity. The colour black indicates a time of lamentation and woe. There is scarcity of food which is indicated by the careful weighing (cf. Ezekiel 4:16–17), causing anxiety. The third rider personifies famine.[25] The voice giving the commission, coming from the middle of the heavenly beings, could be: the voice of God (the ultimate source of these judgements); or the voice of the Lamb (associated with the living creatures in the midst of the throne, 5:6). If it is the voice of the Lamb, it displays his authority and power over death and Hades (cf. 6:8). The famine is not universal, as evidenced by the instruction 'do not hurt the oil or the wine' (6:6). The poverty and famine occasioned by this third seal is partial. Whereas the prices for staple food commodities increases by about eight to sixteen times normal,[26] luxuries such as oil and wine are not affected. The rich were not hurt by the famine. The third seal points to the economic inequity between the rich and the poor.

Revelation 6:7–8 The Fourth Seal

The colour of the fourth horse—that emerges when the fourth seal is broken—is pale green (*chloros*), the yellowish green of decay like a corpse in an advanced state of putrescence. The rider is a personification of death (in Greek Hades means, literally, 'that which is not seen'). Death (the state) and Hades (the place) are

---

25 cf. the order of false Christs + war + famine in the Olivet discourse, Matthew 24:5–7.
26 Beale, 1999, 381.

satanic forces under the ultimate governance of the heavenly throne room (cf. 1:8; 20:13–14).[27] The sword, famine, and pestilence (6:8b) are means that God uses to allow death and Hades to operate. The sword (6:8) is a symbol of a violent death. The wild animals (6:8) represent the violent death to which Christians at that time were being exposed in Roman persecutions. The additional mention of death (6:8b) is because of the pestilence that the fourth rider releases and not, as in the case of the third rider, death in general.[28]

Thus the four seals provide ongoing punishment for the unbelieving world. But the seals also indicate to believers that only through many tribulations will they enter the kingdom of God. God exposes believers to the general evils in the world. Believers must trust God through them.

The disasters of the first four seals could be sequential, but it is more likely that they are simultaneous. The fourth seal appears to function as a summary of the second and third seals: conquest, civil unrest and famine leads to death. These are ongoing categories of disasters in the present world; they are parallel judgements. The same introductory and visionary formula occurs for each judgement (seal). Like the covenant trials pronounced upon faithless Israel (Leviticus 26:18–39), the seals are warning judgements which partially affect the whole world—'a fourth of the earth' (6:8b)—and are designed to induce repentance.

Revelation 6:9–11 The Fifth Seal

When Christ opens the fifth seal, John sees another vision of what is happening throughout human history beginning with Abel. The souls of the faithful are under the altar: those slain for their fidelity to the word of God unto death, and those slain for their faithfulness to the testimony of Jesus in a godless world. John saw the souls of the martyred saints under the altar of burnt offering (cf. 8:3–5; 9:13). The blood of their sacrifice had been poured out at the base of the altar.[29] The blood at the base of the

---

27 In 20:13–14 death and Hades must surrender their dead.
28 cf. Beale, 1999, 382.
29 Caird, 1966, 84.

altar attests their sacrifice. In addition, being 'under the altar' may symbolise divine protection for the saints.[30]

Since the soul is what animated the body, the use of the word 'soul' (6:9) indicates the saints' lives or persons. These martyrs, who recognise that their cause rests with God, can pray a dispassionate prayer for vengeance. Their prayer is for the full coming of the kingdom of God when righteousness and justice will totally prevail. Their prayer will be answered when the voice from the temple announces 'it is done' (16:15-17).[31] These saints are no longer mortal. They await in a conscious state after death for the resurrection of the body.

The prayer of the saints is not vindictive, rather, it is a covenant prayer in keeping with the covenant curses (Deuteronomy 28:15-57; 32:35). The testimony which the saints held was what they had received from Christ for their faithful witnesses.[32] Their cause rests with Christ (6:10). The martyred saints cry 'how long?', the well-known cry of suffering. At the heart of this desperate 'how long' prayer is the belief that God is holy and true, yet what has happened does not seem to be consistent with God's promises. The 'how long' prayer also conveys assurance that God will act to bring in his kingdom and vindicate the saints by judging world Babylon; but the 'how long' prayer also airs their concern about delay.[33] God is not acting quickly enough! By the coming of the kingdom, God will judge the inhabitants of the earth and vindicate the blood of the slain. 6:9-11 sets the agenda for the judgements that follow as a response to the prayers of the saints. These judgements will bring the historical world to its end. A response to these prayers of the saints comes at once with the opening of the next seal.

The saints begin with an affirmation of God's absolute power and authority ('Lord'). They also say that God is 'holy and true', that is, separate from evil. Because they understand the perverted nature of the world and its people, the saints look to God for action on the basis of his faithfulness to his promises in response to their

---

30 cf. Beale, 1999, 391-92, footnote 62.
31 Bauckham, 2004, 8.
32 cf. Tonstad, 2006, 180.
33 Stevenson, 2001, 289.

prayers. They know that God cannot tolerate iniquity and must avenge. In Revelation, 'those who dwell upon the earth' (6:10) are humankind in hostility to God. The phrase refers to humans who are outside of the covenant (cf. 3:10; 8:13; 11:10; 13:8,12; 17:2,8), that is, that portion of the whole human race throughout history who have been rebellious unbelievers.

God answers by act and word. The stole that the martyrs now wear was a robe of state flowing down to the feet. The white robe honours their spiritual purity; it is bestowed on the faithful under divine sovereignty. They will not receive their transformed physical bodies until the Parousia. But they are now wearing white, signifying blessedness and the beauty of holiness. What these saints wear is symbolic of the glory of the reward promised to overcomers.

Satanically inspired evil and suffering will disappear under judgement. So the saints are told to rest a little longer (6:11b) until the number of both their fellow servants (that is, fellow Christians as one group) and their brethren (that is, fellow martyrs as another group) are complete. The final ingathering of the redeemed, at the coming of the kingdom, will include martyred souls, those who die faithful to the Lord (cf. 14:13), and those who will be transformed at the coming of the Lord.

In the midst of all this strife and confusion, Christians are expected to conquer as Christ conquered. Each of the prophetic messages to the seven churches included the promise of a reward for those who conquer (2:7,11,17,26–28; 3:5,12,21). Christ promises the overcomers that they will be enthroned with him. We first meet these victorious followers of Christ in Revelation 7, which continues the theme of the messianic war. The victorious followers of Christ are depicted as the army of the Davidic Messiah.

Revelation 6:12–17 The Sixth Seal

The sixth seal (6:12–17) anticipates the answer to the martyrs' prayer. It involves cosmic and terrestrial disturbances betokening dissolution of the world and thus the judgement and end of rebellious humankind. This is the day of reckoning for the disobedient world. All the items in the judgement are drawn from Old Testament contexts. The earthquake (6:12) is often a sign of God's presence in judgement on his enemies.³⁴ This judgement will bring the world to an end. Self imposed human world judgements over the centuries have failed to move humanity. But the outpouring of these final divine judgements coming from the divine throne as divine interventions will indeed move the world. The pictures of the sun darkened, the rolling up of the sky, and the shaking of the stars (6:12–13) are associated with cosmic action. The pictures signal the punishment of principalities and powers which stand behind human authorities.³⁵ Final judgement will become the vindication of the martyrs. God's glory is to be manifested in natural phenomena. But, protecting his transcendence, God himself is not to be seen. His wrath, associated with the wrath of the Lamb, is the fixed and just and totally visible response to evil. God's fixed response to evil had been seen in the cross. This final judgement of God and the Lamb will be the divine response to the rejection and crucifixion of the Messiah.

This is a vision of the advent of the Day of the Lord. The vision indicates that on the Day of the Lord there will be total disruption of the disordered world and collapse of world political and economic systems. The seven fold (seven = complete) classification (6:15) of all who respond to the final judgement tells us that all humanity is to be involved. The first five responders (6:15) are leaders in the idolatrous, disobedient world (cf. 19:18–19): the kings are the rulers; the chief ones are probably their high-ranking officials; the commanders are those in control of military might; the rich are controllers of commerce; and the strong are those who exercised power and authority by bodily strength, force of personality, or some other means. The sixth and seventh responders are comprehensive for the remainder of humanity: every slave and every free man. All will hide from the presence of God in the same way. All humanity will call on the mountains and rocks to fall on them; it would be better to perish on earth (cf. Isaiah 2:10,21) than to face the wrath of the Lamb! The wrath of the Lamb is the outworking of the consequences of the rejection and crucifixion of the Messiah. The rejection and crucifixion of the Messiah has divided humankind and put the world under judgement (John 12:32).

---

34 cf. Judges 5:4–5; Joel 2:10, Osborne, 2002, 291.
35 cf. Isaiah 34:4; Beale, 1999, 396.

The earth, sun, moon, stars, heaven and every mountain and island—seven cosmic signs—are correlated with the seven classes of unbelieving mankind to be judged by the final judgement.[36] Such figurative imagery is often used in the Old Testament for God's intervention in judgement to bring to an end a phase of history (cf. Isaiah 13:10; Joel 2:10,31). The massive earthquake accompanying the sixth seal is divine intervention in final judgement in keeping with the promise of vindication for the saints (cf. the similarity of this sixth seal to the seventh bowl, 16:17–20). The seventh seal (8:5) will conclude the seals and introduce the trumpets. But the end of the trumpets will be the same as the end of the seals.

'Who is able to stand?' the judged ask (6:17). And their question is in stark contrast to the vision of the Lamb 'standing' in triumph, having been slaughtered (5:6). This is a graphic picture of terror and despair. This is the day of God's great and final judgement. God's judgement is the wrath of sacrificial love. The only option after rejection of God's Messiah is to punish evil and all its adherents with the utmost severity. The cosmic upheavals are the clear sign that God's ultimate wrath has come and the Parousia and judgement will follow. The Day of the Lord (cf. Joel 2:11, 2:30–31) will be followed by prosperity for the righteous (Isaiah 30:23–26; 35:1–10; Joel 3:18; Zechariah 14:6–11). However, this sixth seal is not the actual end: it is an anticipation of what is to come under the seventh bowl.

---

36 cf. Old Testament judgement contexts as cosmic signs, Isaiah 13:10–13; 24:1–6,19–23; 34:4.

Revelation 7

Revelation 7 The Church in Two Modes

Revelation 7:1–8 The Saints Protected for Battle

Revelation 7 indicates the manner in which the saints will always be spiritually protected in the ongoing crises within history. By fighting the good fight of faith within the world (7:1–8), they are protected from ultimate harm and already stand in heaven before the throne of God (7:9–17).Revelation 7 applies to the work of God in the world throughout history and is particularly pertinent to the Christian age. When the fifth seal is opened the martyrs cry out for their blood to be avenged but they are told that they must wait until the full complement of the redeemed is complete. Thus the final judgement upon the wicked waits for the remainder of the Lamb's followers to be called. Revelation 7 presents the victorious followers of Christ in two ways. First, there is the church militant (7:1–8). This first presentation continues the theme from Revelation 5 of messianic war, depicting the triumphant church as the army of the Davidic Messiah. This army is depicted as coming from both Testaments. The life-style of worship through which the number of elect will reach their final goal is also presented (6:11b). The second presentation (7:9–17) is of the heavenly church already assembled but also still being gathered out of the great tribulation and being lead to streams of living water.

The whole church on earth (7:1–8) is presented in the vision as 144,000 from the tribes of Israel. They symbolise God's people who will always be protected. The same church (7:9–17) is then characterised as a multitude from all the nations (that is, including the Gentiles): in communion with the Lamb they are coming through the great tribulation, already enjoying heavenly blessing. The number 144,000 (7:4) expresses the completeness of Old and New Testament believers—12 x 12 multiplied by the largest scriptural number (1,000), used symbolically to suggest a vast number—the entire church of God. The entire congregation (144,000) are members of the new Jerusalem (cf. the numerical references in 21:12–16). Some suggest that 7:1–8 refers to Jewish believers and 7:9–17 refers to the Gentiles believers. Alternatively, the 144,000 are seen as the complete number of martyrs (cf. 6:9–11). But the sealing (7:3) is of the whole people of God throughout history. The servants of God have been engaged in world warfare (7:1–8) leading to heavenly celebration (7:9–17). So the 144,000 is an army of the 'true' Israel, mustered under Davidic leadership to defeat devilish opposition to the purposes of God in the world.

7:4–8 appears to be a census corresponding to a census conducted for military purposes in the Old Testament (cf. 2 Samuel 24, Numbers 1). This numbering of God's people is prompted by the expectation (6:9–11) given to the martyr servants when they were told to remain quiet until the number of their fellow servants and brethren was full. The final state of the redeemed (7:9–17) reflects the efficacy of the divine protection afforded (7:1–8).

Revelation 7, as well as addressing the martyrs' prayer, also provides an answer to the question: 'Who shall be able to stand in the great day of the wrath of God unfolded?' (6:17). The world around is falling apart but God's restraining and protecting hand is outstretched to undertake the cause of the faithful. The opening of the sixth seal (6:12–17) anticipates the final judgement, but this final judgement is delayed until all the servants of God are sealed (7:1–3). This indicates that the judgements of the seal series are anticipatory of what will follow in the sequence of trumpets and bowls.

The four angels (7:1) stand at the four ends of the earth. This points to their universal, worldwide responsibility and control (four = universality). The threefold repetition of 'four' underlines the completeness of the four angels' actions (three = completion). The four winds of heaven are not precisely connected with the four horsemen in Zechariah 6:1–8.[1] The point of 7:1 is the restraint exercised by the four angels, standing in readiness for God's complete saving intervention for the saints (cf. Jeremiah 49:36). The angels hold fast the four winds—biblical instruments of world strife, turmoil and war—in a delaying movement. This provides time for God to put in place measures for the continued protection of the saints throughout history. The winds are strug-

---

[1] Smalley, 2005, 179–180.

gling agents of destruction in this gathering storm,[2] always ready to be destructively released. The message is that the incessant warfare depicted in 7:1–8 is within the decreed control of history by the sovereign God.

The sealing must take place (7:2–4) before the release of the winds. The destructive winds will only affect those who are not sealed (cf. Ezekiel 9:4). If the connection with the four horsemen is sustained, then this sealing of believers points to a divine activity in place for all believers since the Fall.[3] The mark on their foreheads defines them as God's remnant people (cf. Ezekiel 9:4).

The 'sea' (7:1) could mean nations and peoples. 'Trees' could mean the might and pride of the earth. Together, the sea and trees could symbolise the idolatrous worship of the fallen order. But the sequence—earth, sea, tree—is probably literal of the totality of creation, all of which will be affected by the judgements detailed in 6:1–8.

A fifth angel—another angel of the same kind (*allon*, 7:2) as the four (7:1)—comes from the east (7:2). The east is often depicted in the Bible as the source of divine revelation: paradise was in the east (Genesis 2:8); the glory of God returns to the temple from the east (Ezekiel 43:2); the Dayspring from on high, symbolic of the Messiah, rose in the east (Luke 1:78); and Palestine, where God chose to reveal his salvation, was east of Patmos. The angel brings with him the seal 'of the living God'. The servants of God are then sealed, that is, marked with the sign of divine ownership. Revelation 7 is thus a presentation of how God will protect the people of God in, not from, the calamities and distress brought upon the world in the course of history.

John does not say what the seal is, but 14:1 suggests that the seal is the name of God and the Father's name. The title 'living God' (7:2) stresses his unending eternity as assurance. God can accomplish for his people his purposes of eternal life that reach beyond the finite limits of history. The loud cry to the four destroying angels, whose range of power is complete, marks the urgency of the message.

---

2   Tonstad, 2006, 146.
3   cf. Beale, 1999, 406.

The fifth angel's message (7:3) fixes the sequence of the sealing first and then the release of the winds. The angels charged with destruction are not to begin their work against the world (land, sea and trees) until the faithful are sealed from all the effects of divine judgement. The servants of God are to be marked on the forehead—the part of the person by which we are normally identified—a conspicuous sign of their consecration. This sealing on the place of perception also indicates the divine direction of their life (cf. Ezekiel 9:4–6, a similar sealing of the faithful remnant of Israel).

The function of the seal is to authenticate believers. The seal is a sign of divine ownership (cf. 14:1, where the 144,000 have the name of the Lamb and God on their foreheads). The servants of God are, in fact, branded and empowered to serve by this seal of the Spirit. Since believers (cf. 7:3 'servants of our God') are sealed against the final destructive onslaught of the judgements in all the three series (seals, trumpets, bowls), the final judgement upon the wicked must wait for the assembling of the rest of the Lamb's followers (6:11). Believers will be physically exposed to the first four judgements upon the world in the trumpet series. Believers will suffer. But—through 'sealing'—believers will be spiritually preserved. Believers will be brought through the turbulence of the end (the seventh trumpet), and presented faultless before the throne of God. Believers will be able to stand at the throne of God in the world judgement because they have been faithful (cf. 6:17). This is why their victory is celebrated, as an interlude, before the seventh seal pronounces the end. The end is carried through by the seventh item of the trumpet and bowl series (the seventh trumpet and the seventh bowl).

The sealing now takes place (7:4). The numbered tribes (12 x 12 x 1000) constitute all believers of all time (cf. 14:1). The people of God, the true Israel (cf. 7:4), are shown moving towards ultimate fulfilment. However, if they are faithful, believers (the true Israel) are already—before the ultimate fulfilment—enjoying the fruits of salvation.

The order of tribes in Revelation 7 corresponds to none of the nineteen Old Testament lists. Dan, linked with pagan idolatry (cf. Judges 18:30–31; 1 Kings 12:25–33), and Ephraim are omitted.

Levi, Joseph and Manasseh are inserted. Judah—also prominent in the Old Testament tribal lists—heads the list, significantly, as the messianic tribe. Old Testament lists are normally arranged geographically, moving from south to north (Numbers 34:19-29; Joshua 21:4-7; Judges 1:2-36; 1 Chronicles 12:24-37). But the list in Revelation 7 is not geographical. Other Old Testament lists, which put the tribes in their military order, put Judah first (cf. Numbers 2:3; 7:12; 10:14). In the Revelation 7 list, after Judah, the remainder of the order is not in the order of the birth of the patriarchs. Reuben, Issachar, Zebulon, Joseph and Benjamin are correctly placed in birth order; Gad and Asher, Simeon and Levi are correctly paired in birth order, but not correctly placed. So the more probable explanation for the difference in the order in Revelation 7 is that believers constitute the true Israel, hence the clear break from the order in the national censuses of the Old Testament

One of the twelve tribes, Dan, had now been lost. After the crucifixion, the twelve apostles replaced Judas (the apostle who had defected, Acts 1:21-26). Similarly, the lost tribe must be replaced.[4] In the Revelation list: Judah moves from fourth to head the list; Reuben moves to second; and the handmaid tribes (Gad, Asher, Naphtali) follow, with Manasseh replacing Dan. Smith suggests that this elevation of the children of non-covenant mothers represents the inclusion of the Gentiles in Israel. The sons of Leah (Simeon, Levi, Issachar and Zebulon) precede the two sons of Rachel (Joseph and Benjamin). However, the inclusion of both Joseph and Manasseh (7:6, 8) has never been satisfactorily explained. The tribe of Levi is usually excluded from military lists (Numbers 1:49; 2:33; 26:1-51; cf. 1 Chronicles 21:6). Levi is normally numbered separately, according to a non-military principle (Numbers 3:15; 26:58-62). But Levi is included in the Revelation list (7:7). Without Levi the war could not be a Holy War.

The loss of records due to Israel's historical disasters—exile, various destructions of the temple, A.D. 70—made tribal connection unidentifiable. So this list in Revelation (7:5-8) is to be taken as a presentation of all believers as a messianic army brought into being by the blood of the Lamb (7:14) and led by the Davidic

---

4   cf. Smith, 1990, 111–118.

Messiah (whose tribe, Judah, heads the tribal list). As an army, they are engaged in holy war (cf. 1:9; 2:3; 3:10) under the leadership of the Lion of the Tribe of Judah (5:5) who has triumphed (cf. Genesis 49:8–12). In the great battle over who runs the world, believers overcome as their leader Messiah overcame by persistence unto and into death.

The nature of the warfare in Revelation 7 is readily conjectured. It will be against: the world, the flesh, and the devil; spiritual powers in high places; and temptations throughout their earthly lives. Believers will need the whole armour of God to bring them through the great tribulation (7:14). However, believers will triumph by their witness to Jesus, their fidelity under trial and persecution, and their faithfulness unto death. The picture of the redeemed is corporate. But written into this picture is the heroism of countless multitudes of believers who—like Jesus—for the joy that was set before them have taken up their cross, despising the shame.

Revelation 7:9–17 The Earthly Church from a Heavenly Perspective

7:9–17 is a proleptic vision of the faithful: those who have been victors over the dragon and his retinue in the timeless 'messianic' war conducted throughout history (7:1–8). The proleptic vision offers present comfort to readers. By their individual appropriation of Christ's sacrifice, the readers are already included in the total work of Christ. In the heavenly temple, believers of all eras of history—chosen before the foundation of the world—stand in service and worship before God, presenting the work of the cross upon saved humanity.[5] This is a vision of the present of all ages, not the end-time, for in the end-time the temple symbolism will disappear.

At the end-time the existing heaven will cease to exist: heaven and earth will have been fused into one reality. Heaven is the image of the transcendent throughout the Bible. So the fusion of heaven and earth into one reality will mean that the transformed universe will be caught up into transcendent reality. The anticipatory character of 7:9–17 is similar to the concluding section of

---

5   cf. Spatafora, 1997, 157.

Revelation. However, 7:9–17 is not exclusively about the future. Transcending temporal and spatial categories, 7:9–17 describes believers' redeemed existence 'as victorious and joyful in God's proximity'.[6] The location of 7:9–17 is heaven—note the presence of the angels and the four living creatures and twenty-four elders in 7:11—as opposed to the location of 7:1–8 which is the earth. 7:9–17 is a new vision (cf. 'after this', 7:9), reporting a victory which still awaits consummation. This new vision comes at the end of the seal series. The seal series does not declare the final judgement; the seal series declares the present facts of the world case. Likewise, 7:9–17 is a picture of present heavenly reality combined with anticipation of a transformed future.

The innumerable multitude, the redeemed people of God, are coming out of the great tribulation. They had been sealed (7:1–8) in anticipation of the great tribulation. They are now standing—that is, ready for service—in front of God, praising him and the Lamb for the Lamb's victory. The angels and other heavenly beings join the worship of the redeemed. The redeemed are clothed in white robes, the garments given to overcomers in heaven (3:5). John had previously heard the number of those who had been sealed (7:4) but now he sees the reality (7:9). They are not martyrs: they are an innumerable multitude of the people of the slaughtered Lamb (7:17). The vision is of the final church comprised of those to be ransomed from all nations (cf. 5:9). The group that fights the messianic battle within the history of the 'great tribulation' (7:1–8) is the group that is victorious before the divine throne, having come out of the 'great tribulation' (7:9–17).

This innumerable multitude (7:9) echoes God's promise to the patriarchs: that their descendants would be innumerable (Genesis 13:16; 15:5; 32:12; Hosea 1:10; Jub 13:20; 14:4–5; Hebrews 11:12). In contrast with Jewish reflections, 7:9 sees the promise to the patriarchs fulfilled in the great multitude that cannot be numbered. John places *ethnous* (nations) first in this enumeration of mankind (cf. the different orders in 5:9; 11:9; 13:7; 14:6 and variations of the list in 10:11; 17:15). This sets *pantos ethnous* apart from the other three components—tribes, peoples and tongues—enabling 7:9 to emphasise the connection with the promises given to the

---

6   Ulfgard, 1989, 106.

patriarchs: that the world would be blessed through them. *Phulon* (tribes) in second place echoes the repeated *ek phules* of 7:4–8, suggesting that the tribes of Israel are included in the international multitude of Abraham's and Jacob's descendants. The international multitude (7:9) are all members of the true Israel (7:4). Thus 7:9, as the interpretation of 7:4-8, indicates not so much the complete replacement of the national people of God as the abolition of its national limits.[7] This is consistent with the description of the new Jerusalem (Revelation 21), where the gates are inscribed with the names of the twelve tribes of the sons of Israel (21:12) but stand open to all the nations (21:24–26).

This presents all the people of God, including Gentiles, as the true Israel in fulfilment of the promise to Abraham (Genesis 12:1-3). This true Israel enjoys divine spiritual protection during the coming 'exodus' plagues. 'Every tribe', believers from every nation, experience this divine spiritual protection.[8] The white robes worn by the true Israel: attest the heavenly character of the multitude; are festal garments of victory, the victory and righteousness obtained through Christ's death, not merited but given by God; and are given to martyrs as a comfort and recompense as they await the full complement of God's people. In the Sardis letter, the conquerors are promised white robes because they have not soiled their garments and are worthy of walking with Christ in white (3:4). The church community of Laodicea is urged to buy gold, white clothes and eye-salve to make up for their nakedness, poverty, and blindness (3:18). These outward garments attest the inward spiritual participation of the saved in the prospective new Jerusalem, and thus qualify them for life in the heavenly world.

Palm branches are a pagan victory symbol. However, with palm braches in hand (7:9), the true Israel cry 'the salvation belongs to our God' (7:10). This cry is often thought to refer to Psalm 3:8; but the cry could reflect Psalm 118:25 (a tabernacles Psalm). According to the Mishnah, the *lulab* (the Hebrew word meaning palm branch) was waved at the reading of Psalm 118:25.[9] Palm branches were symbolic of the Feast of Tabernacles (cf. *lulab* in

---

7   cf. Bauckham, 1993, The Climax of Prophecy, 224–25.
8   Ulfgard, 1989, 79.
9   cf. op. cit., 1989, 89–92; John 12:13.

Leviticus 23:40). The Feast of Tabernacles celebrated God's protective presence with the people of Israel during their wanderings in the wilderness. In the Christian tradition, the palm branch has become the emblem of Christian martyrdom. Holy warriors of Simon Maccabee's army waved palm branches in celebration of their recapture of the citadel of Jerusalem (1 Macc 13:51).

Thus the victorious army (7:10), according to the standard motif of holy war tradition, cries in unceasing praise for *the* (the Greek article precedes 'salvation') salvation: a totally comprehensive, final deliverance. The saved ascribe their victory to both God and the Lamb (7:10). Sharing in the victory won by the Lamb (cf. 5:6) identifies those who have been ransomed from all nations (5:9).

The angels and others of the heavenly assembly who encircle the throne (7:11-12)—the true Israel clothed as overcomers in white robes—fall down and praise God. The doxology (7:12) contains seven (seven = perfection, completion, fulfilment) characteristics of God (cf. 5:12f.). God and the Lamb are praised in an all-embracing way. The opening 'amen' is the solemn affirmation of the multitudes that the reality of divine action is expressed by their assembled presence. This all-embracing praise for God's character includes: blessing or praise due to God; glory (*doxa*) justly accorded to God for his 'worth'; divine wisdom, the source of all truth and the bestowal of all knowledge as expressed in the plan of salvation; thanksgiving; honour, which is the felt esteem for God shown in worship; God's power, the divine omnipotence which is effective against all opposition (God had delivered the multitude from the 'great tribulation', the most formidable antagonism that earth could muster); and divine strength. The final 'amen' validates the truthfulness of the characterizations of God.

The past, present and future of the multitude clothed in white robes is described in a dialogue between John and one of the twenty-four elders (7:13-17). The dialogue: reveals the identity and origin of the multitude; reveals the comfort and blessings the multitude will enjoy from God and the Lamb; and indicates that the purpose of the vision was to convey information. The present and future tenses used to describe the multitude in 7:13-17 refer to something that has its beginning in the decisive past event

(7:14, Greek aorist tense). The verbs begin in the present and past tenses (7:14–17) but continue in the future (7:15).

The decisive past event was washing in the blood of the Lamb (7:14). Identifying themselves with Christ's sacrifice has made them, through the Spirit, what they are: holy, set apart for Christ's service. This controls the present and the future for believers. The blood of the Lamb 'is the saving sign through which the multitude may stand in God's presence'.[10] The multitude now share with Christ in royal dignity, tribulation and patient endurance. Though in the body, they now have a citizenship in heaven (Philippians 3:20). The multitude share with Christ a triumphant life in the new Jerusalem.

The emphasis is not that the multitude has come through death but that they are safe in God's presence. Despite threats from a hostile world, they may trust in the continued protection of God. But, just like Israel in the desert, they run the risk of falling away if they do not preserve their faith in God's ability to save his people. This throws light on the oscillation between threat and promise in the prophetic messages to the churches.

They are coming out (*erchomenoi*, 7:14) of the great tribulation, a continuing process. For these living saints, the battle is ongoing. They are coming out for one reason only: they have washed (Greek past tense) their robes in the blood of the Lamb. Their robes were not always white.

John is bewildered (7:14). John's reply to the heavenly elder—'My lord, you know'—is both a confession of ignorance and also a request for information. The earthly human situation for believers is described in the continuing present phrase 'they who are coming out of', referring to ongoing transformation from being in the flesh to being in the Spirit throughout a lifetime. Richard Bauckham suggests that 7:14 may depict the army of 7:4–8, now victorious after battle, washing their bloodstained robes; coming out of great tribulation could refer to their victory.[11] However, the continuing present seems to indicate that, having moved into a new relationship in Christ, they are still subject to worldly pressures against their Christian witness until death. The

---

10 Ulfgard, 1989 106.
11 The Climax of Prophecy, 1993, 226.

thought of victory (white robes, 7:9) is fused with that of purification (7:14, washed their robes white cf. 19:8). The Greek aorist tenses of 'washed' and 'made white' look back to their conversion and cleansing from sin on earth; the inward change in their character is now reflected by their outward heaven-worthy garments.

Inward change is produced by the Spirit in regeneration. The multitude clothed in white has appropriated by faith the merits of the Lamb's redeeming death. They exhibit this appropriation by their faithful witness to the point of death. They are still involved in the 'great tribulation', maintaining the witness of Jesus (12:17; 19:10). The Christian multitude washed their clothes just like Israel washed her clothes to appear at Sinai (Exodus 19:10,14). The soiled garments refer to their previous condition of sinfulness and alienation (cf. Isaiah 1:18–20). Washing garments after victory was also part of the ritual purification required before and after the shedding of blood (Numbers 31:19–20,24 cf. Numbers 19:19). Thus, in Revelation the believers are participating as priests in worship. The washing may be seen primarily as a reference to their baptism in the Spirit, that is, their conversion.[12] They are now a kingdom, priests to God. The multitude are not all martyrs: Revelation does not envisage martyrdom for all believers.

Redeemed saints are coming out of 'the great tribulation' and moving in a victory procession to the new Jerusalem. This continues the exodus emphasis, as does the mention of the 'blood of the Lamb'. Christians are to see existence from two perspectives: the heavenly and the earthly. Belief in Christ's victory—that one day will be universally acknowledged—by the seal of the Spirit gives the multitude power to endure hardships that are, paradoxically, earthly consequences of Christ's victory. Those hardships will become even more terrible as history proceeds.

Coming out (present) of the 'great tribulation' refers to the multitude's overcoming. The present participle (*erchomenoi*, 7:14) indicates a continuing state. Normally the participle would take its time reference from the finite verb. But the context makes it clear that coming out of the great tribulation was subsequent to the verbs 'washed' and 'made white'. The 'great tribulation' is an allusion to the time of the end (cf. Daniel 12:1). But, in this

---
12 cf. Dumbrell, 2006, 44–45.

context, the 'great tribulation' may mean no more than pressures to engage in idolatry and compromise; pressures to which believers, in these last days (cf. 1:9; 2:9,22), will always be subject. Despite present difficulties, the multitude are victors continually. Thus they stand now with the heavenly assembly (7:9–11)! This is the situation of believers in the world after the death and resurrection of Christ. But this is also the situation of the earthly life of every believer of every age.

That they are coming out of the great tribulation is indicated by their service, that is, their worship (*latreuousin*, 7:15). They are members of the worshipping assembly in the heavenly temple (7:9–11). Temple and throne (7:15)—transcendent symbols of God's ruling covenant presence—are indications that, while they are on their way to the ultimate goal, they are now with God under his care. Nevertheless they are still on the way, living in this world, on their journey (7:15b–17). The fullness of divine protection can only be realised when they come out of the great tribulation by physical death (cf. 7:14–17).

The tabernacle, as the repository for the ark, represented God's covenant presence with the children of Israel through the wilderness. So, in the believers' journey through their wilderness now, they have God's covenant presence with them: God tabernacles (7:15) with them. Believers are now temple servants in the new covenant. Because they serve God within his new temple, God will spread over (*epi*, 7:15) them his protective, tabernacling, immanent presence. God is journeying with them, guiding the faithful to the final Promised Land (cf. Ezekiel 37:26–28). Believers are on a journey, but their gaze is set upon the goal. There are more exodus motifs in this section: believers have come out from a slavery-type situation (7:14); believers are now travelling through the wilderness; through the wilderness believers are protected and assured of God's glory dwelling with them by the Spirit, as indicated by the tabernacle spread over them (7:15–16; cf. Ezekiel 37:27–28; Isaiah 4:6); finally, and with great joy, they will reach their promised inheritance (7:17).

The verbs in 7:16–17 begin in the present and extend into the future (cf. Isaiah 49:10). When they reach their goal, believers will no longer be threatened by the difficulties of human existence ('hunger and thirst', 7:16) for they will have come out of the great tribulation. The reason for their arrival at the throne of grace (7:17) is a combination of: being protected, led and fed by God and the Lamb; and God's comforting of his chosen people, counteracting all sorrow. The shepherd motifs in Ezekiel 34, Psalm 23 and Isaiah 49:10 may serve as a backdrop for 7:17, but the particular reference is to Ezekiel 37:24 where the new Israel will serve under the Davidic Messiah and 'they shall have one shepherd'.

Their shepherd is also the Lamb. Their shepherd, the Lamb, is now at the centre of heaven, one with God, and also an organic member of the flock.[13] The Lamb has guided believers to the springs of living water, that is, eternal life (Isaiah 49:10). There is still a goal to be reached (7:14) for believers in the world, but it will be reached under divine protection. The goal will be reached because the Lamb is now the shepherd (John 10:11, 14; Hebrews 13:20; 1 Peter 2:25; 5:2–4) beside God on the throne. So the Lamb guarantees their present relief (cf. 7:16), patiently caring for the sheep. Life's lingering pressures are not able to defeat them. God himself will finally counteract sorrow, wiping away all tears of grief (Isaiah 25:8), making Christ's conquest of sorrow and death complete for the multitude of believers.

Thus all the covenant promises and hopes will be fulfilled, though 7:9–17 reports a victory that still awaits the consummation. The vision of 7:9–17 is not just a description of the future, and it does not describe all that John is given to see of the future after the consummation. In this sense the vision is not proleptic as it transcends temporal and spatial characteristics, speaking of the believer's redeemed experience as victorious and joyful in God's proximity. It is proleptic, however, in that the glorious end of the book is anticipated: the ideal communion between God and humanity in the new Jerusalem, in the regained Paradise (7:17).

---

13 Pattemore, 2004, 159.

Revelation 8

Revelation 8:1, 3–5 The Seventh Seal

At Christ's opening of the seventh seal in heaven (8:1), a silence of half an hour occurs to highlight that the seven seals are spent. This unexpected silence is a dramatic pause to symbolise the awe and dread with which even the heavenly hosts await the coming judgements. The judgements will be primarily upon the natural world, but humanity will also be affected tragically. The brief interlude of silence also allows the prayers of *all* the saints to be heard (8:4). The end of history is within reach; the new creation is about to burst in. The sixth seal (6:12–17) had placed the world on the threshold of the end, leaving the trumpets to both retrace the same ground and also further enact the judgements through the bowl series which will follow.

A heavenly response to the prayers of all the saints (8:3–5) not only concludes the seals series but also, importantly, interlocks the seal series with the trumpet series by the overlap of 8:2 and 8:6 before the first trumpet is sounded (8:7). There is the appearance of another angel (8:3, cf. 7:2). The angel facilitates the prayers of the saints, that is, all the believers of all ages who through the Spirit pray especially for the coming of the kingdom. The angel is at the golden altar of incense inside the sanctuary (Isaiah 6:6; Ezekiel 10:2) to offer much incense as an accompaniment to the prayers of the saints, thus indicating that the prayers of the saints are acceptable. When the incense was offered in the Jerusalem Temple, the people outside also offered their prayers (Luke 1:8–10; Judith 9:1).[1] The altar is described as 'near the throne' (8:3b): God is near to the prayers of the saints. The smoke of the incense, together with the prayers of the saints, ascends to God (8:4) and there is an immediate divine response (8:5).

Revelation 8:2, 6–9:21 The First Six Trumpets

The progressive opening of the scroll prepares the reader for, and is presupposed by, the content of the scroll. This preparation governs what follows the opening of the last seal (8:1). There was a

---

1 Stevenson, 2001, 291.

pause between the sixth and seventh seals during which the church age was reviewed on earth (7:1–8) and in heaven (7:9–17). There is a similar pause between the sixth and seventh trumpets (10:1–11:14). The pauses indicate that ongoing world judgements are operating, but the church age must be brought to a conclusion before the seventh item operates. The bowls series of judgements are broadly parallel to the trumpets, but the bowls also lead directly to the end: evil itself is judged as the seventh bowl is poured into the air. The seventh bowl is placed at the end of history in a way that the previous seventh judgements (seals and trumpets) were not.

The divine response to the prayers of the saints (8:4) is judgement (8:5), which is spelled out in detail in the seven trumpet blasts. The interlocking device (8:2; cf. 11:15)—introducing the angels with their trumpets ready to sound the heavenly call to battle—indicates that the trumpets are an outworking of the seals, as does the expanded repetition of the judgement imagery of 4:5 at 8:5. But the trumpets are not the contents of the scroll. On the contrary, whereas the last seal of the scroll is broken at 8:1, the scroll of Revelation 5 first appears open (perfect participle) at 10:2.

Revelation 8–9 present the second of the three sets (seals, trumpets and bowls) of progressive devastations to come upon the human world. In trumpets 1–4 there is the application of seals 1–4 to the natural world. Trumpets 5–6 direct attention to the colossus of deceptive evil in the world, quite beyond the capacity of humankind to counter or conquer. God must win a final victory. The seventh trumpet, anticipated by the seventh seal (8:5), indicates the end of history and the advent of the kingdom.

The angel (8:3) now casts to earth (8:5) the fire of judgement from the altar (cf. Ezekiel 10:2 in which burning coals were taken from between the cherubim and scattered over Jerusalem). The fallen order is shaken to its roots (8:5) at the prospect of this judgement to which the trumpets will lead. The same image of judgement by fire appears in: the seventh trumpet (11:19); the seventh bowl bringing history to an end (16:18); the verdict against fallen Babylon whose destiny is to be burned with fire

(18:8); the fire that falls upon Satan and his hosts as they encircle the camp of the saints (20:9); and the lake of fire (20:14–15).

8:3–5 serves as a conclusion to the seals and an introduction to the trumpets. 15:2–4 performs the same interlocking device between trumpets and bowls. The three trumpet woes (8:13) indicate the trials that are the last three trumpets of the church age. The first six trumpets are parallel in time with the first four seals.

The cosmic imagery in the seventh item of each series, particularly the earthquake, relates the divine judgements (Revelation 6–16) to the vision of heaven (4:5a). This vision of heaven is set within Revelation 4–5, which is the key to the book. The prospect of final judgement on the unbelieving world, integrating the trumpets and bowls with the seven seals, is the answer to the saints' plea. The judgement in the trumpets and bowls will vindicate the saints.

Revelation 8:2, 6–9:21 The Trumpets Sound

To close the interlude, the seven trumpet angels—maybe the seven archangels, since they stand in God's presence—reappear and prepare to sound (8:6). The intercalation of the trumpets (8:2,6) with the seals (8:1–5) shows that the trumpets are the detailed answer to the saints' prayers, especially the seventh trumpet. The answer to the saints' prayers is that God's judgements are to be inflicted on idolatrous powers.[2] The first six trumpets operate while the seals are operating, affecting a third of the world. Thus these first six trumpets are redemptive, warning of the end but not yet the end.

In the first four trumpets (8:6–12)—directed against all humanity because of their persecution and idolatry—God deprives the ungodly of earthly security to indicate their separation from him. The fourth trumpet is the logical emphasis and climax of the first four: darkness, the emblem of unbelievers' spiritual separation from God, is figurative of all that reminds unbelievers of their separation from God. The tribulations of 8:6–12 are throughout the world but do not affect at any one time the whole world or all the people. The creation (cf Genesis 1) is systematically affected:

2　Poythress, 2000, 121.

light, air, vegetation, sun, moon, stars, sea creatures, and humans.

The separation between the first four general judgements and the last three trumpets, directed specifically at unbelievers, is achieved by the proclamation of the eagle (8:13) between the fourth and fifth trumpets. The eagle proclaims a three-fold woe on the earth's inhabitants (8:13; 9:12; 11:14): the three trumpet woes that lead to the final judgement. The third woe (cf. 10:6–7) is the seventh trumpet.

The unbelieving world are spiritually insensitive to the meaning of the first four trumpets. They are in the dark (8:12). The trumpets and bowls are judgements emanating from the natural world throughout history. These judgements are intensified by human mismanagement of creation, interpersonal and international human relationships, and misguided human interventions into the course of nature. But the world just sees natural events; they don't understand.

The trumpet judgements point to the bowl judgements. But the bowl judgements will be total, directed against a hardened unbelieving world that has failed to repent. The unbelieving world will not understand that these distresses in history were presenting the wrath of God against human sin. The parallelism between the three series (seals, trumpets, bowls) may help to identify the nature of the respective disasters. However, the imagery is so stark and often so bizarre that we may have to conclude that the presentation of the detail of the trumpets and bowls is deliberately obscured to disturb readers.

The impression is that the seals and trumpets are successive, but the trumpets are interrelated with the seals. Unlike the seals, the trumpets primarily affect nature with necessary deleterious affects on humanity.

The judgement of the seventh seal (8:5)—encompassing the trumpets and expressing the purpose of the seals—is the world-ending event (like the seventh and final trumpet and bowl judgements of 11:19 and 16:18). Likewise, the judgement of the seventh trumpet expresses the purpose of the seals and encompasses the sequence of the bowls. There is this interrelationship between all three series. The same final judgement is reached in the seventh item of each series: actual in the case of the bowls, prospective in the case of the seals and trumpets.

The seventh seal, pointing to divine judgements always taking place in the world, introduces the trumpets. The trumpets are a more severe application of this continuing divine judgement. Likewise, the seven trumpets introduce the bowls and are explained and intensified by them. The two sequences (trumpets and bowls) feature natural phenomena taking place throughout history deleteriously affecting humanity. The relationship between the trumpets and bowls is parallel (earth 8:7 with 16:2; sea 8:8–9 with 16:3; waters 8:10–11 with 16:4–7; sun 8:12 with 16:8–9; torment and agony 9:1–11 with 16:10–11; the river Euphrates 9:13–21 with 16:12–16; anticipation of the end 11:15–18 with 16:17). There is, however, a chronological movement of the effects of judgements. Nevertheless, the two series are necessarily recapitulative, expanding in their results upon nature and the world.

The figurative character of punishments is denoted by the use of 'as' or 'like'. The threefold woes to come during the last three trumpet blasts are marked by a literary division to indicate their greater harshness. There is a longer description of the woes as climactic trials. The last three trumpets and bowls directly strike at the wicked, for in these judgements God exposes the true nature of their rebellion.

The progressive severity of the trumpets and bowls affirms Paul's warning that God gives the world up to increasingly sinful human control when increasing human idolatry is expressed in independence from divine design for human conduct (cf. Romans 1:18–32). These judgements are God's way of dealing with world and personal evil (cf. the refrains of Romans 1:24,26,28).

The first four items identified in the seals as the basis of continuing world problems—with intensification through the course of history—are taken further in the first four items of the trumpets and bowls series. The last three items of trumpets and bowls represent increasing intensification of world suffering for unbelievers in the post-cross world.

Summary

The continued reference to 4:5 (with expansions) indicates that the same final judgement is reached in the seventh item of each of the three series (seals, trumpets, bowls). In each of the first two series (seals 8:5b, and trumpets 11:19), there is a preliminary glimpse of final judgement (16:18–21) that the following series then approaches from closer range. The progressive expansion of the formula (4:5; 8:5b, adding an earthquake; 11:19 adding heavy hail; and 16:18–21, huge hailstones) corresponds to the progressive intensification of the three series of judgements.

The first four trumpets (8:2; 8:6–11:19) do not form an obvious set,[3] but the last three trumpets are closely related to each other as the eagle proclaims the three-fold set of woes on earth's rebellious inhabitants (8:13). The woes, with their emphatic formulae that signals a sequence (9:12; 11:14), provide additional means—alongside the numbering of the trumpets—to keep the hearer aware of the sequence of the fifth, sixth and seventh trumpets. The reason for this emphasis is the importance of these last three judgements for John's purpose in these chapters. The enumeration indicating the end of the second woe (11:14) heightens the increasing tensions. The second woe fails to evoke repentance. The sequence of woes formula (11:14) then indicates that time for repentance is running out: the third and last woe is coming quickly (cf. Christ's word at 2:16; 3:11; 22:6,12,20).

The trumpet sequence leads to the final judgement, which is emphasised as both the seventh trumpet and the third woe (10:6–7). Revelation 7 and 10:1–11:13 are paralleled by their function as interpolations after the sixth judgement in the series of seals and trumpets (6:17; 9:20–21). These interruptions delay the final judgement. The first delay (7:1–17) is to protect the people of God. The second delay (10:1–11:13) is to report the prophetic witness of God's people in an unbelieving world.

The detailed outworking of the symbolism of the trumpet judgements is uncertain. Michael Wilcock states that the symbolism points to judgements that will be generated by agencies so far

---

3   Bauckham, The Climax of Prophecy, 1993, 11.

'beyond human control that their divine origin should be obvious.'[4]

The first five trumpet judgements broadly parallel five of the Exodus plagues, which had indicated to Pharaoh that he was no more than a steward in God's world. The first trumpet parallels the seventh plague of hail and fire mingled with blood (Exodus 9:23–24). The second and third trumpets resemble the first plague of rivers turned to blood (Exodus 7:19–20). The fourth trumpet recalls the ninth plague of darkness (Exodus 10:21). The fifth trumpet is like the eighth plague of locusts (Exodus 10:12). Just as the Exodus plagues shattered Pharaoh's world of hard-hearted and idolatrous hostility to the people of God, the trumpets now challenge and condemn a world hardened in its idolatry and boast of sovereignty. Like Pharaoh, the world will not repent. But God's intention, in spite of the world's resistance, is to lead his people into the new Canaan.

The first four trumpets (8:6–12) parallel the first four seals. God deprives the ungodly of earthly security because of their persecution and idolatry, and thereby indicates that the ungodly are separated from him. The first four trumpets set in motion the forces of nature: the first three affect earth, humankind, sea and rivers; the fourth affects the sky and heavenly bodies. The last three trumpets are directed specifically against those who do not have the seal of God on their foreheads, to call them to repentance (cf. 9:20–21). God continues to use the world of nature to punish humankind.

To close the interlude of 8:3–5, the seven trumpet angels reappear (8:6) and prepare to sound. This preparatory activity heightens the sense of expectancy. God uses the world of nature to punish humankind; this has been the case throughout world history. The fifth and sixth trumpets sustain the faithful. All of these trumpet judgements culminate in the last judgement described by the seventh trumpet (11:15–19). Therefore, the first four trumpets and plagues indicate typological judgement on the ungodly world, affecting both believer and unbeliever in the age of redemption. The indictments indicate that for the unsealed there is a continued hardening of the heart, and thus a continued punishment.

---

[4] 1975, 94.

The Interrelationship of the Three Series

Recapitulation occurs from seals to trumpets to bowls. The first four items in each series are set off from the last three items by definite markers: the four horsemen set off the first four seals from the last three; the eagle's announcement of the three last woes (8:13) divides the trumpets; and the first four bowls parallel the first four trumpets, with the fifth bowl drawing together the effects of the first four. The sixth item features events leading to the last day: the sixth seal reveals cosmic devastation (6:12–14); at the sixth trumpet two hundred million troops kill one third of mankind; when the sixth bowl is poured, the battle of Armageddon occurs. The seventh item gives a description of the end: when the seventh seal is opened there is awe in heaven at what is to come (8:1); at the blowing of the seventh trumpet, loud voices in heaven announce the coming of the kingdom (11:15); and at the pouring of the seventh bowl a loud voice from the temple announces 'it is done' (16:17).

There are interludes within the seals and trumpets but not within the bowls. Between the sixth and seventh seals, there is the sealing of the faithful (Revelation 7). After the sixth trumpet the church's role in a rebellious world is shown (Revelation 10–11). After the seventh trumpet, before the bowl judgements, there is the conflict between the church and the powers of evil (Revelation 12–14). These interludes alert the reader to the vast periods of time involved in the operation of the seals and trumpets.

The recurring character of the items of the three series (seals, trumpets, bowls) points to the similarity of the historical effects of the Fall. The effects of the Fall are heightened on account of increasing human waywardness occasioned by social, cultural, and inventive development. There is increasing human confidence that their own abilities will bring a better world into being. This historical progression explains the increasing severity of the first four trumpets and bowls over the first four seals.

The end appears to come in the first two series (seals and trumpets), but is postponed. At the opening of the fifth seal, saints ask how long (6:10), and the answer is that they must wait (6:11). After the opening of the sixth seal, the recalcitrance of humankind becomes more evident. But again the end does not happen. The first two series progressively increase from one quarter to one third of humanity devastatingly affected. Then, with the bowls, the effect is on all unbelievers. At the same time, the seals and trumpets judgements are still cumulatively operating on all. Every opportunity for repentance is being provided before the end is ushered in. God's sovereign holiness is vindicated by his patience. However, the plagues of the third (bowl) series are God's final measure (15:1)!

The audience differs in each series. In the seals and trumpets the audience is general: the earth and all its inhabitants. In the bowl series, the final judgements are directed against those who bear the mark of the beast (16:2). The first two series allow repentance. But the prospect of salvation diminishes as the end approaches. No offer of repentance is attached to the seven bowls.

The opening of the seventh seal introduces the trumpets. With the blowing of the seventh trumpet the days of the end have come (10:7): the anticipation of the end is announced (11:15), but the end is still distant. The seventh trumpet is not a single vision but an announcement of a long period reaching to the end. Prior to the blowing of the seventh trumpet only two of the three woes (8:13) have occurred. The final woe does not begin until Satan is thrown down to earth (12:9, 12). Satan's wrathful activity on the earth precedes the end. The song of praise (11:15) that bursts forth from heaven when the seventh trumpet is blown looks forward to the consummation of the kingdom. But the third woe must intervene, involving the persecution of the church followed by the final overthrow of the beast's kingdom.

There is progressive interaction of the three series of divine judgements pronounced from the throne room (Revelation 4). In 4:5, flashes of lightning and rumblings and peals of thunder emanate from the throne as a warning of judgement about to come. In 8:5, an earthquake is added, indicating that judgement has reached the earth. At 11:19, heavy hail is added to the earthquake. At the seventh bowl (16:18,21) the earthquake and huge hail reach end-time proportions, bursting upon the wicked with crushing retribution.

Each series carries forward the content of its predecessors and augments it. The subsequent bowl visions are the elaboration of the end-time events, with believers withdrawn (cf. 11:12). Believers are not affected by the bowl judgements. The pouring out of the seventh bowl is the end. The progression is a literary presentation, with the broad contours of a chronological progression in literary format.

Each series is a record of divine judgements on fallen humankind. Humans are left to the burden of their choices. Each subsequent series is an intensification. The trumpets presuppose more intense human suffering than the seals. The effects of the trumpets are presented as being throughout history, so also during the Christian era. The bowls indicate more intensification of world problems at the end of history. The bowls are specifically concerned with the judgement of the beast and his city.

The trumpets and bowls are differentiated from the seals, being more specific. The use of the exodus plague background and natural phenomena for the trumpets and the bowls indicate the purpose: to inform and bring Christian believers out from a hostile world into a new Promised Land. The first four judgements in the trumpets and bowls series apply to the same four divisions of creation: earth, sea, fresh waters, and heaven. Both series are modelled on the same exodus plagues, alluding to them in roughly the same order. This differs from the seals, in which the first four categories affect humanity. The exodus plagues were mostly warnings to Pharaoh to recognise God's sovereignty, but the trumpets and bowls correlate with judgements now coming upon the world in the period between the resurrection and the Parousia.

The intensification of the bowls over the trumpets attests historical progression within an unbelieving world society and culture. There is a progressive increase in godlessness throughout Christian history. This will be alarmingly so during Satan's ability to deceive the nations in the time between his release (20:1–3) and the Parousia, especially after the withdrawal of the church (11:11–12). Hence the misguided use of our world intensifies, as does the inability for humanity to live at harmony within the framework of nations.

The exodus plagues represent the reaction of divine holiness to world ungodliness present at the beginning of Israel's experience. And the trumpets and the bowls series are modelled on the exodus plagues as typological judgements. So these series of judgements indicate not only the divine holiness that always reacts against human social and cultural transgression, but also that we are in the same exodus situation of hoped-for departure from Egypt and pilgrimage to the Promised Land. Between the resurrection and the Parousia, humans generally are wandering in a wilderness brought on by Babel-like attempts to build a better world. God's latter day exodus judgements continue in these times.

The sixth item of the seals corresponds to the seventh items of the trumpets and bowls. However, a general parallel exists between seals, trumpets and bowls in the fifth, sixth and seventh items. The first four items of the seals affect humanity directly.[5] The last three items of each series affect individuals.

The fifth and sixth items in the trumpets and bowls, which occur with terrible consequences, have specific reference to individuals in an ungodly world. They register the psychological and spiritual effects of unbelief, like the Old Testament prophets who had constantly registered the effect of special divine intervention on worldly Israel for breach of the covenant (cf. Joel 2:30,31; Isaiah 2:12,19; 34:3,4; 50:2–3; Jeremiah 4:23–26; Hosea 10:8).

Revelation 8:7 The First Trumpet

The trumpet judgements are a sequence of six plus a decisive, final one. This sequence is like the sequence in the fall of Jericho (Joshua 6), which was the decisive victory that ensured conquest of the Promised Land. The sounding of the first trumpet, a precursor in the Old Testament to holy war, is followed by hail and fire mixed with blood (8:7). The hail brings to mind the seventh exodus plague; the combination of fire and blood recalls the prophesied Day of the Lord (Joel 2:30–31). A significant part of the

---

5 Beale notes that the first four trumpets and bowls affect the sources of human life (1999, 464).

earth's vegetation is burnt, inducing famine (like the third seal, 6:5 cf. Ezekiel 5:16–17).[6]

Revelation 8:8–9 The Second Trumpet

The second trumpet sounds and the visionary sequence describes a great mountain burning with fire, symbolising the judgement of an evil kingdom (cf. 6:14; 18:20–21; cf. Babylon as a mountain in Jeremiah 51:25, and sinking like a stone into the sea in Jeremiah 51:63–64). The burning mass falls into the sea: a third of the sea—which may be figurative for unbelieving people (17:1,15; cf. Jeremiah 51:55 in which Babylon is described as being engulfed by many waters, the waters being a metaphor for invaders)—becomes blood; a third of sea life is killed; and a third of ships is destroyed. Babylon currently holds sway over the world system, but she will be judged (18:8). Every shipmaster will cry out at the destruction of Babylon (18:11–19). Judgement affects the whole world. The natural world so affected brings calamity to humankind.

Revelation 8:10–11 The Third Trumpet

The third trumpet involves the poisoning of fresh waters, inducing a judgement of famine (cf. Exodus 7:15–24 where rivers and springs of fresh waters were affected; cf. Psalm 78:44). The great star, which Beale identifies as a falling angel,[7] falls from heaven as a burning torch (a fireball, probably signifying famine). The star's name was wormwood. Wormwood is a plant with a bitter taste; it is a symbol of divine punishment in the Old Testament (Jeremiah 9:15; 23:15; Lamentations 3:15,19; cf. Jeremiah 8:13–14). The star will appear again in the world kingdom of Babylon under satanic control (cf. Isaiah 14:12–15). There is bitter suffering and famine affecting one third of the world.

Revelation 8:12–13 The Fourth Trumpet

The language continues to be figurative, referring to all the cosmic disturbances that remind us of our humanity. With the blowing of the fourth trumpet the view of one third of the sun, moon

---

[6] Beale suggests that the first trumpet judgement is equivalent to the judgement of the third seal (1999, 473–4).
[7] op. cit., 474.

and stars (that is, one third of the day) becomes darkened. This probably indicates spiritual darkness throughout the world, affecting all areas of life. Darkness was a symbol for judgement (cf. the ninth exodus plague, Exodus 10:21–22). Darkness was also a feature of the Day of the Lord (Amos 5:18; Isaiah 13:10; Joel 2:2). All life would feel this darkness. Following the analogy of the Egyptian plagues, the point of the first four world disasters heralded by the trumpets is the supremacy and sovereignty of God over all earthly alternatives. However, there is no repentance.

Beale suggests, correctly, that the first four trumpets represent troubled world conditions resulting from idolatrous trust in disordered and evil world systems. This idolatrous trust breaches the fundamental conditions of human occupancy of the planet.[8] However, as stated previously, these disasters have come progressively upon the world since the Fall. The disasters heralded by the trumpets have intensified because of human failure to understand the sequences and function of creation. This was inevitable when humans lost the divine presence at the Fall. Without God, there is no harmony with nature: there are progressive human distortions in the handling of creation.

8:13 forms a transition to the next two trumpets. An eagle flies in mid-heaven where all can see and speaks of judgement (cf. 14:6; and the association of birds with judgement in 19:17 and 18:2). The eagle is a metaphor for destruction in the Old Testament (Deuteronomy 28:49; Jeremiah 4:13; 48:40; 49:22; Lamentations 4:19; cf. Hosea 8:1; Habakkuk 1:8). The last three trumpets will be the most grievous.

8:13 marks off these first four woes from the rest. The remaining three trumpets herald harsher judgements. The plagues become more severe and more specific. The descriptions are longer. And the association of the eagle/vulture as a bird of prey signals greater intensity leading to final judgement. The final three woes strike all people who are intractable in their unbelief. The spiritual nature of the judgements becomes more explicit (cf. 8:12) with the direct involvement of demons. Evil hovers over its prey. The prey of evil is the unbelievers dwelling on earth. The first four trumpets affect three parts of the created order: creation is being

---

8   op. cit., 488.

undone. The judgements are figurative, as indicated by the use of the Greek words *hos* (as, like, 8:8,10; 9:2,3,5,17) and *homoios* (like, 9:19). The people of God were borne on eagle's wings to Sinai (Exodus 19:4). Likewise, the eagle might indicate that the entrance to a new age is near at hand. The woes proclaimed by the eagle are directed only at 'those who dwell upon the earth', that is, the ungodly.

Revelation 9

Revelation 9:1-12 The Fifth Trumpet: Demonic Locusts

The fifth and sixth trumpets offer a frightening, comprehensive picture of evil as a perversion of creation. Evil operates in this form 'immediately' preceding the end. The passage introduces intensification of wickedness at the end of the era of church witness (cf. 11:7-13). The power of evil and the impossibility of human conquest over evil is the subject of the two trumpets in Revelation 9: the hideous and repulsive nature of evil is described in the fifth trumpet; and the unimaginable but real power of evil is described in the sixth trumpet. However, satanic evil is prevented from operating outside God's plan for the universe. The locusts are given limited time, five months; and whereas they are allowed to torture humans, they are not allowed to kill them (9:10). The purpose of the trumpet plagues, descriptive of society increasingly motivated by idolatrous concerns, is for humans to repent (9:20).

Unbelievers are affected by the fifth and sixth trumpet plagues. The intense psychological affects of sin and depravity affect unbelievers only; believers are sealed against such demonic assault.

With the sounding of the fifth trumpet an angel falls (or descends) from heaven (cf. the fall of the daystar, Isaiah 14). Jesus anticipates Satan's fall (Luke 10:18). In 1 Enoch, a similar description of 'falling' is reserved for evil angels. The fallen angel opens the bottomless pit (9:2). The bottomless pit contains all accumulated human evil under divine control. This infernal reservoir of evil is once again permitted to influence humanity for a short period, that is, short with respect to the total history and development of human culture. However, the power to open the shaft comes from God, not Satan. Satan is unable, by himself, to mobilise his forces of evil (9:1-2).

No angel retains permanent possession of the key to the abyss. Christ has the key (1:18); only Christ can give it. God exercises ultimate sovereignty over the satanic realm. The shaft (*abussos*) is bottomless (*a*, privative of the Greek word *buthos* meaning depth). The LXX similarly refers to *tehom* (the deep, Genesis 1:2; 7:11; Psalm 106:9; 107:26) or the depths of the earth (Psalm 71:20). The picture is that of a subterranean cavern connected to earth's surface by a shaft or well (*phreatos*) whose opening has a secure lid. The inhabitants of the abyss, the place of accumulated evil, include the demonic prince (9:11) and the beast (11:7; 17:8). Fallen angels are incarcerated in the abyss (20:1,3). The abyss thus houses awesome, unlimited, cruel and irresistible power.

Non-Biblical creation myths depict the deep as the source of chaotic powers. This mystery of evil, located in the abyss and intrinsic to it, is about to break loose upon the unbelievers of the world. Provoked by divine decree (9:3), the loosing of evil will inevitably lead to the end. Then God, good and order will be clearly differentiated from Satan, evil and chaos. This clarity will afford the world, which is passing away, a final opportunity to repent.

Like the divine judgement of Sodom (Genesis 19:28), smoke arises portending doom and judgement (9:17,18; 18:9,18; 19:3). The smoke may be coming from the fires of divine holiness at work within the pit. The smoke darkens the light of the sun and the air through which the light must pass. The darkness thus points to the loss of spiritual perception in the world. This is the power and terrible consequence of sin over humankind.

Demonic beings materialise from the smoke (9:3–11). They are armoured and have deadly tails; they evoke fear. These demonic beings are reminiscent of Joel's locust plague (Joel 1–2). They are led by the angel of the abyss and they cover the earth. Their animal-like characteristics draw attention to their ugliness.[1] Evil's army, like a locust plague, can be so steadily reinforced that no earthly order is free from attack. Evil is virulent and tenacious and seems to slow up the progress of the gospel. But evil is not overcoming the gospel, rather, the gospel generates a steady hardening of resistance leading inexorably to a last great climax.[2] The human problem of persistent and tormenting evil becomes habitual and demonically entrenched. People become virtually powerless and tormented when in the grip of punishment engendered by human abuses.[3] These evils may not, in themselves, kill. But evil is so noxious and debilitating that it leads to a wish for death (cf.

---

[1] Resseguie, 1998, 119.
[2] cf. Caird, 1966, 123.
[3] Krodel, 1989, 200.

9:5–6). Evil is a frighteningly striking perversion of the natural order. In Revelation 9 evil is so overwhelming that nothing less than a final stand by God will overcome it and break its resistance. John shatters once and for all the notion that the spread of the gospel will drive the tenacious, virulent power of evil into a corner like a wounded animal.[4]

Like the eighth exodus plague (Exodus 10:12–20), the demonic creatures (locusts, 9:3) emerging from the smoke are symbolic of the forces of evil (cf. Luke 10:19). These demonic creatures possess the power to torment. The locusts represent evil: a frightening blend of demonic and human with attractive features but with a sting to hurt. The reservoir that feeds the evil hoard is a bottomless pit. Divine judgement at work in the pit is now transferred to the world: the demonic creatures in the pit now effect God's judgement in the world. The grotesque description of the locusts portrays the character of evil: repulsive and totally abnormal (9:8), incredibly powerful (9:9), and cruel (9:10). These creatures are the irresistible agents of destruction spoken of in the Old Testament (Deuteronomy 28:38; 2 Chronicles 7:13; Joel 2:25). They are limitless in number (Psalm 105:34; Nahum 3:15). The demonic character of the Revelation locusts is evident in their attack on humanity, not nature. But limitations are imposed on them (9:4), for God controls this plague. In this world evil serves divine purposes! These demonic locusts can only go as far as God permits: their venom can only be directed against the unsealed (9:4); their attack is spiritual, not physical. The accumulated evil that these locusts represent is a further warning to the world's inhabitants. The purpose of the evil plague is to drive fallen humanity to repent (9:20). But the opportunity is not taken.

The locusts are limited in their power to hurt: they are not allowed to kill humans (9:10). Evil is prevented from operating outside of God's plan. God does not cut short the reign of evil for evil must be unmasked by humanity (17:16–17). And God is not willing that any should perish. Therefore, in the course of history, saints suffer in the world and the end does not come until every opportunity has been given to an obdurate creation to repent.

---

[4] Resseguie, 1998, 197–199.

The plague of demonic locusts (9:1–12)—with the concomitant physical, mental and spiritual torments—operates unremittingly for five months (9:5) which is approximately the duration of the normal locust life cycle. However, a locust plague only lasts a few days.[5] So the plague of demonic locusts is unique: these locusts are constantly destructive for their whole life cycle;[6] they do not devastate vegetation; but they torment unbelieving humans, their target is rebellious humankind.[7] The plague only affects unbelievers, moving them to desperation (9:6). This is the first woe (cf. 9:12)!

The spiritual difficulty into which unbelievers are plunged by the locusts[8] may be a deleterious life cycle from which they cannot escape (cf. Rom 1:19–32). Tormented, these unbelievers look to death to rescue them. But death is elusive, for God will not grant it. Human commitment to the evil that this attack signifies is the divine punishment!

9:7 is an application of Joel 1–2. The armour clad (cf. 9:9) locusts charged like warhorses: a hostile army on the move whose loud sound is terrifying. The overall picture is invincibility. On their heads the locusts wore what seemed to be crowns (*stephanos*, a victor's wreath, 9:7). The locusts were the victors; evil is dominant. However, the picture is illusory for what they wore were only 'like crowns'. The apparent crown was deception, not reality. The locusts also seemed to possess intelligence and reason, like humans (9:7); evil must always have a human face and mind. The Bible never speaks of 'natural evil' or 'fall of nature'. Evil always requires an evil will. 'Hair like women' (9:8) suggests that the locusts' appearance evokes thoughts of victory, power, intelligence, charm and fascination.[9] 9:7–8 suggests that the demonic evil represented by the locusts is attractive, fascinating and appealing. But the satanic deception has a sting in the tail, at the end. This is like the sting of evil that inflicts its ongoing torture, not to begin with when the lure is still charming and fascinating, but at the

---

5   G. R. Osborne, 2002, 368.
6   cf. Hoeksema, 2000, 319.
7   Beale, 1999, 496.
8   op. cit., 501.
9   Hoeksema, 2000, 319.

end. Their teeth, like the prophet Joel's invading locust army (Joel 1:6), are like lion's teeth: terrifying and voracious.

The commander of the locusts is 'the angel', that is, the satanic force named Abaddon (meaning place of destruction) (cf. Job 26:6; 28:22). Abaddon's name suits the plague. For Greek readers, John supplies a translation: Apollyon, equivalent to Abaddon, means destroyer. The calculated reference to the Greek god Apollo—known as the god of plagues and symbolised by, among other things, the locust—indicates irony obliquely directed against the emperor cult, with which Apollo would later be connected.[10] The Antichrist of the New Testament is called the 'son of destruction' (2 Thessalonians 2:3). Judas Iscariot is also referred to as the 'son of destruction' (John 17:12).[11] 9:12 indicates that the vision of the first woe is now concluded.

This puzzling fifth trumpet appears to present the terrible reality of evil affecting, in its intensity, the future. This evil requires a human face and will. Nothing is said about divine reaction to this evil. The divine response, which will surely come, seems to lie beyond the temporary presence of this terrible evil. The fifth trumpet is powerfully developed by the sixth trumpet.

Revelation 9:13–21 The Sixth Trumpet—Demonic Horses

The sixth trumpet blows, and a voice—probably that of an angel, perhaps the same angel as in 8:3 and 16:7—announces the second woe (9:13–11:14) from the midst of the horns of the golden altar of incense within the heavenly temple. The next woe is another trumpet plague. Like the fifth trumpet plague, this plague is another spiritual attack against non-believers (9:4). The context is the Euphrates, the eastern boundary of the Roman Empire beyond which lay the Parthians. The fifth trumpet's analysis of the seriousness of sin (9:1–11) is now translated into the deadly attack, the increasing severity, of the sixth trumpet (9:13–19).

In response to the sound of the trumpet, a voice relays a divine command (9:14) from the four horns—that is, the four corners—of the golden altar. The sound of the trumpet focuses the power of heaven in answer to the prayers of the saints (6:9–11; cf.

---

10 Krodel, 1989, 203.
11 Smalley, 2005, 234.

8:3). There are four angels at the Euphrates river that have until now been prevented from operating (cf. 7:1). Now they are released to initiate the attack for which they had been prepared (Greek perfect tense, 9:15). If these four angels are the angels referred to in 7:1, then what was anticipated in the destructive four winds is now happening (cf. the sixth bowl, also at the river Euphrates, 16:12–16).

The four evil angels may be representative of pagan powers beyond the Euphrates that were threatening Rome in the early Christian period. The area beyond the Euphrates was the point from which, in the Old Testament, the major attacks came on the people of God. The four angels are dedicated to effect universal (four = universality) destruction. But the sealed saints are secure (cf. 7:1–4). These evil powers had been prepared and bound for a very specific occasion (not duration, since one article governs the four nouns of time, 9:15). The precise moment had arrived. God's actions are carefully planned. Beale relates this sixth trumpet to Jeremiah 46:4, 22, 23 and the judgement coming against Egypt by the cavalry from the north.[12] In the Revelation sixth trumpet, there is a massive cavalry wearing breastplates.

The intensification of the sixth trumpet unleashes against unbelievers a force to kill, physically and spiritually, one third of the population (9:15). The four angels at the Euphrates materialise as a huge, evil, spiritual force of two hundred million demonic cavalry (cf. the mythology of Gog and his hordes, Ezekiel 38:9). This demonic calvary breathes fire, burning sulphur and smoke: three plagues (cf. the destruction of Sodom and Gomorrah, Genesis 19:24,28). The evil emanating at the sixth trumpet is of such a magnitude that it is impossible for humanity to overcome. The progress of the gospel cannot overcome this evil. Only the direct intervention by God will bring this colossus to heel.

Is the army used to accomplish this slaughter (9:16) men or demons? Their horses differ from human horses—fire, smoke, and brimstone proceed from their mouths—so the horses are demons. And it is the horses, rather than the horsemen, that are the actors in the slaughter. The number two hundred million is figurative in biblical usage, like ten thousand (especially when plural, cf.

---

12 1999, 507.

Genesis 24:60; Leviticus 26:8; Numbers 10:35–36; Deuteronomy 32:30). The army is an innumerable multitude. There is meaning in the imagery presented in this demonic army: coming from their mouths, the fire betokens judgement (cf. 1:16); they kill physically and spiritually (9:18), making it clear that unbelievers die in unbelief and are doomed; the fire and sulphur indicates that this judgement is eternal; the colour of their breastplates, deep blue or purple, reflects the colour of the smoke coming out of their mouths; this smoke, and consequent darkness, infers punishment by deception (cf. 8:12; 9:2–3); the focus on the mouth (9:18–19) points to deception or false teaching (cf. 2:6, 14–15, 20–21; also the mouth of the dragon, 12:16); and comparing the tails with serpents emphasises the lethal power of the horses.

Contemporaries of John could have applied this symbolism to the expectation of Nero's return at the head of innumerable Parthian hordes. But, rather, the entire presentation signifies divine judgement. God, controlling all history, turns evil to his own sovereign purposes. The vision of the horses' heads and the fire, smoke and brimstone that proceed from them is probably a reference to the fiery lake of burning sulphur where all evil will be obliterated (20:10; 21:8). The phrase 'in the vision' (9:17) underscores the highly symbolic nature of the judgement presented with the sixth trumpet.

The horses capture John's attention (cf. 9:7). Their majestic heads are like lions and the three destructive plagues (fire, smoke and sulphur) issue from their mouths. The threefold connection of fire, smoke, and sulphur resonates with other biblical destructions (Genesis 19:24–27; cf. Isaiah 30:33; Ezekiel 38:22): a sign of the destructive forces to follow. The colours of the breastplates (9:17), distinguished by definite articles, probably represent the three separate plagues (fire, smoke and sulphur, 9:18). And there are clear affinities with the locusts of the fifth trumpet (9:7–10). The horses' heads, like lions, emphasise their ferocity. The power of their tails is like snakes' mouths. The colour and character of their breastplates (red, blue and yellow) are correlated with the damage they will do with their mouths (fire, smoke and sulphur). So this great demonic assault at the sixth trumpet builds upon and intensifies the horse-like locusts that had been presented in the judgement of the fifth trumpet.

Breathing fire, smoke and brimstone (9:18)—satanic deception pouring from their mouths—draws on the analogy of the destruction rained on Sodom and Gomorrah. The searing power of the deceptive content of the demonic army takes various forms but always leads to death. The picture of demonic horses breathing out fire (cf. Leviathan, Job 41:19-21), with tails like serpents (a satanic allusion), is grotesque. Like the picture of evil presented in the fifth trumpet (9:1-11), the power of evil at the sixth trumpet is also in the tail. One third of the population is deceived and then killed, but probably not by a military assault.[13] Demonic powers are constrained (20:1-3, perhaps until 13:1) from deceiving the nations during the church age, that is, the millennium. But then, later, evil forces will have power for a little while to deceive the nations (cf. 20:1-3) as active opponents of God.

In spite of the plain evidence of God's wrath at work (9:20), the rest of men did not repent 'of the works of their hands' (an Old Testament term of derision for idolatry, cf. Psalm 115:4b-8). Their hearts were hardened. They continued to act as if the world was theirs despite the plain evidence to the contrary. Not even the final plague series of the bowls will make them repent of their world (16:21). By their evil, they continually rob God of the glory that is due to him alone. To worship idols constructed from created materials is, ultimately, to worship demons. So the reference to the works of men's hands (9:20) betokens idolatrous pursuits: idolatrous demon worship.

Unbelieving human conduct—murders, sorceries, sexual immorality, thefts (this fourfold listing appears again at 22:15 for exclusions from the new Jerusalem)—will continue to characterise the human world (9:21). The earth dwellers not only failed to repent of sins against the first table of the law (commandments one to four), but also those of the second (six to ten). Their sorceries and immorality, normally biblical watchwords for idolatry, were in addition to idolatry (9:20).

Following the sixth trumpet, the intensity of divine judgements is levelled on unbelief through evil being released from previous

---

13 Krodel, 1989, 206.

constraint. Whereas the fifth trumpet presented an analysis of evil, the sixth trumpet underlines human inability to deal with the almost indescribable colossus that evil presents in our world. Only God can deal with it. However, as evil grows and captures the entire world, at the end—paradoxically—evil will itself lead to the destruction of evil.

Severe world judgement fails to induce repentance. God's world plan is end-time victory by the Lamb. Victory will not come by world repentance but, rather, under judgements self-imposed by the world.[14] Jesus will, finally, judge by the word of his mouth (cf. 19:21). This word—a saving or damning word—was heard time and again over the years by many who took no heed. Those who persisted to the end in ignoring the truth must perish with their lies.[15] For us all, at the end, judgement will be the final confrontation with the truth of God in Jesus (cf. John 3:17–21; 12:46–49; Romans 2:2; 1 Corinthians 9:10–11). The failure of the sixth trumpet to evoke repentance will necessitate the blowing of the final seventh. Before the end, however, the church age must close and the church must be removed from the world.

---

14 Bauckham, 2004, 6.
15 Ibid.

Revelation 10

Revelation 10 The Open Scroll

10:1–11:13 and Revelation 7 are parallel in that they each speak of the church after the sixth judgement (seals, 6:17; trumpets, 9:20–21). These interruptions record the delay before the final judgement with the church in the world while the judgements of seals and trumpets are simultaneously proceeding. Accordingly, the presentation of the conflict between evil and the church in Revelation 10–15 is literary, not chronological. The reality of history is being viewed from two perspectives.

The first delay (7:1–17) shows that believers are protected; the second delay (10:1–11:13) records the prophetic witness of the church to the world. Two visions preceded the seventh seal (7:1–17); likewise, the vision of an angel with a little scroll (Revelation 10) and the account of two witnesses (11:1–13) intervene before the seventh trumpet (which is also the third woe). There is no judgement in this section (10:1–11:13) but there is consolation to believers.

'And I saw' (10:1) introduces the vision of 10:1–11:13. The church will minister in a disordered world in which the disasters of the seals and trumpets presently operate and proliferate. This interlude between the sixth and seventh trumpets is designed to motivate believers in their struggle with the forces of evil.[1] John is now on earth (10:1). The scroll opened by the Lamb in heaven is now brought to earth to be given to John to eat (cf. Ezekiel 2:8–3:3). God had provided the scroll (5:1), like the sealed scroll containing God's purpose in Daniel. The meaning of Daniel's vision, which predicted the events of the last days, was to be kept secret until the last days (Daniel 12:7,9). In Revelation 10 the angel announces that the last period that leads immediately to the end of history has now arrived: this is the time, times and half a time prophesied in the book of Daniel (Daniel 12:7). This time period appears in several forms in Revelation (11:2–3; 12:6,14; 13:5) but only outside Revelation in Daniel 7 and 12, where this formula for

---

1   Lioy, 2003, 141.

time specifically refers to the period of the last days. Significantly, the indication of the time appears immediately after John has ingested the scroll and begins to prophesy.

The mighty angel (10:1, cf. 5:2), directly from God's presence, comes down and places his right foot on the sea and his left foot on the land (10:2). The angel thus puts the whole world under the sphere of God's judgement. The angel's voice is like the roar of the lion (10:3). The hidden purposes of God in judgement (the mystery, 10:7) are now to be revealed: God's aim is to carry through his covenant with creation. The scroll is sweet in the mouth but bitter in the stomach when John eats it. After John has eaten the scroll, he is recommissioned (10:8–11). The sweet and bitter signifies the mixture of woe and triumph in anticipation of what is to follow (11:1–13).

The open scroll held by the strong angel in 10:2 is the scroll spoken of by the strong angel in 5:2.[2] The scroll (5:2; 10:2) has been opened by the Lamb in heaven and is now brought down by the angel for John to consume. John must absorb and reveal the words of the prophecy (10:10–11), as he does in 11:1–13 and more fully from Revelation 12 onwards. All that precedes the eating of the book is preparatory to the message of Revelation, which is John's commission to prophesy about the ministry of the church in the world. The first angel to mediate revelation to John is the strong angel in Revelation 10. And his message role is completed in Revelation 10 (he does not appear again, except perhaps at 22:6–9 where he shows John the vision of the new Jerusalem, being described in 21:9 as one of the seven angels who had the seven bowls full of the last seven plagues).

All parts of Revelation 6–11 are skilfully linked into Revelation 4–5. The two series of seven (seals and trumpets) develop sequentially out of the vision of the Lamb and the scroll (Revelation 5). The Lamb had opened each seal and the seventh seal opening entailed the onset of the trumpet blasts. Both series are linked at their climactic conclusions (8:5; 11:19) to the vision before the divine throne (4:5). However, the two interpolations (7:1–17 and 10:1–11:13) have their own links with Revelation 5. The second

---

2 Bauckham, The Theology of the Book of Revelation, 1993, 81–82.

insertion (10:1–11:13) contains the event to which Revelation 5 looks forward: the contents of the scroll revealed.[3]

The description of the mighty angel—coming down from heaven clothed in clouds—is normally a sign of a heavenly ascent/descent of God or the Son of Man. This powerful heavenly emissary is presented more elaborately than any other angel in Revelation (cf. 18:1). This angel is, therefore, uniquely important. But doubtless, even though he is similarly described (cf. 1:15–16), he is far less important than Christ.

The rainbow on the angel's head is part of the glory of the heavenly throne (Ezekiel 1:28). This glorious rainbow headdress is also a sign of divine assurance that the creation covenant is being fulfilled (cf. Genesis 9:12–13). The description of the angel is invested with glory and great majesty, with his face—like Christ—like the sun (Matthew 17:2). The cosmic stance of his feet astride land and sea is unparalleled, demonstrating God's sovereignty over all creation. Cloud and fire (10:1) may hark back to God's leading of Israel in the exodus. Pillars of fire, as in the exodus, may indicate divine protection for the saints. But 'fire' is also a sign of judgement, this time on the world as a whole. By planting his feet on the land and the sea the angel declares universal judgement; his gigantic size and posture indicate that his message relates to the whole world.

The scroll in the angel's hand is an opened scroll (10:2,8; cf. the sealed scroll at 5:2), the contents of which are now to be made known. Bauckham suggests that most commentators have been misled by the diminutive (*biblaridion*, 10:2) to suppose that this scroll or book is another scroll. However, like many diminutives of the period, *biblaridion* is probably being used as a synonym for *biblion* (5:2–9; 10:8). Moreover, John carefully equates the two words, so that the distinction is not between a large and small scroll but between a sealed and open scroll.[4] The little scroll of Revelation 10 appears to be the same, or at least part of the same scroll as that of 5:2. Boring draws attention to the Old Testament background (Daniel 12:1–10). The Daniel scroll contained details of a great tribulation, a resurrection and a judgement, all to be

---

[3] cf. Bauckham, The Climax of Prophecy, 1993, 243–57.
[4] Boring, 1989, 140.

sealed until the time of the end. There is to be a time of trouble such as has never been (Daniel 12:1), which must be experienced and overcome by the saints (Revelation 11:1–13).

The Lamb had opened the scroll in God's hand (6:1–8:1). Now the strong angel takes it from heaven to earth (10:1–2) and gives it to the prophet to eat (10:8–10). This movement corresponds exactly to 1:1. In Revelation 10, John is presented as a prophet like Ezekiel: for both John and Ezekiel the prophecy ends with the establishment of the temple and God perpetually present in the temple-city. Throughout Revelation 4, 5 and 10, John is following the inaugural vision of Ezekiel: the divine throne (Revelation 4, Ezekiel 1) prepares for the communication of a message to the prophet; the scroll containing the message (5:1; Ezekiel 2:9–10); God himself opening the scroll (5:5; Ezekiel 2:10); God giving the scroll to the prophet with the command to eat (10:9–10; Ezekiel 3:1–2), symbolising the prophet's absorption of the entire message; and the scroll being as sweet as honey in his mouth (10:10; Ezekiel 3:3). But in Revelation the scroll becomes bitter in John's stomach (10:10) because of the opposition that its proclamation will create.[5] For both John and Ezekiel, the contents of the scroll cannot be revealed until its contents have been ingested by the prophet.

Before the scroll is given to John to eat, its significance is further clarified (10:3–7) by the seven thunders after the angel's arresting shout. The angel's cry was full of power and vengeance, like a lion's roar (*mukatai*, cf. Amos 3:7–8), evoking fear. The seven thunders may be a further series of judgements following the first two series of judgements (seals and trumpets; cf. Psalm 29 concerning God's rule from his throne, when the voice of the Lord—depicted as thunders—is mentioned seven times).

In Psalm 29 the seven thunders sound in celebration of the power of God as ruler of creation. John hears—and perhaps understands—the thunders. He is about to write what he heard when he hears a voice from heaven, direct from the throne, and he is told not to write down the thunders (10:4). This may mean that the thunders are further judgements proposed to display the complete purpose of God in bringing in the kingdom, but they are not

---

5 Resseguie, 1998, 98.

yet required. However, more probably, John is required to seal up what the thunders uttered because these seven thunders are a complete display of God's impending judgement. As such the seven thunders would signal the end. But the end is at present deferred until the ministry of the church in tribulation and victory is completed. Only after the ministry of the church is completed will the finality of divine judgement on the world be felt. This is in accord with Daniel 12:4 where the divine disclosure is sealed since it is not a judgement for the present course of history but one for the end, to bring history to a conclusion. There is more to be revealed about the plan leading to the end. The Greek construction ('do not write') is punctual, meaning, 'do not write at this point but keep it in mind for the future'.[6] The tenor of the heavenly announcement is that the church age must intervene before the final judgement process ushering in the end can begin. This is what is reported in 11:1–13 (perhaps the contents of the little scroll). After the church age, the seventh trumpet will sound and the bowl judgements that inaugurate the end of history will commence.

The revocation of the seven thunders is followed by the angel's solemn declaration (10:5–6), where he 'raised his right hand to heaven and swore'. The oath is 'by him who lives forever and ever': by God as the eternally existent sovereign Creator (10:6). The oath itself—it 'will be accomplished' without delay (10:7)—reflects Daniel 12:7. The oath recognises the immense power of God to exercise judgement over everything created, including his authority over the powers of evil which are about to come upon the Revelation scene. Lifting up the hand signifies acceptance of personal responsibility for the content.[7] Those who invoke the divine name place themselves under the power and judgement of Yahweh. The angel swears by the eternity of God the Creator, since the coming judgements will mean that he who created the world will end it.

The angelic pronouncement that there will be no more time is an indication that the end of history is at hand (Revelation 11–18; cf. Daniel 12:1–13, the prophecy of the end which is now to be com-

---

6   cf. Ruiz, 2006, 100.
7   Osborne, 2002, 398 (with references).

pleted).[8] The Antichrist—the visible presence on earth of evil—is coming, but he will be defeated. Then eternity will commence (Revelation 19–21). However (*alla*, 10:7), at the sounding of the seventh trumpet (11:15–19) the mystery of God will be finally revealed: the divine secrets that have been hidden from past generations will be revealed by God to his people as the conclusion of his plan. The kingdoms of the world will have become his kingdom (11:15). All three spheres of life in this world (heaven, earth and sea, 10:6) will be affected. The angel who swore the oath (10:5) brings the oath into being (10:6). There is to be no more delay, for the time of the eschaton predicted by Daniel has arrived.[9]

Describing God as Creator (10:6) recalls the living creatures worshipping at the throne (4:9–10), just as the rainbow on the head of the angel (10:1) recalls the rainbow around the divine throne (4:3). The work of this angel, judgemental in character, contributes to the stability of the transformed creation. The message and work of this angel is from the God who created the whole world, reigns in heaven, and has bound himself to the whole of creation in the creation covenant.

God himself announced the 'mystery of God' to his servants the prophets (cf. Amos 3:7). Daniel's 'time, times and half a time' (Daniel 12:7) in which God's secret purpose (*mysterion*, 10:7) for the coming kingdom is to be accomplished, has now arrived (11:1–13). Daniel did not understand the words of the man clothed in linen (Daniel 12:8). Daniel was told that the contents of the scroll were to remain sealed until the end (Daniel 12:9). The disclosure is now being made by God to John. What was sealed at the time of Daniel—that is, the purposes of God for the coming of his kingdom—is now unsealed for John. Therefore, the end has now arrived (cf. 10:6 'time will be no longer').

10:7 does not say that God revealed his secret to his servants the prophets, but that he announced it. That God would reveal the mystery was known (as was the promise of the gospel, cf. Romans 1:2). Daniel's 'time, times and half a time', now to begin, will bring in the kingdom. Thus, the content of the scroll is 'what must soon take place' (1:1; 22:6). However, the scroll will not give any more

---

8   Beal, 1999, 540.
9   Daniel 11:29–12:13 (cf. Smalley, 2005, 264).

information about the length of the final period than has already been given by God to Daniel.

However, whereas the scroll does not give any further definition about the length of the end time, it does reveal further information about the nature of the time of the end; that is, the scroll reveals the way in which events that were so mysterious in the prophecies of Daniel and the other prophets will now contribute to the coming of God's kingdom. The 'end of the delay' is not the end, rather, it refers to the days of the sounding of the seventh trumpet covers including the bowl or end-time judgements. The mystery of God (that he will finally bring in his kingdom, 10:7) reaches fulfilment in these days, including: the end-time suffering of the people of God, God's intervention, and the rule of the saints (cf. Daniel 12:7 in the context of Daniel 11:29–12:13).[10] The rule of the saints will not happen until the 'shattering of the holy people' (Daniel 12:7) has occurred (cf. Revelation 12–13).

The further revelation of the contents of the scroll (Revelation 5) must be the outworking of the Lamb's conquest in establishing the kingdom of God. The church is the subject of this little scroll. Therefore the church—already God's kingdom in a world that contests his rule—will be significant for the universal coming of the kingdom.

The church has already been spiritually preserved (sealed) from judgements on the evil world (7:1–3). The account of this spiritual sealing is placed at the same point in the series of seal judgements as the open scroll section (10:1–11:13) in the series of trumpet judgements (that is, between the sixth and seventh items). The relationship between these two passages (the sealing of the saints and the open scroll) is that the little scroll reveals more fully the tribulations through which the church must pass to bring in the end. This seeming triumph of the world (Revelation 13) over the church will end in the world's defeat. This reveals a mystery. The gospel of the advent of the kingdom of God (cf. Mark 1:15), which was communicated to Old Testament prophets, is that the world is defeated at the very point where it seems to be in triumph over the church. The world is always living precariously because of humankind's addiction to evil. But God will vindicate

---

10 cf. Beale, 1999, 541–7.

his people and give peace to them on a transformed earth forevermore. This is the focus of the remaining chapters of Revelation. Judgements have failed to bring the world to repentance and faith in God, so the scroll reveals a more effective strategy.

John is now commanded to take the scroll from the angel (10:8). God's sovereignty and purposes must now be made known. When John is told to take and eat the scroll, he commits himself to an Ezekiel type vision of the shape of the way to the end (10:8–10; cf. Ezekiel 2:9–3:3). The taste is sweet because it is God's word of final vindication for the church. But it is bitter when swallowed because there will be preceding judgement, great suffering and persecution for the people of God. Only when the seven seals have been opened by the Lamb in heaven (6:1,3,5,7,9,12; 8:1)—so that God's plan for history has been announced through them—can the scroll be taken by the angel to earth for John to eat as a fuller exposition of the plan (10:1–2).

Thus the little scroll (Revelation 10) offered by the angel (10:9) indicates the nature of events, including the seventh bowl and the consummation, at the time of the end. It produces world-wide what Ezekiel's ingestion of the bitter-sweet scroll was intended to do (cf. Ezekiel 2–3), that is: the founding of the new Jerusalem, the temple city and the new creation. But in the world the message of this unfolding mystery will be received as negatively as Ezekiel's message was received in exiled Israel. Ezekiel's prophecy is of a reborn Israel, united and now fulfilled with the gift of the Spirit at Pentecost (Ezekiel 37). This new Israel is committed to a suffering ministry—like Jesus—with vindication to come through God, but only at the Parousia.

Having digested the scroll, John is given his prophetic commission: 'You must (by divine necessity, *dei*) again prophesy against (*epi*) many peoples and nations and languages and kings' (10:11). The negative use of this fourfold formula (peoples, nations, languages, kings) in Revelation begins at 10:11 and continues therefrom. This is John's future ministry. The 'again' indicates that this is a renewal of his earlier commission. The prophecies of the remainder of the book are therefore more burdensome, directed against the four groups (peoples, nations, languages, kings) by the believing and witnessing community. After eating the scroll

(Ezekiel 3:3), Ezekiel was given his prophetic commission. Ezekiel's commission was to disobedient Israel, not to many nations and peoples. But the cross displaced national Israel. So the message is now to all the disobedient world. Ezekiel's allusion to 'many peoples' (Ezekiel 3:6) is expanded in Daniel 7:14—'peoples, nations and languages'—to which Revelation adds 'kings' (10:11), making the social adjustment appropriate to the time.

John's fourfold phrase (peoples, nations, languages, kings, 10:11) is one variation of a formula that is used seven times in Revelation to refer to all nations (5:9; 7:9; 10:11; 11:9; 13:7; 14:6; 17:15). However, 10:11 is the only variation where 'many' and 'kings' (usually the formula includes 'tribes') are included in the formula. The use of the fourfold formula and the substitution of 'kings' characterises the subject matter of John's prophecy—the content of the scroll—as that of Daniel 7: the triumph of the saints through the Son of Man. The books of judgement had been opened to bring into being the acknowledged kingdom of God. John's pronouncement is to affect the whole world.

The first mention of Daniel's time period formula—time and times and half a time (Daniel 7:25)—is in the context of the coming of God's kingdom. The theme of Daniel 7 was the transfer of sovereignty over 'all peoples, nations and languages' from the world empires (represented by the beasts) to one like unto a Son of Man and the people of the Most High:[11] the advent of the visible kingdom of God. John's little scroll is about the way in which this transfer of sovereignty is to occur. Before 10:11, the fourfold formula has been used to refer to the church, not to nations (cf. 5:9; 7:9). The church is drawn from all nations and witnesses to all nations. The subject of the church's witness in Revelation 11 is taken further in Revelation 12-15, and includes the final seven bowl judgements introduced within the body of Revelation 15.

John has not been commanded previously in Revelation to prophesy. However, he is being told here to prophesy *palin* (again, 10:11). The earlier command to write to the seven churches (1:19) was, implicitly, a command to prophesy.[12] Thus John's prophecy from Revelation 10:11 onwards is being compared to the earlier

---

11 cf. Beale, 1999, passim.
12 Beale, 1999, 555.

prophecies of Revelation 2–3, which were prophecies to and about churches. The scroll reveals further that the earlier prophecies to the churches were preparing them for their role in the last days. The new concern from 10:11 onwards is the church's prophetic witness to the rebellious nations.

Revelation 11

Revelation 11-13 The Church Age

Revelation 11:1-13 A Summary of Christian Witness

There is a direct link (and, *kai*, 11:1) between Revelation 10 and Revelation 11, that is, *kai* indicates that Revelation 11 is the outworking of the content of the scroll (Revelation 10) in the Christian age. Revelation 11 reviews the church age, showing how the kingdoms of the world become the kingdom of God (11:15). Particular features of the church age follow (Revelation 12-13). But is it possible to reconcile the expectations of Revelation 11 with the realities of church history? 11:1-2 presents the church as always being under threat from the world, yet triumphing (11:3-6). This seems inconsistent with the record of church history. The text presents the church as being phenomenally successful in witness throughout its history (11:3-6). Then the laconic 11:7 has the beast, whose character is seen in his many forays throughout history (cf. Daniel 7:1ff), rising from the abyss (the text seems to indicate a process rather than an event). Under satanic direction, the beast's presence throughout the history of the church finally succeeds to provide a world alternative to the church. The beast then replaces the church with its alternative before the Parousia (11:7).

Revelation 11 moves from the earthly temple under continuous threat (11:1-2) to the heavenly temple from which God's eternal reign over the world is declared (11:15-19, the central message of John's prophecy and the summary of the remainder of the book). A series of enigmatic images, to be drawn out later, is introduced in 11:1-13, including: the great city (11:8); the beast and his war against the saints (11:7); and the symbolic time period (11:2-3) as the period of the church's conflict with the beast. 11:1-2 appear to present a summary of 11:1-13.

The placement of Revelation 11 is to indicate how the church's witness to the nations from Pentecost to the Parousia must proceed before the final judgement (the seventh trumpet, with which God's kingdom finally comes, 11:15-19). This witness of the church—sealed from ultimate spiritual failure—to the world will produce the warfare described in 7:1–8, the great tribulation produced by world idolatry. Christian witness in the face of world opposition must precede the visible advent of the kingdom of God (cf. Daniel 7; 12:1–7). Then Revelation 12–15 speaks of the church's victorious conflict through Christ over the powers of evil. Then, in Revelation 15–22, this victorious conflict is integrated into an extended account of the final judgement.

11:1–13 is about the witness and vindication of the church on earth during the first six trumpets. The first of its two parts is unique in that only here in the whole book is John commanded to perform a symbolic prophetic action (11:1–2). Thus John has begun to fulfil his prophetic commission (10:11; cf. the pattern in Ezekiel 8–9 in which the commissioning was similarly followed by symbolic actions). John's starting point relates to Daniel 12:7–8. The answer of the man clothed in linen to Daniel's question—'how long' would persecution last—was a time, times and half a time. When the shattering of the power of the holy people finishes (Daniel 12:7), then all these things (namely, the events leading immediately to the end) would be accomplished (cf. 11:1). 11:3-14 will implement this scenario.

The sanctuary that John measures must be a temple building containing the holy place and the holy of holies (cf. Ezekiel 40–42). The word *naos* (temple, sanctuary) did not normally include the outer courts. The unprotected court outside the sanctuary—immediately outside the temple building—was called the court of the priests in New Testament times. It contained the altar of burnt offering. However, the altar (11:1) does not refer to the altar of burnt offering. Rather, *to thusiasterion* (11:1) refers to the golden altar of incense in the holy place. The reference to 'those who worship in it' (*en auto*) could mean those who worship 'at the altar' but, most naturally, the meaning is those who worship where the golden altar is situated in the 'sanctuary' (as opposed to the outer courts). When *to thusiasterion* (altar) is used without qualification it would refer only to the altar of burnt offering in the unprotected court outside the temple building (*naos*). But John has qualified *to thusiasterion* in 11:1. So, fulfilling the symbolism, those who worship in the sanctuary must be the priests (that is, true believers) who alone could enter the holy place and offer incense on the altar of incense.

John measures the temple for its protection (as in Zechariah 2:1-5, the measurer is a protector). In this case the measuring 'reed' is a rod. The rod is normally an instrument of dominion and royal power or authority (cf. Psalm 2:9).[1] What is not measured is profane (11:2); what is measured is within the domain of God's holiness.[2] However, John measures both the temple and the worshippers thereby indicating a separation between those who will be saved and those who will be condemned (cf. 2 Samuel 8:2).[3] Spatafora suggests that the outer court represents the sinful, human dimension of the church including those members who reflect the values of the world.[4] However, the measuring actually separates between: the certainty of spiritual protection for the saints who are priests within the new temple structure; and the same group (saints who are priests) when exposed in the outer court to the nations, and thus under persecution. John measures only the sanctuary building (*autoi*, 11:1 = *naos* = church) containing the altar of incense and the priests who worship there, symbolising the failure of the nations—try as they might by defilement and destruction—to prevail against Christ's true church of committed believers (cf. Ezekiel 40:1-6; 42:20; Zechariah 2:5).

Daniel used temple imagery to make the point that the nations had removed the altar of burnt offering (cf. Daniel 8:11; 11:31; 12:11) and erected the idolatrous 'transgression that makes desolate' (Daniel 8:13) or the abomination that makes desolate (Daniel 11:31; 12:11). Presumably the transgression or abomination is in place of the altar of burnt offering. A parallel image in Revelation—'given over to the nations' (11:2)—seems to refer to the termination of public worship (cf. 11:7). The believing community is the holy city (11:2b). The conjunction of the threat to the holy city with a time limit stretching to the Parousia (11:2b) presents a believing church resilient under profound opposition (cf. 11:7) in the period prior to the Lord's return.

---

1   Hoeksema, 2000, 370.
2   cf. Smalley, 2005, 271.
3   Spatafora, 1997, 164.
4   Ibid., 172; cf. also Jaubianinu, 2002, 507-526.

Revelation does not indicate that the Daniel prophecy is to be fulfilled by the temple building itself being given to the Gentiles. Since the daily sacrifices on the altar are to be abolished (Daniel 8:11; 11:31; 12:11), then the court outside the sanctuary must fall into the hands of unbelievers. Revelation states that the outside court is 'given over' to them (cf. Daniel 8:13). John picks up the word 'trampling' from Daniel 8:13 when he states that the nations will trample the holy city and the host of believers (11:2; cf. Daniel 8:13–14 and Daniel 9:24 to interpret the forty-two month period). The 'holy city', always spiritually protected (11:1), is not a place; the holy city is the believing community.[5]

Forty-two months is given for the rebellious world to engage in Satanic persecution against the church. The woman is protected from the opposition of the dragon for the same time period (12:6, 14). This is a period of tribulation for God's people (cf. 1 Kings 16:29–18:46; Jeremiah 52). The trouble is being stirred up by a world in the grip of the sea beast for the same time period (cf. 13:5). Zechariah 12:3 also refers to all the nations coming against Jerusalem in the last days. Thus 11:1–2 interprets two Old Testament prophecies: Daniel 8:11–14 and Zechariah 12:3. So the contents of the Revelation scroll give further light on what had remained mysterious to Daniel in Daniel 8:11–14.

The temple referred to in Revelation is not the temple in Jerusalem which was destroyed in A.D. 70. Neither is earthly Jerusalem or existing Israel referred to in Revelation. Rather, the temple and the holy city are taken up as earthly symbols of the people of God. Furthermore, Revelation takes Daniel 8:11–13 to refer to the same events as those of Daniel 12:7, namely 'the shattering of the power of the holy people' (cf. Daniel 7:25). This 'shattering' is also the 'trampling' of the holy place and city (Daniel 8:13). However, Revelation's view of Daniel 8:11–13 stresses what is no more than implicit in Daniel; throughout the shattering and trampling, the sanctuary with its altar—and the priests who worship in it—are preserved from defilement and trampling by the nations.

Thus the inner, hidden reality of the church as a kingdom of priests (5:10; cf. the 'holy city' in 11:2b) who worship God in his presence is distinguished from the outward experience of the

---

5   cf. the phrase 'the new Jerusalem', 21:2,10; 22:19 (Beale, 1999, 568).

church exposed to persecution by the kingdoms of the nations (11:2a). No inner defilement or hostile outward opposition will bring down the true church on earth (11:2b). It is the church of Christ, therefore it must follow the her Lord in ministry, death, resurrection, and ascension. The term 'holy city' (11:2b) distinguishes the faithful people of God from both apostate people who are now rejected by God and the unbelieving world. 'Holy City' thus refers to the true church in the world: 'measured' and thereby kept safe spiritually but outwardly suffering under persecution, including martyrdom (11:2a). Using different imagery, the measuring of the temple is like Revelation 7 where the servants of God are kept safe by the seal on their foreheads as they soldier on in the world.

11:2 provides a link between Daniel's prophecy and what happens in 11:3–13. The three and a half year time-period of both 11:2 and 11:3 is the time period covered by Daniel's prophecy. But 11:3–13 employs far less of Daniel's imagery (only 11:7, which alludes to Daniel 7:21) than 11:1–2. The message of the scroll is that whereas the divine intention is the 'shattering of the power of the holy people' (Daniel 12:7), even so, their hopes of entering the new Jerusalem will not be shattered.

In the midst of persecution those who truly worship God are kept spiritually safe in the sanctuary, the hidden presence of God. During the same period (but differently represented): the sanctuary is protected; the holy city is trampled; the witnesses prophesy (11:1–3); the heavenly woman who has given birth to the Messiah is kept safe in the wilderness (12:6,13–16); and the dragon in his pursuit of the heavenly woman turns to attack her children (12:17). Her refuge in the wilderness is the same spiritual haven as the sanctuary (11:2). She is kept safe while the beast rules and puts her children to death (13:5–7). The heavenly woman is the mother of the covenant people of God: of Jesus and Christians; of Eve and Mary; and of Israel, Zion and the church. She is the female figure corresponding to the holy city (11:2). From all this it follows that the 'killing of the church' (11:7) refers only to the public expression of the faith.

Revelation 11:3-13 Two Witnesses

11:3-13 is distinct in that it is not a vision or even an interpretation of a vision (cf. 17:7-18 which is the interpretation of a vision). Rather, 11:3-13 is a narrative prophecy comparable in form with Daniel 11. These verses show the ministry of the church to the world in the two spheres identified in 11:1-2 (inner sanctuary and outer world), with the same result for the church in the world. The church is never in spiritual danger and will ultimately be caught up to God. The two passages (11:1-2 and 11:3-13) are linked to each other and to the Daniel prophecy by the time period given in two different forms (11:2 and 11:3). That is, linked by equivalent time periods, but distinguished by different forms of the time period and also different imagery.

11:3-13 is a kind of parable. Two individual prophets represent the church's divinely permitted prophetic witness to the world in the final period of 1260 days (11:3, cf. for the required two witnesses, Numbers 35:30; Deuteronomy 17:6; 19:15). This parallels both the three and one half years of Jesus' earthly ministry and the time of persecution for the whole church (cf. 11:2; 12:6,14; 13:6).[6] The witness of the church is now shown to be effective, even though only two of the seven churches (Revelation 2-3) escaped the Lord's rebuke.

The symbols of the two witnesses representing the church in Revelation are: two lampstands (11:4; cf. 1:20), indicating that the witness of the church is to provide light for the world; and two olive trees (11:4; cf. Zechariah 4), indicating that the church is sustained by the Spirit as kings and priests for prophetic witness. Zechariah 4 includes a vision of a solid gold lampstand with a bowl at the top. On the lampstand there are seven lights with seven channels to the seven lights. In Zechariah's vision, two olive trees stand on either side of the lampstand (Zechariah 4:2-3), connected by pipes to the lampstand (4:12). The olive tree on the right of the bowl is Zerubbabel, the kingly person. The olive tree on the left of the bowl is Joshua, the priest. In Zechariah's vision, the lampstand is the temple and the seven lights are the eyes of the Lord which range throughout the earth (4:10). The message of

---

6   Beale, 1999, 574.

Zechariah was that God would rebuild the temple and that his Spirit would overcome Israel's opponents. Through Zerubbabel, the Spirit would level the mighty mountain (4:7; cf. the opposition described in Ezra 4–5). God guided the two leaders (king and priest) in the completion of their task of temple building. Thus, by analogy, the two olive trees in Revelation (11:4) are the two witnesses. Since the two witnesses are two lampstands representing the true church, they stand before the Lord (Zechariah 4:14) and provide light for the world. The lampstands are the church in an active prophetic role of witness to the world. The Spirit empowers the church in prophetic witness to the world and preserves the established new temple (11:2).[7]

In Zechariah 4 the oil of the spirit is channelled to the community through the two leaders, but in Revelation the Spirit is not channelled to the community through the two witnesses. As prophets, the witnesses must have been anointed with the oil of the Spirit.[8] Signs which afflict their persecutors accompany their ministry (11:5; cf. 2 Kings 1:1–14). The signs include: the shutting of the heavens like Elijah (11:6a; cf. 1 Kings 17:1); turning water into blood like Moses (11:6b; Exodus 7:14–21); and every kind of plague (11:6c; Exodus 9:13–14; 1 Samuel 6). Failure to repent at their witness will result in the death of the persecuting world.

The background of the imagery in 11:3–6 is Moses and Elijah, the two significant 'witnesses' of the Old Testament. But the Revelation witnesses are not a portion of the church, rather, the whole church is equipped with powers like Moses and Elijah (shutting the sky against rain, turning water into blood, smiting with every plague).[9] The witnesses are clothed in sackcloth like Elijah (2 Kings 1:8) and John the Baptist (Mark 1:6). Sackcloth is worn to mourn for the sin of the nations (Joel 1:8; Amos 8:10) or to express sorrow for sin (Jonah 3:5–9). The church's witness is a call for repentance. The witnesses proclaim the coming judgement of the one true God upon evil, to a world addicted to idolatry and evil. Their warning still offers humanity time to repent. Old Testament prophecy identified the need for Israel's witness, but Israel's

---

7   cf. Bauckham, The Climax of Prophecy, 1993, 165; Beale, 1999, 577–578.
8   Siew, 2005, 234.
9   cf. Boring, 1989, 146.

defective witness had estranged the nations. The two Revelation witnesses affect the whole world in their ministry. The people of God have been redeemed out of all the nations (5:9–10) by prophetic witness (11:3–13). The witnesses are committed to overcoming the world through suffering and rejection.

The church is presented in terms of spiritual authority (11:3), protective spirituality (11:4), and prodigious power (over fire and water like Elijah and Moses, 11:5–6). The church advances resolutely against the gates of hell. Nothing is able to break the spirit of the church or to deflect it from its goals or prevent it from accomplishing its God-appointed tasks. The church is the true Israel (11:4), threatened (11:5) but never overcome, calling to its support divine power like that which had been given to Moses and Elijah (11:6). In this era of Christendom, the ministry of the church is remarkable and world-changing.

The witnesses have the power to devour their enemies by the fire of their word (11:5). So the witnesses are spiritually immune from attack for as long as—but no longer than—they need to complete their testimony (cf. 11:7). That is, the concept and expression of their witness is protected by divine provision. The fire coming from their mouths is judgemental proclamation of the word (cf. Jeremiah 5:14). The judgements foreshadowed (11:5) are the series of bowl judgements.

The witnesses call upon God and receive power (11:6) from him to complete their testimony. Through the two witnesses divine judgements are being executed, indeed, their ministry evidences every kind of plague (summarising the first four trumpets and bowls). However, the two witnesses are not Moses and Elijah come to life again since the power of both is attributed to each witness (11:6).

The witnesses have delegated power that signifies the ability of the Spirit through them to complete their mission, even in the face of the beast's persecution of the church. Their signs of divine judgement—shutting the sky, turning the waters into blood, striking the earth with plagues—are commensurate with their preaching of repentance, in accordance with the sackcloth they are wearing (11:3). Like Moses and Elijah (cf. 11:6), the two witnesses confront pagan rulers and pagan religion.[10] The church in prophetic power will confront the world. Indeed, the prophetic power of the two witnesses even exceeds that of Moses and Elijah, for the two witnesses call on their extraordinary ability whenever they wish (11:6). Therefore, the power of the testimony of the two witnesses (the church) exceeds the greatest demonstration of prophetic witness under the old covenant. This power is required because, under the new covenant, the world enters the visible church in a way that never took place under the old covenant.

Beale shows that the two witnesses (11:3) are not individuals but, rather, that they represent the true Israel (that is, the church). Beale's argument is as follows. First, the two witnesses are identified as the two lampstands (11:4; cf. Zechariah 4:1–14), replacing Zechariah's seven branched (all Israel) lampstand. Secondly, the depiction of the beast making war with the two witnesses (11:7) relates to Daniel 7:21 in which the last evil kingdom makes war with the true Israel (not with individuals). Thirdly, the whole world witnesses the death and resurrection of the witnesses (11:9–11). The two witnesses represent God's empowering presence in the world through the unquenchable Spirit (cf. Zechariah 4:6–9) in the church, putting the world on trial (John 16:8–11) during the time in which the church in the world is threatened and persecuted. Fourthly, the two witnesses are the church as kings and priests in faithful witness. The church is like the royal Zerubbabel and the priestly Joshua (Zechariah 4), on either side of the lampstand, through whom the Spirit works to rebuild the temple. Fifthly, in Revelation testimony is a function of the whole church (6:9; 12:11,17; 19:10; 20:4). And, sixthly, 11:3 explains 11:2 which in turn refers to the holy city or total people of God.[11]

The power of the church through the Spirit of Christ is on display in the two witnesses, as the church changes the world in this divinely favoured time for Christian witness. Persecution is mentioned (11:5) but readily quelled. In my judgement this era of the two witnesses presents the golden age of the Christian world movement: the millennium, the thousand years (20:1–3) when the devil—though always active (cf. 11:2)—is prevented from

---

10 Bauckham, The Climax of Prophecy, 1993, 277.
11 Beale, 1999, 574–5.

deceiving the nations (not just unbelieving individuals). During this period there was, as always within the church: inner division, corruption, and general weakness. Church unity was always imperilled; church growth was always blemished. However, the work of God through the church is aptly described in a grandiloquent way for God works his great task through an imperfect church. The blemishes are human but the results are divine.

This golden age of the church will end before the return of Christ. The witnesses finish their ministry when the gospel is preached to all the world. When effective Christian ministry has finished, *the* beast—that is, the well-known ten horned and little horned beast (Daniel 7:7–12)—rises (Greek present tense) from the abyss and kills the witnesses (11:7). This brief description identifies the Revelation beast as the incarnation of evil who wages war against the saints in Daniel's prophecy (Daniel 7:21). The use of the article *to* points to the beast's well-known character in this new phase of his infamous career (cf. Revelation 13). This represents a devilish attack on the church. Caird states, with regard to this passage: 'Wherever men lay claim to despotic power, refusing to acknowledge that they are responsible for the use to which they put it, there the monster rises from the abyss'.[12] Revelation 13 is the height of demonic opposition, it speaks of the apparent victory of satanic might. This 'overcoming' by the world, paradoxically, fulfils the testimony of the two witnesses by their death.

The beast is presented as 'coming up' out of the abyss (chaos, 13:1). The beast comes with the same intent as the four beasts of Daniel 7:1–8, namely, to do battle with the saints and destroy them. 'Coming up' probably refers to the beast's gradual assumption of power. The beast becomes a presence in the world which is gradually perceived to be significant and, finally, dominant. As far as the church is concerned, there will have been many preliminary skirmishes before the beast comes to final prominence with outright restrictions and persecutions imposed on the church. The bald result of the 'death of the church' (11:7) comes after a length of time during which the beast's world power and influence are growing until, finally, it has total control over the world. The

---

[12] 1966, 137.

beast 'kills' the church, that is, it brings to an end the free course of the gospel in the world. Then with the two witnesses overcome, the age of the church will give way to an era of demonic opposition and apparent victory of satanic power. This 'overcoming' of the church by the world is, paradoxically, all in the plan of God (11:1–13). But some form of Christian witness continues until the Parousia (cf. 11:3). So the 'death' of the church must mean that the church is driven underground for the three and one half days of the beast's total control of world authority; during this time period the church is totally banned or discredited. However, the church's spiritual state remains unaffected (cf. 11:1–2). This is the period of the three woes (cf. 8:13). The beginning two woes (Revelation 9) represent the overpowering presence of evil in the world, now directed against non-Christians.

Revelation 13 and 17 elaborate on the role and function of the beast. The puzzle, however, in 11:3–6 is the way in which the ministry of the two witnesses is presented as totally authoritative and totally victorious. There is no hint in 11:3–6 of the abrupt death of the church in 11:7. Despite its success in the preaching of the eternal gospel (cf. 14:6), the ministry of the witnesses will come to an end.

Thus the effective witness of the church had persisted, even though she is always replete with the blemishes and problems of a movement comprising fallen humanity (Revelation 2–3). We can see the great achievements of church history, along with great disappointments. Since it is clear that the beast represents a world system—increasing in influence since the resurrection of Jesus—which finally seizes total control, then the demise of the effective church is not brought about by a final conflagration. Rather, the church's demise in the divine timetable seems to be brought about by the attractiveness of emerging world-embracing materialism. Accordingly, the world expresses profound relief (11:10) with presents when the 'torment of the two prophets' is brought to an end.

The church's witness to the world will be overcome but the church's inner essence and connection with Jesus cannot ever be overcome. There is a divine timetable at work in the ministry of the two witnesses and in the opposition of the beast. In the success yet death of the witnesses, a world situation is being described. Satan is described as the dragon, serpent and deceiver (20:1–3; 12:7–12). By use of the same terminology, Satan's defeat at 12:7–12 is being interpreted in 20:1–3. Being cast out from heaven, Satan cannot deceive the nations until the thousand years is over. Hence, in the millennium there is no significant threat to Christian witness. That is, whereas the beast is active during the 'church age', it is not totally successful until the end of the 'church age'.

During the 'church age', Satan—through his beastly agencies—is unsuccessfully endeavouring to deceive the nations (20:1–3); during this time, Satan is unable to prevent the free course of Christian witness in the world. We cannot present a scenario to precisely identify the rise of the beasts and their final domination of world social, economic and political systems. However, we have witnessed significant impediments erected to Christian witness by the rise of nationalism and the rejection of colonialism in the 20th century with accompanying graduated restrictions being placed on Christian mission. I do not intend to go any further with this speculation. However, the very positive presentation of the church and its abrupt end is associated with the spectacular dominion of the beast who drives the church from society and thereby 'kills' the church. Thus commences a totally pagan age: the great last period of world history, the three and one half days of Satan's world ascendency.

The world, which will 'kill' the witnesses as it killed Jesus, is in the grip of the beast which is always rising from the pit in its last foray. Like Jesus, the witnesses will fulfil their ministry by dying in public humiliation. The world—earth dwellers (cf.13:8), the customary term in the book for rebellious humanity—have welcomed Satanic deception to bring about the end of public Christian witness (11:10).

The powerful witness of the two witnesses ended in their death, but also led to a heavenly reward (11:12). However, behind the direct statement of the 'death of the church' (11:7) comes the expanse of time contained in the beast's coming up (13:1), the first stirrings in the world of the conflict, its protracted worsening and finally the Christian world prostrated by the world won over to the materialistic worship of the beast. The final transformation of the world is to occur after the death, resurrection and ascension of the witnesses.

The martyrdom of the two witnesses moves beyond the prophetic precedents set by Moses and Elijah. Their bodies (*ptoma*, Greek singular noun indicating that the witnesses are a corporate entity) are left unburied (11:8, a great indignity; cf. Psalm 79:2) for three and one half days. This denial of burial is an index of the great scorn shown by the world to the witnesses' prophetic testimony, and a demonstration to the world of the power of the beast. What all this symbolism actually means only the future will unfold. However, that the church is left unburied seems to point to its continuing presence in the world, denuded of all its previous vitality, without valid public witness. Through this death and the prophetic witness that led to it, the victory that overcomes the world will be achieved.

The death, resurrection and ascension of the witnesses (the church) identify them as the covenant people of God re-acting the full ministry of Jesus. The singular 'body' (11:8), and singular 'mouth' (11:5) signifies that the two witnesses are viewed as one church. They lie in the streets of the great city for just three and one half days, a small fraction of their ministry (11:3) of three and one half years.[13] And they are still ministering in their fallen presence. However, in their resurrection after the three and one half days—reminiscent of Jesus' three and one half years of ministry—the three days of Jesus' resurrection have been converted into the three and one half days of conventional apocalyptic (cf. time, times and half a time). The willingness of the witnesses to suffer not only indicates how believers conquer and overcome but also plainly identifies evil and how it operates.

The great city (11:8) in which the 'Lord' of the two witnesses was crucified is called Sodom (renowned for depravity and godlessness, and ripe for judgement) and Egypt (the oppressing beast of the exodus). The reference to the city is spiritual, not literal or geographical. The paradox of the crucifixion is that Jerusalem—the place of the crucifixion of Christ, 'their Lord'—is now the paradigm for an oppressive and rebellious world. The reference to the

---

13 Smalley, 2005, 282.

Spirit (*pneumatikos*, 11:8) refers to Spirit-given perception required for interpretation, that is, spiritual understanding. The death and the lack of burial point to the ineffectiveness of the church's prophetic witness at the end of the church age. It seems that visible Christianity will vanish from the earth at that time. The church may continue to exist in name in the world, but without effective public witness: effectively dead to the world. However, there is a reference to Satan drawing fiery judgement upon himself for attacking the camp of the saints, the beloved city (20:9). This seems to suppose a continuing Christian complement after the 'death of the church'.

Because of the apparent victory of the beast (11:9–10), the idolatrous citizens of what is later presented as 'fallen Babylon' rejoice. The Babelised world exults over the removal of the constrictive influence of the true Israel. The earth-dwellers suppose that the prophetic witness of the church has been refuted by the 'deaths' of the two witnesses. This excites global interest and exultation (11:10). The world rejoices because it is now relieved of the torment of prophetic demand for repentance and warning about judgement (11:10). But the triumph of evil is for a very short period. The church's disappearance from the world marks a short period before the end of history.

The symbolic resurrection and ascension of the witnesses (11:11–13), after three and a half days, continues the parallel paths of the ministries of the church and Jesus. The saints, having been given into the power of the end-time evil ruler, now ascend in a cloud just as Jesus had ascended. God breathes life into them; God also empowers them as his Spirit enters them. These two witnesses—the true Israel, spiritually preserved—are raised to heaven as a mighty army, like the resurrection of Israel in Ezekiel 37:10. Like the resurrection of Jesus, the resurrection of the witnesses is a public event; the saints resurrection is witnessed by all the unbelieving nations of the world (cf. 'seen' in 11:9,11,12 as emphasised). The prophetic witness of the church brings to all the world what Jesus achieved in his own prophetic witness, death and resurrection. The resurrection of the two witnesses is a final witness to the world of the power of the gospel and the judgement about to come.

This conclusion to the ministry of the witnesses is expected since their witness to Jesus is the witness of Jesus in them. The effectiveness of their testimony lies in their witness unto death, that is, their participation in the victorious death of the Lamb. Jesus is the faithful witness (1:5, 3:14) because he maintained his witness unto death, and Jesus' faithful witness was vindicated by his resurrection. The testimony of the two witnesses, following the testimony of Jesus, is likewise powerfully vindicated. Through the Spirit, their witness is the witness of Jesus to the world. Ironically, it is their rejected witness which brings them victory with the final defeat of the rebellious world.

Thus, like the ascension of Elijah (2 Kings 2:11), the two witnesses also participate in a resurrection and ascension when they hear the summons to heaven (11:12). This is the moment when the 'last trump shall sound and the dead shall be raised incorruptible and *all* shall be changed' (1 Corinthians 15:52). The witnesses ascend in a cloud, the same means of heavenly transportation as the Son of Man (cf. Acts 1:9–11), indicating their connection with Christ. The church returns 'from heaven' as the bride with the bridegroom at the onset of the new creation (21:2). The ascension of the church—carried up in a cloud like Moses and Elijah—seems to be triumphant. The testimony of the death and resurrection of the witnesses causes the inhabitants of the earth to give glory to the God of heaven. If people are to be set free from the spell of the beast and the lure of Babylon then, by God's intervention, Babylon must fall and the beast must be dethroned. God's secret plan is to accomplish this by the death of Christians who, in their witness, hold fast to the teachings of their Lord. God does not prematurely bring in the end and cut short the reign of evil for he is not willing that any should perish. Saints suffer and the end does not come until every opportunity has been given to an obdurate humankind to repent. Martyrdom is, like the cross, the cost of divine patience.

Humans witness the divine approval of the prophetic ministry of the church simultaneously with the advent of phenomena that inaugurate the final coming of the kingdom of God. The world must see the triumph of the witnesses over death in order to be convinced of the truth. What happens from their death onwards takes the witnesses beyond prophetic precedents; it is impossible to predict with certainty the course of events for the church after its death.

Because of the resurrection of the church (11:11)—that is, the second resurrection (20:11–15)—believers stand before the great white throne (20:11) for salvation and vindication preparatory to their entry into the new Jerusalem (21:2). Thus the church's spiritual resurrection (11:11) signals the end time: the third woe and the advent of the kingdom, part of the total proceedings of the return of Christ. 1 Thessalonians 4:16–17 refers to the actual second coming of Christ and states that the dead in Christ shall reign first (4:16c; cf. 20:4–6). Is this the 'rapture'? It is certainly not the popular pre-tribulation rapture as the seals and trumpet series of judgements have preceded the church's resurrection. Abject terror now falls upon the world (11:11). It is not likely that the 'resurrection of the church' refers to a spiritual revival in the world because, immediately following the withdrawal of the church, the last series of judgements (the bowls, Revelation 16) is exercised only on unbelievers (cf. 16:2).

When the two prophets were raised to life, great fear fell on the nations. The devastating effect on humanity is numerically represented: one tenth of the city fell; 7000 are killed by the earthquake (7×1000 = a complete large number affected by judgement).[14] The casualties are thus a preliminary judgement on the world leading to the last judgement.[15] Caird and Beale suggest that the 7000 are killed as a *lex talionis* (equivalent retaliation) for the death of the two witnesses (cf. Elijah's 7000 faithful who had not bowed the knee to Baal, 1 Kings 19:18).[16] The figure is, in any case, symbolic of God's exact divine reaction at this beginning of final judgement.

The manner in which the world has delivered itself to godless evil precipitates the coming of the kingdom. In its world-building godless materialism, with all restraints removed, the world will attempt to bring in Utopia. But it will founder, as Revelation will show, because humanity will not co-operate with each other. Thus, the removal of the church turns humanity in on itself and promotes the coming of the kingdom.

---

14   Resseguie, 1998, 151.
15   Beale, 1999, 602.
16   loc. cit.; Caird, 1966, 140.

The great earthquake in the world city (11:13) is a sign of final judgement. Its partial effect indicates that more judgement is to come. At the time of the church's resurrection (cf. 11:13 'in that hour'), God's presence is to be manifested in final judgement (cf. 11:19). Progressively increasing in their intensity of disruption of the cosmos, the earthquakes (6:12; 8:5; 11:13,19; 16:18) give warning of the final establishment of God's sovereignty. At this divine intrusion into history, when the witness of the church is seen to be vindicated as the truth (11:11-13), the remainder of the inhabitants of the city recognise that this is divine judgement. So those who are left now give glory 'to the God of heaven'. But this is not repentance, rather, it is a reaction like that of Nebuchadnezzar when he was alarmed and shaken by the events of Daniel 2 (Daniel 2:44-46).

Revelation 11:14-18 The Seventh Trumpet Sounds the End

11:14 marks the end of the second woe (cf. 8:13; 9:13-11:13). The third woe follows (summarised in 11:15b-19). The detail of final world judgement does not come until the climax of the seventh bowl (16:17-21). Nevertheless, 11:15-19 is the divine pronouncement of the third woe which follows through to 22:5. This expectation is reported in past tenses as an affirmation of prophetic certainty.

An angel sounds the seventh trumpet to pronounce the third woe (11:15), which brings history to an end. The dramatic heavenly announcement (11:15b) inspires a hymn of thanksgiving (11:16-18). God has come in Christ. The kingdom of the world—not kingdoms, that is, the world united under the evil rule of the beast—now became (*egeneto*) the kingdom of the Lord and his co-regent, Christ (11:15b). Christ and his saints have overcome, but the victory is God's. The singular future verb *basileusei*, used to avoid monotheistic confusion, refers to the coming visible joint reigning of Father and Son (cf. Psalm 2).

God's final overthrow of Satan at the seventh trumpet brings forth an outburst of praise in marked contrast to the silence of the seventh seal (8:1). The whole host of heaven sings, and John in his vision is now back in heaven and hears their song. The focus of enthusiasm is the kingdom of God come. The world empires have passed over to their true owner. Satanically usurped authority has been replaced. The vivid description—seen as already accomplished—is proleptic. The time is coming for it to happen but it has not yet happened. The central theme of Revelation is the establishment of the kingdom. This is about to be fulfilled.

The twenty-four elders fall down (11:16) and worship in a song of thanksgiving for this coming reign. The hymn celebrates that the Lord God Almighty—a much used title for God in Revelation, indicating his omnipotence—has completed his plan; God's eternal projected rule has begun (Greek perfect tense).

The proclamation of the establishment of the kingdom is followed by judgement against the enemies of the kingdom. Then there is praise for the visible introduction of the kingdom of God over which God and the Messiah will reign forever and ever (11:17). This is the time that God has chosen to usher in the kingdom of the Messiah; for this purpose the seventh trumpet is blown.

The normal three-fold formula for the uniqueness of God's sovereignty over history—who is and who was and who is to come—is abbreviated in the majority of Greek texts in 11:17, omitting 'who is to come'. The reality expected in the omitted phrase is anticipated. God has now taken (Greek perfect tense) permanent control of the world to judge the wicked and confirm the righteous; God has begun to reign (ingressive Greek aorist tense) and God will show his eternal power in his final overwhelming display by which all enemies are overcome (17–19:10).

The inauguration of the kingdom (11:18) includes the reward of eternal life given to the dead of the prophetic church. The defiant rage of nations that has been directed against the Lord and his anointed is rendered illusory at the coming of the kingdom by the reward given to dead believers (Psalm 2:2). The nations are judged and defeated since God's *orge* (judgmental anger, wrath) operates to bring an end to world rebellion. The judgement of the dead is vindication for the whole sanctified church (prophets, saints, those from both Testaments who fear God): one great family of the saved will reign with God as their reward. And those who destroy the earth (Babylon the Great, the beast, the false prophet,

Satan and all under their control) will be destroyed. Continued human mismanagement and exploitation of the world has been the concomitant of expulsion of the human pair from the Garden. The world outside the Garden had desperately needing God-fearing dominion. The human pair went out from the Garden to make their own choices, like God. But, unlike God, they were not able to discern between good and evil. So they exploited creation by their ability to influence the world with their fallible decision-making power; they subjected creation to servitude under which it metaphorically groans for release (cf. Romans 8:22).

The temple (*naos*, 11:19) in heaven is now opened. 15:5 is the only other place where the temple is described thus, and that verse refers to the seven angels carrying the seven bowls of wrath on a mission of final judgement. So the final transformation of the world is about to occur (cf. 21:1). The opening of the temple and the appearance of the Ark (11:19) indicate that the source of final world transformation is God's throne room in heaven. Therefore, what has been announced will be carried out. The open temple will bring judgement on the world. The seventh trumpet announces that God alone is king and that no enemy may stand before him. God's power is to be openly established and the power of the beast nullified. 11:15–19 celebrates the finality that is to come with the Parousia.

The presence of the Ark of the Covenant (11:19) attests God's covenant fidelity to Israel from Sinai to the end, means that the glory of God is now fully displayed, and is a pledge that—in bringing about his kingdom and judging the world—God is faithful to his covenant promises to his people. The covenant bond between God and Israel ensured his presence among faithful Israelites. The temple served as a central unifying symbol of the covenant bond, visually representing God's relationship with Israel and her elect status.

The third woe which is to come at the seventh trumpet will bring about the defeat of the world system (Revelation 16–19) in the bowl judgements. Lightnings, voices, thunders, an earthquake, and a great hailstorm (11:19)—the accoutrements of the divine execution of the last judgement—accompany both the seventh trumpet and the seventh bowl. These theophanic phenomena and the enthroned twenty-four elders (11:16) are the enactment of the throne room vision proleptically described in Revelation 4. But the extended presentation in Revelation 12–13, beginning in heaven, reveals the inner movements that lie behind this climax of human history. 11:19 closes the trumpet series and opens the second of the heavenly visions that reveals the end.

Revelation 11:19–15:5 Summary: The Centrepiece of Revelation

11:19–15:5 is the middle—the centrepiece—of the three heavenly visions (cf. 4:1–5:14; 11:19–15:5; 19:11–21:8). This centrepiece vision deals with the unfolding contest between God and Satan (11:19–14:20).[17] The transition verse (11:19) is both a response to the hymn (11:17–18) and an introduction to Revelation 12. Seeing heaven opened (11:19), John is being admitted to the transcendent world (not a geographical state). The Ark, the symbolised throne of God and surrogate for his divine covenant presence (Exodus 25:10–22; Deuteronomy 10:1–2; 1 Kings 8:1–13; Hebrews 9:3–5;)[18] is visible in the transition verse. This opening of heaven with the Ark visible and the Sinai theophanic signs of covenant conclusion bears witness to the end. The ark had been the repository of God's will for humankind: the Ten Words. The mercy seat, the sign of God's grace, was over the ark signifying that it was only by God's mercy that his will in the Ten Words could be kept. But God's new covenant has superseded the Mosaic covenant. The symbols of the old covenant now give way to the final reality of the new covenant: sin will be remembered no more (Jeremiah 31:34); and all the redeemed will know God, from the least of them to the greatest.[19]

After final judgement, full access to heaven's holy of holies, to the very throne room of God, will be granted to believers. The centrepiece vision indicates what the reward to the faithful will be: immediate fellowship with God through fidelity to his new covenant. The Ark stands as the footstool of the divine throne. The mention of the instruments of the Sinai covenant (the ark and

---

17 cf. Lioy, 2003, 66.
18 Caird, 1984, 144.
19 cf. Dumbrell, 2002, 144–147.

theophanic signs) reminds us of the continuity of covenant theology, moving from creation to the new creation.

From this point on—implementing what has been declared in 11:15–19—the heavenly temple becomes the centre from which judgement proceeds. In Revelation, the throne room scenes initiate punitive action on earth.[20]

Nothing specifically Christological has been injected in the sequences of the first heavenly vision (Revelation 4–11). The subject has been the difficulties always encountered by believers: in the post-Fall world and amid the political opposition of their times. The advent of the reign of God had arrived with the resurrection of Christ. Believers can enter into intimacy with God at the altar, which under the old covenant was given to priests only. God has now manifested himself as the God of the new covenant.

Revelation 12–22 fills out 11:3–19, highlighting the final drama of church witness and world judgements leading to the Parousia and the advent of the new Jerusalem. The seven bowls of wrath respond to the demonic attack on the church (11:3–13; cf. Revelation 12–13). A much fuller exposition of the conflict between the forces of evil and the witnessing church (11:7) is provided in Revelation 12–13 (cf. 11:7 echoed in 13:1,7); by correspondence, a fuller explanation of 11:3–6 is provided in Revelation 12. The church's witness is given a context in the great cosmic conflict for sovereignty over the world between God and the forces of evil. This conflict for sovereignty began in the Garden of Eden and reaches final judgement for resolution at the Parousia.

---

20 cf. Lioy, 2003, 144.

Revelation 12

Revelation 12-13 The Church Under Persecution

Revelation 12 Satan's Release

Revelation 12-13 presents a history of the church that—always under persecution—experiences satanic onslaughts in the period of three and one half years before history's end (that is, the period during which Satan controls history through the two beasts). Revelation 12 presents the birth of the Messiah, the crucifixion, the expulsion of Satan from heaven, and the gradual extension of Satan's influence on earth. The church, on the way to the Promised Land in a new exodus, is fully protected spiritually. Revelation 13 presents intensification of the struggle under the satanic two beasts who impose their political, social and intellectual wills upon the whole of world society.

The circumstances of Revelation 12 and 13 appear to present two different stages in the battle with evil in the period between the cross and the return of Jesus. Likewise, 20:1-3 presents Satan as initially constrained and unable to deceive the nations for the duration of the millennium (I take that to be the church age). But then, at the end of the millennium, Satan is released with power to deceive. During the millennium, Satan and his representatives—the two beasts—will not succeed in their aim to win over the entire world by deception. But the dragon appears to have the total success that he craves after the millennium is ended. I will suggest (20:1-3) that this means Satan will impede, but be unable to halt, the free course of the gospel and missionary activity during the millennium.

Satan is expelled from heaven (Revelation 12) as a result of his defeat by the cross and resurrection. Human fear of death has been vanquished by Christ's resurrection and the defeat of death. Defeated, Satan—who is described as the deceiver of the world (cf. 20:3)—and his angels are cast down to earth, unable to deceive nations in this primary age of great gospel expansion. Even so, during the millennium, Satan is able to do great harm to individuals

(12:13–17; cf. the description of protection for Christian witness, 11:3–6).

Revelation 13 presents an entirely new situation. The beast is the architect of a fierce regime of world dominion by evil. The beast arises from the 'sea'—in the biblical symbolism of Revelation, the 'sea' is the 'chaos factor' also described as the abyss (9:1; 20:1)—that is, the domain of evil. The church, persecuted but protected (12:13–17), then gives way (Revelation 13). In the plan of God, the church is totally exposed to the world. This, too, is the church bearing witness to the coming victory of God. The beast blasphemes against God and overcomes the saints who had previously overcome Satan (12:11). The world is presented as gradually falling, by human acceptance, under the world rule and control of Satan (Revelation 13).

Therefore, Revelation 12 and 13 echo the situation of the two witnesses (Revelation 11) who, when they complete their powerful witness, are totally exposed and killed by the beast. The Christian world is then at the mercy of the beast: the church lies dead in the street of the great city for the significant period of three and one half days. Then, having been killed by the beast, at the end the church is resurrected.

Revelation should not be read as a book in chronological order. However, the survey of Satan—with measured success in Revelation 12 and then evil taking over the whole world in Revelation 13—summarises Satan's varied success in the world between the cross and the return of Jesus (cf. 20:1–3).

Revelation 12:1–6 The Woman, the Child and the Dragon

Revelation 12–22 explains in detail the generalities of Revelation 1–11 including the opposition to be expressed by the dragon and then his beasts (Revelation 12–13) followed by the victory of the Lamb (Revelation 16–17), fulfilling the seventh trumpet announcement of God's universal reign (11:15–19).

The beginning of Revelation 12 is devoid of literary links to what has preceded. This fresh start is required as the record of the woman and the dragon begins earlier, chronologically, than any previous part of the visionary narrative. In the New Testament, the word 'dragon' only occurs in Revelation. But 'dragon' is used in a number of Old Testament books as a symbol for tyrannous evil. The 'great' sign in heaven (that is, in the sky, cf. 12:4), which introduces Revelation 12, differentiates it from what has preceded and emphasises its eschatological importance. Revelation 12-13 records: the depths of world rebellion that must be overcome before the kingdom of God arrives visibly; and the broadest conception of evil's temporary triumph which is unable to be overcome by the witnessing church.

The issue must be decided in the heavenly sphere, which is where Revelation 12 begins. The genre is that of symbolism, not precise historical occurrence. The woman of 12:1 is no ordinary person, for she is: radiant with heavenly lustre; arrayed in celestial garments wrought with the splendour of the heavens; wearing a crown of twelve stars symbolising God's end-time people, the true Israel, the community of salvation; clothed with creation's luminaries as the light of the world. Her crown of twelve stars indicates her royal dominion (cf. Joseph's dreams, Genesis 37; and the formation of the twelve tribes of Israel). Her progeny will be opposed by evil itself. The evil opponent is girded with brilliant but ostentatious human fabrications worn by the harlot (Revelation 17).

This woman (12:1) is mother Israel: mother of the true people of God from both Testaments. The Messiah is born of her (cf. Isaiah 66:7-9). Her heavenly birth travail (12:2), translated into earthly realities, may represent the earthly persecution of the righteous before the birth of Christ. Her crown (*stephanos*) symbolises the victory of the faithful community from which Christ comes in the ensuing encounter with the dragon. When the woman bears a child, the Christological drama begins (cf. the harlot who holds a cup filled with the blood of the woman's seed, 17:6).[1] The conflict between the mother of Israel and the harlot will be the final illustration of the enmity between the woman and the serpent projected in Genesis 3:15.

The conflict between the woman and the red (for bloodshed) dragon leads into an account of contemporary and continuing conflict between the people of God and the enemies of God. The dragon also appears in heaven—a second sign, to counter the sign

---
1   cf. Paul, 2000, 256-76.

of the woman—indicating that the contest between the dragon and the woman will be played out in the heavenly spheres, with consequences felt on earth. The dragon is a metaphorical caricature of all opposition to God, like the seven-headed chaos figure of apocalyptic tradition in the creation myths of Ugarit and Babylon (Lotan in Ugaritic; Leviathan in the Old Testament). With seven heads and equipped with ten horns, the Revelation dragon is the amalgam of the four beasts of Daniel (Daniel 7:7; in Revelation ten = power in sizeable proportions, for a limited time)[2] from which ten kings would arise (17:12; Daniel 7:24). The dragon is crowned with seven diadems (royal crowns for his claim to universal reign). With this equipment, the 'huge' dragon has a great reservoir of cunning and strength. The conflict between the dragon and the woman leads into the clash of two kingdoms: those who are of the world and the kingdom of God. But the clash is one-sided because the dragon's activity is under divine control (cf. 12:6,14; 13:5). The dragon is Satan and his defeat has happened (12:5–12): he cannot prevail against the church; his future is determined. 12:1–15:4 is, therefore, a more detailed account of the church age (cf. 11:1–13). The conflict ends with the conquerors of the beast (the followers of the Lamb, 14:1–5) triumphant in heaven (15:2–4) after the messianic war (Revelation 12–14).

The call to readers and hearers to conquer by their witnessing faithfulness unto death is fundamental. This call demands the readers' active participation in the divine war against evil. Members of the churches enter the new Jerusalem by conquering. Prior to Revelation 12, the verb 'to conquer' is always left without an object (except 11:7) because the principal enemies of God—who must be defeated to make way for his kingdom—are not identified before Revelation 12–13.

The enemies of God are a satanic trinity. The dragon is the primeval supernatural source of all opposition to God. The dragon works through both the beast or sea-monster (the imperial power of Rome as representative of world government throughout history), and the second beast or land monster (the propaganda machine of Rome's imperial cult, representative of the worldview that supports world government throughout the ages). Babylon,

---

2 cf. Lioy, 2003, 42.

the world system developed under this trinity, is not introduced until Revelation 17. Babylon is not conquered. But Christians are called to come out of her (18:4), that is, to disassociate themselves from her evil before she is destroyed. Finally, the world system—always containing the seeds of its own destruction—turns in upon itself, and implodes (17:16–17).

The initial confrontation between the serpent and the woman (12:1–6) occurs in the Garden of Eden (cf. Genesis 3:15 of the struggle between the seed of the woman and the serpent). The woman's travail in birth (12:2) represents the sufferings of the Old Testament covenant community of faith. The dragon is Leviathan, the many-headed dragon (Psalm 74:13) whom the Lord will punish with his great sword on the last day (Isaiah 27:1).

One third of the stars is swept away by the dragon (12:4), perhaps referring to the original war in heaven when Satan and his followers—one third of the heavenly host—rebelled against God. However, it is more probable that the sweeping away of the stars refers to pre-Christian persecution by the rebellious, devilishly inspired world against the faithful in the covenant community of Israel (the saints, cf. Daniel 8:10).

After the dragon swept away one third of the stars, he then 'stood'. This signifies his readiness to take further action at the birth of the Messiah. The dragon's attempt to devour the child is reminiscent of Herod's slaughter of the children (Matthew 2:13–18) in his attempt to kill Jesus. A male child is born (cf. Isaiah 7:14; 66:7), referring to the spiritual rebirth of Israel out of the travails of captivity.[3] Thus the narrative presents the Messiah as being central to the salvation and deliverance of Israel. The birth of this child—the Messiah—anticipates the consummation of history as he will exercise international judgement, dashing the nations to pieces like shards of pottery in messianic warfare (Psalm 2:9).

But before the consummation of history in the rule of the Messiah there is the church age, which is characterised by demonic persecution becoming more intense at the approach of the Second Coming. So the child is 'snatched up' to God's throne (*harpazo*, cf. Jesus' refused to 'snatch at' deity but humbled himself in death,

---

3   Osborne, 2002, 462.

Philippians 2:6). Christ is rescued from death and enthroned at the right hand of God. At the Parousia when Christ returns to earth, he will be God's king (Psalm 2:6–7), the manifest ruler of the nations. The theme is divine care for mother Israel (Zion) in the desert wilderness (12:6; Deuteronomy 1:31; 8:3; Psalm 78:52; Acts 7:36; cf. Hosea 2:14). The movement from the wilderness to the Promised Land occurs after the church age (1,260 days, 12:6; cf. 11:2; 13:5; 11:3; 12:14; Daniel 7:25; 12:7).[4] The community of Israel in exile is comforted by God and restored to the final Promised Land (Isaiah 51:2–3,9–11; cf. Isaiah 7:14; 66:7–8).[5]

Revelation 12:7–12 War in Heaven

There is war in heaven, which is the counterpart of the victory of the resurrection (12:1–6). Michael, an archangel, is presented as Israel's protector (Daniel 10:13,21; 12:1,8). Michael takes a stand for the people of God in the latter days (Daniel 12:1). In non-canonical writings, Michael is depicted as the chief officer of the heavenly armies who would defeat the enemies of Israel.[6] Michael is the first of the four archangels (with Raphael, Gabriel and Phanuel) who stand before the throne of God (1 Enoch 40:9–10). These four will seize the kings of the earth and cast them into God's fiery furnace (1 Enoch 54:6). In the interaction between heaven and earth, Satan—the deceiver of the world (12:9) on earth and the accuser of the brethren in heaven—is depicted as an angel with a similar retinue to Michael (12:7). This war in heaven could be: the original fall of the angels at creation, according to Jewish tradition; the Genesis account of the sons of God taking as wives the daughters of men (Genesis 6:1–4); in accordance with the account in 2 Enoch 29:4–5, when Satan thought of placing his own throne higher than God's and as a result of his intended usurpation was cast out of heaven; or a situation of continuing rebellion in heaven through the ages to which attention is drawn occasionally (cf. 1 Chronicles 21:1; Job 1–2 Zechariah 3:2).

In this war in heaven, angelic presence is sufficient; the direct presence of God is not required since the battle is for control of the

---

4   4 Ezra 9:38–10:57 also has an account of the birth of a son who dies and is restored to life by a heavenly woman identified as Zion.
5   Beale, 1999, 630.
6   Osborne, 2002, 469.

world above, over which God the Creator stands as sole authority. Satan's power cannot operate in heaven. Satan operates in the earthly realm since he is the god of this world (2 Corinthians 4:4) which is characterised by craft, deceit and implacable opposition to God (cf. Leviathan in Job 26:13; Isaiah 27:1). In this conflict heaven is split into opposing factions: Michael and his angels versus Satan and his angels. Some angels seem to have been practising evil before the creation of the world (cf. Isaiah 14). Hebrews states that heaven had been subjected to defilement and required the cleansing provided by the death of Christ (Hebrews 9:23).

With Jesus' ascension and his overcoming death, Michael finally prevailed with victory over Satan. Satan is cast out of heaven; he now operates entirely on earth. In the Old Testament, Satan still acts in heaven not as an occupant but as a functionary with a carefully supervised, permitted presence (cf. 2 Samuel 24:1; 1 Chronicles 21:1; Job 1-2). But in the New Testament, with the incarnation and the wilderness challenge, Satan is presented as the god of this world who understands clearly the issues at stake for him with the birth of Christ. Because of the victory of the cross and resurrection (cf. John 16:8-13), Satan has been cast out of heaven. Jesus foresaw this when his disciples began to have power over Satan (Luke 10:17-20) by being able to cast out demons. Jesus said that the disciples' names were written in heaven (Luke 10:20). In the context of talking about their power over the enemy, Satan, Jesus said to his disciples that 'nothing shall by any means hurt you' (Luke 10:19).

Whereas there is no place in heaven for the rebellious dragon, he has authority to operate in this world under divine control. For the period of the millennium (20:1-3), the dragon will endeavour to but will not be able to deceive the nations. During the millennial age, Satan's victories will be over individuals. However, at the end of the millennium, Satan is released from this constraint; he will act to deceive the world, and the indications from the remainder of Revelation are that he will have world success. The millennium is therefore the world reign of Christ through the church during which there is free course for the Christian gospel throughout the world. If this is so, when will or when did the millennium conclude? No indication is given. However, we now live in a world in which nations are being deceived, when the course of the gospel is restricted.

The Satan (12:9, ὁ *Satanas*) the slanderer (*diabolos*)—the article designating his function as accuser of the brethren—is cast out of heaven to the earth with his angels as an anti-God force. Satan is also called the ancient serpent: the agent responsible for the primal deception of Genesis 3. Excluded from heaven, Satan will inflict his deception on the whole world. After the Fall, Satan and his angels do what Satan had done in Eden on a world-wide scale: they deceive the whole earth, continuing Satan's work of deception after the cross even through agents of Satan in the churches.[7] The dragon's activity is directed against all, the whole inhabited earth (12:9), but his operation is carefully monitored by heaven.

The victory already celebrated in heaven must now be played out on earth. Satan casts down the saints (Daniel 8:10; 10:20–21) but this sin is turned against him. Satan will succeed for a time on earth, for the world is characterised by its refusal to worship God. On earth, the crucifixion was the historical manifestation of God's victory in heaven. The results of this victory must now be seen in the interplay between the people of God and the dragon. However, this interplay will take a paradoxical form, as believers will be tempted, often persecuted, and—by the power of the Spirit—believers will be overcomers even unto death.

Heaven had been the home of God and Satan where good and evil co-existed (12:7–8). Now Satan and his angels are cast out and good alone remains in the new heaven. God previously permitted the devil to accuse his people of sin (Job 1; Zechariah 3:1). Old Testament texts portray Satan as accusing saints of untruthfulness and of not deserving God's salvation blessings (Zechariah 3:1–5, 9). Implicit in the charge was that God's own character was corrupt: Satan implied that God had bribed Job (Job 1)![8] The two kingdoms of Satan and of God demonstrate the mystery of the presence of evil, according to God's purpose (Isaiah 45:7), in a world that is intended to be a universal Eden. The kingdom of Satan on earth henceforth signifies Satan's rule as authorised by God. In his kingdom Satan is the deceiver of the whole world

---

7   Beale, 1999, 656.
8   cf. op. cit., 659.

(12:9). This is how Satan works on earth. He convinces humanity that the world of rebellious and disobedient people is life as it should be: natural and beautiful.

12:10–12 comments in summary on the fall of the Devil and proclaims woes on earth during the short time still left for him. The decisive battle between God and evil is described as having taken place already. The consequence of Satan's defeat in heaven is that his activities on earth are intensified. But human beings can defeat Satan on earth, anticipating the eschatological end battle, by virtue of Christ's saving death and their steadfast confession of Christ. God's faithful people are protected from all Satanic attacks.

12:10–12 is a hymn from heaven that interprets 12:7–9. The hymn is introduced by the loud voice of the heavenly court. The defeat of Satan by the cross signals the coming of the kingdom of God and the reign of Christ. The hymn celebrates the arrival of this messianic kingdom of God and Christ by Christ's death and resurrection (12:10). This *soteria* (salvation, 12:10) is God's final defeat of the dragon. Probably Satan and his hosts had fallen before the creation of the world (cf. Isaiah 14:11–16). But Satan still had some access to heavenly circles and has some temporary victories over believers. However, the believers' victory over Satan will be final and eternal (12:10a). So the heavenly host rejoice because of the work of Christ.

The casting down of the 'accuser' signals the forensic nature of the heavenly 'courtroom' battle that Satan has lost.[9] Up till now Satan has been accusing believers in heaven. But, because of the victory of the cross, Satan will not be able to lay any more accusations against the brethren. Believers, as 'those who tabernacle' here (10:12)—that is, in God's presence, the place of security and protection where Satan is not at liberty to accuse—may now rejoice. Henceforth believers overcome Satan by their faithful verbal and life-style witness to Jesus unto death (12:11; cf. 6:9–11). Believers conquer through trust in the blood of the Lamb that has atoned for all sin and through his resurrection that attests his victory over death. Satan knows he has lost (12:12), clearly demonstrated by his frenetic attempts of persecution against the people

---

9   Caird, 1966, 154–6.

of God. This is compelling reason for the heavens and those who dwell in them (that is, believers) to rejoice. But the 'earth' is now under the control of evil powers; it must bear with hope the promise of a wonderful future (cf. Romans 8:18–25).

The devil, cast down, has great wrath. He had lost his place in heaven and only has a short time on earth. He is now using his limited time productively for his purposes. But Christ has been lifted up. Access to heaven itself through Christ is now available for believers (John 16:23). The uninterrupted accusations of Satan against the brethren of all ages have been replaced by the access now available for the brethren into God's presence through the exaltation of the Messiah. 12:11 shows, by anticipation, the redemptive historical victory of Christ on earth in Christians who win against the serpent—in history—by testifying to their faith. So Christ's cosmic victory is repeated in the victorious witness of the faithful.[10] The faithful did not love their lives unto death: they persevered in their witness and conquered in the end by their death, trusting in Christ's death for them and in their involvement in his resurrection. 12:11 thereby summarises the victorious conflict of Revelation 12 (especially 12:7–12). The heavens now celebrate (12:12) with the angels and saints whose dwelling (*skenountes*, tabernacling) is in heaven. The heavenly status of faithful believers is accomplished despite (or, rather, through) their earthly tribulation.

Now cast down from heaven, Satan musters his forces in the shape of imperial power (12:12; 13:2). The beast was able to make war on the saints and conquer them, but this merely secured their eternal future through death (11:7). The real victory was won on earth for the saints through the redemptive act of the crucifixion and resurrection (Revelation 11) to which, even in martyrdom, saints give testimony. The beast may kill the saints, seeming to defeat them by physical death. But he cannot suppress their Christian witness, which will be rewarded by eternal life.

The earth and the sea are the totality of the world (12:12) in which the dragon's power to deceive, tempt and persecute believers now operates. But that power, as the dragon well knows, is only for a 'time' (*kairos*). There will be an end to the dragon's

---

10 Ulfgard, 1989, 54.

power with the return of Jesus. Until then, the conflict will be intense. Later, with the death of the church, the beast will take full control of the world. The dragon's attack upon the child emphasises the two realms of existence. All are either in Christ tabernacling in heaven, or in the world as inhabitants of the earth (cf. 12:12).

The woe addressed to the earth and the sea relates to the concentrated efforts of the devil against all, believers and unbelievers, but especially Christians (12:12,13–17). He can no longer wreak havoc in heaven, so he expresses great wrath for the little time that he has on earth (the symbolic three and one half years, cf. Daniel 7:25; 12:7). Finally, the kingdom of God will be consummated and Satan will go to final defeat.

Excursus: The Fall of Satan

The fall of Satan comes as a result of the crucifixion. Satan and his agents will now work within history but will not achieve their aim to deceive the nations—that is, they will be unable to secure full control in the human world—until the end of the millennium. In my view, the millennium is the church age. I propose that the church age is not the full time between the resurrection and the return of Christ (11:7–12) but, rather, the time from the resurrection until the mission of the church is terminated by the beast arising from the sea (11:7). Satan is always about his task. But for the short time after the end of the church age, before the Second Coming, Satan will have great success. It is difficult to predict what forms his deception will take. But in the 21st century there is the promotion of apathy in previously Christian nations. There may come national repudiations of Christianity. Persecution and suppression of the faith in countries with religious alternatives may also occur. The millennium context of 20:1–6 will discuss these propositions further. However, such conclusions will not be countenanced by those who hold to a pre- or post-millennialism position.

Revelation 12:13–18 The Pursuit of the Woman

12:13–18 provides details of the dragon's pursuit of the woman (12:1–4), that is, the dragon's pursuit of the community of the people of God. The birth of Christ totally changed the dragon's situation. His time is now short. 12:13–16 considers the dragon's earthly pursuit from a heavenly perspective; 12:17 turns to the earthly reality. The persecution inflicted by the dragon will be extensive and partially successful but it will not achieve the global success that will come with the appearance of the beast (Revelation 13). Thus 12:13–18 reports the tensions of 11:3–6. There is no place for the dragon in God's realm. But there is a necessary place for the woman in the dragon's realm. The dragon's assault is triggered by identification of the woman as mother Israel with her worldwide people. Daniel's period of tribulation (12:14) is applied to the church, which flees as Israel had fled before Pharaoh. The church is under spiritual protection (12:13–16) as Satan's opposition continues.

The woman is given the two wings of the eagle. The definite articles point to the eagle in God's protection of Israel (cf. Exodus 19:4; Deuteronomy 32:10–11). Soaring above earthly trials, the eagles' wings (Isaiah 40:31) provide expansive strength and rapid flight to escape into the wilderness (cf. 12:6) to be nourished by God's care. The church is nourished in the wilderness during the persecution under Satan's reign for Daniel's time, times and half a time. This is where believers live by the word of God and have the sustaining tabernacling presence of God (12:14). Believers partake of the heavenly manna (cf. John 6:32) with the triumph of redemption to follow (cf. Isaiah 40:31 for future Israel). Hoeksema suggests that the wilderness (12:14–16) represents the people of God in the world pursuing a policy of spiritual separation from the world, as historical Israel had been called to do when commissioned as the people of God (Exodus 19:5–6).[11] However, the main purpose of the wilderness is to show that the church at this time is under ongoing persecution whilst enjoying divine protection. The dragon, now styled 'serpent' (and thus identified with the Genesis 3 deceiver)—intensifying his effort in pursuit of the saints—spewed out water like a river to flush the church out from the protective separation which isolates them from worldly

---

11 2000, 444–5; cf. Dumbrell 1984, 85–87.

threats.[12] Persecution is likened to an overwhelming flood in Psalms 32:6; 42:7; 124:4 (cf. Isa 43:2).

A further allusion to Israel's exodus deliverance is the earth 'swallowing' (12:16, Exodus 15:12) the enemy's river (cf. also Isaiah 51:10).[13] The saints' wilderness persecution is ended by divine intervention. This is a precursor to entrance into the Promised Land. The church being in a wilderness relationship to society identifies the divine protection that enables the church as the people of God to always survive in its materialistic age. Old Testament Israel was commissioned to live this way (Exodus 19:5–6), but she violated her commission by treaties and alliances with world powers.

12:17 turns to the suffering of individual believers as distinct from the previous focus on the church as a whole (12:13–16). The dragon now directs his anger against individual believers who keep the commandments of God (12:17), keep the testimony that Jesus bore, and preach the gospel that comes from the testimony of Jesus. This important theme of witness and the testimony of Jesus runs throughout the book of Revelation (1:2,9; 12:17; 19:10; 20:4; cf. 6:9; 11:7; 12:11; 15:5).[14] Believers stand by the witness that Jesus bore to the truth of God, the Creator and Lord of history. 12:17 concludes the chapter but also introduces a new portion of the vision (Revelation 13).[15] The dragon stands by the sea waiting for the arrival of the sea beast to make war against those who bear the testimony of Jesus (cf. Daniel 7:3).

---

12 Witherington, 2003, 171–72; cf. Caird suggests that the 'river' is a river of lies, the catalogue of deceits with which Satan fights the church 1966, 159.
13 Beale, 1999, 676.
14 Lioy, 2003, 71.
15 Osborne, 2002, 489.

Revelation 13

Revelation 13 The Worship of World Power

Revelation 13:1-10 The Antichrist

Revelation 13 expresses more elaborately the dragon's wrath (cf. Satan freed from restraints for a time, 20:1-3; and the rise of Antichrists, 1 John 2:18; 4:1-6). There is drastic and successful persecution of the church in the world (cf. 11:8). Through human governments, institutions and agencies there is indication of the active presence of Satan in the world.

There are two major symbols for Rome—and similar world powers to arise in the future—representing different aspects of state control. The first symbol is the sea monster (the beast of Revelation 13 and 17) which represents the military, social and political power of both the Roman State and other governments throughout time. This demonic power undergirds empires and power structures throughout time, but achieves popular acceptance in the final period of history. The second symbol is the land beast (the false prophet). The activity of the demonic pair (sea monster and land beast) corresponds to the two witnesses (11:1-13), that is, the demonic pair ape the church's Spirit-inspired prophetic witness. The false prophet provides false communication on behalf of and in support for the sea beast. In this way the false prophet undermines the spiritual, political and philosophical underpinning of human governmental and social structures of the day.

In Revelation, the sea beast operates in the Christian age (cf. 13:5, 7); but it is not worshipped by Christians in the Christian age (cf. 13:4,7; and 11:7 referring to the activity of the beast in the Christian age). The work of the second beast starts after the first beast is firmly in control, that is, after the church has been 'killed'. Hence no activity is recorded against Christians in 13:11-18.

Satan, not Rome, is the primary enemy of the faith. The rule of the beast represents Satanic influence. A transcendent perspective is thus provided to readers of Revelation, with a new understanding of Christian existence.[1] Christians are at war for their witness. This is the theme of Revelation. Opposition to Christians is presented starkly. The sea beast in the church age—through earthly kings and governments—opposes God, the Lamb and their faithful followers on the issue of who rules the world. In the post-Christian age, the world seems to be under the complete control of the dragon. The dragon then gives authority to the sea beast (13:2b,4a). The sea beast goes on to provide derivative authority to the land beast (false prophet, 13:12). This evil trinity (dragon, sea beast and false prophet) ultimately, ironically, performs the will of God (13:5,7). Compromise and idolatry may provide a comfortable existence; but it will prove false. Revelation declares that God rules this world, God is faithful to his covenant, and God will defeat his enemies and bring in a totally just society.[2]

The conflict between the churches and those who worship the beast dominates the latter half of Revelation. However, the conflict is not between two equal communities. There is a small network of faithful witness against the powerful world.[3] This small network is backed by the power of God. But the beasts of Revelation 13 are shaping society in the absence of the church; the beasts shape society with the assent of unsaved humanity.

The second beast (arising from the land, 13:11) is later styled the false prophet (16:13; 19:20; 20:10). Unlike the sea beast, the false prophet does not operate in the Christian age. Rather, the false prophet makes the earth and its unbelieving inhabitants worship the first beast and make an image of it (13:8). The false prophet: deceives the world with mighty signs; gives 'spirit' and speech—that is, ability to operate with intelligence—to the man-made image of the beast; calls fire down from heaven (13:13), like Elijah; and generally promotes the anti-Messiah as the public presence of the beast. But he is a false prophet, a false spiritual leader, promoting worship of a false god (the first beast), and thus committing the ultimate blasphemy. The false prophet is not seeking to promote an emperor cult in Ancient Rome, rather, his aim is to direct the ethos of the whole of society.

---

1   Stevenson, 2001, 282.
2   ibid., 282–3.
3   Siew, 2005, 272.

The sea beast seems to operate all of the machinery of state. In a perversion of true authority (cf. Romans 13:1-7), the sea beast is bent on leading the world into the public affirmation of all that is inimical to God and Christ. The land beast gives to what is genuinely evil a publicly plausible face: organizational genius to shape the thought of government and society.

Initially, the beast is continuously coming (Greek present participle) out of the sea. This continuous coming indicates continuous world rebellion by 'chaos' forces. In this last 'rising', the beast uses its human adherents to perpetuate rebellion through human institutions of every age. The rising of the sea beast also refers to his gradual, insidious, rebellious anti-God pressure being imposed over the world. The sea beast: renews the old conflicts between order and chaos (Psalm 74:13-14; Isaiah 27:1; Daniel 7:3); wears ten diadems (ten = of sizeable proportions, 13:1), an assertion of his false claim to world sovereignty (cf. Christ's unnumbered crowns, 19:12); and carries blasphemous names (13:1), like the divine titles of Roman emperors in John's day. But Christ bears the title of King of kings and Lord of lords (19:16).[4] The servants of Christ are marked with his Father's name (14:1). The sea beast also marks its believers with his name (13:16-17). The critique is political in Revelation 13 and economic in Revelation 17-18. But in both passages the critique is, essentially, religious.

The sea beast represents a horrifying and hideous amalgam of the four beasts from Daniel 7:1-7. No doubt, for John, the sea beast was embodied in the devilish features that typified the Roman Empire. The reference to Daniel (13:1-2) confirms that the appearance and purpose of evil throughout history is always the same, with the same end in view: world domination. The beast has seven heads (13:1)—the sum total of the heads of the four beasts of Daniel's vision—to indicate influence and control.[5] Likewise, the seven horns represent the accumulation of power expressed by Daniel's four kings (Daniel 7). The sea beast is the complete expression of evil intention and power. Thus, just as in Daniel 7:1-8, the beast will finally be overthrown. Thus, in this final period of

---

4 Resseguie, 1998, 124.
5 Lioy, 2003, 72.

human history, the beast from the sea is the incarnation of the devil who is the prince of the power of this world.

The sea beast (13:1–2) adapts features from the first three beasts (the lion, the bear, and the leopard) of Daniel 7:1–6: the terrifying roar of a lion's mouth (the lion also mimicking the Messiah of Judah); the power of a bear (feet); and the evil cruelty of a leopard. This incarnation of the beast not only sums up all of Daniel 7:4–7 but also exemplifies the fourth beast of Daniel 7, namely, the maliciously destructive little horn (Daniel 7:8; cf. 13:5).

The blasphemous name—indicative of his claims to power and rule as an anti-God (cf. the little horn, Daniel 7:8–11)—is on the sea beast's heads (13:1). The beast receives worship (13:4) that endorses its materialistic approach to life and power. Worship of the beast is the antithesis of worship of God and Christ (5:8–10). Through this Antichrist the dragon has become blasphemous, rebelling against God's very existence. The dragon takes God's name in vain, thereby pitting himself against God's being. The focus on the mouth of the beast indicates its role in promoting blasphemous claims. False and deceptive teaching was a characteristic manifestation of Antichrist figures in the early Christian age (1 John 2:22; 4:3; 2 John 7). Such deceptive teaching had resulted in the apostasy of many professing Christians (cf. Matthew 24:10–12; 2 Thessalonians 2:3; Mark 13:14).

The combination of four beasts from Daniel 7 (the lion, the bear, the leopard and the little horn) into one (13:1–10) highlights the extreme ferocity of the Revelation sea beast.[6] The fourth beast in Daniel 7 stands for the last king (Daniel 7:17) or kingdom (Daniel 7:23) before one like a Son of Man (Daniel 7:13–14) takes power; that is, until the holy ones—true believers—of the most high (7:18,22,27) take possession of the kingdom (7:22). The Revelation beast (13:1–2) is a symbol of oppressive and evil world kingdoms, the floruit of the anti-Christian world system. He is both a king and a kingdom. Hence, worship of the beast is worship of the state (13:8).

The sea beast is the incarnation of Daniel's fourth kingdom (Daniel 7): the manifestation of evil world power after the Christian era; the last devilish expression of total world power before

---

6   Beale, 1999, 685.

the kingdom of God takes dominion over all (cf. Daniel 2:40–44). The kingdoms of the world are vested in this undisputed ruler (cf. 11:15) for the three and one half day period during which the church is dead in the world (13:5; cf. 11:2–3; 12:6,17). As the Antichrist, Satan's vice-regent, the sea beast is incarnated in world power throughout the Christian era but, climactically, the eschatological figure (13:1–10) rules over the kings of the earth (17:12–13; 19:19). The beast must be overthrown before the kingdom of God will come.

The dragon gives its great power to the beast (13:4). Therefore the beast is the manifestation of the dragon. The dragon shares his authority and power (13:2) with the sea beast. So the sea beast is to rule over every tribe, nation, people and language (13:7). He will blaspheme (cf. Daniel 7:8) by giving himself a divine name and thereby claiming divinity (13:1,5). Thus the beast will be the consummation of evil in its final attempt to control the world. Perhaps this attempt to take control will be through the promotion of universal worship of materialism and human potential, thereby taking worship from God and, instead, directing worship to the Caesars of the day (13:4,8). The beast's diadems—crowns claiming authority, power and control—had moved the point of control from the head of the dragon to the horns of the beast (13:1), indicating the brute power of Satan's rebellion.[7] The beast will manifest the usurped authority, power and deity given to him by the dragon.[8] Though he had already lost his rights in heaven, Satan still has a throne and great power which he gives to the beast (13:2).[9] Satan now has the beast to impose his world rule. Evil draws all its power from one supreme master-spirit.

In its parody of Christ's death, one of the heads of the beast seems to have received a mortal wound (13:3), like the crucifixion! Though amazingly resilient to the mortal wound, the wound is nevertheless an indication of the beast's final annihilation: it was inflicted in heaven, the point of final decision, as a result of the judgement of the crucifixion. But the wound affected only one of seven heads. This indicates that whereas Satan retained his power

---

[7] Smalley, 2005, 336.
[8] Beale, 1999, 684.
[9] Caird, 1966, 163.

he was, nevertheless, vulnerable. The beast's healing and derivative power is of Satan.

The mortal wound was thought to be a reference to Nero whose suicide, though not a defeat, was a mortal wound to the beast (Rome). And Nero's rule—and the rule of Rome generally—was certainly a manifestation of the beast. Nero's death was followed by a chaotic year of four emperors. But recovery took place under the Flavian dynasty. From the brink of collapse, the Empire emerged as apparently invincible.

The essence of idolatry is demonstrated by the people of the earth who don't understand the indication of the beast's defeat but who, instead, marvel at the beast (13:4) and identify with his world aims and recognise his sovereignty. In their worship of the beast—that is, their worship of the satanic power behind the beast—they chant, mocking the Old Testament absolute acclamation of Yahweh and monotheism, 'Who is like the beast?' (Exodus 15:11; Psalm 71:19; Isaiah 44:7; 46:5; Micah 7:18). So the unbelieving peoples of the world reject the living God and instead give sovereignty, in the time of the beast's ascendancy, to the respective world powers under which they live. But in worshipping the beast (that is, world powers), the people of the world are giving their allegiance to the underlying power behind the beast. And the underlying power of the beast is the dragon (Satan).

The beast is Satan's mouthpiece (13:5, cf. the little horn of Daniel 7:8 who also 'spoke great things'). This Satanic expression of evil in the world lasts only for an express period of time and is under the permissive will of God (cf.11:2–3; 12:6,14). The beast makes unceasing war with the saints (13:7; cf. Daniel 7:8, 20). He seduces all those whose names are not written in the Lamb's book of life (13:8). His defeat, however—by the Lamb and the 144,000 overcomers who stand on Mount Zion (14:1–5; 15:2-4)—is certain. Therefore the beast's authority, though destructively powerful, is temporary (13:5).

The beast blasphemes the divine manifestation of God's character throughout history (13:6–8). This blasphemy was, in the first instance, through the divine pretensions of Rome and her emperors. But the blasphemy has been perpetrated by all world governments throughout history when they fail to acknowledge the source of their power. The beast's blasphemy is also directed against those who dwell (as God's tabernacle) in heaven, that is, those on earth who are members of the new covenant and therefore citizens of heaven (13:6; Philippians 3:20; cf. 11:1–2; Daniel 8:10–13). Heaven is the permanent abode of members of the new covenant. The beast's blasphemy (13:6)—its demand to be the focus of world worship—is logically followed by war on the saints (13:7; cf. Daniel 7:20–21). This war is exercised with subtlety through the deceptions of the land beast (13:11–18). Exercising authority over the human world, the beast is allowed to overcome the saints (cf. 11:7). The rule of the beast and the forces of evil will prevail (Daniel 7:21) until the Ancient of Days (cf. 1:12–16) comes to take possession of the kingdoms of the world. The paradigmatic examples of the failures of the seven churches (Revelation 2 and 3) demonstrate that the beast's victories will be by cultural subversion. That is, the beast will induce in the church an accommodation to worldly culture and compromise to worldly standards. Insidious domination through human structures (13:7) will be the means by which the beast will finally overcome the church (11:7) and receive universal acclaim from the whole unbelieving world (13:8).

The beast's authority is, for a time, universally accepted except by those whose names were written in the book that attests those ordained to life (3:5; 17:8; 20:12,15; 21:27; Philippians 4:3; cf. Daniel 7:10). The inscription of their names in the book of life is dependent on the activity of the Lamb. The proximity of 'written' and 'slain' (13:8, cf. 17:8) suggests that the cross, historically expressed in Christ's surrender to death, is part of the eternal order of God from the foundation of the world (cf. 1 Peter 1:19–20).

The warfare of the beast is happening in the context of churches in the world (13:9–10b). Hence the exhortation to believers, like the exhortations to the seven churches: 'if anyone has an ear, let him hear' (13:9). Satan has been actively persecuting and opposing the church in the post-cross world from the time of his expulsion from heaven (12:7–10). Old Testament Israel was never exposed to the beast's opposition for commitment to the kingdom. This requires discernment. This view of the evil reality of the present world will not be easily be easily accepted by some members of the covenant community. Through the beast, an arrogant, humanistic Babylon is again building its way to heaven.

A warning is now given to the saints (13:10). They are to submit with 'perseverance' (NASB)—that is, with courageous endurance (*hupomone*)—to the persecution that is now in process as part of the divine purpose. The church must not attempt to counter the sword with human weapons. No matter what, the saints must not yield to the temptation to succumb and join in the worship of the beast. 13:10 appears to quote or allude to Jeremiah 15:2 and Jeremiah 43:11. The Jeremiah quotes were, in the first instance, directed against rebellious Israel. The punishment for rebellious Israel, according to Jeremiah, will be death by the sword.

Revelation 13:11-18 The Land Beast and 666

The second beast, the earth monster (13:11-18)—also called the false prophet (16:13; 19:20)—arises from the dragon's realm (the earth) and thus is under his direct control. The formula for the rising of the sea and land beasts is the same (13:11; cf. 13:1), indicating that the work of the two beasts overlaps. But the land beast arises after the church had been killed. None of the land beast's activities is directed against Christians. The final bestial control of the world in the three and one half days after the killing of the church, through the land beast, is more sophisticated. Earthly inhabitants will be much more responsive to the beast than was possible before the death of the church.

The land beast's age is characterised by spiritual deception (13:11). The tenacity of Christian presence in the world prior to the death of the church requires the land beast to simulate the testimony of the church. So the land beast has two horns like a lamb, but it spoke like a dragon. In the controlled materialistic age of the land beast there is still a need to make power look beneficent: gentle and harmless like the Lamb, masquerading as meekness and goodness (2 Corinthians 11:3). But the truth is that the land beast expresses the will of the dragon. It is the 'little horn' of the fourth beast of Daniel 7. This deception gives authority to the beast by compelling and cajoling the whole earth and its citizens to worship the beast, not God. This is the satanic admission that evil, expressed in raw power, is always insufficient to capture people's allegiance. Evil must have the weapon of deception (13:14) to give power a benign veneer. The use of the present tenses in this sequence (cf. 13:12–14,16) may indicate contemporaneous application of the passage to the imperial Roman cult. The second (land) beast brings human life under the power of the first (sea) beast. It was the first beast which had waged war (13:7; 11:7) on the saints. Yet the fact that this beast is later called 'the prophet' suggests that its function is also to shape human opinion and attitudes in the absence of Christian values after the witness of the church in the world has died. Therefore, just as the sea beast is the reality of the final age, so the land beast is the spirit of the final age.

The false prophet (land beast) is the first beast's (sea beast) prophetic witness. The sea beast represents humanity in a depraved form. The land beast controls institutions that point humanity to depravity. It is the voice of humanism seeking the capitulation of humankind to the worship of secular power. The land beast may symbolically stand for any religious system that allies itself with the hostile forces of the world against the faith of Jesus Christ.

The land beast gives diabolical prophetic witness to ape true prophetic witness (Revelation 11). Resseguie has pointed out the following parallels: both contexts (church and beasts) present prophets (true 11:10; cf. false 16:13; 19:20; 20:10); the true and false prophets both perform signs (true 11:6; cf. false 13:13,14; 19:20); the true and false prophets both receive authority (true from God 11:3; false from the sea beast 13:12); and whereas the true prophet tormented the inhabitants of the earth (11:10), the false prophet deceived the earth's inhabitants (13:14).[10] There is another parallel. There are two Christian witnesses: two olive trees and two lampstands (11:3–12). Similarly, there are two beasts: the sea beast and the land beast. The prophetic activity of the land beast—stressed by the ninefold use of *poieo* (13:12–16)—is to persuade the state by its deceptions to support political, religious, and economic values that persecute the church and deceive the ungodly (13:11–17).

The land beast, posing as a representative for truth, may take many forms. It convinces the world to make an idol of the

---

10   1998, 127.

blasphemous sea beast (13:15). Through false and deceptive worldviews, at times, the land beast even deceives the faithful (cf. 2:15,20). When the church is defeated, the land beast successfully garners the support of all unbelieving humanity (cf. 13:12; 11:7). The idolatry promoted by the land beast will involve commitment to materialism and atheism. The land beast produces apparent (world) miracles (13:13), like the Old Testament prophets (cf. Elijah's fire from heaven: 13:13; 1 Kings 18:38–39). This stimulates false worship. Life and vitality is thus given to the political apparatus so that it appears as though it's alive and speaking (13:15). Under the land beast's false prophetic witness, the authority of the state becomes like the authority of Old Testament prophets (13:14).

When John wrote Revelation, pagan priests produced deceptive signs and wonders. But deceptive signs and wonders are substitutes for the truth of God in any age (cf. Mark 13:22; 2 Thessalonians 2:9)[11] And when believers are not overwhelmed by the deceptive signs and wonders when pressured to engage in idolatrous worship, then they are threatened with death (cf. 13:15; Daniel 3:3). Christians were being pressured to worship the image of the Caesars in John's day (13:16–17). Propaganda put out by contemporary authorities which reflect the spirit of the last age are also a pressure on believers in our day to engage in idolatrous worship. Those who worship the beast are sealed with the invisible mark of the beast, identifying them with their contemporary power structures.

The executive authority of the second (land) beast is derived entirely from the first (sea) beast (13:12). The second beast secures, by coercive cultural and social pressure to conform (cf. 'it made', 13:12), the world's submission to and worship of the first beast. The sea beast's wound—inflicted by the sword of divine judgement (cf. John 12:31–32) which issues from Christ's mouth (1:16; 2:12,16; 19:15)—had healed (13:12). This healing is explained in resurrection terms: he came to life, like Christ at the resurrection (13:14).

The land beast refers to the perceptual framework which promotes an unbelieving lifestyle. It communicates the pervasive

---

11 Beale, 1999, 711.

worldview of governmental powers of the day which are insidiously imposing the values, structures, and dynamics of fallen Babylon (Revelation 17). The second beast presents the sea beast as a saviour messiah, like the Lamb, bringing benefit to human life. The land beast is, therefore: a false apostle; a false angel of light; deceptive and seducing (cf. Genesis 3). The land beast beguiles with its promises all but the earnestly faithful. The characteristic of the first (sea) beast was blasphemy. But the characteristic of the second (land) beast is action (*poieo*, 13:12–16). The resulting world structures look right; they appeal and are convincing. These political and social structures were created to serve. But, under the second beast, they seduce and enslave.

The fire brought down from heaven (13:13) by the second beast (like Elijah, 1 Kings 18:38), is presented as a counterfeit second Pentecost. There are miracles like those at the birth of the Christian church. Thus the earth dwellers are enrapt by the deception that they had chosen (9:20–21). They are delivered up to Satan (1 Corinthians 5:5). With Christian influence already withdrawn from the earth (11:11–13), humanity now demonstrates its fallenness by deifying the beasts (13:14).

The land beast (13:15) breathes life into the image of the sea beast: a satanic parody of the gift of the Holy Spirit. The land beast is thereby able to provide a persona for the sea beast. The sea beast is healed, attractive and convincing. This validates, by cunning deception, conduct in accordance with the anti-Christian values of the day. John was probably thinking about emperor deification in his day. But there is ongoing application where pretence at reality has no substance. The image of 13:15 provides a choice to unbelievers who remain (by this time, Christians generally seem to have been withdrawn from the world, 11:12). Unbelievers who remain will either worship their altered social world or die. The second (land) beast—generally responsible for the final state of the world—has induced apathy and direct unbelief throughout the world (13:7–9;14–17). There is a totally non-Christian world at the time of the end.

The second beast monopolises the global economy: none can participate without the mark of the first beast on the hand or forehead (13:16–17; cf. the relationship between Christ and the Holy

Spirit written on the foreheads of believers, 14:1). The beast's mark is symbolic for requiring total commitment to the sea beast. Since the mark of the beast is the name of the beast, the mark is compliance with the ethos and expression of the prevailing secularism of the day. Spiritual imperceptiveness wins a great victory at the end of history, brought about by the deceit of the land beast.

In every age we are bound up in the battle between the two kingdoms of light and darkness. We are in the world, but Jesus cautions us not to be of the world. Historically, being of the world is the cause of ruin and decline of much visible Christianity. Worship the beast and live; recant Christ or die: this choice was the historical reality of John's times as well as the end-times. Those who worship the beast are sealed: either on the forehead, the seat of perception (Ezekiel 3:8–9; 9:4; Jeremiah 3:3; Isaiah 48:4; Numbers 24:17); or on the right hand, the custom to identify slaves, where the faithful Jew wore signs of consecration to God (Exodus 13:9,16; Deuteronomy 6:8). This branding of the beast was a parody of Christian baptism. In John's day a satanic counterpart to the church was being erected in emperor worship. And this is a paradigm for what will happen in the last days.

The worship and reverence for secular authorities is destined to become a world movement in the time before the end. The transforming power of deceptive evil, with the church killed (11:7), will leave its mark on unbelieving humanity and world institutions. The mark of the beast on the right hand envisages action; the mark of the beast on the forehead indicates perception. Both marks indicate submission to the name or character and person of the beast. The sealing of the believer (7:4) and the sealing of the unbeliever are both invisible. But those who are sealed as believers, and also those who are sealed with the mark of the beast, can be publicly identified by attitudes and actions. Those without the mark (*charagma*) of the beast will be excluded from participation in society. Since the *charagma* was a commercial seal, this could refer to the divine claims made by Roman coins that bore the Emperor's image.

All economic transactions were restricted to certified worshippers of the beast (13:16–17). Absolute power moves towards totalitarianism. Enforced conformity shapes both the worldview and the lifestyle. Alternative structures are not tolerated (13:16–17). This is the pagan counterpart to the sealing of saints (cf. 7:2–4).

The situation to come calls for wisdom, that is, careful Christian discernment by which the signs of the times must be understood (13:18, cf. Daniel 12:10). The number of the beast, 666—representing economic, political and social pressure to worship the beast—would identify those who espoused the Antichristian spirit of the world. The number has often been related to Roman Emperor Nero (A.D. 54–67). Neron Kaisar (the translation of the Greek form of the name into Hebrew) by gematria, using letters as numbers, amounts to 666; and Nero Caesar (the Latin form) equates with the alternate textual reading, 616. In this interpretation the Roman Emperor is the incarnation of the beast. However, the number 666 falls three times short of complete perfection (777). The number 666 thus means continued human failure when God is excluded from the structures of society. This amounts to idolatrous imperfection being expressed through the trinity of evil: Satan, the beast from the sea; and the beast from the land. The 666 trinity is apparently wonderful in achievement, but falls short of perfection as evil brings on future judgement.

Absolute power on earth is, therefore: satanic in its inspiration; destructive in its effects; and idolatrous in its claim to ultimate loyalty. It claims divinity, not in heaven but on earth. But it is utterly unlike divine sovereignty. God's judgements are true and just (16:6; 19:2; cf. 15:3). The sovereign God is the only holy one (15:4). Only God has righteousness as his very nature. God is the source of all value. False worship is false because its object is not transcendent mystery; the object of false worship is mystification of something finite. But the transcendent God is not one finite being among others. He is therefore able to be incomparably present to all, closer to them than they are to themselves. So the transcendent God can make his home with all human beings (21:3). The image of the throne in the new Jerusalem is an expression of God's closeness to his people (22:3–4). However, God's glory is not yet manifested in this world because it is dominated by injustice. Only when God prevails over evil can he be said to have come to earth

(11:15). And when God has prevailed over evil, he will make his dwelling with men and women (21:3).

Summary of Revelation 11–13

Revelation 11–13 is a record of the church between the resurrection and the Parousia. Revelation 11 summarises the period of the millennium: positive and aggressive witness in the church age. Nevertheless, throughout this church age the witness of the church is not perfect, as indicated in the prophetic messages of Revelation 2–3. Revelation 12 also indicates resounding advances of the church in an idolatrous and difficult world, hindered by persecution and apostasy.

The millennium is therefore the age of great blessing to the world through church witness and Christian advance. This is necessary in the purposes of God to bring the eternal gospel to the whole world, despite Satanic opposition. But this age of great blessing is to be terminated before the Second Coming. The gospel proclamation finishes when the sea beast—who had been present throughout the church age, growing in power—'kills' the church. The visibly dead church is left in the world for the shortish span of three and one half days. In this period the sea beast is supported by the land beast. The humanistic world is no longer inhibited by Christian witness. The church has always been rejected by the majority world because her gospel and life is incompatible with humanity's desire to develop their own lifestyle, unfettered by divine authority. Under the rule of the land beast, the world rejects Christian faith entirely and gives itself openly to the blandishments of the beasts.

Under the rule of the land beast, the world will probably reach the floruit of human ingenuity, technology, medical and scientific advance with global interrelationships basically under one world system. This is like the eve of the great flood when God saw that 'the wickedness of man was great on the earth, and that every intent of the thoughts of his heart was only evil continually' (Genesis 6:5). Jesus' remarks on the times of the flood and Sodom and Gomorrah (Luke 17:26–33) indicate that what was happening in these anti-God societies was normal human conduct: eating, drinking, marrying, buying, selling, planting and building. It was life as usual within the narrow range of self-centred human concerns. But the world was brought down by the flood, and in Luke 17 the end of national Israel is in view. The issues of Revelation 11–13 are raised again in Revelation 16–18 when, at the end, the unbelieving world seems convulsed by problems which have driven a rift between the whore of Babylon and the sea beast (the world system on which she sits). Babylon is then destroyed as the beasts are triumphant over her. The last battle, Armageddon, is projected and settled (19:11–21) by the Lamb. In this victorious battle the Lamb uses the word of his mouth, that is, his final judgement of unbelievers.

The point of this long history of the world is that—in spite of great epochs of human progress, social elevation, technical advance, and multiple demonstrations of what seems endless ingenuity—humanity has always sought to run its own world, just as individuals have always sought to run their own lives. For humanity as a whole there has only ever been a titular recognition of God as Creator. God has allowed history to continue, to exhaust all human possibilities of building an ideal world. However, God's own purpose for humanity will prevail. Only God can produce the new Eden.

I argue that the millennium defines the length of the church age. This is time enough for believers to bear testimony and make changes in the world so that the world acknowledges that history is under divine control. Humanity has never been able to do this, notwithstanding the presence of the Spirit of God. This is because of the effect of the Fall (Genesis 3). And the effect of the Fall on the churches is yet to be removed also. Paul states that creation is in travail, groaning under human administration, waiting for the revealing of the sons of God (Romans 8:21–22). In the world outside the garden, human exercise of the power of being 'like God' will bring the world to the point of extinction. Only a complete transformation of humanity can control a new creation. This control is to be vested in redeemed humanity.

Revelation 14

Revelation 14–15 Victory and Judgement

Revelation 14 indicates the outcome of the war on evil. Revelation 14–15 records God's judgement to be imposed on the beast and his followers. Both chapters are set in heaven but conclude with final world judgement coming from the heavenly throne room. In 14:1–5 the Lamb is assembled with believers on Mount Zion. They have been victorious in spiritual warfare and now await the advent of the new creation: the historical and eschatological restoration of the true Israel.[1] The assembled believers have been brought together for the proclamation of the eternal gospel (14:6–7), the fall of world Babylon (14:8–12), and final judgement (14:13–20). Revelation 15 retraces ground. The beginning of the bowl judgements is interrupted by drawing attention to exodus parallels in the defeat of the beast, summarised by the new victory song (15:2–8) which is like Exodus 15:1–18. Then the temple is opened, and angels carrying the seven bowls of final judgement come out from the throne room of heaven.

Revelation 14:1–5 The Lamb and His Army on Mount Zion

The vision—a reply to what seemed to be the success of evil in Revelation 13—turns to the Lamb standing on Mount Zion. Mount Zion is the site of the heavenly temple in the new creation. The Lamb is standing with the faithful. The faithful bear God and the Lamb's names on their foreheads (14:1–5; cf. Isaiah 4:2–6; 11:11ff; 27:13; Joel 2:32; Ezekiel 40–48). With a forward look at the consummation and indication of how the victory of the Lamb and his warriors would be achieved, there is hope (14:1–5). The emphasis is on the contrast between the believers' position during the activity of Antichrist (Revelation 12–13) and their condition when standing in the place of final triumph. The believers, Israel with the Lamb, are now victorious. The assemblage on Mount Zion means that the nations are defeated and the kingdom of God is established (cf. Psalm 2:6). Those who were persecuted are now

---

1 Wall, 1991, 179.

triumphant. There is no more danger from the beasts. Believers are secure forever in the Lamb's presence (cf. Greek perfect tense of 'standing', 14:1). So in John's vision of victory over the dragon, the citizens of the new Jerusalem have already been called into existence. Victory over the world is already being celebrated towards the opening of heaven at the Parousia (19:11–21). Believers are standing on Mount Zion with the messianic king (Psalm 2:6). The unruly world has been defeated. The 144,000 assembled represents the final fullness of membership of God's new covenant (12 times 12 times 1,000 representing the fullness of God's people, a very large number cf. 7:4ff).

Thus, in reply to the world authority of the beast, the messianic army is visibly triumphant in heaven. The 144,000 is the completion of God's plan for the final assembly of his chosen people (cf. Isaiah 24:23). So the final end is now anticipated.[2] The victory over evil (Revelation 12–13) refers to Psalm 2:6, depicting the triumph of the messianic king and his warriors over the hostile nations. It was prophesied that God would inaugurate his eschatological reign on Mount Zion (cf. Isaiah 2:2–4; 24:23; 52:7; Obadiah 21; Micah 4:7; Zephaniah 3:16; Psalms 146:10; 149:2). On Mount Zion the Messiah's reign is to be confirmed and there he will receive the sceptre from God in an investiture of power. This power will then be expressed in executing judgement on the nations that trampled the holy city (cf. 11:1–2; 14:17–20).

Thus the redeemed army of the Lord are assembled on Mount Zion as the new Jerusalem (cf. Hebrews 12:18–24) in the presence of the Lamb. They are first fruits (14:4), the whole harvest of the redeemed, offered to God (cf. the whole of Israel redeemed from Egypt were first fruits to God, Jeremiah 2:2–3). The angelic hosts accompany the Lamb as singers and harpists. All the demonic strategies to destroy the church have failed.

The names of God and Christ sealed their foreheads as belonging to God (14:1; cf. 7:2; also the contrast between the 'seal' of God and the 'mark' of the beast, 13:16). The seal of God signifies what the names on the ephod of Israel's high priest signified (Exodus 28:9–11): their priestly status and access. Believers can enter the final holy of holies, the new Jerusalem. Their use of 'Father' for

---

2   Ulfgard, 1989, 75.

God indicates that under divine ownership they have been protected from apostasy. Hence their covenant righteousness (14:5). God has cared for them as their Father. The saints, the Lamb's army, have successfully resisted the attack of the two beasts. The assemblage therefore reflects the triumph of their witness through the work of the Spirit. Despite all satanic opposition, the true Israel finally emerges. The citizens of Babylon have the beast's name on their foreheads. The citizens of the new Jerusalem have the name of God and the Lamb on their foreheads; they are shaped in their being and doing by the divine nature of their Father and the Lamb.

There is a shift from vision (14:1) to audition (14:2). What John hears (14:2) is associated with what he has seen (14:1), namely, the triumph that is always being celebrated in heaven. The new song with which heaven reverberates (14:2–3) is a response to the redemption of the great throng. John is still on earth when he hears the thunderous voice of the harpists, the heavenly source of the song from the multitudinous (cf. 'many waters') redeemed (cf. 7:9–11). The assembly of the redeemed stand on the sea (cf. 15:2), representative of the rebellious order. The heavenly song (14:3) is a response to earlier statements of the Lamb's triumph (5:6–14) and the triumph of his followers (cf. 7:9–12). The new song celebrates a new victory. Angels, the redeemed, and those around the throne (5:13; 7:9–10) all hear the song of the 144,000 who are both on earth (cf. 7:1–8) yet already in heaven (cf. 7:9–11). Their song is theirs alone since the experience that their song celebrates has been solely theirs. The 144,000 have participated in the victory of their Redeemer's death, so they now join to sing his victory song.

The assembly is the new covenant community of all peoples, purchased by the blood of the Lamb, out of 'the earth', and 'from humankind' (14:3,4). For now and forever, they belong to the Lamb. John describes (14:1–3) and then interprets (14:4–5). The explanation for the victory of the saints contains three identifying statements (14:4): they did not defile themselves with women, they are virgins; they have followed the Lamb wherever he has gone; they were first fruits to God and the Lamb. The 144,000 have learned their song through sacrifice and struggle and, above all, by coming out of the 'great tribulation' (7:14). Just like John's original statement about the Lamb's victory (5:5–6), so the three explanatory statements about the 144,000 move from holy war imagery to sacrificial imagery to faithfulness of Christian witness.

That the 144,000 did not defile themselves with women (14:4) points to: their purity and faithfulness; and their holiness, making them fit for messianic warfare. Their fitness for messianic warfare is supported by their identification as 'virgins', echoing the holy war demand that all warriors keep themselves free from sexual defilement (1 Samuel 21:5; 2 Samuel 11:9–13; Deuteronomy 23:9–14). This has been their witness. As 'virgins' (*parthenoi*, masculine) they are ready for the marriage of the Lamb with the bride (21:1–2). They have avoided the pollution of spiritual adultery, that is, false worship. Their virginity is in contrast to the great harlot (Revelation 17). Their freedom from defilement with women (14:4) represents their refusal to participate in the life of fallen Babylon. The 144,000 have not been subverted by Babylon's persuasions.

That the 144,000 have followed the Lamb wherever he has gone implies that they have been released from the deception of the world and, instead, imitate the Lamb's faithfulness unto death. By following the Lamb they have been led to the heavenly city. Their chastity represents their faithfulness to the Lamb.

As first fruits, the 144,000—that is, all believers (cf. Jeremiah 2:2–3)—are the true Israel, the best of their kind (Numbers 18:12). They are not merely an initial offering from the remainder of humankind. They are a symbolic exhibition of what is still to come in the historical unfolding of the new Jerusalem, their final home. Ready for harvest, the 144,000 first fruits are offered as sacrifices to God. Under the old covenant, Israel's first-born were redeemed. Their place was taken by Levites as first fruits for all Israel. But the 144,000 are all priestly worshippers in the new temple. They serve God in the temple, having been agents of God's presence in Babylon.

14:5 deftly ties together all three of the explanatory statements (14:4). The cultic purity of 14:4a is interpreted as moral purity, namely. Like the Servant who was put to death as a sacrificial Lamb, pure and without deceit in his mouth (Isaiah 53:9), no lie was found in the mouths of the Lamb's servants. *Amomoi* (4:5, without blemish)—used to describe the 144,000—could mean without physical defect, in which case it specified that perfection was required for inclusion to witness in the Lord's army (as was required for Levitical priests, Leviticus 21:17–21). However, *amomoi* could also point to fitness for sacrifice demonstrated by complete commitment (Leviticus 1:3; 3:1; Hebrews 9:14; 1 Peter 1:19). The conflict in which Christians were engaged was of cosmic proportions. Hence the holy war imagery. They had resisted, not by violence but by faithful witness. Following the Lamb wherever he had gone meant imitating Jesus Christ's truthfulness as the faithful witness (1:5; cf. the deceit of the forces of evil, 2:20; 12:9) and accepting the sacrificial death to which following the Lamb could lead. So *amomoi* applies to the 144,000 followers of the Lamb, either in holy war or as sacrificial victims.

Revelation 14:6–13 The Process of Judgement

Chronologically, the order of Revelation 14 and 15 is: first, the proclamation of the gospel, putting the question of worship and world control to the rebellious order (14:6–13); secondly, the harvest judgement of the earth (14:14–20); and, finally, the victory that follows the final harvest of the earth (15:1–5). The victory, chronologically last, has already figured at the commencement of the section (14:1–4). The victory will be won through the triumph of the gospel (14:5–12) resulting in the fall of the world system, Babylon. This divine sequence will bring access for the saints to the new Jerusalem (14:1–5).[3]

The judgement outcome—the saints victorious in the presence of God (14:1–5)—precedes the extensive judgement scene (14:6–20). Judgement has been pronounced (14:5–12) and is about to take place (14:13–16:21). The end-time environment is in conformity with Jewish tradition: the saved people of God are on Mount Zion (14:1–5). God's deliverance of his people and the establishment of his kingdom are described using themes such as temple, covenant, and Israelite heritage.

Three angels announce the onset of the judgement (14:6–12). They proclaim that: the hour of God's judgement on a fallen world has come (14:7); therefore, Babylon has fallen (14:8); and God's

---

3   cf. Tonstad, 2006, 162–4.

wrath and anger (*thumos* and *orge*, 14:10) will come upon the beast and upon all who bear his mark. The judgement scene that follows is like Joel's description of a single judgement involving both harvest and winepress (Joel 3:13).

'And I saw' indicates the beginning of a new movement in the vision (14:6). Six pronouncements of judgement (14:6–20) bring on the victory scene (14:1–5). Another angel—a distinct and separate basis for judgement—flies in view of all, continuously, in mid heaven. This other angel has the eternal gospel (14:6). The gospel is eternal because God's character and purposes never change; God's will is eternally valid. This is a gospel of judgement for all nations, proclaimed to those who 'sit' (perhaps in complacency, apathy, or unconcern) on the earth. The order of the four-fold formula (14:6, nation, tribe, tongue and people), is not repeated in other similar references (5:9; 7:9; 10:11; 13:7). The order of 14:6 is the order of communication: the general (nations); to the constituents of nations (tribes); then language differences between tribes (tongues); and, finally, individuals (people). The 'eternal gospel' is always a divine announcement and is operative throughout human history (cf. Psalm 96:2b, the whole of Psalm 96 celebrates God's righteous judgement).[4] Psalm 96 calls on its hearers to proclaim to the nations that God is king (96:10). Blessing follows the acceptance of this core submission. The one biblical, eternal gospel is the proclamation of God as universal sovereign over nations, tribes, tongues and peoples (cf. Romans 1:2). The demand of this gospel, to accept the sovereignty of God, is presented to a world that is facing judgement for its failure to respond to the demand.

14:7 presents the demands of the gospel which are relevant because judgement (*krisis*) is proceeding. First, the one biblical eternal gospel requires fear of God—that is, the inner posture of reverence to God offering due submission to God—without which humankind will face the terrible, final judgement. The definite article (*tes kriseos*) signifies the impending final judgement. Secondly, the one biblical eternal gospel requires humankind to give God glory: to acknowledge his nature, to affirm his sovereignty, to allow God and his realm to be the shaping power of life. Thirdly, the one biblical eternal gospel requires humankind to worship

---
[4] Bauckham, The Climax of Prophecy, 1993, 287–288.

God; to affirm his sole control as Creator over all creation and to turn away from any other worship.

14:8 presents the final result of opposing and refusing this one biblical eternal gospel. God's verdict establishes the eternal demise of Babylon's materialistic regime. The world city Babylon is described as a harlot. While she is ruling, Babylon is already regarded as fallen (14:8; cf. Isaiah 21:9). Her rule was always totally insecure.[5] The verdict has been issued so the matter has been concluded even though there have been many historical eras beyond the day that John heard the verdict. Babylon's distinguishing characteristic was her fornication, that is, her idolatrous worship in place of true worship of God. She intoxicated her age by her demands for apostasy and persecution against Christians. Those who worship Babylon will be forced to drink the undiluted intoxicating wine of the wrath of God (14:10).

A third angel applies the judgement of 14:7 to the gospel demand for those who worship the beast (14:9–12). Rebellion against God is possible but escape from the presence and judgement of God is not possible (14:10–11). God's holiness is the reality upon which unbelievers will be broken. There is eternal (cf. 20:10), uninterrupted, tormenting punishment for all unbelievers; the description of the punishment is reminiscent of Sodom and Gomorrah or the fires of Gehenna in the valley of Hinnom south west of Jerusalem. The fire and brimstone (14:10) represents the presence and action of God's holiness in the midst of what is unholy. God's holiness is directed against all who bear the mark of the beast. The wine of God's wrath—that is, punishment directed by God's holiness against sin—is potent, prepared at full strength with everlasting effects. Judgement on all who have ever worshipped the beast who comes out of the chaotic sea throughout the ages will take place in the presence of the Lamb and the angels. They are to be continually reminded of the Lamb they rejected. The description of eternal punishment (14:11a) is the same as God's forever visible punishment of Israel's typical enemy, Edom (Isaiah 34:9–10). But Revelation adds that there will be no rest day or night (14:11) for those who worship the beast. Therefore, total destruction (or annihilation) is excluded. Believers can

---

5   Beale, 1999, 756.

rest from their labours. But rest is denied to those who are separated eternally under divine judgement from the divine presence.

14:12–13 is an aside to the churches. The patience of the saints is exhibited by keeping God's commandments as an index of their covenant faith and exercising trust in Jesus as the author and finisher of their faith. It is possible that the two categories—those who keep the commandments, and those who exercise trust in Jesus—indicate the saints of each Testament. The second of seven blessings from the Spirit in Revelation comes at the end of the message of the three angels (14:13). The citizens of heaven, presently in the midst of fallen Babylon (that is, the anticipated fall which is yet to come), are called to endurance. Christ has defeated death. So, for all who believe in Christ, death has now become (cf. 1 Corinthians 15:54–57) the beginning of final blessedness. Believers who die before the Parousia enter God's rest (Hebrews 4:1–11). The 'henceforth' (14:13) is not 'from now on' (NIV) but 'forthwith'. That is, the blessing for those who die in the Lord occurs immediately after death. The deeds of those who die in the Lord follow them. The result of their witness to the truth, and their willingness to suffer and endure, are seen in the converts who come after them.

Revelation 14:14–20 The Divine Harvest

A twofold harvest scene—two different aspects of the one reality, a single event (14:14–16 and 14:17–20)—reveals the consummation of God's purposes. The double image of final judgement is like the two stages of the grape harvest in Joel 3:13. These two stages are the two aspects of the Parousia, positive and negative: the verdict for the converted nations; and the judgement against the unconverted nations. The description of the figure seated in a kingly position on the white cloud is, like the Son of Man in Daniel 7:13. Daniel's Son of Man is the symbol of God in theophanies[6] and the sign of God's coming in judgement (cf. Matthew 24:30; Acts 1:11). The Son of Man is wearing the victor's crown of gold (14:14, *stephanos*). All authority in heaven and earth has been given to the Son of Man: he is 'sitting' enthroned as judge;[7] he is equipped with the sickle, the instrument of final judgement, by which he reaps the fruit of the gospel (Matthew 9:38). The harvest of the faithful, the citizens of the new Jerusalem, is a grain-type harvest (14:15–16; cf. Isaiah 27:12; Joel 3:13; Matthew 3:12). But the harvest for unbelievers, the citizens of fallen Babylon, is a grape harvest (14:18–20; cf. 19:15; Isaiah 63:1–6). The righteous are harvested (judged) by the Son of Man; the rebellious are harvested (judged) by an angel.

The people of God (14:1–5) have been presented as first fruits, that is, the first sheaf reaped that was then offered to God as a sacrifice (Leviticus 23:9–14). Significantly, the Old Testament first fruits were to be accompanied by the offering of a lamb without blemish (Leviticus 23:12; cf. 14:4–5). The image of first fruits (14:4) implies a final full harvest of all categories: the faithful and unbelievers.

The order for Christ to harvest the faithful comes from the temple—that is, from God's throne—through an angel (14:14–16). Another angel came from the altar. The altar expresses the demand of the consequences of Christ's sacrifice, the demand of the one biblical eternal gospel. The prayers of the saints are also offered on the altar (cf. 8:3–5). This angel from the

---

6 cf. Spatafora, 1997, 188.
7 cf. Hoffman, 2005, 55.

altar orders another angel who has come out of the temple to gather the grapes from the earth.

The grapes (unbelievers) are then cast into the winepress of God's wrath (14:17–20). The time for judgement has now come. The angel from the heavenly altar comes with power over the fire; that is, with God's authority to spearhead the judgement against unbelievers. The citizens of fallen Babylon are first gathered for judgement and then trodden in the winepress (an Old Testament image of judgement). The winepress is the crushing finality of God's wrath outside of the city (cf. 22:15; 21:27), that is, outside the new Jerusalem (14:20). The final abode of judgement for unbelievers is absolute separation from the gathered saints in the city. Like the crucifixion to which their judgement relates, the winepress is located outside the city. The severity and global scope of God's judgement is pictured vividly, like 1 Enoch 100:3 which states: 'the horse shall walk through the blood of sinners up to his chest'.[8] The death blood from judgement flows for 1600 stadia, which is the approximate length of the holy land from Tyre to the border of Egypt.[9] 1600 may also have numerical significance (4^2 = universal, x 10^2 = of sizeable proportions), referring to universal judgement.[10]

The two harvests are two facets of the one final judgement. The righteous (14:1–5; cf. 14:13) and the wicked (14:8–12) have been differentiated throughout Revelation 14. The first harvest, requiring a single movement of reaping, is redemptive. Indeed, the gathering of the saved has already occurred before the Parousia (cf. 11:12). The second harvest requires two actions: the gathering performed by an angel; and the trampling outside of the city by the Son of Man, cf. 19:11–16).[11] This second harvest is condemnatory.

---

8   Krodel, 1989, 276.
9   Beasley-Murray, 1974, 230.
10 Lioy, 2003, 83.
11 Smalley, 2005, 372–6.

Revelation 15

Revelation 15 The Seven Bowls and the New Exodus

The vision of seven bowl angels (15:1) initiates the foreshadowed judgement sequence (14:14–20). The angels' bowls are poured out like the exodus plagues (15:2–8), thereby bringing about the final exodus overthrow of evil and providing access to the Promised Land. The bowls are poured out as the wrath of God; his reaction against evil. The command to pour out these bowls of wrath is issued from the throne room. The bowls conclude the content of the third woe; they are the final warning to human society before the end of history. This vision of the bowls is described as great and marvellous: the heavenly temple is open (15:5); the angels who are to pour out the wrath of God come out (15:6); and history is about to be concluded. One of the living creatures gives to the seven angels the bowls full of the wrath of God who lives for ever (15:7). There is direct continuity between the throne room vision (Revelation 4–5) and the bowls sequence. The golden bowls (5:8) contain the prayers of the saints. This final outpouring of wrath is God's complete response to the prayers of the saints. God is the eternal one. Evil must perish under his judgement. After the bowl sequence, there will be no further occasion for the issue of God's wrath.

Revelation 15:2–4 The Song of Moses and the Lamb

The vision of the people of God in heaven, triumphant over the beast (15:2–4), is sandwiched between the introduction of the seven angels with the seven bowl plagues (15:1) and the preparations to pour out the bowls on earth (15:5–8). The seven bowls are the last punishment on the world (15:1). The vision is inserted to draw attention to the reason for this final bowl series of judgements, namely, the redemption of the saints in a final exodus. It is not one quarter or one third of the world that is at risk in the bowl judgements, rather, the totality of the unbelieving world is affected as Christians have already been withdrawn (cf. 11:11–13). Redemption is now complete (15:2–4). Pharaoh was overwhelmed by the waters of judgement. He was at that time the beast, that is, the potential devourer of the people of God. Judgement is to be administered against the beast within his own domain (a sea, 15:2). Before the bowl judgements, the saved will have already been rescued from the world; by then, the world had for a time been under the beast's total control. But, at the end, the saved will stand on the chaotic cosmic sea—Satan's own domain—now mingled with the fire of divine judgement. The chaotic sea is now calm (cf. 4:6). The exodus victory has been won. But the fire in the sea is a reminder that the complete elimination of evil occurs at the final general judgement (cf. 20:11–15). The true Israel is now able to enter the Promised Land, following the bowls which are God's covenant intervention (15:5–8).

The world may now be destroyed as opportunities for forgiveness have finished. The victory necessarily precedes the final judgement (14:14–20). There are two exodus-type events celebrated in Revelation: the passage of the Red Sea; and the triumph of the exodus plagues (Revelation 16).

The seven angels are introduced by: 'I saw another sign in heaven, great and wonderful' (15:1). This introduction is a variation of the formula used to introduce the woman and the dragon (12:1). The reference to 12:1 connects the narrative begun in Revelation 12 with the seven bowls. Hence, the seven bowls are the divine reply to persecutions from the fallen trinity and a fuller version of the seventh trumpet (15:5 echoes 11:19a; 16:17–20 expands 11:19b). Thus Revelation 15 is the point where the narrative of the history of the church (begun in Revelation 12) converges with the narrative of the divine trumpet judgements (begun in Revelation 8). Both narratives (church history and divine trumpet judgements) reach provisional conclusion in the pouring out of the seven bowls (pending a further conclusion in 19:11–21:8). The seven bowls refer—unlike the seal or trumpet sequences—to the opposition posed to the people of God by those who had the mark of the beast and worshipped its image (16:2). Opposition to the people of God has come from: the throne of the beast and his kingdom (16:10); the dragon, the beast, and the false prophet (16:13); and, finally, from Babylon the great (16:19).

The outcome of the Revelation exodus event (15:2–3) is that the saints conquer the beast. They have refused to follow the beast like the rest of the world (cf. 13:3). As worshippers of God the saints refuse to worship the image, choosing death instead. They reject the mark of the beast (13:16–18) and, instead, accept economic deprivation. They choose hunger over Babylon's delicacies. The victorious Christian army on Mt. Zion (14:1–5) is the people of the new exodus standing upon (*epi*, 15:2) a heavenly Red Sea of glass mingled with fire. The sea is the home of the chaos dragon (Psalm 74:12–14). But chaos is now defeated and the sea through which the Christian army had passed—the chaotic world with great tribulations—is now calmed. Believers have triumphed over the beast's deceptions in his heartland, the sea. But whereas the end-time plagues are yet to come (Revelation 16) in this new final exodus victory, the song of Moses and the Lamb is the heavenly celebration for the assured success yet to be realised in history. The sea of glass is now the floor of heaven, so those overcoming the sea beast stand on the sea before the throne associated with the Lamb in the victory over the world.

In heaven the true Israel sings the exodus song of praise for deliverance, celebrating the divine attributes. The passage of true Israel through the sea has now brought them into the new Eden (cf. 22:1–5). The song's content is mostly drawn from faith statements in the Old Testament: God alone is king and his judgements are just. The salvation of the true Israel has been God's work entirely. Just as Old Testament Israel had been liberated to be a priestly nation (Exodus 19:6), so the Lamb redeems a new nation of kings and priests commissioned to conquer the beast's empire. The singers hold harps of God—identical to the harps held by the 144,000 who stood with the Lamb on Mount Zion (14:1–5;15:2)—indicative of the deep harmonies of redemption.

Moses and Israel sang a song on the shores of the Red Sea (Exodus 15:1–18) to commemorate deliverance from Pharaoh. Likewise, those who are in the process of conquering (*tous nikontas*, 15:2) stand as victors on the fiery sea of glass and sing the song of Moses and the Lamb. The exodus of the people of God that began under the leadership of Moses was completed by the death of Jesus. This new song is still the song of Moses since the redemption of Israel had begun with him. But it is also the song of the Lamb because it commemorates the final redemption of believers from the beast and the judgement of the wicked: the exodus of the true Israel in anticipation of their full new citizenship in the new Canaan. This is the highest moment in Christian redemption: the enemies defeated by God and chaos tamed. Mere words could not capture this triumph; that is why it is expressed in song.

God's mighty act of deliverance of his people in Christ (cf. Exodus 15:3) was also a judgement on his enemies (cf. Exodus 15:1–10,12) and the beginning of his liberation of the true Israel from their enemies. Exodus 15 previewed the whole course of God's redemptive purposes for his people, that is, a new creation with the worship of God in his holy temple in the new Jerusalem. The completion of redemption is 'great and marvellous' (15:3). The purposive action of the seven angels by which the old world will pass away is, likewise, 'great and marvellous' (15:1) because from the judgements will come the new creation.

The Lamb's song opens with the most comprehensive term in Revelation to recognise God's universal sovereignty: Lord God Almighty (1:8; 4:8; 11:17; 15:3; 16:7; 19:6; 21:22, cf. 16:14; 19:15). The song celebrates the conclusion of God's covenant faithfulness (15:3). This song by Moses evokes images of Sinai, exodus, ark, covenant and the tabernacle. But, in addition to Moses, this song is about the Lamb's new exodus by the cross and resurrection. The song is about the course of biblical redemption from Moses to the cross. It is not the full story of redemption; it does not begin with the Fall. But it is the full story of Israel's exodus redemption. It is sung to the Lamb because the Lamb's victory (redemption) explains the implications of Moses' song. Like the ancient Israelites, Christ's people had been brought through their Red Sea exodus. The Lamb's followers know that the victory that is now theirs has been won by the blood of the new Passover Lamb (cf. 7:14; 12:11). The new song by Moses and the Lamb is sung with harps from God: divine instruments necessary for new divine cadences of final redemption celebrating new deliverance under a new covenant. What God did in Moses was a preview of what God was to do in the Lamb. But the song does not praise the victory itself—it is expected that God would prevail to protect the people he had chosen—rather, praise is given for the manner in which God achieved victory. So God is praised for his holiness, which is his manner of acting. And what God does in his holiness can never be anticipated.

Richard Bauckham has pointed out that the new song by Moses and the Lamb—celebrating the exodus—is influenced by Isaiah 12, with exodus detail from Psalm 105.[1] On the great day of eschatological salvation, the true Israelites will sing a victory song like the song at the Red Sea. They will praise God for threefold deliverance from the beast, the beast's image, and the number of the beast's name (cf. Deuteronomy 32; Exodus 15).

The exodus had shown God's might, God's judgement over his enemies, and God's clear superiority to foreign gods by bringing his people into his temple (Exodus 15:13,17).[2] The new exodus will, likewise, lead to God's eternal kingdom. The controlling motif of the Revelation exodus song is celebration of the divine attributes of God and his incomparability. God's great and marvellous works are interpreted as righteous and therefore true. God's actions of historical deliverance reveal his fidelity to his covenantal promises. It is by God's wondrous acts that his people will finally occupy the always contemplated new Eden (cf. Genesis 2:4–17). The exclamatory 'King of the ages' (15:3) extols God's divine greatness. These Old Testament exodus themes present the victory of the one true God evoking worship from the nations. The song of Moses is also called the Song of the Lamb because in the Lamb's death is the completion of the exodus redemption by which it is possible for the saints to occupy the real Promised Land: the new sanctuary in a new world-Eden (22:1–5). The victory song of 15:2–4 also refutes the beast's invincibility (cf. 13:3–4 in which the mortal wound of the beast and his recovery is taken to attest his deity). The death and resurrection of the Lamb demonstrates the deity of the true God.

God's mighty act of judgement filled the nations with fear (Exodus 15:14–16). This fear is the attitude of awed reverence appropriate for humankind at the revelation of God (15:4) and his unique superiority to pagan gods (Exodus 15:11). In the new

---

[1] 1993, The Climax of Prophecy, 296–307; cf. Steve Moyise, 2004, 347–60.
[2] cf. Bauckham, The Climax of Prophecy, 1993, 300.

exodus, God's incomparable deity that refute the beast's claim to deity and world rule is demonstrated to the nations. All nations will come and bow down to God's incomparable deity (Psalm 86:9). All nations will fear God as the universal King (cf. Jeremiah 10:7). All nations will give God glory (14:7), that is, declare his uniqueness (15:3–4). All nations will bow to God's uniqueness in both salvation and judgement. The song (15:2–4) thus negates the hollow exodus parody with which the world worships the beast: 'who is like the beast and who can fight against it?' (13:4; cf. Exodus 15:11).

God's mighty act of judgement on his enemies also constitutes deliverance for his people (Exodus 15:1–10). God's judgement and deliverance demonstrate his incomparability (Exodus 15:11; cf. Jeremiah 10:6–7a; Psalm 86:8–10), fill the pagan nations with fear (Exodus 15:13, 17), and bring his people into the temple. The significance of the new exodus is that it leads to the temple of God and the Lamb (21:22).

The effect of the Lamb's sacrifice is the redemption of a special people from all the nations who will worship and acknowledge God. The result is reconciliation of the world to God and the purchase of the true Israel. The Lamb's victory is dispensed throughout the world by Christian witness. Christian witness also testified to God alone as holy, distinct from his creation, and thus beyond comparison in judgement (Jeremiah 10:6–7; Psalm 86:9–10).[3] God reveals his incomparability by judging people in righteousness; these are his 'righteous acts.' God's ways are contrary to expectations;[4] the goal of the world kingdom of God is beyond human comprehension or implementation. The continual attempt of humans throughout history to bring in their kingdom of God has been the great world error. At the end—whether willingly or unwillingly—all nations will worship God and honour him as the one true God.[5]

Finally, the link between this new song and the bowl judgements show the two reactions to the judgements that accompany the church's witness and God's call to the world to repent. The

---

3   Beale, 1999, 797.
4   cf. Tonstad, 2006, 153.
5   Beale, 1999, 799.

first reaction is the worship of God: the divine judgements, if recognised as the vindication of the witness of the church, lead to repentance and worship. The second reaction is blasphemy of the divine name: those who still refuse to heed the church's witness and God's call take up a position of stubborn opposition from which they cannot be converted. God's judgements vindicating the elect and punishing the godless reveal his uniqueness.

Therefore the judgements in the seven last plagues (16:2–21), like the plagues of Egypt and culminating in an earthquake, characterise both the witness and vindication of the two witnesses (11:6, 13) and the destruction of the godless. 15:5–19:21 shows that the continued refusal of the world to heed the church's witness hardens the opposition of the world to God. This hardening pinnacles in a final climactic attempt to prevent the coming of his kingdom.

The Song of Moses and the Lamb was anticipated at the end of Revelation 14 (the positive image of the Son of Man's harvest followed by the negative image of the winepress). This victory song (15:2–4) must be followed by God's action that leads to the fall of the world system. Babylon the harlot must give way to the new Jerusalem, the bride of the Lamb.

Seven angels carrying (cf. 15:7) the seven last plagues now appear from the open temple of the tabernacle of testimony (15:6), where the Ark of the Covenant contained the two tables of the Decalogue. Thus what follows is God's execution in judgement of the unchangeable divine law. The tabernacle—with its Ark of the Covenant and two tables of the Decalogue—merges in symbolism and divine purpose with Zion and the temple. Drawing on Israel's wilderness experience of the accompanying tabernacle, God is revealing his sustained presence with his covenant people throughout history. The seven angels bear the bowls of God's wrath (cf. 14:10; Isaiah 51:17, 22) which the unbelieving world must drink.

Continuing the exodus motif, the heavenly temple is parallel to the wilderness tabernacle as its function is to contain the testimony (that is, the Ten Commandments). The tabernacle is a covenant repository. God will call the world to account for its flagrant disobedience to his laws. God's covenant law contained in the tabernacle, by which the world was to be regulated, comes fully into play in the final judgement. God's demand for obedience to his declared will—a demand which was fully and finally communicated in Jesus, the faithful witness (1:5)—takes centre stage in the final judgement. God rules from the heavenly temple. This rule of God is continually demonstrated through divine control of history, but God's rule is seen pre-eminently in and through the witness of Jesus through the Body of Christ.

The heavenly temple (cf. 7:15) thus represents the fulfilment of symbolic presentations of the divine presence in the Old Testament.[6] The seven trumpets had found their climax in the vision (11:19) of the open heavenly temple. With the temple now open prior to the bowl judgements (15:5), God's just covenant decrees are about to be fulfilled as his kingship over the nations is imposed.

The seven angels are robed in pure white linen and clothed around the chest with golden girdles (15:6) like priests (cf. Exodus 28, 39; Lev 16:4, 23, 32). These angels are almost identical in appearance to the Son of Man (1:13). This similarity in appearance indicates that these seven angels are acting as Jesus' royal representatives. God is now responding to the saints prayers (in golden bowls of incense, 8:3) with golden bowls full of wrath (15:7; cf. Isaiah 51:17, 22). God's wrath is to be directed against Babylon, the world city. The temple is filled with smoke, just like: Sinai mountain had been wrapped in smoke in the exodus;[7] and the judgement vision of Isaiah 6:1–4. The smoke is indicative of the unapproachable glory of God and his power at a critical 'moment' (cf. 1 Kings 8:10–11; Ezekiel 44:4). No being, not even heavenly beings, can stand in God's awesome presence till the seven angels have completed their task (15:8).

The section between God's temple opened (11:19) and the temple of the tabernacle of witness opened in heaven (15:5) is the centrepiece of the book. 11:19–15:5 is in the middle of the three heavenly visions (4:1–5:14; 11:19–15:5; 19:11–21:8).

The Ark of the Covenant was seen by John within the opened heavenly temple (11:19). This signifies that in the final transformation, with the descent of believers as the new Jerusalem, the

---

6 Spatafora, 1997, 239.
7 Smalley, 2005, 392.

full covenantal purposes of God (to place his people in an Eden setting) will be achieved by the seven bowl judgements to which the seven trumpet judgements had pointed. The seven angels come from the temple with the seven plagues (15:5–6). The accompanying theophanic constituents of 11:19 (lightnings, noises, thundering, earthquakes, great hail) are expanded in the account of the seventh bowl (16:17–21). The intervening chapters (Revelation 12–14) reminds the reader that the assembling of the people of God must proceed apace with the restoration of creation preceding the final judgement (cf. Romans 8:20–22). The sequence of bowls is thus marked as a development of the seventh trumpet. That is: the seventh trumpet is followed by the centrepiece vision (11:19–15:5); the centrepiece vision is enclosed by the marker of the opened temple; and the centrepiece vision is followed by the bowl sequence. Unlike the seals that anticipate judgements, the trumpets and bowls implement the judgements.

The temple was filled with smoke from the glory of God as evidence of his powerful presence (15:8; cf. Exodus 40:34; 1 Kings 8:10; Isaiah 6: 4; Ezekiel 44:4). The smoke of the glory of God prevented anyone from entering, just as Moses had been prevented from entering the tabernacle by the cloud of God's glory at its consecration (Exodus 40:35; cf. 1 Kings 8:10–11). God, in his awesome sacredness, had taken possession of his sanctuary. An allusion to Isaiah's vision (Isaiah 6:1–4)—which began when the living creatures cried holy, holy, holy is the Lord God Almighty (4:8)—is completed with the smoke filling the temple (15:8). But whereas Revelation 4 was the vision of the throne, Revelation 15 is the vision of the opened temple. The use of 'temple' differs slightly from 'throne'. Both 'temple' and 'throne' are used as authority symbols. On the one hand, 'temple' is used in Revelation only in regard to a world that disobeys God's commands. On the other hand, 'throne' is used as a royal judicial symbol indicating that God's glory is to be manifested in natural phenomena. But God himself, now acting in this terrible judgement, cannot be seen.

The smoke prevents access to the temple until the seven plagues of final judgement run their course; the old order must be transformed before the new order is accessible. Nothing else takes place until this world judgement finishes. The smoke is reminiscent of the dedication of Solomon's temple when, after the Ark of the Covenant was brought in, Solomon's temple filled with a cloud and priests were unable to enter (2 Chronicles 5:7, 13–14).[8] After Solomon's prayer of dedication, God's glory filled the temple again. And, again, entrance into the temple was prevented (2 Chronicles 7:1–2; cf. Isaiah 6:4). God's judgements on a fallen world are designed to restore the everlasting covenant between Creator and creation. The judgements will lead to an open heaven and the descent of the new Jerusalem. The bowls of wrath are delivered from the throne to the angels by one of the four living creatures (4:6). The living creature is a representative of the four guardians of nature. Here nature is being surrendered for destruction with a view to transformation. The final judgement expresses the glory of God (*doxa*, the manifested holiness of God 'who lives forever', 15:8) and the power of God (*dunamis*, the manifested might of God in judgement, 15:8). The affirmation of the throne room is that the God who lives forever exercises his control over a godless world (15:7; cf. 4:9–10). When God's glory is manifested in heaven, the effect on earth is the destruction of evil (15:7–8).

Heaven Excursus

The term heaven originally meant the firmament: the physical space above the earth with everything that was in that space. But heaven is not a geographical space. The Bible does not place God in a space above the earth. Heaven also acquired a metaphysical meaning (cf. 11:19): the divine sphere, the transcendent world, where man does not normally have access. In the Revelation John has access to God's dwelling in heaven; John is allowed for a time to experience the transcendent.

In the Old Testament: the flood gates of heaven were opened to flood the earth (Genesis 7:11); God commanded the gates of heaven to open and rain manna on his people (Psalm 78:23–24); and the prophet cried out to God to open the heaven (Isaiah 64:1), to manifest himself in a new theophany so that the divine word would be open to the human person. Heaven will cease at the

---

8   Stevenson, 2001, 298.

inauguration of the new creation; heaven and earth will no longer be two distinct realities, rather, they will be united as one.

The opening of the heaven in the New Testament is associated with Christ. The Synoptic Gospels indicate that heaven was opened at Jesus' baptism, indicating that the kingdom of God had broken into this world. All the promises given to Israel are fulfilled in Jesus. So heaven is now open and in faith the believer can see the divine glory (Acts 7:56). Heaven is open for the Seer in the Apocalypse, that is, John is in the divine presence and given a knowledge of divine revelation. The opening of the heavenly temple signifies accessibility. Whereas heaven is still a symbol of the transcendent sphere where God can be found, because of Jesus heaven is now also the place where man can encounter God and be present with him. The open temple means that humans can now have direct relationship with God. In the Old Testament, God was only accessible to the priestly class. But the open heaven means approach to the Deity is open to all. The old economy of salvation based on the temple in Jerusalem with its cultic system is now abolished. Instead, God is now worshipped in the heavenly temple. So the crowd worshipping in the heavenly temple (7:9–12) is a vision of the people of God in this age; this is the transcendent reality for Christians in the present age.

The heavenly temple is a symbol for another reality. Whereas heaven has cosmological and theological meaning, the image of the heavenly temple cannot be interpreted literally. The Bible says that God dwells on high above the clouds beyond human sight. But Scripture uses the language of above and below to speak of God's utter difference from human persons, that is, his superiority. 'On high' is not a physical location. To describe God as dwelling in heaven is to recognise the transcendence of God, his separateness from the created order. Scripture itself recognises the inadequacy of metaphorical language used to describe God's dwelling place: 'But will God indeed dwell on earth? Behold, heaven and the highest heaven cannot contain thee' (1 Kings 8:27).

So heaven is the symbol of the divine world beyond human senses and, therefore, unattainable to humankind. In 4:1 John is invited to go through an open door and enter into heaven. It is not a physical entering but, rather, a raised awareness of being in the presence of God. John was in the Spirit. When the Bible speaks of heaven, the sacred writers are trying to express in words what is beyond human thought and experience. God utterly transcends the normal human boundaries of time and space. God is everywhere. But the limits of space and time which God transcends are all around us. So the truth about heaven is neither the image nor the language. The reality which Bible words are trying to convey is that heaven is the breaking in of the wholly different end-time into history. In the end-time, the temple will consist of God and Christ and the faithful who are united in them.

In this now and not yet time there is a heavenly temple which is not the temple of the eschaton. God and the Lamb are not the temple in 7:15 since the text says that the elect will serve God in his temple. The now and not yet heavenly temple is: a transcendent reality where the person is united with God; the breaking in of the transcendent into our world; the church in all its reality. To be in heaven does not mean being in a geographical place. Rather, to be in heaven is to be united with God. Heaven is a quality of human life, that is, full maturity and perfection in the presence of God. Heaven is sharing in the life of the resurrected and glorified Christ. Christians reach the perfection of heaven in death. But Christians are already in heaven in this life inasmuch as they are united with God in Christ. Christians enjoy on earth in an imperfect way the life which will be manifest in the final age. They cannot see or fully experience yet the transcendent reality but, in a veiled way, Christians are already participating in heaven. In this way the kingdom of God is already present in the world (1:9; 11:15; 12:10).

Revelation 16

Revelation 16:1–19:5 World Judgement: The Fall of Babylon the Great

This section of Revelation presents the fall of the world system and the final defeat of evil. When the church has been removed from the world, Satanic evil turns on itself. At the end of Revelation 16, the world system implodes and God's rule is ushered in without final conflict.

At 16:1 God is alone in the temple since the temple had been filled with God's glory (15:8). God's glory (the sense of his aweful majesty) is ubiquitous (Numbers 14:21). But there are critical moments when God's glory is displayed and becomes tangible to the senses in all its overwhelming intensity. At critical moments when God's glory fills his temple, some great new beginning or ending is taking place (cf. Isaiah 6 at the beginning of Isaiah's great ministry; Ezekiel 8–10). The great end accompanying God's glory filling the temple (15:8) is probably the end of the age of the Gentiles; the new beginning is the ushering in of the new creation. At the end of the bowls series a great voice (of God) comes out of the temple from the throne saying 'it is finished' (16:17). This announcement is the end of God's wrath. This is also the last *naos* (temple) passage in Revelation.

In Revelation 16–19 judgement falls on the beast and his followers. With the final bowl, judgement is complete (16:17). Babylon the Great is destroyed. Revelation 17 details the judgement when all who are evil turn on themselves and their system. Revelation 18 presents lamentations from those who had benefited from Babylon. In 19:1–2 the prayers of the saints (6:9–11) have found their fulfilment. In Revelation 19 two different futures are envisaged: the marriage banquet of the Lamb (19:7); and the great supper of God (19:17), which is the defeat of all opposition.

Revelation 16 The Judgement of the Bowls

The seven bowls correspond to the seven trumpets and the exodus plagues. The first trumpet/bowl has to do with the earth (8:7;

16:2). The second trumpet/bowl has to do with the sea (8:9; 16:3). The third trumpet/bowl has to do with rivers and fountains (8:10; 16:4). The fourth trumpet/bowl has to do with the sun (8:12; 16:8). The fifth trumpet/bowl has to do with darkness, torture and anguish (9:2; 16:10). The sixth trumpet/bowl has to do with the Euphrates (9:14; 16:12). And the seventh trumpet/bowl has to do with loud voices in heaven (11:15; 16:17). The consummation is revealed at 19:6–22:5. So the vision of the bowls repeats the trumpets but with added emphasis. The operative problems in the world have greatly intensified from tribulation and warning (the trumpets) to total world judgement (the bowls).[1] The drama of the first exodus from Egypt is being replayed but in a different key towards the final entry into the land of promise.

The divine order for pouring the bowls of judgement comes from the temple, that is, from God himself. In Psalm 11:4–7 God looks down upon the wicked from his heavenly temple and brings judgement on them in the interests of justice. Isaiah 66:6 announces: 'A voice from the temple! The voice of the Lord, dealing retribution to his enemies' (RSV). The voice from the temple (16:1) promises similar retribution.[2] Following God's command, the seven golden bowls filled with the wrath of God are poured out. The prayers of the saints are in golden bowls (5:8). So the outpouring of the golden bowls on the earth is the fulfilment of the saints' prayers for justice. The saints' prayer arose from the altar (6:10) and finds fulfilment in the proclamation from the altar.

The bowls are concerned specifically with the judgement of the beast and his world-city. The first four judgements apply to the fourfold division of creation: earth, sea, fresh waters and heaven. In 14:17 the angel called on all peoples who dwell on earth to worship 'him who made the heaven and the earth, the sea and the springs of water'. But this call had not been observed. So the bowls of judgement are poured out. In the first four bowl judgements, those who worship the beast are shown the evidence that God the Creator is sovereign (not the beast).

The bowl judgements must be interpreted as occurring after the chorus of the saved praising God for the completion of the new

---

1   cf. Talbert, 1994, 72.
2   Stevenson, 2001, 299.

exodus conducted by the Lamb (15:3–4). The reaction of the world to the final bowl judgement is blasphemy (16:21). Unlike the seals and trumpets series which each have a lengthy interruption between the sixth and seventh items, all seven bowls are delivered with only a brief interruption. The account of the sixth bowl is interrupted by a prophetic oracle which Christ addresses to his people (16:15). This interruption does not signal delay, rather, the oracle signals the suddenness of the Lord's coming. Humanity's failure to repent, noted in the sixth trumpet (9:20–21), is no longer a cause for delay. This structural difference marks the finality of the bowls series.

There is a contrast in the unbelieving world's response to the same judgements. Pseudo-belief (11:13) is contrasted with those who finally harden themselves against all witness to the truth of God (Revelation 16). Thus hardened, unbelievers are destroyed in their last assault on God's kingdom so that God's kingdom may come. No one is said to die from the plagues of Revelation 16, instead, final world judgement follows immediately.

The judgements administered by the seven angels will result in the total collapse of the world structure and its institutions. Each angel, with the exception of the fifth, pours his bowl on an element of nature. The pouring of the bowl brings on the associated plague. And creation is thereby transformed.

The bowls series is the intensification of the trumpets series of judgements, directed against the same world problems (idolatry and disobedience). The bowls represent the conclusion of the third woe, that is, the seventh trumpet (11:14). The bowls usher in world judgement in preparation for God's new social and world order. One of the angels who pours out this final expression of wrath (the bowls) is John's guide both at the beginning of the Babylon section (17:1) and the new Jerusalem section (21:9). Thus the two sections—Babylon and new Jerusalem—are related: the judgements are followed by salvation; the destruction of Babylon and the advent of the new Jerusalem are the interrelated conclusions to which the whole process of judgement has been moving, commencing at Revelation 6.

The punishments imposed by the bowls are consistent with the way that God has always responded to evil in this world:

humankind is permitted to suffer the consequences of its own evil. The exodus plagues parallel the bowls series of judgements. These parallels identify these punishments as being from God for the failure of the world to honour God. The plagues on Pharaoh and his land were an open statement of the character and power of the God of Israel, a deliverance of God's people, and entry into their Promised Land. In Revelation the exodus-type happening accomplishes: God's liberation of believers; God's transformation of the believers' world; and, in a way that could not have been predicted, their entry into a new Promised Land. God's blessings for the future (Revelation) take the form of the blessings for the faithful in the exodus: a Promised Land in which there will be eternal rest; and final, perfect security in divine fellowship for all believers who conquer the beast. Revelation takes a special interest in martyrdom (13:15); but the book does not promise the martyrs special privilege. The martyrs reward will be their knowledge that their sacrifice glorified God.

The response of unrepentant sinners to the seven last plagues is not craven fear and enforced worship. On the contrary, they curse God. Their response (16:9,11,21) is antithetical to the response of the believing community (15:3). In the subsequent account of the fall of Babylon, the Parousia and the battle of Armageddon (Revelation 18–19), there is never any suggestion that those who suffer final judgement acknowledge God's rule. Revelation seems to offer only two possibilities for the nations: repentance, fear of God, genuine worship (11:13, 14:7; 15:4); or persistence in worshipping the beast, refusal to repent, refusal to worship, cursing God, and final opposition to God's rule leading to final judgement (14:9–11; 16:9,11,21; 17:14; 19:17–21).

After the judgements of the seals and trumpets, the wicked fail to repent (9:20–21). The response of the unrepentant to the seven last bowl plagues is even worse: they curse God (16:9,11,21) and then gather for a determined last act of opposition to God (16:13–16; 17:14; 19:19). The first four of the seven bowl plagues (16:2–9) show God to be the Creator. The unrepentant cannot avoid recognising that God is Creator. They could make the connection between effect and cause. But instead of responding to the invitation to worship the Creator (14:7), they refuse to repent and—probably recognising who God is—curse him.

The loud voice from God (16:1) from the temple is an imperative in the aorist tense: 'go'. The directive is urgent. The angels are to empty (pour out) their bowl judgements. These bowl judgements are not only a recapitulation of previous punishments (seals and trumpets) but the bowl punishments are also more universal and more intense. The judgements of Revelation 16–19 destroy the world's political, economic, and religious systems (symbolised by the beast, the false prophet, the world city of Babylon, and the kings of the earth). Humans who support these world systems will perish with them. The world continues to reject what the church faithfully proclaims. But finally the world must concede that God is sovereign.

Inexorable doom must now reach its climax. The bowl narratives move to a rapid conclusion without significant interlude (16:15). The final three bowl plagues (16:10–21, parallel with the last three trumpets) bring about the collapse of the world system. The plagues in the two series (trumpets and bowls) reach their climax after small beginnings and gradual development.[3] No further series of judgements is to follow. There is no further possibility of repentance. The seventh seal and seventh trumpet anticipate and refer to the climactic seventh bowl.

The first four bowls may be simultaneously poured out on creation—earth, sea, rivers, sun (the factors for life, growth, and commerce)—directed against those who bear the mark of the beast. These first four bowls bring about the further gradual but very threatening dissolution of creation. All areas necessary to sustain human life (earth, sea, rivers, sun) are brought to the point of collapse. God has endangered and removed necessary components for human survival. World hunger, thirst, deprivation, and suffering ensue. But world reaction to these plagues is not repentance; rather, the world curses the Creator (16:9). The failure of the unbelieving world to repent is noted (16:9,11). But the unrepentant in this final series of judgements do not cause further delay (cf. 9:20–21). There is no further possibility of repentance available.

---

3   cf. Hoeksema, 2000, 542–5.

The first four judgements of the bowls (16:2–9) apply to the same four divisions of creation (earth, sea, fresh waters, heavens and sky) as the first four trumpet judgements. The last three bowls are poured on the beast, on the great river, and on Babylon (the city that is representative of systematic world unbelief). The first four bowls having regard to the four divisions of creation show that God, not the beast, is the Creator. The first six trumpets and first five bowls also serve to explain in detail the woes of the age. The last trumpet and last two bowls narrate the last judgement.

The focus of the trumpets was that they were incomplete. They gave continuous warning to the world by the threat to life posed by a fallen created order. Creation's purposes had been distorted. But whereas the trumpets were incomplete and gave continuous warning, the emphasis of the bowls is terminating the world of human existence.

Revelation 16:2 The First Bowl

The first bowl is poured on the earth, humankind's habitat, which is now ruled by the beast and his followers. The unbelieving world is then repudiated for their idolatry in worshipping the image of the beast. The first bowl becomes a foul and festering sore (*elkos*, cf. the similar sixth plague in Exodus 9:8–11) on those who had the mark of the beast. They already had the mark of the beast; now they have a penal mark of another kind.[4] The bowls thus deal comprehensively with all the disobedient—all who followed the beast—before the advent of the final heavenly Canaan.

The plagues demonstrate that the holiness of God is active on earth in judgement. Creation had become other than what it was meant to be. The bowls emphasise that, in the presence of God's holiness, the mark of the beast leads to pernicious human problems.

Revelation 16:3 The Second Bowl

The sea (16:3; cf. the second trumpet 8:8–9) on which the next bowl is poured is the realm of rebellion. The sea is the counterpart of the earth, symbolising rebellious humankind (cf. 17:1, 'many

---

4   Beale, 1999, 814.

waters' = multitudes of peoples). The plague symbolically presents a dire blow to the ungodly economy of the Empire, which depends on trade and commerce (cf. 8:9 where a third of the ships were destroyed).[5] The sea turned to blood parallels the first exodus plague (16:3; cf. Exodus 7:17–21). Trade and commerce was the life-blood of the great city (world Babylon). Initially it was probably thought that Rome was world Babylon. But ongoing ungodly social and economic systems will always be in conflict with the final city of God.

Revelation 16:5 The Third Bowl

The angel of the waters (16:5), who apparently pours the third bowl, may be some kind of divine superintendent of part of the material creation.[6] He pours out the bowl on the fresh waters, rivers and springs (cf. the third trumpet, 8:10–11). Humankind depends on these waters for life. The water turning to blood, like the second bowl, is reminiscent of the first Egyptian plague and may refer to economic suffering.[7] Blood is a figurative symbol for both death and suffering. This is a grim requital for all those who have subjected the Christian church and its leadership to persecution and death.

The hymnic interlude (16:5–7) is a theological reflection on the nature of the judgements in the first three bowls. These judgements affect people, firstly, then world trade and finally the fundamental necessities that sustain human life.[8] Smalley points to the close relationship of the hymns in 16:5–6 and 15:3–4, both of which point to the judicial righteousness of God's response. God's judgements are never capricious (16:5) but, rather, are always holy and just. The penalties of the bowls are deserved. The bowl judgements are products of God's righteousness. In these judgements God is being faithful to his creation. God's holy judgement executes his wrath against the persecutors. The persecutors—those who had shed the blood of God's servants—are themselves, metaphorically, given blood to drink (cf. Isaiah 49:26). This blood drink may refer to either the internecine conflict among the

---

5   op. cit., 815.
6   Aune, 1998, 884.
7   ibid., 1999, 816.
8   Smalley, 2005, 402–4.

persecutors (17:16–18) or the polluted waters rising from the second bowl. Hence this third bowl judgement is *lex talionis*: the world has shed the blood of believers; the persecutors get what they deserve (16:6). These end-time judgements are the answer to the prayers of the saints and prophets whose blood had been poured out (16:6–7; cf. 6:9–11). A second voice from the heavenly altar, probably one of the martyrs underneath it, affirms that the exercise of this punishment has been true: consistent with God's revealed righteous character and, therefore, the judgement itself is righteous.

Revelation 16:8–9 The Fourth Bowl

The fourth bowl is, figuratively, poured out on the sun. The sun is the source of heat and life for the human-occupied earth. Life is impossible without the sun. The figurative 'scorch' inflicted by this bowl judgement is repeated (16:8,9) to indicate the severity of the judgement. All four divisions of natural creation (earth, sea, rivers, heavens) have now been subjected to judgement. Beale suggests that cosmic change repays humankind for altering God's moral laws, that is, the cosmic structure of the earth has been affected by human disobedience throughout history.[9] The world responds to these bowl judgements with blasphemy, attributing the plagues to anything but God. Hence there is no repentance. The blasphemous earth dwellers have been changed more and more into the likeness of the blasphemous beast (cf. 13:1,5,6; 17:3). They affirm the beast's character in their actions and lifestyle. Unmoved by this bowl judgement, the earth dwellers don't give God glory: they don't acknowledge the judgements of God as the source of their problems and repent. Instead of repentance, they responded with anger.

Revelation 16:10–16 The Fifth and Sixth Bowls

The last three bowls induce full scale devastation on fallen humanity, overthrowing the governing structures of the world.[10] The fifth bowl highlights the power of God and reveals the illegitimacy of the beast's claims to royalty and power. The images of gnawing tongues, pain and sores (16:10–11) collate the effects of the first

---

9   Beale, 1999, 821–22.
10 Lioy, 2003, 144.

four bowls: the sores have come from the first bowl; the gnawing tongues, representing thirst from the waters turned into blood, have come from the second and third bowls (16:3–4); and the pains from the scorching sun have come from the fourth bowl (16:8). Believers will be protected from these effects of judgement (16:2; 7:16).

The heart of the idolatrous world—the throne of the beast, the centre of the beast's sovereignty, the source of the power of evil in the world—is affected. The kingdom of the beast is now in disarray. Darkness, reminiscent of the ninth exodus plague (Exodus 10:21–29), indicates the withdrawal of God's presence. Evil now prevails; spiritual darkness covers the entire kingdom. People now begin to recognise God's curse as the cause of their suffering but they do not turn to God (16:11). Darkness is also a metaphor for judgement (2 Peter 2:17; Jude 13) and coupled with the shadow of death in the Old Testament (cf. Jeremiah 13:16). 16:10 is the first direct mention of the 'kingdom' of the beast, although the beast's kingdom is implied by his 'throne' (13:2). In unity the citizens of the beast's kingdom blaspheme the God of heaven: they blindly continue to war against all that reveals the true condition of their kingdom.

The sixth bowl resumes the effects of the sixth trumpet with the image of the Euphrates (16:12–16; cf. 9:14). The Euphrates was the border of both the Promised Land and Rome's extremities. Beyond the Euphrates was a region from which danger would come for Rome. The symbolic army of 9:13–19 historicised the contemporaneous threat of Parthian invasions. Rome quailed at this threat and, indeed, the destruction that shook the empire came from this source. The drying up of the waters of the Euphrates—historically used of judgement upon Babylon (Cyrus diverted the river to capture Babylon, Isaiah 44:27; Jeremiah 50:38; 51:36)—is now taken up to foreshadow the coming demise of the world city at the hands of assembled 'kings' and their forces.

The dried up 'waters' suggests a picture of Babylon's adherents throughout the world becoming disloyal to the city (cf. 17:1 for Babylon's world control and 17:17–18 for her demise from within the system).[11] Babylon's fate, alluded to in the sixth trumpet (9:20), is consummated in the sixth bowl. The sixth trumpet and the sixth bowl both refer to the demonic deception of unbelievers.

16:13–16 spells out the details of 16:12. A further vision (16:13–14) involves all three members of the evil trinity. The third member of the evil trinity is designated as a false prophet. As false prophet, his activity extends to within the churches as well as within the world.[12] The river of lies—his attempt to overwhelm the church—had come out of the mouth of the dragon (13:12–15). Out of the mouth of the beast had come blasphemous pretensions. Out of the mouth of the false prophet had come seductive propaganda supportive of the rule of the beast.[13] The title false prophet suggests that this seductive propaganda supporting the rule of the beast will also affect covenant communities. All three members of the evil trinity are involved in this deception leading to a consummate, final, world scale crisis. By their deception the evil trinity gathers its evil army for battle (16:14; cf. 19:19; 20:8).

Three unclean spirits are spewed out of the mouths of each member of the satanic trinity like frogs, emphasising the demonic character of evil propaganda. The ritually unclean frogs recall the exodus frog plague (Exodus 8:1–15). The frog plague, directed against the Egyptian goddess Heqt, was one of two Exodus plagues that the Egyptian magicians were able to duplicate.[14] The Egyptian goddess Heqt represented resurrection and fertility as a frog.[15] These frog pagan deity emblems coming from the mouths of the unholy trinity 'travel' world-wide. In this way the spiritual deception of the dragon is made effective through the beast's blasphemy and operative in human life and society by the false prophet's mandated control of world values, structures and dynamics. Human world leadership is drawn into the martial service of the dragon by the demonic forces of the unholy trinity. Throughout history unregenerate humanity has been in rebellion against God. But this final war is the great day of Almighty God

---

11   Beale, 1999, 828.
12   cf. Beale, 1999, 831.
13   Caird, 1966, 206.
14   ibid., 1999, 832.
15   A.F. Johnson, 1981, 551.

when the world force of unbelief is assembled (19:19; 20:8) against Christ at his Second Coming for *the*—that is, the expected—war. In this final battle the Messiah and God will destroy the forces of the dragon and the beast (17:14; 19:14–21; 20:7–10).

The frogs are presented as 'doing signs'. The frogs represent great deceptions calculated to stimulate unbelievers to defend what they see as their vital interests. This false view causes the world's political leadership—that is, the kings of the whole inhabited earth—to gather armies for the great denouement of the Day of the Lord, the Parousia, when unbelievers will be finally judged and believers given their reward of the crown of life.

A charge is given to the saints in the parable of the 'thief' (16:15; cf. 3:2–3; Matthew 24:43; Luke 12:39–40; and, associated with the Day of the Lord, 1 Thessalonians 5:2,4). The saints must keep their garments, that is, the saints must maintain sanctifying conduct (cf. 3:4–5,18; 19:8)[16] that is detached from idolatrous conduct with the world. The saints must be clothed ready for instantaneous action. For the end will be unforeseen, unexpected, probably when the human world and its systems are at the height of their power and achievement. The world will be unprepared (cf. 'nakedness', 16:15). Like the action of a thief, the end cannot be predicted. But there is a blessing (the third of Revelation's seven blessings) pronounced on the faithful. However, this blessing is combined with a warning. The combination of blessing and warning emphasises the finality of what is to come. Failure to prepare will mean shame and exposure. Saints who are enticed by the human achievements of the idolatrous world will be left naked, exposed to judgement (2 Corinthians 5:3; cf. Israel at Ezekiel 16:39).

Demonic spirits of the evil trinity ('they', 16:16) gather the kings of the world and their armies ('them', 16:16, the world army) at Armageddon. Believers are not involved. If the location is given a Greek rough breathing it could mean Mount (*har*) Megiddo; but there is no mountain there. If the location is given a Greek smooth breathing (without an initial plosive *h*), it could mean Megiddo city; and there was such a place near the Plain of Esdraelon. The location could also mean *har* (mount) Magedon (of

---

[16] Smalley, 2005, 412.

slaughter).[17] Megiddo, as the site of over two hundred battles, may be symbolic of titanic world collapse. Megiddo was the location of decisive battles: Lord Allenby in 1914–18; Thutmoses III in 1468 BC; Judges 4–5; and the defeat and death of king Josiah by Pharaoh Necho in 609 BC (2 Kings 23:28ff). But the outcome of this final battle will not be decided by action between two armies. Rather, this final battle—symbolically projected at Megiddo, the centre famous for battles in world history—will be won by the Messiah as he applies the sword of his mouth (cf. 19:15).

Revelation 16:17–21 The Seventh Bowl

The battle of Armageddon leads to the ultimate destruction of the evil world system (anticipated at 16:17–21 and 17:14–18; presented in detail at 19:11–21).[18] When the seventh bowl is poured, the voice comes from the temple to announce completion of the judgements. 'It is done!' (16:17) signals God's final direct divine intervention to transform his own created universe (cf. 21:6). Thus commences the concluding section of Revelation (16:17–22:5). Even the air—the realm of Satan (Ephesians 2:2) upon which the contents of the seventh bowl are poured—seems to be affected by the evil rebellion. This element that sustains life is thus subject to judgement. Holiness from the throne of God (16:17) affects the totality of the rebellious animate order. The voice of either God or Christ comes from the temple and the throne, from the very centre of world authority, with a proclamation: 'it is done'. And this proclamation means that the human rebellion which has distorted every aspect of creation has now been overborne!

The third woe, announced prior to the seventh trumpet (11:14), is now fulfilled. The proclamation 'it is done' says that God's wrath has been fully expended. The end has come, as foreshadowed, with the sounding of the seventh trumpet (10:6–7). The bowls have thus been interpolated within the seventh trumpet. No part of the world realm has been exempted from judgement, and God is present in the midst of the rebellious order. Lightnings, voices and thunders tie this dramatic end into the

---

17 cf. Aune, 1998, 898–899.
18 Beale, 1999, 841.

throne room vision (4:5; cf. 16:18; 8:5; 11:19). The cosmic phenomena at the final judgement (16:18) are unparalleled in human experience. These phenomena, especially the earthquake, speak for the presence of God shaking (16:19) the world as the consummation of his wrath (cf. 15:1) wreaking destruction on the realm of rebellion (6:12; 8:5; 11:13; 16:19). Whereas this is still visionary, it nevertheless reveals the dire consequences of God's act in Christ's death. The attendant circumstances of the end are revealed but the end itself is not revealed. The destruction of the Great World City (Rome, representative of the Babylon of all ages), now dissolved into three parts, is complete. The whole orientation of the rebellious realm is radically overthrown (16:20). God had remembered Babylon (16:19), for her sins had reached even unto heaven (18:5)! But the evil trinity has not yet been destroyed. The fall of evil (Revelation 6–16) and the onset of the new creation (19:11–21:8) are thus linked: the latter as a consequence of the former.

The total cosmos (16:20) is affected. Islands and mountains vanish, perhaps a result of the earthquake. The terrors of the divine encounter with the world are compounded with the last physical judgement in which tremendous hailstones—like those that fell on Gog, the end-time enemy of Israel (cf. Exodus 9:22–26; Ezekiel 38:19–22)—drop from heaven (16:21). But the citizens of fallen Babylon continue to blaspheme. The first four bowls reveal the detrimental consequences, personally, in the lives of those who persist in rebellion. The last three bowls reveal the detrimental consequences for the rebellious kingdom of the beast. God had touched the centre of the beast's kingdom which is now totally overthrown. The destructive consequences of the cross and resurrection for a world under judgement have now been completed. Yet unbelievers, hardened in their sinfulness, continue their stance in blasphemy to the end. The mighty shout from heaven, 'It is done', anticipated the end (cf. 21:6). The effect of this judgement is described in the following chapters.

The collapse of world imperialism is due to fornication, that is, the consequence of idolatry (cf. 17:1–2). This collapse takes place as the climax of Revelation is approached. Babylon is the name chosen to exhibit world imperialism (world structures), which makes sense in the light of Israel's experience. The empire ideology nominated as Babylon finds continuity in Rome and other world empires which are all destroyed as the end comes (17:1–19:10). The closing chapters of Revelation exhibit details of the end viewed from different vantage points. The end of the present world order (17:1–19:10) synchronously gives way to the picture of the final judgement of God in Christ (19:11–20:15) and then moves to the advent of the new Jerusalem (21:1–22:9).[19]

The dire consequence of God's act in Christ's death is fragmentation of the entire human structure of rebellion. Historical, particular human organizations will crumble. Fallen Babylon's entire edifice is removed, compounded by the terror of the hail (16:21). But the citizens of fallen Babylon continue to blaspheme to the end, which is the rebellious world's attitude to the cross and resurrection.

The parallel phenomenon associated with the last item in each of the three series (seals, trumpets, bowls) indicates that they are parallel, overlapping judgements which come with increasing intensification. The earthquake accompanying the seventh bowl is described as unique in all history (16:18b); the hailstones accompanying the seventh bowl are described as having the weight of a talent (16:21). Also, in each of the three seventh items (seals, trumpets, bowls) there is a connection with the altar or temple, indicating that God is in complete control of world history even though it may seem at times that history is being fully directed by human decision.

---

19 cf. Mulholland, 1990, 276.

Revelation 17

Overview of Chapters 17–19

Revelation 17–19 traces the nature and fall of Babylon, after the fall of Babylon. If people are to be set free from the spell of the beast and the lure of Babylon, then the city must fall and the beast must be dethroned. God's secret plan to accomplish this end is through the death of Christians who hold fast to the teachings of their Lord. By death they defeat death. Christians are included in Jesus' resurrection life: they are in death with Christ (Philippians 1:21).

The decadence and demise of the Babylon/Rome/world structures is reported in repulsive images (Revelation 17). The threat posed by Babylon is neither her persecutions nor her blatant authority but the insidious power of her seduction.[1] The beast and Babylon have to be unmasked because, in a distorted world, apparently benign Babylon institutions seem normal and culturally acceptable. Babylon and the beast had ruled the world (17:1–2). Babylon's success had been founded on the evil, but seemingly acceptable, ideology represented by the sea beast. Babylon is identified as the harlot (17:5), seducing her world to godless idolatry and immorality (cf. Romans 1:18–32). But absolute power corruptly applied must end in the abyss from which it came (17:6–8).

Aggregation of world power is symbolically represented by the seven mountains on which the beast sits (17:9–11). In John's time, power was concentrated in imperial Rome. In Revelation, the final evil reign is a short-lived united world power structure (17:12–14). But the inevitable end, characteristic of evil, is that the adherents of the evil structure (Babylon) will turn against Babylon's political dominion even though these adherents had once worshipped Babylon and been nourished by her. The evil power eventually collapses in upon itself (17:15–18). The final collapse comes in the abortive attack against the kingdom of God (19:19–21). This final attack is a devastating persecution of Christians and Christianity.

---

[1] cf. David L Barr, 2006, 205–22.

The Old Testament background to the Revelation lament over Babylon (Revelation 18) is the lament over mercantile Tyre (Ezekiel 27) and the demise of conquering Babylon (Jeremiah 51). This Old Testament background indicates that the source of Babylon's/Rome's world authority was commercial (Tyre, Ezekiel 27) and military (Babylon, Jeremiah 51) power. The end of the final world city, with its commercial and military power, will mean the end of the world social system as we know it. Political authorities (18:1–10) and commerce and trade (18:11–20) will wail over the end of the world social system. This end of the world system will also bring about the demise of crafts and culture (18:21–24). The end of the kingdom of Antichrist moves the world into the advent of the kingdom of God. The destruction of Babylon is the end (19:1–8), but it also marks a new beginning.

Following the triumph over the evil world city, heaven celebrates the coming reign of God and the marriage of the Lamb. Babylon (the godless world structure of any age) sits on the beast (the undergirding power throughout the ages). So when Babylon falls, the new society is inaugurated. This resolves the New Testament's eschatological tension. The bride, the new Jerusalem, the church, is—on the one hand—the wife of the Lamb. But, on the other hand, the church is yet to be married. Likewise, the followers of the Lamb constitute the bride (19:7) but they are also guests at the wedding (19:9).

Revelation 17 The Great Fall of Great Babylon

Introduction

Babylon is the great harlot, the godless spirit pervading all unbelieving world structures (17:1). She is seductive. She intoxicates the inhabitants of the earth, influencing them with economic power and dominion. World history evolves in pursuit of these two elements. The whole realm of humanistic existence will rest on the beast (17:3) and is carried by the beast (17:7). From John's perspective, the beast is future. The beast is therefore not one of John's contemporaries, neither Nero nor Domitian. The sea beast reigned as seventh king of the world (17:8) then died but is raised from the dead as the eighth king (cf. 20:1–3). So Satan's power which was forfeited by the cross (12:7–10) is resuscitated in the beast (13:1). The beast is also one of the seven kings, expressing continuity with them (17:11). The seven heads are seven mountains. These seven are not Rome, rather, they represent the world power structures upon which the woman sits (17:9). The presentation is not literal; the heads are not literal. As the great mountain of Daniel 2 is the symbol of the all-powerful kingdom of God, 'mountain' in Revelation (17:9) is also a symbol for 'kingdom'.

The woman—who is the harlot—sits dominant on seven mountains (17:9), which are also many waters (17:1). The seven mountains symbolise kingdoms (rule/rulers) throughout history (cf. Jeremiah 51:24 in which the destroying mountain is a symbol for Babylon). The seven mountains (seven = completion) symbolise the woman's world rule and influence throughout the ages 'upon the many waters', that is, the human world (17:1; cf. Revelation 12). The eighth king is the last world ruler. He will be the manifestation of Satan's representative, that is, the beast from the sea. So the seventh and eighth rulers are one and the same, that is, the beast who rules through all seven rulers and who suffers a mortal wound but is resurrected and rules again as the eighth 'king'. The seven kings rule with law and order. But the eighth ruler discards law and order, capitalising on human reaction to the bowl judgements, thereby making his idolatrous opposition to God very clear. This last world rule/ruler will demand submission, in obvious and subtle ways, to him and to his worldview. But in the end the beast will go into perdition.

The beast represents the humanistic ethos of the Roman Empire—based on its military and political power—that is, the world imperium including all of Babylon's successors such as Rome. There is political critique of world structures in Revelation 13 and economic critique in Revelation 17. But the political and economic critique is also religious critique. The harlot rides on the beast since she is maintained by Roman and successive imperialism (17:3). Local ruling classes received the Empire well (these seem to be the 'kings of the earth' of the time) and the *pax Romana* was celebrated. This ordered government is the wine with which the harlot intoxicates the nations. The exterior of the cup offered by the woman is attractive (golden), but it is filled with abominations (17:2,4).

It is a serious error to think that Revelation opposes Rome only because of oppression and persecution of Christians. Rather, Revelation implicitly advances a thoroughgoing prophetic critique of the Roman system as Rome is part of a continuing false world. This makes Revelation a powerful piece of resistance literature.[2]

Bauckham points out that, whereas there had been martyrdoms, full scale persecution of the church was not yet happening (2:13; 6:9–10; 16:6; 17:6). The prophetic messages to the seven churches suggest that persecution was only sporadic and local. But Revelation suggests that the nature of Roman power is such that, if Christians are faithful witnesses to God, then there must inevitably be suffering for them. Rome's divine pretensions clashed with Christians' witness to the true God. Indeed, Rome—that is, representative world government—will be judged not just for martyrdoms but for the slaughter of all innocent victims ('the blood of prophets and saints and of all those who have been slain on the earth', 18:24). Those who bear witness to the one true God will expose Rome's idolatrous self-deification. In the light of God's righteousness, Rome's oppression and exploitation stand condemned. Rome does not hold ultimate power and will not be allowed to continue her unjust rule indefinitely. And all similar future governments will have this inevitable end.

The deep reality of the collapse of Babylon needs special interpretation which is provided by one of the seven angels that had the seven bowls (17:1). The angel began his interpretation to John with the words, 'Come I will show you' (17:1). These words are, ironically, the very words that introduce the Bride when the demise of the world system means the introduction of the new creation (21:9). The judgement of God in Christ is the focus of the visions of both the harlot and of the Bride, the results being judgement sentence or blessing. The fallen world order is presented as a human-centred city with humanity generating values as if it owes allegiance to nothing beyond itself. With the Tower of Babel humanity sought to bring God and heaven within their own self-generated agenda (Genesis 11:1–9); this is always the aim of

---

[2] Bauckham, The Theology of the Book of Revelation, 1993, 38.

humanity in building their own world. The scattering at Babel meant that humanity lost its centre and thus lost their unity. Henceforward humanity has always shown a propensity to fragmentation, for there can be no wholeness or unity without a centre. But when the new Jerusalem comes down its citizens are given a new name on their foreheads. There is a new social cohesion embracing new values.

Thus Babylon and the new Jerusalem represent the two alternatives for humankind. Babylon is the satanic dominated parody of the ideal city/civilization, the earthly counterpart to the new Jerusalem. Babylon strives to exercise heavenly dominion over the universe. But Babylon cannot be heavenly. Rather, Babylon simply symbolises human lust for deification. Babylon is an idolatrous city-world, opposed to God, consumed with itself, and a 'brothel' for kings and merchants. Babylon's luxurious lifestyle, insatiable greed, and use of human life as merchandise (18:13) are symptomatic of the worship of power and wealth. Babylon is allegorical for the idolatry that any human power commits when it succumbs to the powers of evil. Babylon elevates material abundance, military prowess, technological sophistication, imperial grandeur, racial pride and other glorification of the creature over the Creator. Babylon is not a human city gone wrong; Babylon is humankind gone wrong, characterised by self-deification and attempting to live apart from the one true God. Babylon is the pre-eminent city where the beast is enthroned and Christ is dethroned. The negative language of John's description accentuates the depravity of Babylon: it has lost its greatness, goodness and glory. Babylon is unclean, a desolate dwelling place of the demonic. Babylon is a symbol of death for the world.

Contrariwise, the new Jerusalem is described in terms of what it is not. The new Jerusalem is not like the human city that we know. The heavenly city (new Jerusalem) is altogether new. General positive terms are used to describe the new creation because there are no comparisons in the human world. The new creation will not be an improvement or enhancement of what is in this world. Rather, the new creation will be altogether new. That is why the new creation is virtually indescribable. Hence Revelation

21 introduces the new creation (21:1) but then, without expanding, continues with pictures of the new life in the New Jerusalem.

Revelation 17:1-6

One of the seven bowl angels elaborates on the fall of the incarnation of harlotry: Babylon, the prostitute of misused power who seduced her world into idolatry.[3] The beast and the harlot (17:1-2) are intimately related, for the harlot rides on the beast (17:3). In contemporaneous terms, Babylon is supported by the system and communicates the prosperity of the city of Rome at the Empire's expense; her corrupting influence over the Empire rests on the power achieved and maintained by the imperial armies. The picture of the kings of the earth in Revelation relates to the regional ruling classes whom Rome co-opted for participation in her rule; the picture of the merchants of the earth relate to those who benefited from and gave their support to Rome's economic prosperity. Rome's subjects were persuaded by the ideology of Empire to accept and welcome her rule. In Revelation, the ideology of Empire corresponds to the two different aspects of the beast and the harlot. The harlot offers herself to her clients and then thrives at their expense. Representatively for all ages, the benefit of the ideology of Roman rule (17:4)—the *pax Romana*—was vigorously pressed during the first century A.D., providing world peace and thereby engendering prosperity throughout the Empire. The self-proclaimed eternal city of Rome offered to her subjects security, wealth and a prosperity in which they could share. But this ideology, according to Revelation, was a deceitful illusion. The illusory ideology was the wine with which the harlot (the city and the Empire) intoxicated the nations. The gift of security, wealth and prosperity is offered in a golden cup; but the cup contains abominations (17:2,4). So the security, wealth and prosperity of Rome's ideology are spurious attractions; the inner reality behind the facade is filth and pain.

17:1-19:5 reveals the cup of God's wrath for the harlot who has blasphemed the human relationship with God. There is: a vision of the great harlot (17:1-6); interpretation of that vision (17:7-18); the significance of her great fall (Revelation 18); and

---

3   Smalley, 2005, 437.

praise to God in heaven for his judgements (19:1–5). In summary, the cup of God's wrath for the harlot is the effects of the trumpet and bowl judgements, with projected human reaction. When John is called up to look on the judgement of Babylon, he sees the great whore sitting as overlord on many waters (17:1). The many waters are a physical reference to historical Babylon astride the Euphrates and its canals. The Old Testament background is Jeremiah's oracle on Babylon astride the waterways of the Euphrates—with its many canals—greatly multiplying its wealth by trade (cf. Jeremiah 51:13). The contemporaneous expression of Babylon, Rome, had promoted materialistic world apostasy. Rome was the intensified expression of world power. Rome drew wealth from its many waters of peoples, tribes, nations and tongues. The acquiescent kings of the earth and the earth's inhabitants (17:2) had all become shaped in the image of the harlot. Deliriously intoxicated by the wine of her fornication, the kings and inhabitants were emboldened to commit the harlot's apostasies of idolatry and godlessness. Hence the world exhibited the effects of idolatrous political leadership, namely: economic materialism and immorality.

John is then carried to a desert wilderness by the Spirit (17:3; cf. Ezekiel 40:2). John sees the woman clad in fine, colourful garments: purple (the colour of empire); scarlet (the colour of royalty, wealth, prestige, and also the colour of persecution); but not the white of the saints. John sees the woman seated, as royal, on a scarlet beast. The beast is a manifestation of the dragon with seven heads and ten horns (12:3; 13:1; 17:7) representing the fullness of power held by the 'kings', that is, the power structures who persecute Christians.

John is free from the charms and attractions of Babylon to which the world so easily succumbs. Nevertheless, he needed to understand Babylon's true nature for even he might be enticed by her. John is in a wilderness, which is an appropriate setting for a vision of judgement. Finally, Babylon becomes this desert wilderness.[4] Blasphemous names which speak of her arrogant self-deification and her claim to universal power and rule covered the harlot's entire body (17:3). In John's day the city god (Roma) 'sat firmly' on the sea beast (the devilish powers that underlie the

---
4   Beale, 1999, 851–2.

godless world system). Rome was the contemporaneous incarnation of the dragon's rebellion manifest in the influence of world empires and governments throughout the ages.

Like the dragon (12:3), the scarlet colour of the beast is not only indicative of its kingship pretensions aiming at universal sovereignty but is also emblematic of its murderous, bloodthirsty, persecuting nature. The harlot also wears fine linen (18:12,16), but not the white and pure fine linen of the saints (19:8). Purple and scarlet are the colours of this world's honours; they signify the woman's earthbound nature.[5]

Thus the harlot Babylon presents herself as a desirable, enviable state. She is resplendently garbed and adorned with jewels, displaying her wealth and power (17:4). She holds out a golden cup to the inhabitants of the earth to make them drunk with the wine of her fornication: abundance, power, pride, violence, and especially idolatrous false worship. She intoxicates the world by her malign influence. Her cup is full of abominations, that is, all that is utterly contrary to the will of God for the world. Her cup is in stark contrast to the golden bowls which are the prayers of the saints (5:8). Her resplendent dress is the antithesis of the bride's pure linen that is the righteous deeds of the saints (3:18; 7:9; 19:8).

John is 'carried away in the Spirit' at both 17:3 and 21:10, pointing to broader parallels between the two cities of Babylon (the harlot, 17:1–19:10) and the new Jerusalem (the bride of Christ, 21:9–22:9). Together these two 'women' form the climax towards which the whole book has aimed: the destruction of Babylon (the godless human world); and replacing the harlot with the bride of Christ, the new Jerusalem. The interconnection is emphasised by the announcement of the Lamb's marriage to his bride immediately following the rejoicing in heaven over the fall of Babylon (19:7–9a). Between these two climactic sections about the harlot (17:1–19:5) and the bride (21:9–22:9) comes another section which describes the transition from the harlot to the bride via the victory of the Lamb. The Lamb's victory effects the bridge between the fall of Babylon and the descent of the new Jerusalem.

---

5   Dale R. Davis, 1973, 149–158.

The name etched on Babylon's forehead (17:5) stated her character: 'mother of harlots and abominations of the earth'. Roman practice required courtesans to wear their names on a headband. Babylon's headband identified her as the harlot achieving profound fallen unity within all successive political and world governmental structures. The mystery of the name is the previously veiled essence of the person: intrinsically evil. Her known, symbolic name was Babylon. 'Babylon' is code for Rome: the mother who spawns harlotries and abominations throughout the world.

Revelation infers that Babylon exists throughout history as satanic deception to capture the world. Babylon embodies total world culture astray from God. She is the archetypical representation of every idolatrous manifestation in time or space. And she is attractive, enticing and makes sense to fallen humankind in their perversion. But there is a great contrast between her apparent beauty and her degrading effects. Her name Babylon the Great (17:5; cf. Daniel 4:30) was mystery, that is, it required revelation to combat her obvious eminence. Babylon is the great mother of harlots and the source of all idolatry. Her contribution to mankind is wrong goals and aims and desires. But her aims are there for all to see, proclaimed on her forehead (17:5) and perpetuated in her 'progeny' throughout history. Nevertheless she is desired and sought after by all the inhabitants of the earth. John's picture of the great harlot is like Paul's advice to Timothy about the latter days: the doctrine of devils will be promulgated; men will give heed to seducing spirits and so depart from the faith; and marriage will be forbidden throughout Babylon's dominion with the consequent abandonment of society to general dissolution (1 Timothy 4:1–3). The great harlot will always be the persecutor of the church. But at the end, she herself will be rejected by her world. This rejection will visibly bring on the kingdom of God.

Christians in Rome who did not submit to world economic and religious idolatry were murdered (17:6). Victory over the slain saints (17:6, where *kai* = even), which displayed the naked power of the state, began in earnest with Nero's persecution of A.D. 64. John had expected to see judgement (17:1), but instead he is amazed at this parade of power and magnificence and giddy intoxication.

Revelation 17:7–18 The Interpretation of the Mystery

The angel undertakes to reveal the mystery (17:7) concerning the identity of the woman and the beast—the incarnation of world evil through the ages—but then reverses that order (beast then woman) in what follows.[6] The beast's equipment of satanic power (17:8) includes the seven heads (17:9–11) and the ten horns (17:12–17). In spite of himself, John had marvelled at the might of Rome. He may have been baffled by her continued existence and anxious to know how and why her influence continued and prevailed. The angel now reveals that the beast upon whom Babylon sits is mortally flawed. The beast cannot provide an eternal foundation for the harlot.

The terms used to describe the beast mock its spurious claims to deity. The beast had a past rule ('was', 17:8) but, despite his claims, he did not have any present rule ('is not'). And yet the beast also has a future continuous role (is coming up from the abyss). This description of the beast is in stark contrast with the eternity of control in God's hands ('he who was, is and is to come', 1:4). It is also an intended parody on the Lamb who was and now is and will be alive for evermore (1:8; 2:8). The past role of the beast—the earthly representation of the dragon—points to his power before his confinement at the cross to deceive nations, including Old Testament Israel. During the millennium after the cross in which he is confined, the beast will not be able to deceive the nations (20:1–3). As John writes, the beast is not exercising the full extent of his control but he is always vying for it. After the millennium, at a 'second coming', Satan and thus the beast will be given greater power to deceive the nations for a short time before the end (20:1–3). When that occurs, the world will disown the Christian message (11:7–13). In the short time of three and one half days before the end (11:11), the beast exercises decisive power: continually present (13:1), the beast is always coming up out of the abyss with intent to deceive. This presentation of Rome (as the woman and Babylon) predicts the shape of future evil days.

Thus the beast is to have his own ascension from the pit in the last days (11:7). But the beast ascends for the purpose of his

---

6   Smalley, 2005, 433.

destruction. He will make war upon the saints (13:7), but then he will be thrown into the lake of fire (19:20; cf. Isaiah 27:1). All humankind, except believers, will be awed by the beast who is the Antichrist. The beast ascends from the abyss—after the period of Satan's restraint (cf. 20:3; 11:7; 13:1)—to rule the world. This ascent is a parody of Christ's Parousia from heaven. All the evils of fallen world government leading to further enticing godlessness will be manifested in this closing period of world history in the beast's presence. But the beast and the false prophet are both destined for the lake of fire. The final coming of the beast will be greeted with wonder since under his world government there will be unparalleled materialistic achievements, technological advances and scientific discoveries. But the spectacular successes are distorted under his influence. The wonder expressed by an unbelieving world lacks basic understanding. The beast will end up in the lake of fire! But those whose names are not written in the book of life (13:8; 17:8; 21:27) marvel at the beast's ascension and the achievements of his world government.

17:9 is connected with 13:18 by the use of the expression 'this calls for a mind that has wisdom'. Thus the imagery of 666 is applied to the beast. So the future identification of the beast will call for deep spiritual perception. The beast on which the woman is seated has seven heads (17:7,9). These seven heads are also seven mountains. The seven mountains are not the hills which surround Rome (*oros* is always 'mountain' in Revelation, not 'hill'). Rather, the seven mountains are symbols of kingship or rule (cf. Babylon in Jeremiah 51:25; Zechariah 4:7). Commentators have suggested that there is a correlation between the seven mountains and Roman history, but attempts to provide a suitable sequence of Roman Emperors are unconvincing. The seven heads signify the completeness (seven = completion) of this continued demonstration of demonic power in world rule; they are symbolic for the supreme authority exercised by the beast through the sequence of oppressive anti-God secularism throughout history. These heads or mountains may represent the total civilised world reaching Babel-like heavenwards. This forms a striking parody to the new Jerusalem that comes down to sit on the world mountain (21:10).[7]

However, the seven heads are also (17:10, *kai*) seven kings. They represent in historical authority figures the complete world expression of the evil power of the beast. These historical authority figures endorse and manifest the evil secularism of the beast on which they are based. These 'seven kingdoms' express the fullness (seven = fulfilment) of satanic domination through time. The eighth kingdom most clearly expresses satanic domination but only for 'a little while' (cf. 11:11). The kingdom of the beast—that is, his absolute rule—will come not only as part of the continuum but also as the seventh, climactic consummation of Antichrist world rule (cf. John 12:31). However, as the eighth kingdom, he will come with a new beginning of entirely universal authority (cf. 13:1). The beast's new beginning will have continuity with previous rulers for he is of the seven, having played through time his evil role in their human power structure. The eighth kingdom will be the incarnation of all that is evil in its final fling. All eight kingdoms have the same Antichristian bent.[8] But the 'resurrection eighth' kingdom of the beast will be a demonic total recrudescence of evil power, a 'new creation' of evil, a last days 666.

After ruling the eighth kingdom, the beast goes to destruction. His eighth rule has no succession. This period of rule is, therefore, the end of the age. The ten horns seem to belong to this final stage of history when the power of the beast is complete. So the ten horns who receive authority for one hour are to be associated with this final rule and thus stem from what Daniel had seen (Daniel 7). These ten rulers have not yet received worldly power (17:12) so they cannot be Roman Emperors. They will be active for only 'one hour' (Daniel 4:33; the time in which Nebuchadnezzar became like a beast)[9] so they cannot be trans-temporal. These ten rulers represent the 'totality of the powers of all nations each of which is to be made fully subservient to Antichrists'.[10] They fully implement, for a relatively short time, the direct rule of the beast during

---

7 Resseguie, 1998, 58–59.
8 Beale, 1999, 876.
9 ibid., 1999, 879.
10 Beckwith cited by Smalley, 2005, 437.

his reign as the 'eighth' (cf. 17:14). However, the paradox of 17:12 is that the authority that they have received comes from God and is only derivatively from the beast. Thus, the mysterious place of evil in the divine scheme of things from the beginning of creation will draw the history of the world to its final end.

The rule of the ten horns or kings (ten = of sizeable proportions but indefinite) is significant but not indefinite; their force is formidable but not irresistible. The ten horns will be defeated by the Lamb who, with his seven horns (seven = perfection), is omnipotent. Therein is the finality of the eschatological world clash. It is a battle which the beast and his allies cannot win. Prior to this final battle, the beast and his allies will have 'killed' the church (11:7). But the victory of the church over the world is seen by all when the church is 'caught up to heaven' (11:12). Then comes the final defeat of the beast's kingdom (11:13–15) by Christ at his second coming. World authority (17:13) is the beast's final aim. This is the Babel mentality: building Utopia—with God's authority removed—by human ability, ingenuity, and technology. With Babel in view, the world gives its authority to the beast as an endorsement, presumably, of expected 'benefits'. So the authority of the ten horns becomes an expression of the beast's aims. But the ten horns and the inhabitants of the earth are in a world where they and the evil they represent are created beings; their future is ultimately at divine disposal.

There must now be a final confrontation in which evil will be defeated and eliminated at the last battle between God and evil (17:14). Thus the angel reminds John that it is the Lamb who will make war with the beast and prevail because he is Lord of lords and King of kings (cf. Daniel 4:37). The Lamb will prevail through his followers (17:14) who are overcomers because of his final victory; they are called, chosen and faithful. This is in contrast to the waters on which the harlot sat which were peoples, multitudes, nations and languages (17:15) who—in their acquiescence to the system that the beast represents—were complicit in the harlot's fall.

The angel then shows how evil serves God's purposes (17:16–17). The consistent theme of Revelation has been that the rebellious order is still shaped by the sovereignty of God.

Accordingly, the inherently unstable dynamics of godless government serve to break the power and wealth of the harlot. Evil is self-destructive: its very nature is to use, consume, and then discard. The very beast that had supported the harlot with absolute commitment (17:3) now gathers his allies, the ten horns, and together they devour her (17:16).[11] Satan has cast out Satan and is thus coming to an end (Mark 3:23–26)! The conspirators have turned against world Babylon—perhaps in the deluded pursuit of human world reform—they have stripped her of her power and exposed her. But whatever their intentions may have been, these revolutionary powers are acting according to what God had put into their hearts (17:17). God used systemic organised evil in the world to defeat world Babylon. Nakedness is the state not only of decimated Babylon but also the apostate church (3:17) endowed with economic gain. With no apparent need, the wealthy apostate church does not know the wretchedness of her worldly state. The apostate church is marked by compromise with the world and disingenuous worship. Hence the apostate church will suffer punishment and demise with the world harlot.

Babylon is thus devoured by a fierce world before her final destruction by fire, which is the Old Testament penalty for harlotry (cf. Leviticus 20:14). Beale suggests, probably correctly, that the political side of the ungodly system will turn against the socio-economic-religious side and destroy it.[12] The prostitute will be hated by her former lovers, that is, the beast and the kings. In turning against the world city, the beast and the kings fulfil Old Testament expectations of judgement upon faithless Israel (Ezekiel 16:39–40; 23:25–27; 28:18; 38:21). Babylon (17:18) was the symbolic archetype of all evil that had held sway over all world authority.

Hence the book reveals the world's final disenchantment with the godless materialism that world rule offers. World rule, erected on destructive and greedy competition, cannot offer universal peace. Directed by human rules and godless spiritual principles, world rule may have provided amazing technical development, solving many world problems, making great medical advances,

---

11   Resseguie, 1998, 140.
12   1999, 883.

and removing inequities in the world. But the basic problem is human godlessness, that is, human direction of the world without reference to its Creator. There is no mention in the Revelation assessment of human history of any profound search for kingdom of God values, or any attempt to enthrone God as the rightful ruler of the world. Rather, the world is misguided in its reliance on human ingenuity to secure human survival. Even so, by its godlessness, the world has forfeited all hope. The visionary presentation of Revelation 17 is that the final dethronement of the woman harlot Babylon comes about by world disillusionment: materialism has not brought the hoped-for Utopia.

Wonderful world competence has not provided satisfying answers for life. However, humanity refuses to accept the sovereignty of God over all creation and creatures. So humanity brings to an end its barren world system that has no enduring values. The system finally implodes as evil turns in upon itself. The Second Coming and the power of forgiving love and inner peace is always at hand. But in order to receive forgiving love and inner peace, all the world would be required to surrender their personal aims and ambitions to the one true God.

Hence there are two great cities in the book: Babylon, which had dominion over all earthly rulers (17:5), deceiving the nations by her sorcery (18:23);[13] and an even greater city, the coming new Jerusalem. The multitudes over which Babylon rules turned against her, as portrayed by the sixth bowl judgement with its symbolism of drying up the waters indicating disloyalty to Babylon. But the end of Babylon had in fact been the work of God (17:17), exhibiting God's monistic control of history. God had given world rule over to godless leadership to effect the destruction of evil. So in the end, the human world recognises the evil of evil and attempts to destroy it in a humanistic ethic to reform world control. But humanity still fails to capitulate and recognise God's future for creation (cf. Genesis 2). Revelation thus describes how the Rome of the first century will end. But more than that, Rome had honed with precision how to govern with a godless political base in a fallen world. And Rome's successors would follow her example and meet the same doom.

---

13   Smalley, 2005, 442.

Excursus: Worship in Revelation

The worship of God and the Lamb in the new Jerusalem has a significant parallel in the lament of the kings over Babylon (Revelation 18). Throughout Revelation, in worship that climaxes in Revelation 21, worshippers stand around God at the centre; in Revelation 18, the rest of creation stands viewing the dominant culture (18:10,15,17). New Jerusalem worship is enduring, directed to the one true God; but Babylon worship is a sad refrain of misery and lament directed to the false god, materialistic idolatry. New Jerusalem worship is characterised by the smoke of the glory of God (15:8); but Babylon worship is characterised by the smoke of devastation and destruction (18:9) giving rise to human grief at the collapse of its world. In new Jerusalem worship there are songs of praise and thanksgiving; but in the lost cause of Babylon worship there is loud weeping and mourning (11:15; 18:9). New Jerusalem worship is ceaseless because the centre of worship is eternal; but Babylon's worship of her past is momentary because her centre has dissipated. There is magnificent order and symmetry that includes the entire cosmos in new Jerusalem worship; but there is a collapsing centre in Babylon worship. The message of Revelation is that the worship of the Creator is the only worship that lasts. Misplaced worship, the idolatry that disorders creation priorities, characterises those who are persuaded by the claims of the dominant culture. But Christians are also prone to worshipping the dominant culture, just as John was enticed—greatly amazed (*thaumazo*, 17:6)—when he saw the whore. John's amazement was identical to the stupefied response of the inhabitants of the whole earth as they, 'in amazement', followed the beast (13:3).

Jewish monotheistic worship distinguished between the one God who is Creator of all things and God's creatures; God must be worshipped, but the worship of creatures is idolatry. The polemical significance of Babylon worship in Revelation is that the root of the evil of the Roman State is seen to be in the idolatrous worship of human power. Indeed, lines of conflict are drawn between the worshippers of the beast and the worshippers of the one true God. The high importance of monotheistic worship is illustrated by the angel's rebuke when John attempts to worship him (19:10;

22:8–9). The angel is only a vehicle of communication and not the source of revelation. Therefore the angel cannot be worshipped. Hence the worship of Jesus in Revelation must demonstrate that he is included in the being of God. Likewise, the worship of God by the heavenly court (Revelation 4) is necessarily connected with the acknowledgement of God as Creator of all things (4:11; cf. Genesis 1:1). This is the basis for all worship.

The Lamb is the centre of worship in heaven, receiving the obeisance of the living creatures and elders (5:8). The circle then expands and myriads of angels (5:11) join the living creatures and elders in a form of worship clearly parallel to the worship offered to God (5:12; 4:11). Finally, the circle expands further to include the whole of creation in a doxology addressed to God and the Lamb together (5:13). The scene is structured so that the worship of the Lamb (5:8–12) leads to the worship of God and the Lamb (5:13). Jesus is not an alternative object of worship; rather, he shares the glory due to God. Jesus is worthy of divine worship because worship of Jesus is worship of God.

This inclusion of Jesus within monotheism accounts for the peculiar grammatical usage in Revelation, where the mention of God and Christ together is followed by a singular verb (11:15) or singular pronouns (22:3–4 and 6:16–17[14]). John defies grammar for the sake of theology (cf. 1:4): God and Christ are not ever the subjects of a plural verb in Revelation. A plural pronoun is never used in Revelation to refer to both God and Christ. Thereby Christ is placed on the divine side of the divide without in any way sounding polytheistic. The consistency of usage expresses the relationship between Christology and monotheism.

The worship is heavenly and eschatological (5:8–14 and 15:3–4). The doxology addressed to Christ alone (1:5b–6; cf. 2 Timothy 4:18; 2 Peter 3:18) shows that the churches practised the worship of Jesus. Doxologies were a form of praise by Jews to the one God. Hence the doxologies to Jesus, offering to him the worship due to God, ascribed deity to Jesus. In this way, Jewish Christians in the New Testament identified Jesus as presenting the reality of the one God. Jesus is praised for his redemption (5:9–10). Indeed, it was because Christians owed salvation to the

---

14 *Autou* is the better reading there.

risen Jesus that he was worshipped. But salvation came ultimately from God. So Jesus was not worshipped independently. Jesus was worshipped because—in his life, death, and resurrection—he functioned as God. In his ministry, Jesus had exercised divine functions on God's behalf in relation to the world as Saviour, Lord and Judge. But Christians would not have been content with worshipping Christ as a functional divinity. Though Jesus is not called God in conformity with the general slowness of that usage to become established in Christianity, the one who is worthy of the worship due to God must belong to the ontological reality of the one God.

Revelation 18

Revelation 18 The World Lament over the Fall of Babylon

Revelation 18:1–8 Introduction

The Revelation oracles against Babylon (18:1–19:8) echo Old Testament oracles against Babylon (Isaiah 13:1–14:23; 21:1–10; 47:1–15; Jeremiah 25:12–38; 50:1–51:64) and Tyre (Isaiah 23; Ezekiel 26:1–28:19). But Revelation is not only in the tradition of the prophets; Revelation is also the climax of that tradition, that is, the fulfilment of all the eschatological oracles of the Old Testament prophets. Whilst Revelation 18 is a message for history generally, its particular focus is Rome.

The Old Testament background to the lament over Babylon (Revelation 18) is the lament over mercantile Tyre (Ezekiel 27) and the demise of conquering Babylon (Jeremiah 51). This detailed dirge over the fall of Babylon—the great antagonist of the Christian faith—follows next in the sequence of the vision ('after these things', 18:1). The vision reveals the fall of Babylon but not the ultimate demise of the evil structure that undergirds her. The ultimate demise for the undergirding evil structure is reserved for the lake of fire. Heaven is the source of this compelling revelation. The angel who descends is bright with the radiance that comes from proximity to God (cf. Ezekiel 43:2). The voice is loud with a message that the whole world must hear. The angel's splendour and loud voice will capture the world's attention. Babylon has fallen (18:2–3) and is desolated ('fallen, fallen'; cf. 14:8). Babylon has become the dwelling place for unclean birds, beasts and demons. This is entirely different from the new Jerusalem, which is characterised by an abundance of life (22:1–2).

In a world controlled by divine order, it is inevitable that—given the pernicious nature of her influence through wealth and sensuality (18:3)—Babylon must fall. Babylon's idolatrous and seductive social, economic, and moral actions will bring about her fall. Babylon's blatant paganism will bring about her fall. And the leaders and peoples of Babylon's world will fall with her. Indeed, all the Babylons throughout history must fall (cf. Isaiah 21:9). It is remarkable that divine patience permits the Babylons of history to endure until they collapse under the weight of their own excesses.

Isaiah 13, directed against historic Babylon, states that once Babylon is fallen she will never be inhabited again. Instead, Babylon becomes the dwelling place of demons and a prison of unholiness (18:2; cf. Isaiah 13:20–21). The multitude of her apostasies (18:3) affects her world, enriching and degrading the world's inhabitants. Hence the world's inhabitants will drink the wine of God's wrath against Babylon.

But another heavenly voice reverberates throughout history, calling the people of God to come out and be separated from sinful society (18:4; cf. Isaiah 48:20; 52:11; Jeremiah 51:6). Those who associate with the rebellious world will share her punishment (18:4). God in heaven is fully aware of Babylon's sins (18:5; cf. Jeremiah 51:9). God has remembered Babylon's iniquities, that is, God will take action against Babylon's sins. There will be judgement against military, economic, cultural and political systems of this age which reflect the rule of the beast and the guidance of the false prophet.[1] And when the world system has fallen, there is the advent of the new creation.

The voice from heaven is directed to those who have been commissioned to take vengeance on Babylon (18:6; cf. 18:4). The city that shed the blood of prophets and saints throughout her history will now receive equivalent recompense in kind (not double as in 18:6; cf. Psalm 137:8),[2] suffering the fate of those whom she tormented. Babylon will be totally humiliated for her proud boasting (18:7) as she drinks the wrath of God from her own golden cup (18:6). Babylon will experience deprivations (18:7) as the totality of biblical punishments are employed against her (18:8). She will be seared suddenly and completely by the fire of divine judgement and plagues bringing death, mourning and famine (18:8). Thus the sovereignty of God is expressed in unassailable strength. So, whereas the judgement of individuals is reserved for the Parousia,

---

1   cf. Bauckham, 2004, 11.
2   Beale, 1999, 701.

nevertheless world powers and institutions are judged within history.

Revelation 18:9–20 The Lament of her World over Babylon

Three dirges over Babylon's fall, all based on self interest, are chanted by: the kings of the earth (18:9–10); the merchants who had been made rich by Babylon (18:11–17a); and the maritime trade (17b–19) that had so wonderfully benefited from Babylon.

The kings of the earth (18:9; cf.17:2) are heads of government who had shared Babylon's pervasive atheism. The kings had been materially enriched by Babylon. They will witness, experience and mourn Babylon's fall because they are concerned about the loss of their power structures. Whereas they knew that her judgement must come, they are amazed at the suddenness of God's visitation (18:10).

The merchants mourn (18:11) not out of sympathy for Babylon but because of their personal distress at the loss of commercial advantage—and the consequent effect upon their prosperity—brought about by Babylon's fall. The merchants were the major commercial forces within the empire that sustained Rome's economic system and distributed a bewilderingly luxurious list of commodities to her world (18:12–13; cf. Ezekiel 27:7–25). The merchants' luxurious cargo bound for Rome indicated that social fulfilment in the Roman Empire had been sought in materialism. Rome's indulgent value system, greed and manipulation condoned the pursuit of whims and desires, including the twenty-eight listed luxury items (4 = universality times 7 = completeness, 18:11–13:4). The twenty-eight items are grouped in six batches: precious metals and jewels; costly fabrics; ornamental items; aromatic herbs and spices; foodstuffs; animals and people. The list makes it clear that humankind itself had become a commodity. As the world became rich, it lost its soul.

The exotic foods and dainties that had been commonplace in Rome's daily life are never to be seen again when Babylon falls (18:14). The merchants take up their dirge over Babylon from a safe distance (18:15–17a). They survey the sudden collapse of Rome from the perspective of their own interest. Babylon's former glory and wealth is presented as resplendent attire and adornment (18:16).

The shipping industry—shipmasters, sea travellers, sailors and others who derive their living from the sea—also laments (18:17b–18), echoing the Old Testament lament over Tyre in their lament over Rome (18:19; cf. Ezekiel 27:32). The industry grieves because it had grown rich through the city's wealth applied to ship-borne trade.

In a dramatic change of tone (18:20), heaven and members of the church triumphant are told to rejoice over Babylon's fall. And in this summons to rejoice, the voice from heaven reveals that these judgements against Babylon had been inflicted by God.

The Revelation account of Babylon's doom, proclaimed by the angel (18:21–24), is like Jeremiah's vision of Babylon's fall (Jeremiah 50–51). Babylon will be totally removed from history (18:21). But her fall, like Rome, is still future. Babylon will be cast into oblivion, like a huge millstone cast into the sea. The historical judgement of Babylon will be a particularization of the final judgement of God on the unbelieving world. Babylon suffers the judgements she had delivered against Christians. Hence, in the fall of Babylon, justice will be seen to be done (18:20).

The mighty (strong) angel—the guardian of the great scroll (5:2) and of the little scroll (10:1)—announces the consummation of the contents of both scrolls and underscores in detail the effects of Babylon's judgement (18:21–23). This third appearance of the strong angel interrelates the three pronouncements, communicating the total purposes of God and the consummation of the contents of both scrolls.[3]

The great millstone violently hurled into the depths of the sea (cf. Jeremiah 51:63) symbolises Babylon's sudden demise and complete disappearance into the chaos from which she had come. Finally, this will be Rome's end. Mirth and music (18:22), associated with festivals and feasts, will vanish. The economy will grind to a halt. Silence and darkness prevail, like what Jeremiah had foretold for Judah in exile (18:23; Jeremiah 25:10): no mirth; no weddings; no industrial grinding of millstones; and no habitation as lamps are not lit. Put together, this indicates the collapse of this

---

3   Caird, 1966, 230–231.

world. The contemporaneous interpretation is focussed on Rome's merchant magnates who had become princes through trade, exploiting and deceiving the nations.

Untold Christian lives (18:24) had been sacrificed in Rome; that blood had to be requited (cf. 6:10). So the world city, Babylon, is totally obliterated except for the memory that she had shed the blood of prophets and saints and all who had been slain on the earth. This bloodshed will be the abiding legacy of the 'Babelized' world.

Revelation 19

Revelation 19:1-6 Hallelujah by Heaven and the Saints

The three lamentations by the rulers, merchants and mariners (18:9, 16, 19) is followed by three adulations—praise in great magnitude and power—from those who rejoice over Babylon's fall (18:20): the heavenly multitude (19:1-3); the twenty-four elders and the four living creatures (19:4); and the voice from the throne inviting the whole world to join the chorus of praise for divine judgement upon Babylon (19:5; cf. Psalm 135:1,20).

This praise in heaven is in response to the injunction (18:20) to rejoice over the eternal fall of Babylon, which had been anticipated previously (16:19). The word hallelujah ('praise Yahweh', 19:1,3,4,6) is not used anywhere else in the New Testament. Saints and angels burst forth with their hallelujahs, praising God for his redemptive plan of salvation which has been concluded through his righteous judgements (19:2). And beyond judgement, the renewal of creation (cf. Romans 8:18-22) will reveal God's glory and power (cf. 4:11; 5:12; 7:10,12; 12:10). The praise in heaven that is occurring now anticipates and projects what is or will be due to God and the Lamb for the great work of salvation, that is, what will become the final reality. God's judgements, in conformity to his promises, are true and righteous (19:2; cf. 15:3; 16:7). Human godless dominion over the earth lacks the basic God-given knowledge and direction required for ecological control. In self pursuit of human aims—especially economic gain—human godless dominion over the earth will totally corrupt (destroy) the earth (cf. Jeremiah 51:29 on the judgement of historical Babylon).[1] Human godless dominion has also been responsible for bloodshed in its persecution of believers. Accordingly, Babylon's reward is her eternal demise (19:3). The final annihilation of the city is by the heavenly divine judge and warrior (cf. 19:11), and invokes the second hallelujah. The overthrow of Babylon will never be forgotten (19:3; cf. Isaiah 34:9-10), and this too is cause for further praise.

---

1 Beale, 1999, 927.

The twenty-four elders (19:4) and four living creatures fall down and render their praise to God who is sitting, enthroned. This is the final reference to the twenty-four elders and four living creatures in Revelation. Their amen and third hallelujah confirm their worship and the worship of heaven. A voice from the vicinity of the throne (19:5) then calls upon all faithful believers—'all who fear him', that is, those who in faith acknowledge the nature and sovereignty of God (cf. 1:15; 14:2)—to join in this ascription of praise.

Heaven and earth (19:6–8) provide not only the fourth hallelujah response but also anticipate the coming marriage of the Lamb. God's reign has been visibly established by the fall of usurping, godless Babylon. A mighty roar from the saints and the heavenly beings—like many waters and mighty thunders—celebrates the reign of the Lord God, the Almighty, which had begun (ingressive Greek past tense).

Revelation 19:7–10 The Marriage of the Lamb

The reward for the faithful is participation in the heavenly wedding feast at the marriage of the Lamb. This marriage is the conclusion of the biblical covenant process. It follows the announcement of the visible commencement of the universal kingdom (19:1–6). The bridegroom, by his Parousia, is to return to earth for his bride (*gune*, 19:7). The bride is clothed as befits her sacrificial faithfulness. By the grace of God she had made herself ready, by her faithfulness, during the tribulation. The wedding feast, this great occasion of final vindication, has always been her goal (19:7).

The harlot wore gaudy purple and scarlet with jewellery and blasphemous claims. The contrasting array of the bride is fine linen (19:8). The bride's clothing is given to her by God. The clean and bright fine linen is woven by the pardoning action of God's justifying judgements for the saints (cf. Isaiah 61:10). The church is the Bride. God has clad the church in righteous deeds that have conformed her to the image of Christ. These righteous deeds demonstrate her covenant fidelity. By these righteous deeds, the saints have overcome the world. The deeds do not effect the saint's final salvation, but they do demonstrate the saint's perseverance in holding to the testimony of Jesus (cf. 19:10). So God's final vindication of world judgement is their reward. In this way, Israel's Old Testament covenant imagery is brought to consummate reality.

The fourth of seven Revelation beatitudes is uttered by the angel (19:9). The first (1:3) and sixth (22:7) beatitudes have to do with obedience to the word. The second (14:13) and fifth (20:6) beatitudes proclaim blessing on those who die in the Lord. The third (16:15) and seventh (22:14) beatitudes are concerned with purity, that is, with faith demonstrated by deeds. The fourth, central, beatitude (19:9) is extended to all who are called to share in the blessedness of the new age. Readers must consider the question of their future.

The call to the church is corporate, as a bride. But the call is also to individual believers to be present at the wedding. As the bride, the church is the intended partner of the Lamb. But it is only by grace that the church is present as the bride. The benediction (blessing, beatitude) is upon all who are invited to the marriage supper. The cup containing the wine of the new age will be drunk at the marriage supper, fulfilling Jesus' pledge (Matthew 26:29). The revealing angel affirms the truth of what God has said: the time for the wedding supper has come. This will mean eternal intimacy of believers with Christ. The bride, faithful and vindicated, is ready.

Responding to the glory of the vision, John falls at the feet of the angel in an act of worship (19:10). This is understandable, but forbidden; worship must be offered to God alone as he is the source of revelation. Moreover, the angel is also a creature, a fellow servant. Worship offered to the creature instead of the Creator is idolatry. John's worship is rejected, for the angel and John serve and bear testimony to the same Lord. The angel says that the testimony borne by Jesus provides what the prophetic spirit must proclaim. The name Jesus—which occurs fourteen times in Revelation—is used principally with regard to his humanity, referring to his faithful witness (1:5). Believers have the prophetic spirit by which they must proclaim the testimony of Jesus.

Revelation 19:11–20:15 The Splendour of the End: The Transition from Babylon to the New Jerusalem

Revelation 19:11–21 The Messianic War

19:11 introduces another vision: a scene in heaven (19:11–16). In heaven, God and Christ share the throne (cf. 20:11; 22:1, 3; Hebrews 1:3). 19:11–21 expresses the sixth of seven cycles of judgement in Revelation (cf. 4:1–11; 8:1; 8:2–11:19; 12:1–14:20; 15:1–16:21; 17:1–19:1). This judgement cycle deals with the beast and his followers who overthrew Babylon (17:12–18). The seventh judgement cycle (20:7–15) is connected with the Second Coming. The judgement cycles all move toward the same end: the new creation. The later cycles focus on the most intense phases of the cosmic battle and especially on Christ's second coming.

In this new vision, heaven is open (19:11; cf. 4:1) and thus accessible. The open heaven indicates a major revelation. After 19:11, nothing more is heard of what happens in heaven. Everything needed has been disclosed. Only the details of the end (21:1–22:5) remain to be revealed. So 19:11 is both the climax of what has preceded and also a new, decisive moment in the movement to the new creation. The description of Christ (19:11–16) is like the first vision (1:12–17) and thus connected with the messages to the churches. The vision describes Christ: as faithful and true (cf. 3:14); with eyes like a flame of fire (19:12; cf. 1:14; 2:18); with a sword out of his mouth (19:15; cf. 1:16; 2:12,16); destined to rule the nations with a rod of iron (19:15; cf. 2:26–27).

Mounted on a white charger (19:11)—exercising the power of purity, righteousness and vindication—with the doors of heaven flung wide open, Christ rides on to victory. He comes to take over the kingship over all creation that had been usurped by evil. Called faithful and true,[2] Christ is the divine figure who executes God's just and vindicating judgement to fulfil the covenant promises. He is faithful: he always absolutely expresses God's will. He is true (*alethinos*): in his world rule he expresses the divine will with divine authority. Christ had demonstrated the will of God in his death and his witness, and now he climactically shows God's

---

2   A description of God in 3 Maccabees 2:11

will in judgement. Christ is the divine warrior, the Word of God, the supreme revelation of the One who is eternal (cf. John 1:1–18). The decisive moment in Revelation has arrived: the Warrior King returns to earth with his heavenly entourage. Christ is riding forth in triumph to acclaim the sure defeat of his enemies by judging them in righteousness. His righteous judgement is in fidelity to previously expressed divine standards and intentions (cf. Psalm 72, of the king; Isaiah 11:4 and Zechariah 9:9–10, of Messiah). Christ's victory has already been won but is now to be universally proclaimed. This universal proclamation will bring final salvation to the faithful. Christ rewards the faithful with the eschatological banquet (19:9) and with freedom from affliction. And Christ installs the faithful as kings and priests in the new creation.

The sequence from 19:11–21 to 20:1–10 represents a literary—not a chronological—account.[3] Revelation provides varying descriptions of the final battle (19:11–21; 20:7–10; 16:14,16; 17:14). 19:11–21 and 20:7–10 are parallels in that they both allude to Ezekiel 38–39. The sword that comes from Christ's mouth (1:16; 2:12,16; 19:21), with which he strikes down the nations in judgement (19:15), alludes to the Messiah of Isaiah 11 (Isaiah 11:4; 49:2). The child who is to rule the nations is snatched up to heaven (12:5), but then he returns in triumph to rule as stated (19:15; cf. 12:5). The root of David (Isaiah 11:1) will have the seven-fold Spirit of God (Isaiah 11:2) and shall strike the earth with the rod of his mouth (Isaiah 11:4). Isaiah's messianic images are present in Revelation. The Messiah thus discloses the fullness of the purposes of God now being worked out in history. His conquering victory of the cross had enabled the opening of the scroll and the disclosure of the divine plan which is now to be consummated. 19:11 begins the direct transition to the new Jerusalem.

With eyes as a flame of fire, Christ has authority to judge. Christ is the impartial arbiter of final human destiny (19:12; cf. 2:18–23). Christ is the Son of Man qualified to judge because of the character of his life and death and faithful witness. Christ rightfully wears many diadems, the crowns of royalty. Unlike the seven crowns of the Dragon (12:3) or the ten crowns of the beast (13:1), Christ wears many crowns by virtue of his true claims to

---

3   Beale, 1999, 925.

unassailable, universal authority. The new name which no one knows but Christ (19:12) will be revealed in the final redemptive-historical experience. In the full revelation of the end, all mysteries (1:20; 10:7; 17:5) will be revealed.

The new name to be granted to the overcomer (3:12) is the name of the city of God, the new Jerusalem. So the overcomer's new name is not directly connected with Christ's yet to be revealed name (19:12). Isaiah applied the image of an unknown name and a diadem (crown) to Jerusalem, the crown figuratively representing Israelite saints (Isaiah 62:2–3). The name and crown promised to believers represent: Israel's new, covenantal relationship with God; the kingly status promised for them at the end time; and Israel's new, intimate relationship with God (62:4–5) in which Israel will be the bride and God will be the bridegroom. It is Christ who establishes this new Jerusalem, his latter-day people.

But Christ's new name is not yet known, so Isaiah 62:2–3 (cf. 65:15)—which speaks of Israel's 'new name' and crown, denoting covenant relationship with God at the end-time[4]—has not yet been fulfilled. When the saving acts of God in Christ have been completed and the new Jerusalem is finally revealed, when believers experience the new consummated marriage relationship with Christ, then believers will know Christ's name. But even then believers may not know the full significance of Christ's name. For Christ's name reveals his totally faithful character fully in this age. But then believers will know him in all the fullness of the redemption that he has accomplished at the consummation, at the end of the age.

Perhaps the new name is YHWH (cf.22:4), since the new name is written on the head (diadem): just as the divine name Yahweh was written on a gold plate on the High Priest's forehead; just like the blasphemy names were written on the beast's diadems (13:1; cf. 17:3; cf. Babylon's names, 17:5). But Christ's name represents his significance for the saved. Through Christ's final coming, God will fulfil all the biblical promises: God will restore Israel and reveal his character in an even greater way (Ezekiel 37:6,13; Isaiah 49:23; 52:6). So the divine name YHWH ('he will be what he will be') can only really be 'known' when salvation history has been

---

[4] Smalley, 2005, 490.

fully achieved and the character of God—in creation and redemption, in the totality of history—has been fully displayed.

The rider's (Christ's) clothing, a garment sprinkled with blood (19:13), alludes to the one who obtains victory over Edom (Isaiah 63:1–6); a victorious army of one. Edom represents all the defeated enemies of Israel. Victory over Edom is victory over the nations. Victory over the nations is compared to treading grapes in a winepress. Garments are stained with juice whilst treading the grapes (cf. 14:17–20). However, whereas 19:13 points to victory over the world, it is a different sort of victory: Jesus trod the winepress of God's wrath, alone, for the lives of his persecuted saints.[5] Victory is to be expressed in the final judgement of the nations. The name of Christ which is borne into this symbolic battle is 'The Word of God' (cf. 17:16–17). Coupled with the Old Testament prediction of God's last great act of judgement, this name—'The Word of God'—achieves both thoroughgoing destruction of the ungodly as well as the final construction of the community that Christ leads to victory. Christ is the divine warrior who marches out to battle, thereby expressing the final fullness of God's saving purposes. Christ brings God's word against the world to its full conclusion by administering: punishment upon the ungodly; and redemption for God's people (cf. Isaiah 63:4).

In the New Testament, angelic armies accompany Christ from heaven in executing judgement (Matthew 13:40–42; 16:27; 24:30–31; 25:31–32; Mark 8:38; Luke 9:26; 2 Thessalonians 1:7; Jude 14–15). But in 19:14 it is the saints alone, wearing fine white linen, who follow Christ. The saints' faith and righteousness will be vindicated by Christ's judicial activities. However, whereas the saints participate in Christ's victory, they take no part in the battle. This is because the Lamb's victory over kings and the beast is won on behalf of the called and chosen (17:14).[6] The saints' pure white linen priestly garments suggest that the cause of truth is being celebrated. With one exception (15:6), only saints (not angels) wear the pure white linen garment in Revelation (3:4–5,18; 4:4; 6:11; 7:9,13–14). The final battle effects the Old Testament prophecy of judgement on the deceived nations (Psalm 2:7–9).

---

5   Boring, 1989, 196.
6   Smalley, 2005, 493.

Christ's name as he rides out—'Word of God' (19:13)—is metaphorically explained by the sharp sword (19:15) by which Yahweh's rule will be established (cf. 19:21). Old Testament allusions[7] refer to the Servant's ability to accomplish the restoration of Israel by the sword of his mouth (Isaiah 11:4 LXX = sword, MT = rod; 49:2) and the saving of the nations by means of the word (Isaiah 49:6).

The rod-like words proceeding from his mouth (cf. Psalm 2:9) are God's accusations condemning the ungodly and consigning them to perdition. Thus the word is judicial: the rider will judge by the word and that judgement will vindicate the testimony borne to Jesus (19:10). In Revelation, the Word of God—his revelation of himself—is always equated with testimony of Jesus (1:2,9; 6:9; 20:4). So Christ himself will tread down his enemies in the winepress of the wrath of God and thoroughly destroy them. The fall of Babylon demonstrated this predicted fulfilment (17:17). Thus Christ will execute final judgement on God's enemies.

Another name is added to explain the identity of the Messiah (19:16; cf. 19:11,13). But still all that Christ means for salvation history remains to be revealed. The name is written on the rider's garment and thigh, that is, either in two places or on that part of the garment draped over the thigh (where *kai* carries the alternative Greek meaning 'even', which would be explanatory). The thigh is the typical location of a warrior's sword and the symbolic place under which the hand was placed to swear oaths. The name written on the garment is the title of God—King of Kings, Lord of Lords (Daniel 2:47)—now applied to Christ. This name applied to Christ is the subject of the entire New Testament revelation. But still the name that completes the totality of Christ's instrumentality in ushering in the new creation as the bridegroom awaits confirmation (19:12). If the unrevealed name is Yahweh then, at the end of history, Jesus will demonstrate his oneness with God by judging the beast that carried Babylon the Great.

Revelation describes the fate of the beast associated with Babylon and the false prophet (19:17–18). The beast and false prophet have been the public face of evil in the world, seducing and deceiving. The descriptive language of Ezekiel is alluded to in the

---

7   Beale, 1999, 963.

judgement that was previously depicted as evil's self implosion (17:16–17): God's great feast (19:17–18) is reminiscent of Ezekiel's sacrificial feast over the slain in the last great battle where birds and beasts ate the human victims (Ezekiel 39). In this further vision (19:17), John sees an angel standing in the sun and crying out with a loud voice (cf. 18:1). The macabre invitation to the great supper of God is a parody of the invitation to the marriage supper of the Lamb (19:9). Resistance is futile; the birds of heaven are forewarned and invited to feast on the coming carnage (cf. Ezekiel 39:17) at the great-end time battle between God and the enemies of Israel.

By this battle and feast, God will make known his holiness so that the unbelieving world will know that he is the Lord.[8] God will attest his character by assuming world rule through the salvation of his people. The angel updates Ezekiel 39 by announcing that the birds are summoned *before* the carnage of human society. So Christ is the agent of the defeat of Gog and Magog. And Gog and Magog are identified with the beast, the false prophet and their armies. Ezekiel 39 states that God would make his name—'I am the Lord' (Ezekiel 39:7,22,28)—known to both Israel and her oppressors by the defeat of Gog and Magog. God's glory will then be recognised by all (39:21). The real essence of his name will be made known to Israel by saving them and being present with them; the real essence of his name will be made known to the nations by judging them (19:11–16 and Ezekiel 39).

A further vision of the judgement (19:19–21) presents the beast, the kings of the earth and their armies gathered to make war (cf. 16:14; 20:8). But these anti-God forces can't resist a heavenly army. The list of those who hid from judgement because the great day of the Lamb and God had come (6:15) is reproduced, with slight variations, as a list of those slain in battle and eaten by the birds (19:18). In Revelation, the order of introduction of God's enemies to be destroyed is death and Hades (cf. 1:18), the dragon (Revelation 12), the false prophet (Revelation 13), and Babylon (Revelation 17). But their final destruction now occurs in the reverse order: Babylon (Revelation 18), the beast and false prophet

---

8   cf. Beale, 1999, 966

(Revelation 19–20), the dragon (20:1–10), death and Hades (20:14).

Satan comes out to deceive the nations to gather them together for battle (20:8; cf. 16:14). The divine passive (19:19) shows that this gathering is also under divine control. The beast is named first, implying that he has been instrumental in gathering the world forces. They battle against Christ and his heavenly armies (19:19) and against God, his saints and the beloved city (16:14; 20:8–9). But neither saints nor angels are mentioned as participators in the campaign.

The kings of the earth and their assembled armies are Gog and Magog (20:8; cf. Ezekiel 38:2–8; 39:1–2). So, ultimately, God is the assembler (Ezekiel 38:1–6; cf. Zechariah 12–14; Zephaniah 3). God gathers the nations together for the final battle. 16:14, 19:19 and 20:8 all use the definite article for this final encounter, hence the same battle is referred to in each verse. The beast and false prophet are captured and destroyed (19:20), then their followers are executed (19:21). And the reader is reminded of the reasons for the judgement (19:20): the beast claimed that he was divine, and the false prophet supported the beast's claims. So they are both cast alive into the eternal lake of fire and brimstone (20:10). They endure thus forever. There is no resistance. This end of the world system and its prophet is the final result of the battle that had already been fought at Calvary. So, likewise, all who corporately represent the world system and its prophet and function for them will, at the end, be consciously aware of their punishment eternally (cf. Isaiah 14:10–11). The armies who followed the beast and the kings will be killed by the sword proceeding from Christ's mouth, that is, by the decree of death at the final judgement. This final decree follows the accusation of the word of God. And birds of prey gorge themselves on the slain.

The similarity between the eschatology of Ezekiel and the closing chapters of Revelation is evident (19:7–21 and 20:7–10 with Ezekiel 38–39; 20:4–6 with Ezekiel 37:1–28, pointing to the future of a saved and united Israel; and 21:1–22:5 with Ezekiel 40–48).[9] In the eschatology of both Ezekiel and Revelation, judgement leads to ultimate blessing for the saints.

---

9   cf. Lamprecht, 2000, 362–85.

Revelation 20

Revelation 20 The End of World History

Revelation 20:1-3 The Release of Satan

In the last stages of world history, after the conclusion of the millennium, Satan is released and is then able to deceive the nations for a short time (20:1-3). But the culmination of history is the final defeat of evil. The dead in Christ reign with Christ for the millennial period, and beyond (20:4-6). Satan's last assault on the saints is defeated (20:7-10). Then there is the final judgement (20:11-15). The binding of Satan is marked as a major incident by the reference to an angel coming down from heaven (cf. 10:1; 18:1). Satan had been cast out from heaven (12:7-9 and 20:2-3 have similar vocabulary including dragon, deceive, serpent, Satan; cf. Isaiah 14:12-15; Luke 10:18). Satan is not able to deceive the nations while he is bound. However, even in this period of 'confinement', he will use various means to prevent the free course of the gospel and to attack its witnesses.

The consequence of the Parousia is the destruction of all evil (Revelation 20). The destruction is not an immediate consequence of the cross. Whereas the cross accomplished the means to destroy all evil, the destruction of evil is delayed by a symbolic thousand years—an indefinite period of long duration—the millennium. Following the millennium there is the short period of the beast's rule (11:7-13). During this short period there is dire persecution for the church.

There is a problem of sequence between 19:11-21 and 20:1-15. Satan is prevented from deceiving the nations in 20:1-3; but the nations were destroyed in 19:19-21, as a result of Satan's deceptions (16:13-16). Those who presume chronological sequence opine that the nations of 20:3 are the survivors of the battle of 19:19-21. But in 19:18-21 the finality of Christ's victory is emphasised.[1] And if 20:1-6 is later—chronologically—than 20:7-15, then there would be no one left to deceive in 20:3. Hence the preferred

---

1   Fowler White, 1989, 321.

view is: 20:1–3 precedes 19:11–21;[2] 20:7–10, with reference to Ezekiel 38–39, recapitulates 19:11–21; and 20:11–15 is a description of the final judgement.

The resurrection affects evil (20:1–6). The key of the abyss (20:1) may be equated with the keys of death and Hades, which are held by Christ (1:18). As indicated in the Synoptic Gospels (Mark 3:27; Matthew 12:29), Satan is bound so that he cannot deceive the nations during the millennium. Now Satan cannot deceive the elect in any period since they have been sealed (7:1–8). Nevertheless, at the end of the millennium, satanic persecution through world unbelief will break out against the church. There will be, for a little while, further worldwide deception of the nations that had been curtailed during the millennium. Also during the millennium there is the free course of the gospel. The gospel ought to have been freely available in Old Testament Israel. But Israel had been deceived along with the world. This period of deception was brought to an end by the cross.

So the beast's ascent (11:7; 13:1; 17:8; 20:3,7) appears to be placed 'shortly' before Christ's second coming.[3] Therefore, since Satan is bound in the church age (that is, the millennium), Satan cannot deceive the covenant community in the way that he deceived Adam and Eve and Israel—along with the rest of the human race—before the cross. Satanic oppression against the covenant community climaxed with Christ's death. But the resurrection provided a new turning point in which Satan is bound for the millennial period, during which time he cannot *successfully* deceive the nations. Satan will continue to try to deceive during the millennial period, but with limited success. In this millennial age, when Satan is bound, evil is still nevertheless operative (cf. 1 Timothy 4:1; 2 Timothy 3:1–7). Now the veil of deception is lifted by the cross and resurrection and this enables the church's witness to the nations, beginning at Pentecost. Therefore, whereas 20:1–3 speaks of the free course of the gospel during the millennial age, other sections of Revelation (cf. 11:7–12; 13:1–18) speak of the success of evil at the end of the millennium. The result is the elimination of public Christian witness for some 'shortish' time

---

2 cf. Beale, 1999, 984.
3 op. cit., 987.

before the Second Coming. This seems to be the most plausible construction of Christian history in Revelation.

Revelation 20:4–6 The Rule of the Saints

In the contest between the beast and the witnesses of Jesus, the beast appeared to triumph and the saints—by physical death—appeared to be defeated. But when the heavenly perspective finally prevails on earth so that the truth of things becomes evident, not only must the beast be seen to be defeated but also the saints must be seen to triumph. Thus 20:4–6 speaks of the beginning of the transference of the kingdom to the saints. Before the Parousia, on the clear evidence of the New Testament (cf. Philippians 1:21) and inferences in Revelation (cf. 14:13), the triumph of the saints begins with their physical death by which temptations and torments of the flesh are eliminated. After physical death, the saints appear to enter a purely spiritual existence. This spiritual, heavenly existence is totally controlled by the Holy Spirit. Thus the saints wait for the final gift of salvation that will arrive with the Second Coming transformation. At the Second Coming, the saints will receive a body appropriate to their new spiritual condition: a spiritual body, that is, one that is totally controlled by the Holy Spirit.

The prayer of these saints (6:9–11) asks for vindication for human suffering, but it is not a bitter cry for revenge.[4] God's justice is at stake. The saints need to be justified before the world to vindicate God's name. God's answer to the saints indicates that suffering is all within the execution of God's plan (6:11), in accordance with the 'chronology' of the divine timetable. Earthly saints are suffering, and yet they will overcome the world. And the suffering of earthly saints must continue until the number of those called and chosen is complete. This assurance becomes the motive for perseverance. Moreover, 6:9–11 depicts divine protection for heavenly saints under the altar. But, in addition to this divine protection for heavenly souls, 20:4–6 states that there is a heavenly function for these heavenly saints between their physical death and the coming transformation.

Judgement—that is, a judicial vindication (20:4, *krima*)—was given for the saints (cf. Daniel 7:22). This vindication fulfils Jesus'

---

4 op. cit., 392.

words about a future reign of believers (Luke 22:30 and Matthew 19:28, not just referring to New Testament disciples). Saints are representatively depicted as beginning to reign; their vindication following death was a necessary prerequisite for them to assume kingship with the Son of Man. The judgement upon the evil world kingdoms by the cross paved the way for the Son of Man and his saints to reign. They are reigning in heaven, not on earth (cf. Daniel 7:9). These reigning heavenly saints are all the believers who have died before the Parousia of Christ, not just martyrs. However, martyrs are accorded primary position since the church is defined by 'overcoming': a willingness, if necessary, to be faithful unto and into death.[5]

Two groups are described as coming to life beyond physical death (20:4). The 'souls' (Greek feminine) of those who were beheaded—the customary death for martyrs in John's time[6]—refers to the disembodied state of believers between physical death for the faith (that is, martyrdom) and the general resurrection at the Parousia. A second group is described using the Greek masculine nominative (20:4b, *hoitines*), 'such'. Thus two groups are on view, namely, martyrs and those who had not worshipped the beast. The two groups are also separated by the coordinating function of 'and' (*kai*) within the clauses of 20:4a and 20:4b. The coming to life of both groups of saints (20:4) is described as the 'first resurrection' (20:5). Thus a 'second resurrection' is postulated at the general judgement (20:11–15). It is often argued that *zao* (live, 20:4b) must refer to physical life (as in 16:3). But in Revelation *zao* is mostly used spiritually (3:1; 7:17; 13:14). Moreover, within a single New Testament context, *zoe life* can carry a dual meaning of both physical and spiritual life (cf. John 5:24–29; Rom 6:4–13).

The term 'second death' (20:6) refers to the spiritual death of the unrighteous in the lake of fire (20:10 with 20:15). The 'first death' of the unrighteous is their physical death (20:5). The first physical death of saints ushers in their spiritual resurrection (20:4). The resurrection of the wicked ('the rest of the dead', 20:5)—some time after the end of the millennium (20:5), presumably at the Parousia—leads to their second, spiritual death (cf.

---

5   cf. Pattemore, 2004, 114–116.
6   Beale, 1999, 998.

21:8). The resurrection of the righteous leads to eternal blessedness as kings and priests (20:6). Those persevering unto death are given the reward of the crown of life that prevents them from being harmed by the second death (2:10–11). The reward of immediate heavenly life following death is the seal on their earthly regeneration. Regeneration is spiritual resurrection (John 5:24–29; Romans 6:4–13). But this regeneration in the course of earthly physical life would be no solution to death if the regenerated state were not continued after death.

The saints will reign with Christ for the millennial age (20:4–6). But, irrespective of the view taken with regard to the millennium, this does not mean that the saints' reign will cease at the end of the millennium. The focus of 20:1–6 is the millennial age, answering questions about saints who have died before or during the millennial age (20:4–6) and the fate of unbelievers after physical death (20:5).

Revelation 20:7–10 The Attack on the Camp of the Saints

19:17–21 and 20:7–10 are probably parallel passages as each passage majors on allusions to the Gog-Magog revolt (Ezekiel 38–39). If they are about different events, they would not refer to the same imagery and location.[7] So 19:17–21 narrates the demise of the beast and the false prophet at the second coming; and 20:7–10 narrates the demise of Satan at the same time (the second coming). 19:19–21 concludes what had begun in the gathering for the battle (cf. 16:12–16) and thus is a parallel passage to the seventh bowl judgement (16:17–21). The international campaign of Christ and his people is called *'the'* battle (16:14; 19:19; 20:8). The phraseology in the three passages is roughly the same (for example, *sunago* 'gather together' is used in each passage).[8] This battle at Christ's return is the final battle. The dispensing of the bowl plagues brings to an end God's wrath against the unbelieving world (15:1). This is followed by the description of preparations for the final battle (16:14–16). Thus, God's wrath against the Gog-Magog rebels (20:7–10) cannot be placed after Christ's

---

7   Fowler White, 1987, 327.
8   Fowler White, 1989, 328.

return. Otherwise the 'wrath of God' has not been completed, as stated (15:1), in the 'last plagues' (Revelation 16).

The relationship between 20:1-3 (the chaining and imprisonment of Satan, followed by his release for a little while) and 20:7-10 (the last attempt of Satan to destroy the beloved city, the camp of the saints, after his release from prison) is more difficult. The attempt of Satan to destroy the beloved city (20:7-10) will take place at the end of the millennial age. So the two episodes (20:1-3 and 20:7-10) span the length of time between the end of the millennial age and the Second Advent. Satan will deceive the nations (20:8) and gather them for the final assault on the kingdom of God.

But the parallelism of content between 20:1-3 and 20:7-10 is superficial. The ultimate enemy, the dragon, is constrained; Satan is locked in the abyss for the duration of the church age (20:1-3). And the last attack of Satan against the millennial congregation (20:7-10; cf. 19:11-21) comes to nothing. Then, at the Parousia—the beginning of this new era—there is world judgement (20:11-15). All humanity is raised, the new world of God is made, and there is final salvation. This series of events fulfils both Jewish nationalistic hopes and Christian expectations.

If 19:17-21 and Revelation 20 cover the same events, then the messianic era (20:1-6) belongs to the church age (the millennium). During this age the faithful have entered a heavenly, transcendental reign with Christ (20:4-6). Nothing is said about the reign of the saints beyond the millennium or the relationship of the reign of the saints to the Parousia. 20:1-6 merely indicates what is happening throughout the 'church age'. The unrighteous dead did not rise until the end of the church age (20:5), that is, some period after the end of the millennium for the last judgment.[9]

The devil is cast into the lake of fire where the beast and the false prophet are already (20:10). Many argue that this indicates progression from 19:17-21, signalled by *kai otan* (and whenever,

---

9   The earliest attestation of a thousand year reign is found in 2 Enoch 33:1ff. 2 Enoch depicts a world pause between death and the new life before the advent of the new world. This world silence is based on a world week of 7000 years, with the period closed by a 1000 year Sabbath.

20:7). But 20:8 speaks of the end of Satan's ministry after the biblically short period—three and one half days—when, through the beasts, Satan has been in world control (11:7,9). So the castings into the lake of fire (19:20; 20:10; 20:14–15) will be more or less simultaneous, with the beast and false prophet cast in first.

The recapitulation of 19:17–21 in Revelation 20 is divided into four scenes covering the period from the ascension to the second coming, namely: the binding of Satan for the church age (20:1–3); the heavenly rule of the saints from the resurrection of Christ into the church age and beyond (20:4–6); the release of Satan at the end of the church age, and the final end of Satan and his rule through the beasts (20:7–10); and the great white throne judgement (20:11–15). These four visions are related. The recapitulatI've nature of Revelation does not require chronological connection between 19:11–21 and Revelation 20. But there is overlap. Similar connections about the defeat of Satan can be identified in Revelation 12–13 and 20:1–3. In both passages Satan's deceptive activity will prevail in the world during the short time following the church age until the Second Coming.

The millennium is to be equated with the church age. In the church age: the church is able to proclaim the gospel of God's sovereignty over all creation to the world; the church ameliorates the creation disorder in the world; the church introduces public order based on God's will; and the gospel is circulated in the Christian led world freely. The church age is the great age of world mission (cf. 19th and early 20th centuries). But the free course of the gospel—which has always encountered opposition and persecution, even between professing Christians, even throughout the church age—will become more and more limited as the church moves towards the close of its age (the millennium). However in the present time, even though the great age of world mission appears to be closing, the reflex outcome from world mission is significant growth in national Christian groups everywhere in the world.

Revelation 11 also describes the end of the church age. The beast from the sea arises to (gradually) end the church age of Christian witness (11:7–10). Satan, freed from constraint, successfully (gradually) deceives the nations. By gradual dismissal of its claims, Christianity is unable to maintain a credible public witness in the world. The message in this symbolism is poignant: at the stage when Christian influence in the world is receding, 'warfare' between state and church (11:7) moves to a conclusion with the 'death' of the church. Gradually, Christianity is replaced by other belief and value systems. The death of the church is evident in the great city. For a biblically short but definite period (three and a half days), there is a stark contrast between the unrestrained godless world and the vibrant church age. There has been Satanic attack and persecution during the symbolic three and a half years (11:3, an extension of the three years of Jesus' ministry). But now the godless world rejoices at the absence of Christian constraint (11:8–11).

There will always be persecution of the church in the world (11:2). Further explanation of the survey of the church age (11:1) reveals that the time will come when it will be very difficult for the visible church to function in a hostile world of materialistic values (11:3–13). The whole world will then lie in the hand of the evil one. Attrition in the visible church's influence may result from either persecution or world apathy caused by world satisfaction with human progress (technical, medical, economic and social). Even more disturbing is the opportunity for the nations to build their 'one world' (cf. Genesis 11:1–9), with humankind at the centre and no acknowledgment of God.

When the church's testimony is divinely judged to have finished (11:7), by divine authority the beast from the sea will 'kill' the church. That is, in public view, the witness of the church will probably become ineffective. Beyond this death will be the mystery of the resurrection of the church, in public view, and her heavenly investiture. The church as the true Israel resurrected (cf. Ezekiel 37:10) will be seen to have been vindicated. The details are final but tantalising (11:11–12). The resurrection of the church takes place either before or, more probably, at the final collapse (11:13–14) of the organised world structure. Revelation does not reveal the consequential relationship between the resurrection of the church and the collapse of the world. However, the phrase 'in that hour' (11:13) suggests that they may be simultaneous. Thus, together, 11:1–13 and 20:1–3 reveal a glimpse of the course of the role of the church in the world.

It is interesting that the passage that reports the collapse of world Babylon (19:1–6) presents the church only in heaven. Similarly, the church is in heaven prior to its descent from heaven as the new Jerusalem. However, the church's vindication must be presented to the world as well (19:11–16; 20:7–10). This vindication of the church will contribute to the amazing and climactic character of the end.

Have I been too precise in dealing with what is elaborate symbolism? I think not. John is writing under divine inspiration to reveal, not to conceal. The trans-temporal character of Revelation required the generality of symbols. Hence, precise identification of details cannot be known or understood. The use of symbols also provides a warning to be cautious in interpretive approaches. Even so, the details of Revelation are sufficiently clear to posit a coherent position that contributes to a meaningful exposition of the book.

So 19:17–18 and 20:7–10 both draw on the Gog and Magog details of Ezekiel 38–39 and are therefore parallel expansions of Revelation 15–16 where the same imagery of the last battle takes the reader to the end. 20:7–10 climactically portrays: the release of Satan; the mobilization of Gog and Magog (the assembling of all unbelieving forces, 19:19); the attack on the church; and the final end of Satanic attack with Satan being cast into the lake of fire. This portrayal serves to magnify the power of Christ in the final era and totally reassures the reigning saints of their security.

I have noted the relationship between 16:12–16, 19:19 and 20:8 where the forces of the deceived nations are gathered for battle. This battle at Armageddon (16:16)—the final battle (20:7–10)—is followed by the destruction of the cosmos (16:17–21). There is no indication that the forces in 19:17–21 are demonic; nor is there any indication that the forces in 20:7–10 are human counterparts of supposed demonic forces in 19:17–21. There is no suggestion that the nations gathering for battle in 20:1–3 are either survivors of the Revelation 19 battle or remnant forces that did not enter the first battle. So the deceiving of the nations and the gathering of Gog and Magog (20:8): partly summarises Daniel 7:15–28; is the recapitulation of 16:14–16 and 19:17–21; and is the fulfilment of Ezekiel 38–39, Zechariah 12–14 and Zephaniah 3.

20:9 continues the allusion to Ezekiel 38–39 where a likewise multitudinous enemy had been judged from heaven by fire and brimstone (Ezekiel 38:22). In Revelation the fire of God devours the enemy on the breadth of the earth, that is, a worldwide area (cf. LXX Habakkuk 1:6).[10] The 'camp of the saints' (20:9) is saved Israel, the 144,000 believers. The attack against Jerusalem is anticipated in the Old Testament (Zechariah 12:3; 14:2). In the Old Testament, 'camp' is often used of Israelite tribes camped around the tabernacle (cf. Deuteronomy 23:14).[11] The 'camp' is also called the 'beloved city', that is, what will be the new Jerusalem. The assembled attacking nations will be destroyed by God before they can harm the saints (20:9). God will deliver his people by judging their enemies. 20:7-10 seem to cover the beast's activity from 11:7 to the end of Revelation 19, namely: the deception of the nations; the world influence of evil for a shortish period; and then the details of the final defeat of evil.

The deceiver (20:10) will have been cast into the lake of fire with, or immediately after, his two fiendish allies (19:20). They suffer eternal torment. They know that they are permanently removed from the blessing of the divine presence. The lake of fire (20:10) is not literal. But the lake of fire is spiritual punishment as Satan is a spiritual being. Likewise, the beast and the false prophet are not literal. The beast and false prophet are unbelieving institutions composed of people. Similarly, day and night are not literal. Day and night indicate the unceasing character of the unending punishment (cf. 'forever and forever', 20:10). The Satanic trinity is not abolished, rather, they are tormented forever. All the ungodly suffer the same fate. There is eternal punishment, whatever the character of that punishment may be. The dragon and all who ally themselves with him will suffer this second death. All unbelievers who experience the first physical death are held in Hades to experience the second spiritual death: the lake of fire after their judgement. But the saints move from the 'first resurrection' (a spiritual resurrection) to the 'second resurrection' (a physical resurrection). Then the saints will stand before the great white throne for acquittal.

---

10   Beale, 1999, 1026.
11   loc. cit.

Revelation 20:11–15 The Last Judgement

At the last judgement, Christ as God or God in Christ is seated on the heavenly throne as judge (Matthew 25:31–46; John 5:22; 2 Corinthians 5:10; 2 Timothy 4:1; Romans 14:10; cf. God as judge by Christ in Acts 17:31). When the great white throne appeared, the old creation 'fled away'; that is, the old creation was destroyed or transformed (20:11; cf. Psalm 102:25–27; Isaiah 51:6; Mark 13:31). At the last judgement all the dead are raised and judged according to their works, according to the open record books. The books contain what God decides to remember and what he decides to forget (18:5). Yet the gracious predestining purposes of God are also operating, for the Lamb's book of life is also opened. Death and Hades—as the true and final enemies of humankind and God—are, with their inhabitants, cast into the lake of fire (20:14). Nothing more is said about the details of the judgement of the unsaved. However, since death and Hades will have lost their power, the character of this world is undone and this world must then be replaced by the new Jerusalem.

Thus, the great white throne is set (20:11) following the release of Satan after his imprisonment during the 1000 years (the millennium). Satan had been restrained from deceiving the nations but was then free to do so; indeed, by divine necessity (*dei*, 20:3), Satan must deceive the nations. Even after a 'thousand years' of the glorious activity of the church in mission and free passage for the Scriptures, the universal heart of mankind is still inclined to evil. But when the great white throne appears, then the end of the age has come. Corruption and sinfulness have been so thoroughly entrenched in humanity that millennia of the experience of goodness and divine grace would not eradicate it. The church has not converted the world nor could it do so. The church had, however, borne witness in the world of the need for humanity to be converted; the church has given its evidence of God's intrusions into the world, climaxing in God giving his only begotten son Jesus on the cross and Jesus' subsequent resurrection.

Satan's attacks not only blinded humankind at large to the truth but also caused them to assemble in an attempt to annihilate God's people on earth. Evil continued to advance in the populated world. But this advance of evil does not necessarily mean that the church has failed during the millennial period. Rather, the ongoing advance of evil even during the millennium points to the fact that only God is able to overcome evil. And, at the end, God will do just that. The task of the church had been to call the world to repent. However, it seems that the visible church through compromise and idolatry failed to commend itself to the world. Eventually, like Israel, the church ceased to be sufficiently distinct from its world. There is no reason to suppose—as some suggest—that the millennium would be a period of unmixed good, for Satan is only restrained during this period; evil is not eliminated until the end. Evil is resilient. Unless it is entirely eliminated, evil will spring up again even when it has been restrained. When Satan is released after the millennium, he deceives the nations by once again helping them mistake evil for good and good for evil in our sad world that is never able to see its way forward to a better age.

John now saw this vision of a great white throne (20:11), just as he had mentioned visions of the throne in previous chapters (4:2; 5:7; cf. Daniel 7:9; Ezekiel 1:26–28). Revelation 4–5 referred to the reign of God through Christ to be felt in the world by the witness of the church. God's reign is also characterised by the continuing series of judgements on the unbelieving world. However, the appearance of the great white throne heralds the final judgement to which all other intermediate judgements pointed. The white colour of the throne connotes holiness and vindication. From this throne, sin is punished and God's plan is vindicated. Every prophecy has now been fulfilled and every earthly expectation will have to be jettisoned in the face of God's reality. All are gathered in the one great assembly: every saint, every angel, every sinner, every devil. All created intelligences stand before the throne and all will be revealed; they will see what they really are. No suppliants or penitents can sue before the great white throne, for no new pardons will be issued from it. It is a tribunal: God has prepared his throne for judgement.

The throne is not an empty throne. There is one who sits on the throne, although there is no description of his form. This adds to the mystique of the throne. The Judge is God in Christ. His qualifications to judge are his infinite knowledge, his wonderful compassion, his unsullied justice, and his unlimited power. Christ comes as king in the glory of his Father. And Christ comes in his own glory, the glory of his Godhead, and the glory of his beatified manhood. Believers must also appear before this judgement seat of Christ (2 Corinthians 5:10). Such is the awe and terror of the throne that heaven and earth flee away from it. Even things inanimate and incapable of feeling are smitten with strange panic. Evil is so ingrained in creation that the whole world must be replaced.[12] The heaven of prospect and the earth of calamity sink again into ancient disorder and chaos. They were the scaffolding of the old order but now they flee away because their work is done. But no place was found for them, that is, there is no alternative position. They are completely destroyed or replaced.[13] Everything that opposed the establishment of God's universal kingdom will have been eliminated.[14] This is the end of the old created order and the beginning of the new. But before the great white throne, the realm of the dead is left exposed (20:12).

The godless who are standing before the throne and want to flee away, cannot. There is no place before the great white throne where the godless may hide. The books—a metaphor for God's memory—are opened. Not even a sparrow falls to the ground without divine knowledge. So no one can doubt the justice or equity of God's judgement. The judgement is objective, in accordance with the books which contain a total record of each life (cf. Daniel 7:10; 12:1).

---

12 Talbert, 1994, 71.
13 Morris, 1987, 234.
14 Matthewson, 2003, 37.

Revelation 21

Revelation 21–22 The New Jerusalem as The New Creation

Revelation 21:1–8 The New Heaven and Earth: The Church as the Bride of Christ

The description of all things made new (21:1–8) is very like Isaiah 40–66. There is a new heaven and new earth (cf. Isaiah 65:17–18), a completely new cosmos (21:1–2). The new Jerusalem is described as the holy city, with everything unclean or unworthy abolished. Paradise is now regained and Eden re-established. The new Jerusalem is paradise—city and temple, people and the presence of God—fulfilling the ideals of the city as the place where heaven and earth meet, the place from which God rules and to which the nations are drawn.[1]

21:1–22:5 provides the marks of the true and perfected community contrasted with the false. The warning of 21:8 is addressed to churches in which Babylon has a foothold. Faltering churches plagued by compromise with the whore are exhorted to stop the slide that is leading to the removal of their lamp. They are to reflect their hope in their conduct.

This vision of the perfected people of God in unending fellowship with him is intended to comfort and motivate God's people to persevere through interminable invitations from Babylon to compromise. John tells us that this future has already been inaugurated in Christ. The goal of Revelation is to magnify and glorify God. Divine glory reflected in the people of God, which is central to 21:1–22:5, is the aim of biblical revelation. As God's people, the new Jerusalem can only be defined in relation to the luminescent reflection of God's glory. The central feature of the city of God is God and the Lamb. God illuminates the city and the Lamb shines as a lamp in the city. The new Jerusalem is the image of God's people in fellowship with God and the Lamb, reflecting the glory of the divine pair. A further visionary picture of the divine city (22:1–5) sums up the hope expected in Judaism. John saw a new

---

1   Bauckham, 1993, 132–3.

heaven and a new earth in 21:1, but he only saw a city in the remainder of the vision. Therefore the new heaven and new earth is the new Jerusalem, both representing the tabernacle of God's dwelling with men (21:3).[2]

There are two visions conveyed in 21:1–8. First, there is the vision of the new creation (21:1). Secondly, there is the vision of the bride (21:2–8)—that is, the church—who, with God, will form the final expression of new covenant relationship in the new Jerusalem. The new creation of a new heaven and a new earth will continue to be distinct, but biblically they belong together.[3] The limitations of the old world have been transcended in this totally transformed new world order, fulfilling Isaiah 65:17 (cf. 66:22). The first heaven had 'gone away' (*erchomai*),[4] signifying judgement of the old era and replacement of that world with the new. The replacement world was there before creation (cf. the perfect participle *hetoimasmenen*, 21:2); *kaine* (new, 21:1) suggests qualitative continuity with the expectations of the old creation, but all is renewed in total transformation.

It is argued that 2 Peter 3:10–17 teaches the expectation of a totally new creation. But this contradicts Paul's contention that the whole creation is now groaning in 'child-birth' (cf. Romans 8:22), waiting for the final transformation. 2 Peter 3:10–16 (cf. 2 Peter 3:6–7) may, rather, be referring to metaphorical fire that cleanses and refines in a visionary representation of final judgement.[5] Moreover, in his use of the flood analogy Peter states that the world was 'destroyed' (2 Peter 3:5–7, *apoleto*). Like the world after the flood, this could suggest world renewal beyond the judgement (cf. 20:11–15). Further, the stronger verbal reading at 2 Peter 3:10 is 'will be discovered' instead of 'will be burnt up.' This suggests that the purgative action of the final fire of world judgement provides final release for creation from bondage.

The 'newness' is also, finally, a new Eden (22:1–5). This must mean a renewed, transformed world since Eden was already in the old system. The eschatological city is to be filled with the divine

---

[2] cf. Beale, 2004, 367.
[3] Smalley, 2005, 524.
[4] cf. Heide, 1997, 37–56.
[5] cf. loc. cit.

presence. Therefore heaven, the place of the transcendent, is abolished.[6]

In the vision, John sees that the sea will be no more (21:1c). In the Old Testament, the sea is the source of chaotic evil powers that threaten God's kingdom (13:1; cf. 17:1,15; Psalms 18:11,16; 29:3; 74:13–14; 77:16; 89:9–10; Jeremiah 5:22; 51:36; Nahum 1:4; Habakkuk 3:8). The satanic beast (13:1)—the second member of the evil trinity, an amalgam of the four beasts of Daniel 7:1–12—rose from the sea. The sea was also, until the great white throne judgement, a realm of the dead (20:13). In the Old Testament, God dries up the sea (Psalms 18:15; 106:9; Isaiah 44:27; 50:2; 51:10; Jeremiah 51:36; Nahum 1:4; cf. Psalm 114:3). Furthermore, in a combination of creation and exodus motifs, the metaphorical drying up of the sea enables God's people to return from exile (Zechariah 10:10–12; cf. Isaiah 44:27; 50:2c–d; 51:9–10). The exodus at the Red Sea had thus been a victory over primordial chaos and evil that opposed and repressed God's people. The subduing of the sea in Isaiah 51:9–10 is a prelude to re-entry into Zion with everlasting joy and gladness, without sorrow and mourning. But in the new order the sea, with its chaotic extent, is not merely subdued. Rather, there was no more sea. Therefore the chaotic sea will no longer constitute a barrier to entrance into the new Jerusalem that is established on earth. This victory over the chaotic powers represented by the sea is also seen in the glassy sea like crystal before the divine throne (4:6). The cosmic reality is that the defeat of chaos is continually apparent.

The new Jerusalem is established in heaven.[7] John sees the new Jerusalem coming from God, indicating that God is totally responsible for what descends. 'New' signifies the origin of a new human order belonging to the new creation. The new creation is an amalgamation of the transcendent (heavenly) and the earthly reality. The saints who are in heaven (20:4–6) return as the new Jerusalem with those who have been caught up to heaven at the Parousia (11:11–12; cf. 1 Thessalonians 4:16–17). Furthermore, the new Jerusalem is new because Old Testament prophecies re-

---

6   Spatafora, 1997, 230.
7   cf. Pilchan Lee, 200, 270–271; cf 4 Ezra 7:26; 2 Bar 4:2–7.

lated to the future of the city will have been fulfilled.[8] The new Jerusalem is not the church. Rather, the new Jerusalem is God and the church: the fulfilment of the new covenant relationship; a new, intimate relationship that God shares with his people.[9]

In the New Testament—by the cross, resurrection and ascension—the new creation had already been inaugurated as the new, invisible, heavenly Jerusalem. The new Jerusalem had already begun to replace the old Jerusalem (Galatians 4:26-31; Hebrews 12:22; cf. Philippians 3:20).[10] The advent of new Jerusalem means the fulfilment of eschatology associated with Old Testament Zion expectations, with the world united in redemption. The saved community are the one new people of God, no longer divided by the disruptions of Genesis 3-11. The advent of new Jerusalem also means the fulfilment of temple theology (21:3): the dwelling and rule of God is permanently in the midst of his people (Ezekiel 37:27-28). Prior to Revelation 21, there is no biblical anticipation of a city descending.[11]

The holy city—separate and undefiled—represents in concrete form all that is new, bright and pure, since God is now in the midst of her. New Jerusalem, the holy city (cf. Isaiah 52:1), is the much anticipated new and glorified Jerusalem (Isaiah 2:1-4; 54:11-17; 60:1-62:12; 65:17-25; Zechariah 12:1-14:21; Ezekiel 40:1-48:35). The symbolism of coming down from heaven suggests pre-preparation; transcendence now becomes visible. Isaiah had spoken of Jerusalem's new name (62:2). The new Jerusalem was to be a magnificent replacement; her exodus return had reversed her exilic situation (62:3-5).

The church is identified as the Bride of the Lamb (21:2; cf. Israel as the bride in Isaiah 61:10 and 62:3-5). The nuptial imagery relates to the city made up of the redeemed (21:2). In Isaiah 40-55, Jerusalem had become a synonym for the people of God (cf. Isaiah 40:2). Jerusalem's new name (Isaiah 62:2) connotes a new,

---

8 Walker, 1996, 249; cf. Smalley, 2005, 535.
9 cf. Smalley, 2005, 536.
10 Beale, 1999, 1044.
11 In Jewish non-canonical literature there had been some speculation that the heavenly paradise would appear on earth for the Messiah as the Last Adam (Charles, 1920, Vol. II, 158, quotes 1 Enoch 90:29; 2 Baruch 4:3ff; 4 Esdras 7:26; 10:54; 13:36).

intimate married relationship between Israel and God.[12] This new eschatological union is marked by beauty, intimacy, purity, devotion, readiness and joy. This marriage imagery of the people of God in covenant fellowship had a background reaching back to Sinai (cf. Jeremiah 31:32). That background was particularly evident in Isaiah's consistent use of the metaphor to refer to the eschatological relationship between God and his covenant people when he restores them from exile (Isaiah 54:5; 61:10). The metaphor of Jerusalem as a woman (Isaiah 1:8; Jeremiah 4:31; see also Revelation 12:1) transposes to Jerusalem as the bride of Yahweh (Isaiah 49:18; 61:10). Thus Stephen Smalley points to Jerusalem in Isaiah 52:10 as the holy city, liberated and restored from captivity, rejoicing in covenant fellowship forever with God.[13]

The chaste bride is prepared in heaven. The whore committed fornication with the kings of the earth (17:1–2; 18:9). The primary function of the nuptial imagery (Revelation 19–21) is this contrast between: impure Babylon, the harlot, with her sexual misconduct (Revelation 17–18) and consequent judgement; and the salvation of the elect, the bride (with her purity and devotion, 21:2–8), fulfilling Jewish eschatological expectation. The robes of the bride and the harlot, over which adornments are added, are an index of fundamental character. The harlot's eye catching purple and scarlet attire adorned with jewels (17:4) masks her inner disposition of blatant infidelity. The bride's fine linen attire (19:7–8) is indicative of the righteous acts of the saints.

The bride and the harlot are both world cities bearing their names on their foreheads. Their names personify their characters (22:4; 17:5). Babylon is full of heinous evil (17:3–4); the bride of Christ is pure (21:2, 9). The names of Babylon's citizens are missing from the book of life (cf. 17:8; 21:27). The names of the inhabitants of new Jerusalem are written in the book of life (21:27). Kings who submitted to Babylon's sovereignty (17:18) also strip her of her glory (17:16). At the end, the macabre defeat of Babylon's kings is to be contrasted with kings of the earth who show their submission to God by bringing their glory into the new Jerusalem. Healing and life characterise the saints of the new Jerusalem.

---

12 cf. Beale, 1999, 1014.
13 2005, 536.

Babylon characteristically slaughters the saints, shedding their blood (17:6; 18:24). Ancient Babel attempted to link heaven and earth through self-glorifying pride (Genesis 11:1–9). Latter day Babylon, manifesting the Babel rejection of the Creator, piles up her sins as high as heaven (18:5). But the new Jerusalem will come down from heaven to link heaven and earth. Babylon had glorified herself (18:7). But the new Jerusalem manifests God's glory (21:11). Babylon had become the dwelling place of demons (18:2). The new Jerusalem is the dwelling place of God (21:3,22; 22:3) and the total image of the new creation.

Throughout Revelation false images have been identified: false apostles (2:2); false synagogues (2:9; 3:9); false prophets (16:13; 19:20; 20:10); the Satanic figures, including one with horns like the lamb (Revelation 13) who spoke blasphemies like the dragon; and the use of God's threefold name (1:4,8) for the beast (17:8, 10–11). Babylon had attempted to appear benign and attractive. Evil never presents itself as what it really is. Evil never proclaims what it will result in. Babylon had always been totally corrupt. As the 'world city', Babylon was beyond the possibility of redemption.

Babylon and the new Jerusalem are the only alternatives for humankind.[14] Babylon is the satanic parody of the ideal city. Babylon's luxurious and idolatrous lifestyle and insatiable greed are symptomatic of the worship of power and wealth. Babylon is allegorical of the idolatry that nations commit when they elevate material abundance, military prowess, technological sophistication, imperial grandeur, racial pride and other glorifications of the creature over the creator.[15] The city is the hub of human society. The world city vividly manifests humanity gone wrong. But the heavenly city, the new Jerusalem, is remarkably different; it is altogether new. Indeed, the new creation is beyond description for it will not bring a mere improvement or enhancement of what is in this world. It is impossible to anticipate the details of the new creation.

John's vision becomes audition (21:3–4). A voice speaks with loud emphasis from the throne, interpreting the preceding vision (21:2). The throne is the place from which universal sovereignty is

---

14 Resseguie, 1998, 77–78.
15 Metzger in Resseguie, 1993, 88.

exercised. The voice is not God, since God is later identified as speaking in first person from the throne (21:5a). God's tabernacling with the saints fulfils his covenant (21:3; cf. 7:15; Ezekiel 37:26-28; Zechariah 2:10-11). The Greek plural *laoi* (12:3) indicates that, in the composite people of God, there will be Jews and Gentiles in fulfilment of Abrahamic covenant promises (Genesis 12:1-3). Indeed, God's people—with whom he dwells—will be drawn from many nations (Zechariah 2:10-11; Isaiah 19:25; 56:7; Amos 9:12).

The relational covenant understanding of God in eternal fellowship with his people is now consummated. The new Jerusalem is the image of this new covenant consummation.[16] God tabernacling with his people (21:3; cf. Ezekiel 37:27) in the new Jerusalem indicates that the divine protective presence in the years of wilderness wandering has reached its conclusion. In addition, the tabernacle is the city (21:2-3).[17] So the tabernacle of God being with men completes and transforms Ezekiel's temple allusions and imagery (37:26-27; 40:1-48:35): the new Jerusalem becomes the place where believers are gathered in fulfilment of the new covenant in the eternal presence of God and Christ.

Thus evil is defeated in the new exodus by the death and resurrection of Jesus (cf. 15:2-8). And the marriage relationship of Christ and the church is celebrated (21:2; 21:9ff). Since marriage was the depiction of the Sinai relationship (Isaiah 54:4-6; Jeremiah 2:2) which the new covenant renewed and transformed,[18] then the historical commission of Israel (Exodus 19:5-6) to be God's witness to his intention to renew the world will reach its end in the marriage of the bride and the Lamb.

Believers of both Old and New Testaments—now the new Israel—are placed in their Promised Land to enjoy their longed for *Sabbatismos* (Hebrews 4:9). Believers will celebrate eternal Sabbath rest forever in God's presence, offering continuous worship by unceasing dedication of their persons. There is new covenant oneness of the people of God (Ezekiel 37:15-28; cf. Jeremiah 31:31-33). Old divisions have been surmounted by the Davidic

---

16 cf. Smalley, 2005, 537.
17 Koester, 1989, 124; cf. Mathewson, 2003, 55, note 100.
18 Dumbrell, 2002, 145.

Messianic leadership of Jesus. At the end of history, when death is vanquished, the kingdom of the Messiah is surrendered to the Father who then becomes all in all (1 Corinthians 15:24–28).

As indicated by the use of the old Sinai covenant formula—'they will be his people and God himself (emphatic) will dwell with them and be their God' (21:3)—the new Jerusalem is the consummation of the new covenant. John 'sees' God in his dwelling place (tabernacle) with his people (Ezekiel 37:26) in the new sanctuary. Initiated by the death of Christ, this new covenant is now fully operative; it requires no mediation (cf. Jeremiah 31:34), and sin will be no more. Jew and Gentile are in perfect harmony, redeemed in the community of the city.[19] The long exile from the Promised Land that the people of God had endured is redressed in the wonderful intimacy of this new relationship that fulfils all covenant expectations.[20] The long pre-nuptial preparation is now over and the intimate union of God and his bride has begun.

The bride has been identified with the saints adorned with their righteous deeds (19:7–8). The bride is not Old Testament national Israel but the totality of the redeemed (21:3), the perfected community of the new creation. Creation has been waiting with eager longing for the redeemed community to be revealed (Romans 8:18–23). The wedding had been announced (19:7–9) with preparations put in train; now comes the beginning of eternal experience with God for his saved people.

The covenant union between God and his people is explained in 21:4. There can be no more sorrow, no more grief, no more pain: these were features of the old sinful order and the tribulation of its times. Sorrow and sighing will flee away when the second exodus occurs (cf. Isaiah 51:11). Sin and sinning, and the death they caused, have gone forever (cf. Isaiah 65:17–20; 25:8).[21] All tears have been dried (cf. 7:17; Isaiah 25:8). New exodus language (Isaiah 43:18–19; cf. 65:17–18) is taken up in the vision of the new Jerusalem: 'the first things have passed away' (21:4). The second exodus began with John's preaching in the wilderness (Luke

---

19 Guthrie, 1987, 90.
20 cf. Smalley, 2005, 536; Beale, 1999, 1043–44.
21 Dumbrell, 2002, 146–147.

3:4–6) and found its fulfilment in Jesus' death (cf. Luke 9:31). Revelation reveals the necessary outworking of the cross. The church of God has journeyed through the wilderness during its history. But after the great white throne judgement, the Promised Land has now been reached.

John hears the voice of God (22:5–8) providing reasons for the previously announced new creation and new covenant delights (22:3–4). God's word—'behold, I am making all things new' (21:5; cf. Isaiah 43:19; *kainos* meaning new in quality and in time)—brings the new creation totally ('all') into being. The new exodus has reached its final goal (cf. Isaiah 43:19).[22] The saints have been delivered from Babylon (Revelation 17–18) and they are now placed in the new creation, their pilgrimage finished. God commands John to record the extended vision since what has been seen (21:2–5) is faithful and true: God's words are charged with divine reliability and authenticity. This is the consummation of the divine plan fully revealed. The God of truth (Isaiah 65:16) has done what he had undertaken through Christ, who is faithful and true (1:5): in Christ's death, resurrection and ascension. And God has now completed the history of Israel by bringing the new covenant into full operation (65:17–19).[23] Now that sin is eliminated, it is possible to bring the new covenant into full operation with the new creation in the new Jerusalem.[24]

God announces the end (21:6; cf. 16:17) with the words 'It is done'. God's purposes for the world of humanity have been achieved in the new creation. This is followed by the fullness of life given freely by God to all in the new Jerusalem (21:6b). God is the Alpha and the Omega (cf. 1:8), so he is the source of the divine plan from its beginning, the one who has progressively revealed the plan, and he is the one who concludes his plan. All spiritual thirst for him will now be met. The water of life will quench all spiritual thirst and provide ultimate joy and satisfaction (21:6–7; cf. Isaiah 49:10; 55:1). Eternal fellowship with God as sons (Isaiah 55:3) is given to the saints in God through Christ. And the blessings of the Davidic covenant with its filial relationship will be applied

---

22 Matthewson, 2003, 63.
23 Dumbrell, 2002, 146–147.
24 cf. Mathewson, 2003, 76.

individually to all the saints reigning with Christ.[25] Indeed, the believers' expectation for the future is fulfilment of all promised Old Testament covenant blessings.

God's promise to the overcomers (21:7) is the fulfilment of the hopes of the historical church embodied in the promises to the seven churches, namely: eating from the tree of life (2:7); not being hurt by the second death (2:11); a new name (2:17); authority over the nations (2:26); the name recorded, not blotted out, in the book of life (3:5); being a member, eternally, of the new Jerusalem (3:12); reigning with Christ (3:21). The promises to the overcomers in the seven churches are all summed up in the gift of the life-giving water (21:6). The promise of divine sonship and kingship to the overcomer is part of the restored new covenant relationship (21:7; 2 Samuel 7:14). The new covenant is now consummated through the direct presence of God in the new Jerusalem.[26] The saints have received the divine sonship—forfeited by Israel because of their disobedience (cf. Deuteronomy 32:5, 6, 20; Hosea 1:1–11)—through identification with the Son of David. This provides assurance for the overcomers of their kingship (and priesthood) by identification with David's messianic covenant in the new Jerusalem (2 Samuel 7:14).

The nature of the new relationship in the new Jerusalem is that any transgressor is automatically excluded (21:8). The exclusion list is a warning to John's congregations. Each of the eight categories identifies apostates for whom the alternative to life in the new Jerusalem will be the second death and the lake of fire.[27]

Revelation 21:9–21 The Bride and her Adornment

One of the seven angels who had poured the bowls to bring about the demise of Babylon presents to John a detailed description of the bride and her adornment (21:9–22:5), which is an amplification of 21:1–8. This reveals both the purpose behind the divine judgements and the great contrast between the two cities, Babylon (Revelation 16–18) and the new Jerusalem (Revelation 21–22). 21:9–11 expands 21:2. John 'saw' the bride (21:2); now he

---

25   cf. Mathewson, 2003, 83; Dumbrell, 2002, 126.
26   cf. Lee, 2001, 274.
27   Smalley, 2005, 544.

'sees' the new Jerusalem descending (21:10). The new Jerusalem is the heavenly Jerusalem, descending from heaven: thus the contrast between heaven and earth disappears in the new creation.[28] The heavenly Jerusalem—the heavenly Zion—is now, as the new Jerusalem, the righteous in their eschatological dwelling place.

John is carried away under prophetic inspiration ('in the Spirit', 21:10) to a great and high mountain, which is the location of the city (cf. Isaiah 2:2; 24:23; Ezekiel 40:1–2). The mountain to which the city descends (21:10) reflects cosmic mountain symbolism. As the cosmic mountain, the new Jerusalem is the meeting point uniting heaven and earth. Eden (Genesis 2), destined to be universalised (cf. 22:1–5), was the holy mountain of God (Ezekiel 28:13–14); Jerusalem was the impregnable dwelling of God. The mountain, therefore, has theological—not geographical—significance.[29]

In the Old Testament, the new Jerusalem was to be the site of paradise restored (Isaiah 11:9; 65:25). This fulfils the age-old desire of humanity to join heaven and earth (cf. Genesis 11:1–9).[30] The cosmic setting is described by two adjectives: 'great' and 'high'. These adjectives describe the new Jerusalem (21:9–14; cf. Ezekiel 40:1–11), which is made great and high by the divine presence (cf. Ezekiel 48:35 which states that the city's name is: 'The Lord is there'). Zion is generally deemed to be located on a high mountain (Isaiah 2:2–3; Psalm 48:1–2).[31]

21:11–22:5 describes the bride city with images of beauty and grandeur. Intimate fellowship is to be enjoyed throughout eternity in the new covenantal relationship that God, the Lamb, and his people will share now that sin will be no more.

Believers had shone imperfectly as lights in the world (Philippians 2:15). But now the city shines (21:11) not only with the believers' light but also—primarily—with the radiance of divine glory. Hitherto, in the Old Testament, the radiance of divine glory had been restricted to tabernacle and temple. The glory had also been seen in Jesus (John 1:14). But now the restricted Old

---

28 cf. Lee, 2001, 270.
29 cf. Mathewson, 2003, 100.
30 Bauckham, The Theology of the Book of Revelation, 1993, 132–133.
31 Witherington, 2003, 268.

Testament tabernacle and temple access to the divine glory has been lifted, as prophesied (Isaiah 60:1–2). The beauty and purity of the city are like precious stones or a priceless jewel (21:11–12). The new Jerusalem city is the pearl of great price for which everything must be surrendered.

The city's wall and gates are described (21:12–14; cf. Ezekiel 40:5). The wall and gates symbolise the city's spiritual security and covenant inclusiveness. Gateways infer both the necessity of the right to enter and also the city's separation from all that would defile. The number twelve—used often in describing the new Jerusalem—represents divine completeness and absolute harmony (twelve = fullness of God's people):[32] twelve gates suggest absolute accessibility to a perfect city; twelve angels at the twelve gates welcome incoming pilgrims; the perfect wall providing perfect security has twelve by twelve dimensions .

An angel stationed at each of the twelve gates provides eternal vigilance (cf. Isaiah 62:6). The city is a dwelling place for overcomers only. The twelve gate towers (*pulon*, 21:12) of the eternal city (cf. Ezekiel 48:31–34), representing the twelve tribes of Israel, indicate that salvation is 'of the Jews' (John 4:22). In the Old Testament, the name of the twelve tribes was inscribed on twelve precious stones affixed to the breastplate of judgement of the high priest. This high priestly breastplate provided access for Israel into the divine presence. The high priest carried the names of Israel into the holy place (presence), symbolically, on his breastplate. The twelve foundation stones bear the names of the twelve apostles of the Lamb (21:14; cf. Isaiah 54:11–12; Ephesians 2:20). But wouldn't it be more logical for the tribes to be the foundation, and the apostles the gates? The reversal highlights that the fulfilment of Israel's promises has come in Christ and his body, the church. The church forms the one foundation of the new temple; the church is the foundation of the new Israel.[33] The orientation of the gates (21:13) differs from Ezekiel 48:30–35, distinguishing the new Israel. The names of the twelve apostles on the twelve foundation stones indicate that the new covenant rests on the apostles' teaching. Apostolic doctrine leads to the completion of the new

---

32 Resseguie, 1998, 65.
33 Beale, 1999, 1070.

temple (Ephesians 2:19–22). And Jesus Christ, the slain Lamb, is—by his death—the chief cornerstone of the new temple. The history of Israel and the church comes to fulfilment in the new Jerusalem. The names of the twelve tribes on the gates of the eternal city (21:12) indicate continuity between Old Testament Israel and the new city. God's purpose in creation, which is a world peopled by those who love and honour him, has been fulfilled in the new Jerusalem.

The measurement of the city by an angel (21:15; cf. 11:1–2; Zechariah 2:1–2) signifies that the total city is under divine protection. The length and breadth of the city are about 2,200 kilometres in each direction, which was about the same size as the contemporaneous Hellenistic world.[34] With equal length, width and height, the city is a perfect cube (cf. Ezekiel 45:2–3). Symbolically, the dimensions measured by the angel are vast (21:15–17). These heavenly, symbolic measurements indicate: symmetry, perfect order and the ideal complement of inhabitants. In proportion, the dimensions of the wall are symbolically small (66 metres, 21:17). No protective wall is necessary, but the wall signals completion of the city[35] and delimits its sanctity.[36]

Ezekiel's temple was a square (Ezekiel 45:1–2). But the eternal city is a perfect cube on a square base embracing heaven and earth. The eternal city is the new holy of holies. The divine presence—formerly liturgically related to the inner recesses of the temple—fills the new creation, thus consummating Genesis 1. The city as a cube is all temple, like the holy of holies in the earthly temple. The holy community is constantly involved in the eternal city, the new temple; not just episodically as was the case with the Old Testament Israelite High-Priest.

21:18–20 focus on the materials used in the construction of the city of God, namely, the precious stones and metals of Eden (Genesis 2:11–12; cf. Ezekiel 28:13). Tradition suggested that the jewels of the high priest's breastplate came from Paradise. These pre-

---

34 cf. Mathewson, 2003, 109.
35 Hoeksema, 1969, 697–9.
36 Mathewson, 2003, 111–112.

cious stones would also be used to build the new Jerusalem (cf. Isaiah 54:11–12).[37]

The features in the structure of the city were: its wall gleaming of jasper, and the pure gold like glass signifying transcendence. But gold and jasper were not the only building materials.[38] The structural features all reflect the glory of the divine presence. The Solomonic Temple (1 Kings 6:20), overlaid with gold, furnished the pattern for these features.

The twelve foundations of the wall encasing the city were composed of precious stones (cf. 1 Kings 5:17, the foundation of the temple; Isaiah 54:11–12, the new Jerusalem).[39] Pilchan Lee identifies three references to the jewellery motif in the Old Testament.[40] The precious stones on the breastplate of the high priest are almost identical with the twelve foundation jewels in the eternal city (21:19–20; Exodus 28:17–20; cf. Ezekiel 28:13).

The tabernacle/temple motif (Exodus 28:17–20) relates the precious stones to both the temple and the Garden of Eden (Ezekiel 28:13). The jewel motif defines the new Jerusalem as an eschatological symbol adorned with the most precious materials of Paradise.[41] But only eight of the twelve stones correspond to the Exodus list (Exodus 28:17–20).[42] So there is general continuity with Old Testament Israel, but significant difference as well. Mathewson points out that the notion of bridal adornment is also present.[43] The overall picture is the glory of God (cf. 4:3) radiantly reflected with the city adorned by the redeemed. The walls and foundations link the city into a universal community of the people of God.[44]

The gates are constructed from twelve single pearls (21:21, Isaiah 54:12). Pearls once adorned fallen Babylon (17:4; 18:16). But now the eternal city's adornment with pearl gates is 'a picture of opulence and unimaginable beauty that is comprehensible only in

---

37 cf. Bauckham, The Theology of the Book of Revelation, 1993, 134.
38 cf. Smalley, 2005, 553.
39 Beale, 1999, 1083.
40 2001, 286.
41 Bauckham, The Climax of Prophecy, 1993, 134.
42 Beale, 1999, 1080.
43 2003, 141–3.
44 Smalley, 2005, 554.

spiritual terms'.[45] Saints reflecting their priestly character will walk on a street paved with translucent gold befitting the resplendence of the divine presence in the city (cf. the gold in Solomon's temple, 1 Kings 6:21,22,30). In this glorious city, the saints will also reign as kings (22:5).

Revelation 21:22–27 The New Temple

The distinction between the sacred and the profane has gone in the new city; all are priests with access to the divine presence (cf. Zechariah 14:21). John had anticipated but did not see a temple in the city because the Lord God Almighty and the Lamb are its temple (21:22, *naos*).[46] Temple language is important throughout Revelation, but now the nature of the temple city is being redefined as a spiritual rather than a physical temple. In the Old Testament there was limited, conditional access to the physical temple. But in the new Jerusalem there is no physical temple, so there is no mediation.[47] Rituals are no longer required for access into new Jerusalem, and named courts are not needed to distinguish levels of purity. Limitations have now been abrogated. But there is a temple: God and the Lamb.[48] Universal sovereignty, for which the temple was a symbol, has now occurred. The biblical temple—with its restricted, mediated access to the covenant God—has been transcended. The new creation is all temple; inhabitants of the new creation offer constant worship (that is, undivided service). The city, totally holy, is a temple city (cf. Ezekiel 48:35). The temple city is sacred space. Nothing impure or unholy is allowed into the temple city. Just as the biblical temple had been a point of contact between heaven and earth, so the temple city links heaven and earth (21:1–2). This vision of the new Jerusalem is therefore the consummation of biblical expectation with regard to the temple.[49]

The city and temple resemble Ezekiel 40–48. In Ezekiel a voice comes from the temple (Ezekiel 43:6–7), promising to live with the people forever (cf. 21:3). Ezekiel's new temple represents the

---

45 Smalley, 2005, 555.
46 op. cit., 556.
47 Stevenson, 2001, 269.
48 loc. cit.
49 op. cit., 270.

restoration of Israel around the divine spiritual centre (cf. Ezekiel 37:26–27). In new Jerusalem, the temple city is the final covenant symbol, the place where God's covenant promises are fulfilled.

In the old order, a temple provided special geographical points of contact between the Holy God and fallen humanity. In new Jerusalem, when people are no longer fallen, God can live with them directly. Agents of mediation, no longer necessary, would be considered to be counter-productive and even profane. Hence there is no physical temple in the new creation.

But how can Revelation's temple city (without a physical temple) be reconciled with Ezekiel's prophecy of an eschatological temple (Ezekiel 40–48)? The answer is progressive revelation in which: the context of both visions of the end (21:9–22:5; Ezekiel 40–48) is the aftermath of the destruction of Gog and Magog; both John and Ezekiel are brought to a high mountain to view the new creation (21:10; Ezekiel 40:2); both John and Ezekiel watch an angel make measurements; Ezekiel has minute description of the outer and inner courts, but scarcely says anything about the house itself; and John describes the walls, foundation and gates of the city, but not its interior (Revelation 21). So the outlying elements of Ezekiel are transferred to Revelation's new Jerusalem; the house is downplayed in Ezekiel because it does not exist in Revelation (cf. 21:12; Ezekiel 48:30–35). Also, in both Ezekiel and Revelation the river flows from Gods' throne (22:1; Ezekiel 47:1ff) and trees are on both sides of the river (22:2; Ezekiel 47:12). The emphasis in the description of the temple in Ezekiel is not communion or fellowship but, rather, inclusion or exclusion. But Revelation emphasises both: communion and fellowship, and exclusion and inclusion (21:8, 27; 22:15; cf. Ezekiel 44:9). The matter of ritual purity in Ezekiel becomes moral purity in Revelation. God's glory fills temple and city (21:11a; Ezekiel 43:5; 44:4) because God himself is there (21:3; Ezekiel 37:27; 48:35). It would not have been possible for the exiles in Ezekiel to receive the revelation that, in the end, the temple was to be abandoned.

Even so, the reality towards which the Old Testament temple looked was a temple—the entrance into the holy of holies—in which the redeemed dwell: the universal King's palace. So a physical temple should not have been expected.[50] The Old Testament Zion/Jerusalem image could be both place and people (cf. Isaiah 40:1; 52:1-2). This is the Revelation vision of the citizens of the new Jerusalem, that is, city and new world are one just as Christ and his people are one. God and the Lamb constitute the temple since, reigning, they are the authority and presence which the temple symbolised. At the end as at the beginning (Genesis 2-3), there is no need for a physical temple as the new Jerusalem fulfils that biblical concept.

The building of the new temple is completed (21:22): Christ and his people, completely assembled, are the new city and God is dwelling with his people (21:3). The divine presence fills the city and can be encountered directly. So a sacred place is no longer needed to mediate the divine presence. There was no physical temple in Eden (Genesis 2) since the temple—a substitute for the divine presence—was only required in a fallen world. And in a fallen world there must be limitations to access into the divine presence. But now in the new Jerusalem, inhabited by the people of the Messiah and the Messiah himself, there is eternal fellowship. So God's new temple is not a building; rather, the New Testament anticipates that the temple of God is the saved community in eternal fellowship with Christ and God (cf. Ephesians 2:19-22). Accordingly, the place of worship is no longer the mountain of the house of the Lord to which the world comes in pilgrimage (Isaiah 2:2-4); rather, worship now occurs in the heart of every believer.[51] God's tabernacle is now with his people (21:3). Transcendence is now being communicated through immanence. There is no longer any need for symbolism to express the perfect; the perfect has now come.

Just as the new Jerusalem does not need any physical temple, in the same way there is no need for sun or moon in the city. The fullness of God's light—that is, Christ, the light of the world—illuminates the city. The sun and moon may be there, but they are not needed (21:23; cf. Isaiah 60:19) because the Lamb is a lighted torch. The nations will walk by this light (21:24), that is, the nations will walk in the consciousness of the divine presence

---

50   Lee, 2001, 283.
51   Spatafora, 1997, 238.

enlightening ultimate reality. This is the ideal government of the ideal world. Believers, representing the nations of the world and the kings of the earth (Isaiah 2:2–4), will make contribution to the splendour and honour of the holy city (cf. Isaiah 60:6). This reverses the historical subjection of Old Testament Israel to the nations. But the real wealth which believers bring into the city, unlike Babylon's false pretensions, is the believers themselves.

21:24 describes the long expected (Isaiah 60:3–5; 60:11; Zechariah 14:16–19) pilgrimage by the world to the holy city. The final state of the city is the purity required of those from the present world who are permitted to enter the city. And the saints have been prepared to enter the holy city from the foundation of the world. The gates to the city shall never be closed (21:25 cf. Isaiah 60:11) as all opposition to the city has been defeated forever. There is no darkness in the city; there is no time, days, calendars or years. But the unrighteous who love darkness are necessarily excluded (21:27).

Revelation 22

Revelation 22:1-5 The New Eden

Revelation now focuses on personal existence in the city of God. The description of the blessedness of redeemed covenant life is reminiscent of both Old Testament prophets (Ezekiel 40–48, especially 47:1–12; Zechariah 14:8–11) and Eden (Genesis 2:8–17). Ezekiel's river of life, symbolic of the Spirit, will be the fertilising force to bring abundant life in the new Eden. The motif of kings and priests (cf. Exodus 19:5–6) reappears in 22:4–5.

The influence of life pervades the city and its citizen occupants. Living waters—pure as crystal (22:1; cf. 4:6; 21:11)—are symbolic of eternal life given through the Spirit to believers. The living waters spring from the heart of the temple city (a Zion theme, cf. Zechariah 14:8). Indeed, living water springs from the temple itself which is now the joint throne of God and the Lamb at the centre of the city (not from the threshold of the temple, cf. Ezekiel 47:1–12). This is after Christ finished his work. Christ is now, for the first time, seated on the joint throne (22:1; cf. 5:6). God had been, seemingly, far removed; but he was present in his world in Jesus Christ, whose presence among his churches in the Spirit had also been God's presence.

God and Christ are the source of the river of blessing: eternal blessing of divine life to the redeemed (22:1). In Ezekiel, a river flowing from under the temple becomes a mighty body of water fertilising the deadness of creation—flowing into the Dead Sea, transforming its waters into fresh water—divine life from the shared throne for all saved humanity (Ezekiel 47:1–12). This is like the river going out in the Eden narrative (cf. Genesis 2:10), re-expressed by Jesus as the river flowing out from the new temple (John 7:37–39). This is the complete benefit of the new covenant: earthly faith has now become this new inner expression of the presence of God and the Lamb.

The flow from the throne passes through the centre of the city (22:2), so the river of life is centrally available and the flow of the life of the kingdom of God through Christ is constant. This constant available flow of life in the middle of the street is a striking contrast with the street of the earthly great city, where the bodies of the two witnesses had been cast (11:8). The river flows through the new Jerusalem (cf. Isaiah 35:6–9).[1] The Genesis tree of life —positioned, perhaps, in the middle of the street—is no longer forbidden (22:2; cf. Genesis 2:9). The symbolic picture is the renewal of Eden relationships, that is, the eschatological life which had been in the mind of God from the beginning.[2] The river and the tree are both emblematic of the complete fulfilment of God's creation covenant.[3] Like Ezekiel's river that 'heals' (Ezekiel 47:8–9), the leaves of the tree heal the nations who come to the city. The perfected church is drawn from peoples, tribes, languages and nations. The perfected church is gathered and sustained through the healing redemption of the cross.

There is no life beyond the city. The river of life does not flow beyond the city. Indeed, the city is all there is in the new creation. The tree of life in the middle of the city bears twelve kinds of fruit every month. So there is continued abundance and freshness of blessing—freely available, in a location in which time is no more —in covenant fulfilment for those who dwell in the city. The redemptive blessings of the new Jerusalem have, indeed, already been applied to believers as the body of Christ throughout history. Yet the total picture points to future fullness for the gathered church (the number twelve signifies the people of God). The picture of twelve kinds of fruit every month speaks of new covenant blessings that are both diverse and permanent. And beyond this reception of full redemption there is no need for further healing (cf. 21:4; 7:17).

This healed, sin-free society comes with the removal of the curse. Without the curse, the future of Jerusalem is sure (cf. Zechariah 14:11). The elimination of curse from the new creation reverses Genesis 3:17. In the city there is one throne and thus only one sovereignty. The sovereignty is the unity of the Godhead —note the singular pronoun 'his' servants, 'his' face and 'his' name (22:3–4)—Father and Son communicating through one Spirit. The response from those who dwell in the city is worship

---

1 Beale, 1999, 1105.
2 cf. Dumbrell, 2002, 18–22.
3 op. cit., 2002, 25–26.

(that is, 'service'). Those who dwell in the city offer priestly service (Isaiah 61:6); they are bound to obedience by free commitment. God's kingdom is entirely different from the beast's kingdom. In the beast's kingdom, all are ruled and subjected. But God's servants rule. Moreover, God's servants do not reign over anyone; rather, their rule is a participation in God's rule.[4]

In the presence of the Godhead, those who offer priestly service will see God's face (cf. Matthew 5:8). Previously, no mortal could see God's face and live. The face expresses who a person is, so to see God's face means knowing him in his personal being. Now, in new Jerusalem, the distance that was between the God who rules and the world that is ruled has disappeared. Believers will see 'his' (God's) full glory (cf. Psalms 11:4–7; 27:4); not even Moses was able to do that (Exodus 33:18–23; cf. John 17:24; 1 John 3:2).[5] The face of God, which was at times withdrawn or hidden in the Old Testament (Deuteronomy 32:20), is now visible to all (22:4). The redeemed who serve in the new Eden do so in the revealed presence of God, even as Adam did (Genesis 2).

The name of God and the Lamb on the foreheads of new Jerusalem citizens (22:4) indicates: the new relationship of divine ownership (cf. 3:12); their reflection of the divine character; their priestly relationship to the throne (the name 'holy to Yahweh' had been written on the forehead of Israel's high priest, Exodus 28:36–38); and their demonstration of the totally purified life. This is to be contrasted to the 666 on the foreheads and right arms of those subjected to the beast (13:18).

There can be no vestige of darkness (cf. John 9:4; 11:10) or evil in the holy city because the Lord God will 'shine' by his presence on them. 'Shine' is an Old Testament expression signifying God's favour (Psalms 4:6; 31:16; 67:1; 119:135). This may or may not mean the redundancy of other light (sun and moon). Irrespective, the message is the totally surpassing effect of divine illumination in the city. This is the fulfilment of the Aaronic blessing on Israel (Numbers 6:24–26) in which the Lord is besought to make his face

---

4   Bauckham, The Theology of the Book of Revelation, 1993, 142.
5   Smalley, 2005, 565.

shine in favour on Israel.[6] The citizens in the eternal city will not only be priests but also kings. Their reign (22:5) fulfils the expectation of Revelation (1:6; 5:10; 20:4–6); their reign also realises fully the commission given to Adam and Israel (Genesis 1:26–28; Exodus 19:5–6; cf. Dan 7:18, 27).[7] The saints participate in kingdom rule with full dominion. Perfect service will mean perfect dominion over creation in the new world. God brings about the end but, in the end, God is the end.[8]

Revelation 22:6–9 The Epilogue to the Book

The final encounter with the revealing angel (22:6–9) functions as the conclusion to the new Jerusalem vision, the beginning of the epilogue, and an affirmation of the reliability of the account which has led to the 'faithful and true' revealing of the completeness of the new creation (cf. 1:5).[9] God will perform, in the end, what he has promised in the beginning. Accordingly, 1:1 is echoed in 22:6 ('the Lord, the God of the spirits of the prophets has sent his angel to show his servants what must soon take place'); and 1:3 is echoed in 22:7. Consequently, 'these things' (22:8) which John saw and heard refer to more than the final vision of the new Jerusalem. Rather, 'these things' refer to the whole of Revelation. Furthermore, the angel who showed 'these things' to John is probably neither the angel who interpreted the new Jerusalem visions nor the angel who showed the Babylon vision. Rather, the angel of 22:6 is most probably the angel of 1:1 and therefore the angel of Revelation 10.

The interpretation of the vision of the coming of the kingdom is pronounced true and faithful (22:6; cf. Daniel 2:45)[10] by an angel. The prophetic content of the book ('these words') is thus endorsed. And punishment is promised for anyone who mishandles the book (22:18–19). God had revealed himself, mediated by an angel through John to further 'bondservants', namely, the witnessing seven churches as a prophetic community (cf. 1:1). And

---

6   op. cit., 566.
7   Dumbrell 2002, 17, 21–22, 37–38.
8   cf. Boring, 1989, 215–217.
9   Mathewson, 2003, 74–76.
10 Beale, 1999, 1124.

Jesus tells us that the end of history and the advent of the new creation is always near as an ongoing and ever-present reality.[11]

Revelation has been the visionary experience of John (22:8) and thus contains connected prophetic utterances through John controlled by the Spirit of God. Therefore, Jesus' coming is assured and always to be expected. The sixth blessing (22:7) is pronounced on those who obey the prophetic message of Revelation. The prophetic message is hope in dependence on God's control of history. Then John is rebuked for attempting to worship the revealing angel (22:9; cf. 19:9–10). Smalley points out that John's prostration before angels occurred at the end of the accounts of the opposed world cities, Babylon and new Jerusalem.[12] The message in the rebuke for the seven churches—some of whom were deferring to other channels of revelation instead of the source of revelation—is that, whereas the words of the prophets are to be kept, worship is not to be offered to the prophets. 'Worship God' is the demand for he alone and no one else is the source of true revelation.

Revelation 22:10–17 The Final Prophecy: A Call to Holiness of Life.

The final oracle of Revelation (22:10–17)—unlike Daniel's vision which was to be sealed up in his time (Daniel 12:4)—releases John to open this vision to all readers since the time is at hand (22:10). Unsealings (or sealings, 10:4) throughout Revelation indicate progressive movement towards the final goal. Daniel's message about the overthrow of godless nations and the onset of the kingdom of God has now been fully explained. As it has been fulfilled in Christ, Daniel's message is now to be recorded and made available. The imminence of the time (22:10) makes John's message always urgent.

The angel issues a challenge to the readers of Revelation (22:11): the book is now before them, but what is to be their reaction? If they stay unrighteous, then their destiny is sure. But they may move into the sphere of certain inclusion in the new Jerusalem through right relationship with God. Throughout history

---

11 Smalley, 2005, 568.
12 op. cit., 569.

there will always be the wicked and the righteous. But Revelation has drawn distinct lines between them. So the challenge must be answered. And right relationship must be demonstrated by conduct that is 'right', for the final day will declare it (22:12).

Jesus says that he is coming 'quickly' (22:12–13), that is, suddenly and unexpectedly. At the end, Jesus will reward the obedient faithful with full salvation blessings (as Israel had expected). Divine reward is not dependent on self-effort as all Christian effort is motivated by the Spirit. Nevertheless, the reward is 'according to the work of each'. Salvation blessings are correlated with growth in holiness and works of the Spirit 'that follow' (14:13). Jesus identifies himself with God in the title Alpha and Omega (22:13; cf. 21:6–8).[13] Jesus thus claims dominion over the universe. Believers who 'wash their robes'—evidencing the continuing process of sanctification—in accordance with the seventh and final blessing of the book, will receive the blessings of new Jerusalem citizenship and the right to the tree of life. But the destiny of the ungodly is the lake of fire (21:8). Those whose disobedience is obvious (22:15; cf. 21:8,27) will not be able to enter the new Jerusalem.

Revelation 22:16–21 Finale

Jesus said that he had sent his angel to the angels of the seven churches for them to bear witness to John's letter (22:16). This final call from Jesus is for the churches to be faithful. But the letter is not just for the seven churches of Asia Minor; the letter is for all churches, all Christians. As the Davidic Messiah—that is, the root and offspring of David—Jesus has effected the complete fulfilment of messianic hope (Isaiah 11:1). As the dominant morning star, Jesus will fulfil the promise to the overcomer (Numbers 24:17). Jesus will bring in the new day (Isaiah 60:1–3) which has already begun in his resurrection.

The Holy Spirit (through the book of Revelation) and the bride—that is, the church which testifies to the revelation—address Jesus with the imperative of faith: come (22:17)! Those who testify to the Revelation, who earnestly hear the Revelation, likewise address Jesus with the imperative of faith: come! Some

---

13   Michaels, 1997, 254.

commentators have difficulty with 'come' being addressed to Christ in the first two clauses.[14] However, this request to 'Come' is abject petition. These commentators also suggest that the transition to invite the thirsty to come (the third clause of 22:17) is too abrupt. But this is an invitation towards the eschatological future. The Lord speaks his invitation three times to all who will listen and come into the new Jerusalem, as Jesus tells all who listen to the Revelation: 'I am coming soon' (22:7,12,20).

Two invitations are issued to come to the waters of life found in the new Jerusalem. The living water in the new Jerusalem is freely available, without money and without price (Isaiah 55:1). This is an invitation both for the present and the eschatological future. The promise presupposes that a pilgrimage of faith in Jesus has already begun (John 7:37–38). So the invitation to freely partake of the living water is a call to endurance, with the prize of the new Jerusalem before their eyes. This promised free water of life belongs to the new creation (21:6), indeed, the river of the water of life flows through the streets of the new Jerusalem (22:1–5).

Jesus issues warnings through John to the hearer: don't go beyond the text of the book, either adding to or taking away from the message of Revelation by false teaching. False teaching would distort the message of Revelation (cf. 2:14; 2:20–23).[15] And a distorted message would mean loss of access to the tree of life, loss of citizenship in the new Jerusalem, and exposure to the plague judgements (15:5–16:21).

Jesus, the real author of Revelation, addresses the hearers in the penultimate verse. Jesus is coming soon (quickly, 22:20 cf. 1:1,3; 2:16; 3:11). The human, congregational response is repeated in almost identical terms in the Didache (10:6, *Marana tha*, 'Our Lord come' or 'come Lord Jesus').

The traditional liturgical grace conclusion to a letter is pronounced on its congregational reading (22:21).

---

14 Bauckham, The Climax of Prophecy, 1993, 167–8.
15 Beale, 1999, 1152.

Summary

Gregory Stevenson cogently suggests that Revelation offers a new way of viewing the world which is thoroughly biblical and yet not our normal assessment. Revelation emphasises world opposition to the kingdom of God throughout world history.[16] Stevenson states: 'In Revelation, the world is a place where appearances are deceiving'. Our social context is, therefore, a place of oppositions. The war is waging. And, by their witness, Christians are caught in the middle. Christians do not always identify this reality and, in any case, Christians cannot by themselves achieve the necessary victory over the world. The drama of Genesis 3 against the background of Eden in Genesis 2 has been played out throughout world history. However, the message of Revelation is that the cosmic encounter against evil was won at Calvary. This was the ultimate witness of Jesus. And heaven has now been cleansed by the ascension of Christ (Hebrews 9:23). So Revelation is the unfolding of the significance of the cross through the witness of Jesus given by those who belong to him.

---

16 2001, 301.

Bibliography

Aune, D. E., *Revelation 1–5*. Nashville: Thomas Nelson, 1997.

Aune, D. E., *Revelation 6–16*. Nashville: Thomas Nelson 1998.

Aune, D. E., 'The Form and Function of the Proclamations to the Seven Churches (Revelation 2–3)', *New Testament Studies* 36/2 (1990), 182–204.

Barr, D. L., 'The Lamb Who Looks Like a Dragon? Characterizing Jesus in John's Apocalypse', *Rhetoric and Politics in the Book of Revelation,* edited by D. L. Barr. Atlanta: Society of Biblical Literature, 2006, 205–220.

Bauckham, R. J., *The Climax of Prophecy: Studies in the Book of Revelation*. Edinburgh: T&T Clark, 1993.

Bauckham, R. J., *The Theology of the Book of Revelation*. Cambridge: Cambridge University Press, 1993.

Bauckham, R. J., 'Judgement in the Book of Revelation', *Ex Auditu* 20, 2004, 1–24.

Beale, G. K., 'The Influence of Daniel upon the Structure and Theology of John's Apocalypse', *Journal of the Evangelical Theological Society* 27/4 (1984), 413–423.

Beale, G. K., 'The Interpretative Problem of Rev. 1:19,' *Novum Testamentum XXXIV* (1992), 360–387.

Beale, G. K., 'Eschatology', *Dictionary of the Later New Testament and Its Developments,* edited by P. H. Davids and R.P. Martin. Downers Grove: Intervarsity Press, 1997.

Beale, G. K., *The Book of Revelation: New International Greek Testament Commentary Series*. Carlisle: Paternoster, 1998.

Beale, G. K., *The Temple and the Church's Mission: A Biblical Theology of the Dwelling Place of God*. Downers Grove: Apollos, 2004.

Beasley-Murray, G. R., *The Book of Revelation*. London: Oliphants, 1974.

Blass, F. W. and Debrunner. A., *A Greek Grammar of the New Testament and Other Early Christian Literature*, edited by R. W. Funk. Chicago: The University of Chicago Press, 1961.

Boring, M. E., *Revelation*. Louisville: John Knox Press, 1989.

Caird, G. B., *The Revelation of St. John the Divine*. London: A & C Black, 1985.

Carnegie, D. R., 'Worthy is the Lamb: The Hymns in Revelation', *Christ the Lord: Studies in Christology presented to Donald Guthrie*, edited by H. H. Rowdon. Leicester: Inter-Varsity Press, 1982, 243–256.

Charles, R. H., *A Critical and Exegetical Commentary on the Revelation of St. John, I-II*. Edinburgh: T&T Clark, 1920.

Davis, D. R., 'The Relationship between the Seals, Trumpets and Bowls in the Book of Revelation', *Journal of the Evangelical Theological Society* 16 (1973), 149–158.

Dumbrell, W. J., *Romans: A New Covenant Commentary*. Eugene: Wipf & Stock, 2005.

Dumbrell, W. J., *Covenant and Creation*. Exeter: Paternoster, 1984.

Dumbrell, W. J., *The Search for Order*. Grand Rapids: Baker, 1994.

Dumbrell, W. J., *Faith of Israel*. Grand Rapids: Baker, 2002.

Dumbrell, W. J., *John: Gospel of the New Creation*. Caringbah: New Covenant Publications, 2006.

Fekkes, J., *Isaiah and Prophetic Traditions in the Book of Revelation*. Sheffield: JSOT Press, 1994.

Fiorenza, E. S., 'The Words Prophecy: Reading the Apocalypse Theologically', *Studies in the Book of Revelation* edited by S. Moyise. Edinburgh: T & T Clark, 2002, 1–19.

Forster, W., *'axios,* Theological Dictionary of the New Testament, Volume 1. Grand Rapids: Eerdmans, 1964, 379 .

Guthrie, D., *The Relevance of John's Apocalypse*. Grand Rapids: Eerdmans, 1987.

Hall, R. G., 'Living Creatures in the Midst of the Throne: Another Look at Revelation 4:6', *New Testament Studies* 36 (1990), 609–613.

Heide, G. Z., 'What is New About the New Heaven and the New Earth? A Theology of Creation from Revelation 21 and 2 Peter 3', *Journal of the Evangelical Theological Society* 40/1 (1997), 37–56.

Hemer, C. J., *The Book of Acts in the Setting of Hellenistic History*. Tübingen: Mohr, 1989.

Hendriksen, W., *More than Conquerors: An Interpretation of the Book of Revelation*. Grand Rapids: Baker, 1962.

Hoeksema, H., *Behold He Cometh! An Exposition of the Book of Revelation*. Grandville: Reformed Free Publishing Association, 2000.

Hoffmann, M. R., *The Destroyer and the Lamb*. Tübingen: Mohr Siebeck 2005.

Hurtado, L. W., 'Revelation 4–5 in the Light of Jewish Apocalyptic Analogies', *Journal for the Study of the New Testament* 25 (1985), 105–124.

Jauhiainen, M., 'The Measuring of the Sanctuary Reconsidered', *Biblica* 83 (2002), 507–526.

Johnson, A. F., *Revelation, Expositors Bible Commentary*. Grand Rapids: Zondervan, 1981.

Koester, C., *The Dwelling of God: The Tabernacle in the Old Testament*. Washington, DC: Catholic Biblical Association of America, 1989.

Krodel, G. A. *Revelation*. Minneapolis: Augsburg, 1989.

Lamprecht, J., 'Final Judgement and Ultimate Blessings: The Climactic Visions of Revelation 20, 11–21, 8', *Biblica* 51 (2000), 362–85.

Lee, P., *The New Jerusalem in the Book of Revelation*. Tübingen: Mohr Siebeck, 2001.

Lioy, D., *The Book of Revelation in Christological Focus*. New York: Peter Lang, 2003.

Mathewson, D., *A New Heaven and a New Earth: The Meaning and Function of the Old Testament in Revelation 21:1–22:5*. London: Sheffield Academic Press, 2003.

McKelvey, R. J., 'The Millennium and the Second Coming', *Studies in the Book of Revelation*, edited by S. Moyise. Edinburgh: T & T Clarke, 2001, 85–100.

Metzger B. M,. *Breaking the Code*. Nashville: Abingdon, 1993.

Michaels, J. R., *Revelation,* Downers Grove: InterVarsity Press, 1997.

Morris, L., *Revelation*. Grand Rapids: Eerdmans, 1987.

Moyise, S., 'Singing the Song of Moses and the Lamb: John's Dialogical Use of Scripture', *Andrews University Seminary Studies* 42 (2004), 347–360.

Mulholland, M. R., *Revelation: Holy Living in a Unholy World*. Grand Rapids: Francis Asbury Press, 1990.

Osborne, G. R., *Revelation*. Grand Rapids: Baker, 2002.

Pattemore, S., *The People of God in the Apocalypse: Discourse, Structure and Exegesis*. Cambridge: Cambridge University Press, 2004

Paul, I., 'The Use of the Old Testament in Revelation 12', *The Use of the Old Testament in the New Testament,* edited by S. Moyise. Sheffield: Sheffield Academic Press, 2000, 256–276.

Resseguie, J. L., *Revelation Unsealed: A Narrative Critical Approach to John's Apocalypse*. Leiden: Brill, 1998.

Robinson J. A. T., *Redating the New Testament*. Philadelphia: Westminister, 1976.

Rowland, C., *The Open Heaven*. New York: Crossroad, 1982.

Ruiz, J., 'Hearing and Seeing but Not Saying: A Rhetoric of Authority in Revelation 10:4 and 2 Corinthians 12:4', *The Reality of Apocalypse: Rhetoric and Politics in the Book of Revelation*, edited by D. L. Barr. Atlanta: Society of Biblical Literature, 2006, 91-111.

Ryken, L., and Longman, T., *A Complete Literary Guide to the Bible*. Grand Rapids: Zondervan, 1993.

Smalley, S. S., *The Revelation to John: A Commentary on the Greek Text of the Apocalypse*. London: SPCK, 2005.

Smith, C. R., 'The Portrayal of the Church as the New Israel in the Names and Order of the Tribes in Revelation 7:5–8,' *Journal for the Study of the New Testament* 39 (1990), 111–118.

Spatafora, A., *From the Temple of God to God as the Temple: A Biblical Theological Study of the Temple in the Book of Revelation*. Rome: Gregorian University Press, 1997.

Stevenson, G., *Power and Place: Temple and Identity in the Book of Revelation*. Berlin, New York: Walter de Gruyter, 2001.

Sweet, J. P. M., *Revelation*. London: SCM Press, 1990.

Talbert, C. H., *The Apocalypse*. Louisville: Westminster John Knox, 1994.

Tonstad, S. K., *Saving God's Reputation*. London: T&T Clark International, 2006.

Ulfgard, H., *Feast and Future: Revelation 7:9–17 and the Feast of the Tabernacles*. Lund: Almqvist & Wiksell, 1989.

Walker, P. W. L., *Jesus and the Holy City:. New Testament Perspectives on Jerusalem*. Grand Rapids: Eerdmans, 1996.

Wall, R. W., *Revelation*. Peabody: Hendrickson, 1995.

White, R. F., 'Re-examining the Evidence for Recapitulation in Rev. 20:1–10', *Westminster Theological Journal* 51(1989), 319–344.

Wilcock, M., *The Message of Revelation*. Downers Grove: IVF, 1975.

Witherington, B., *Revelation*. Cambridge: Cambridge University Press, 2003.

www.ingramcontent.com/pod-product-compliance
Lightning Source LLC
Chambersburg PA
CBHW050615300426
44112CB00012B/1510